THE ENCYCLOPEDIA OF
HERBS
and
SPICES

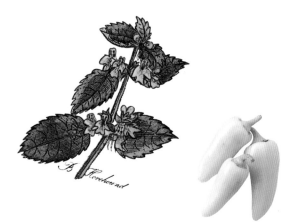

THE ENCYCLOPEDIA OF
HERBS
and
SPICES

ANDI CLEVELY, KATHERINE RICHMOND,

SALLIE MORRIS AND LESLEY MACKLEY

HERMES
HOUSE

This edition published in the USA by Hermes House
27 West 20th Street
NY 10011 New York

HERMES HOUSE books are available for bulk purchase
for sales promotion and premium use. For details write or call
the manager of special sales: Hermes House,
27 West 20th Street, New York, New York 10011, (800) 354-9657

© 1997 Anness Publishing Limited

Hermes House is an imprint of Anness Publishing Limited

ISBN 1 901289 06 0

Publisher: Joanna Lorenz
Senior Cookery Editor: Linda Fraser
Indexer: Hilary Bird
Photographers: William Adams-Lingwood, John Freeman and Michelle Garrett
Home Economists: Lucy McKelvie and Liz Trigg

Previously published as two volumes, *The Complete Book of Herbs* and *The Spice Ingredients Cookbook*

1 3 5 7 9 10 8 6 4 2

Abbreviations: FR. (French), G. (German), SP. (Spanish), IT. (Italian), AR. (Arabic), DU. (Dutch), ETH. (Ethiopian),
FIL. (Filipino), IN. (Indian), IND. (Indonesian), JAP. (Japanese), MAL. (Malaysian), SINH. (Sinhalese).

Contents

Introduction

Herbs and spices have been used since the earliest times. As cooks we depend on fresh and dried herbs and spices to liven up our daily meals and to bring fragrance to our lives. We use them to decorate our homes, to scent our clothes and bodies, and as ingredients in a wide range of medicines, cosmetics and alcoholic drinks.

The Encyclopedia of Herbs and Spices is a comprehensive guide to the huge range of aromatic plants, seeds and berries. The book is divided into two main sections.

The herb section opens with a brief general history of herbs, which highlights their importance as an ingredient in medicines. There is then a complete, practical guide to growing herbs, which includes information on choosing herbs for your garden; the different types of herb garden, from formal to ornamental; planting herbs for color, fragrance and clipping; flowering herb plants, salad herbs and herbs for seasoning, healing and dyeing. There's information on planning a herb garden, with practical guidance on how to structure, design and pre-

pare the site. There are facts about looking after a herb garden and how to grow healthy herbs in pots and containers, with essential tips for growing herbs indoors on a window sill, and practical advice on pruning and training, plus a guide to harvesting and preserving fresh herbs.

A comprehensive A-Z of Herbs follows. This section is arranged in botanical name order and is packed with facts about all the common and less well-known herbs. Each entry includes such essential information as common names and related species, a description of the plant and how it is used, and how and where it is cultivated.

The herb recipe section includes a delicious selection of aromatic dishes, both classic and contemporary, which

use a wide range of flavorful herbs. There are wonderful savory recipes including soups and starters, delicious pies and pastries, warming casseroles and stews, roast, grilled and fried dishes, delightful summery recipes for barbecues and picnics, flavorful dressings and preserves, and a variety of vegetables and salads. Of course, herbs aren't only used in savory recipes: you'll find a delightful selection of desserts, fruit sauces and sweet preserves, aromatic recipes for home-baked scones, breads, muffins, cakes and cookies, and a wonderful selection of drinks and punches.

The final chapter in this section offers a complete guide to using herbs in the home to make aromatic gifts, decorations and scented oils, with instructions for a herbal wreath, a fabulous rose and herb basket, home-made pressed flower cards for special occasion gifts, herbal skin tonics, and scented bath oils to relieve the stresses and strains of a busy day.

The second half of the book is a complete guide to spices and how to use them in the kitchen. It opens with a fascinating history of the spice trade

Left: *A fresh, scented wreath of herbs and flowers makes a delightful wall decoration.*

and an introduction to the use of spices in the kitchen, both past and present. There is information on choosing and preparing spices, and the best equipment to use, and facts about how to store them.

The reference section opens with a spice index, arranged in botanical name order. It is a comprehensive guide to the world's spices and aromatic flavoring ingredients. Each entry includes the history and folklore of the spice, how and where it is grown, its aroma and flavor and its culinary, medicinal and other uses, together with storage and any special preparation tips.

A chapter on spice mixtures follows. This colorful, pictorial guide contains practical information on how to make a wide range of spice mixtures, from simple curry powders to exotic spice pastes from the Far East.

There are recipes, too, for flavored aromatic oils and vinegars, and wonderful spiced drinks, such as Southern Iced Spiced Coffee and Mulled Wine.

The small section on using spices in the home includes delightful decorations and scented gifts, such as pomanders, ginger-flavored tree decorations and delightfully scented pots pourris and spice baskets.

The rest of the book contains a fabulous collection of tasty, aromatic recipes from around the world, with spicy soups and appetizers, fish and seafood dishes, tasty meat, poultry and game, delicious vegetables and salads, and perfect pizza, pasta and grains. There are recipes for home-baked treats, such as breads, buns, quick breads, cakes and cookies, delectable desserts, plus preserves and chutneys.

With a plethora of practical information, fascinating facts and inspira-

Above: *Cotton bags, filled with dried herbs or aromatic spices, were traditionally used to scent linen cupboards and drawers.*

tional recipes, *The Encyclopedia of Herbs and Spices* is the essential reference guide to using and cooking with aromatic plants and ingredients.

HERBS

ANDI CLEVELY AND KATHERINE RICHMOND

Introduction

Juniperus lycia

The history of herbs is as long as the story of mankind, for people have used these plants since earliest times. Wars have been fought and lands conquered for the sake of plants, and even today we continue to depend on exotic species for many of our newest medicines and chemicals.

Today herbs are so pervasive that we take them for granted and barely give them a thought except when cooking or gardening – in contrast to the past when people had a more intimate relationship with the plants around them.

In medieval Europe, country people had always gathered wild harvests of useful plants, but it was in the monastic herb gardens that plants of known virtue were transplanted and organized in beds and borders, and their usefulness studied. This was then catalogued in such early works as the tenth-century book of 'simples' (herbal medicines) sent to Britain by the Patriarch of Jerusalem, and the major treatise on herbs written by a thirteenth-century Franciscan monk, Bartholomaeus Anglicus. Berries, seeds and barks from distant parts of the world were dried and imported as spices to increase the range of flavors and fragrances available to the few who could afford them.

Values change as settled societies become wealthy and less involved in the daily struggle for survival. Before

long herbs were being cultivated in Europe, not just for their availability when needed but also to be enjoyed as amenity plants. This growing appreciation of what is now termed their 'garden merits' seemed to coincide with a gradual decline in their practical use.

In the nineteenth century, prepared medicines, dyes and cosmetics had become widely available, and better methods of food preservation and distribution meant there was no

need to use strong herbs and spices to disguise the flavor of rank meat and stale fish. Old herbal wisdom became suspect as primitive and unreliable, so that today in Western societies, herbalism has become synonymous with cranky superstition.

Below: *Illuminations of herbs and flowers were commonly used to decorate medieval Books of Hours.*

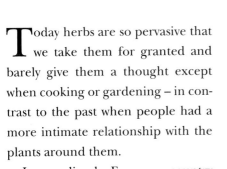

Left: *An elegantly spiraling clipped yew, flanked by the leafy stems of angelica.*

Happily, changing fashion is restoring herbs to their former importance. Alternative medicine has rediscovered some of the skills of phytotherapy (the use of medicinal plants), and the ancient pedigree of healing herbs. Concern for the precarious status of many wild species, especially those that grow exclusively in threatened tropical rainforests, has highlighted the unique properties that might be lost with their extinction. An interest in international cuisines has made us familiar with the flavors of oriental lemon grass, leaf coriander from the eastern Mediterranean, and South American

Left: *An intricate herbal border in the fifteenth-century* Siege of Tripoli *by Guillelmus of Tyre.*

maté, the restorative tea brewed from the leaves of a holly, *Ilex paraguayensis.*

Histories of herbs and herb gardens used to be written from a European viewpoint, ignoring the important fact that global human dependence on plants is

Far Left: *An example of the popular Victorian art of arranging pressed herbs and flowers.*

Left: *Nicholas Culpeper, the great seventeenth-century herbalist, who produced the* Theatrum Botanicum *in 1640.*

Below: *Heartsease and wild strawberry are among the decorative motifs adorning this Book of Hours by Simon Marmion, c. 1480.*

characteristic of all societies in tune with their surroundings, yet Kuna Indians in Panama reserve parts of their forests as sanctuaries in which their healers can gather the medicinal herbs so important to their way of life; the Antasaka and other coastal tribes of Madagascar exploit forest plants for all their clothing, medicines, food and building materials; fishermen on the island of Socotra throw wood chips from the Adenium tree into pools to sedate fish for an easy catch; Arab horsemen treat their mounts with a whole pharmacopoeia of herbs developed by medieval Arabian physicians; and European Romanies still gather wild garlic and wayside herbs as they have done since their migrations began long ago.

Most modern gardeners need to relearn this instinctive affinity with herbs, but growing them in the garden will inevitably lead to an understanding of their qualities. None of us can grow them all, for the choice is vast and increasing as new species and their properties are discovered.

GROWING HERBS

Herbs as Garden Plants

There are many definitions of a herb, none altogether satisfactory. To the botanist it is a plant that dies down to ground level at the end of the growing season; medicinally the word refers to any plant that can assist in the prevention or treatment of illness; while in the kitchen it means a part of a plant that is used in the preparation of food.

Arctium lappa

Paradoxically many gardeners grow only a limited choice of herbs for use, planting others according to their ornamental merits. An essential collection might contain parsley, sage, thyme and mint, with rosemary, lavender or marjoram as optional extras.

How far to explore the treasury of herbs depends on your available space, and on the type of climate and terrain enjoyed by your garden. Plants of tropical origin need warm walls or greenhouse protection in temperate regions, while Mediterranean herbs and shrubs with grey or white leaves prefer dry, sunny places similar to their natural habitats. There are herbs for moist dappled shade, parched banks or the boggy margins of pools, for rock gardens, window boxes and patio pots, climbers to train on arches and trellises, and prostrate leafy mats for embellishing the edges of paths and tops of walls.

Many herbs have varieties and cultivars with colored and variegated foliage, and these can be planted to create a satisfying tapestry of contrasting shades. They are usually a little less vigorous than the normal types from which they were bred. The plainer forms might not rival modern hybrid

EARLY HERBALS

The earliest books about herbs are a fascinating subject for collection and study. Apart from their obvious curiosity value, they are evidence of the beliefs and understandings of particular eras, and chart changing attitudes to plants, the ways in which they act, and their importance in diets, medicine and daily household life, as well as contemporary issues of astrology, alchemy and divination. The earliest scientific works were Theophrastus' Enquiry into Plants *and* Growth of Plants *(c. 300 BC). Seminal texts of the Middle Ages were Avicenna's* Canon Medicinae *(c. 1020) and the Anglo-Saxon* Leech Book of Bald *(c. 950).*

Left: *Even a small herb garden can supply a wide range of aromatic, edible and medicinal material for everyday use.*

Right: *Herbs are so diverse in shape and color that they deserve a garden to themselves, although it need not be classically formal and restrained, as this kitchen herb garden reveals.*

USEFUL UMBELLIFERS

Fennel is a typical umbelliferous herb, with a branching stem system and flattened umbels – heads of little flowers – which are followed by long, aromatic seeds. Many other members of the Umbelliferae family are useful plants, including herbs such as European sweet cicely (Myrrhis odorata), parsley, chervil and angelica, vegetables such as carrots and parsnips, and medicinal herbs such as asafoetida. Unfortunately, some close relatives are extremely toxic – poisonous hemlock is perhaps the most notorious, but there are also others – so it is unwise to gather umbellifers from the wild without accurate identification.

flowers and shrubs for brilliance of color, but their worth lies in their effectiveness as teas, tonics and ointments, for their fragrance, and for the complex flavors they impart to other foods. They are also easier to tend than most choice ornamentals.

USEFUL WEEDS

The nineteenth-century American writer Ralph Waldo Emerson defined a weed as 'a plant whose virtues have not yet been discovered', which is fairer than the common assumption that weeds are unwelcome plants. All plants should be judged by the same criteria, and if they have a pleasing appearance and known virtues they merit room in the herb garden. Wild chamomile, for example, used to be known as the 'plants' physician' for its ability to revive ailing plants nearby, while alliums such as wild garlic and Welsh onions are companion plants for roses, which seem healthier in their presence. Common comfrey has pretty purple flowers, and can be harvested as a compost activator and remedy for skin ailments, while even the ubiquitous chickweed is a valuable salad ingredient with some tonic properties.

There is little difference between garden weeds and wild flowers other than where they grow. Many wayside plants deserve to be grown in gardens, being attractive enough to stand beside cultivated plants, and able to guard them from the threat of pollution and loss of habitat.

HERBS AND WILDLIFE

Bees, butterflies and other wild creatures depend on an enormous selection of plants for their survival. Herbs are ideal conservation plants because their strong perfumes and simple flowers attract browsing insects. In particular, bees love the sweet-scented blooms of thyme, sage, lavender, bergamot, mint, hyssop and rosemary, and it is no coincidence that a beehive was often the centerpiece of medieval herb gardens. Not only butterflies but also hoverflies, whose larvae are voracious allies in controlling pests, enjoy open single flowers or herbs with flat heads of blossom, such as sedum, catmint, sweet rocket and purple loosestrife.

A Place in the Garden

Visiting herb gardens is the best way to decide on which plants to choose and where to grow them. If they are primarily intended for use, it may be enough to gather your favorite kinds in a small accessible bed, which might be a cook's garden of basic culinary herbs, a formally arranged medicinal border, or a relaxed collection of dye herbs in cottage garden style. Some of the more colorful herbs can be planted among ornamental flowers rather than kept separate in a distinct herb garden, while culinary varieties blend happily with kitchen garden crops.

Chironia centaurium

Whatever your intentions, the cultural needs and habits of your plants must come first. It is no good trying to grow a majestic woodland herb such as angelica or lovage in a small, neat bed, for it will dominate the other plants and look hopelessly out of scale. Strictly geometrical designs must be created from evergreen perennials with similar heights and growth rates if the pattern is not to lose its clean outlines or disappear in winter.

Remember, too, that some herbs are very choosy about the soil and aspect they need, whereas others are almost infinitely adaptable – rosemary, for example, thrives almost anywhere, except in cold winters, and may be clipped as an informal flowering hedge or into simple evergreen topiary. A tall variety such as 'Fastigiatus' ('Miss Jessop's Variety') left to grow naturally will grace any shrub border and even support a small clematis for

variety; semi-prostrate 'Severn Sea' is perfect for cascading over a bank; while 'Tuscan Blue' or 'Majorca' with neater growth and brighter flowers are ideal as multi-purpose culinary, medic-

Below: *Whether your garden is a large expanse of soil and shrubs or a small front patch in front of a city house, herbs can be happily combined to produce an attractive display – space need not be a limiting factor in a herb garden.*

ROYAL PRECEDENT

Far from being a modern phenomenon, collecting aromatic herbs can be traced back as far as ancient Egyptian times. Around 1500 BC, Queen Hatshepsut ordered the mass felling of fig trees in her kingdom to build rafts that were poled up the River Nile for hundreds of miles in search of exotic trees and aromatic herbs for the royal gardens. Sennacherib, son of Sargon II of Assyria, constructed magnificent gardens and planted them with myrrh and other aromatic shrubs collected from the lands of the Hittites. Once gathered they were treasured for their great value, and widely used, traded or offered – the Queen of Sheba, for example, is recorded as taking a present of balsam seeds to King Solomon, and King Gentius of Illyria in the second century AD was renowned for his healing exploits with the roots of *Gentiana lutea,* which was named after him.

inal and ornamental container shrubs for a prominent position on the patio.

FITTING IN THE PLANTS

Unless you plan to assemble a comprehensive herb collection immediately, perhaps arranged in classically formal beds, it is best to begin with the few herbs you know you will use constantly, and add others later. Your own needs and preferences must decide which herbs to select, while experience will reveal whether they thrive in the chosen situation. A start could be

Below: *A robust flamboyant climber with ornamental leaves and interesting 'cones' in autumn, the hop plant earns a place in the less formal herb garden as an edible, medicinal and aromatic plant.*

made with essential culinary herbs, planted together in the vegetable garden, leaving until later the option of expanding the collection and moving plants to a dedicated site elsewhere. Most simply, individual herbs may be tucked into existing beds and borders to make their gently colorful contributions, providing an effective foil for brilliant herbaceous plants.

Herbs are irresistibly collectable, however, and finding room for later acquisitions is often a problem, especially in a small garden. A score or so of essential varieties will grow comfortably in a bed about 10 x 3 ft in size, especially if annuals and invasive kinds are confined to containers. Enclosing the bed with a tapestry hedge of evergreens that tolerate clipping permits the addition of hyssop, germander, lavender and similar herbs, while at their base dwarf prostrate kinds (such as pennyroyal, thrift and woolly thyme) can be allowed to billow over the edge of the path. Instead of hedging, you could surround the garden with rustic fencing to support a rose

Above: *Aromatic herbs such as thyme and lavender arranged around the house as dried flowers or pot-pourri make inexpensive and efficient air fresheners, combining the ancient tradition of strewing herbs with modern principles of aromatherapy.*

such as 'Zéphirine Drouhin', which is early to flower and one of the last to finish. Fastigiate (slim and upright) or standard shrub varieties can be added to the bed as an extra tier above ground-level plants.

If your ambitions extend further, you may want to consider planting a larger border or separate herb garden. Collections in botanic gardens are often arranged systematically according to use or family, and these will give you an idea of the amount of room needed. Less congenial parts of the garden may be ideal for larger numbers of herbs – a dry bank, for example, is the perfect site for a collection of thymes, an arrangement of decorative pots in a courtyard might house some of the many available kinds of mint in partial shade or basil in full sun, while a simple heap of rubble and soil could be transformed into a herbal rock garden of mat-forming varieties and dwarf shrubs.

Different Types of Herb Garden

Herbs have always been an important ingredient of domestic country gardens, where they were grown almost exclusively for their practical uses. It is only comparatively recently that the cottage garden has been appreciated and become fashionable. Classic cottage garden herbs include the essential culinary species, perhaps with the addition of coriander, garlic and one or two specimens of southernwood or curry plant to brush in passing. On the whole, the authentic range of cottage herbs was fairly conservative.

Veratrum viride

Most herbs can be grown informally, even 'muddled up' with other plants as the garden designer Vita Sackville-West (1892-1962) preferred them to be, although this should not mean total neglect. Like any other plant, herbs become straggly and unkempt if left to themselves or if they seed themselves too liberally among their neighbours, and it is important to keep them in their place by pruning, division, dead-heading or harvesting as necessary.

Some species blend remarkably well into a flowering border, especially more robust kinds such as angelica, foxglove, and bronze fennel which partners prettily the broad leaves of irises and the rich autumn shades of helenium, dwarf sunflowers or rudbeckias. Rue, santolina and lemon balm succeed in the middle of borders, while sage, marjoram, violets and lady's mantle are compact plants for growing near the front.

Annual and biennial herbs can be sown *in situ* or transplanted from elsewhere to fill space in beds and borders. Try sowing pinches of dill, borage, parsley and marigold seeds in pots for emergency use where gaps appear, and add young marjoram, savory and feverfew plants to edgings of pinks and other low perennials. Container-grown mints such as *Mentha* x *gentilis* (ginger mint) and *M. suaveolens* 'Variegata' (pineapple mint) may be plunged into the soil, with the pots buried up to their rims, to fill gaps with their decorative seasonal foliage.

FORMAL GARDENS

Herbs lend themselves most to a formal layout, as they have done since, in Tudor times, gardeners translated embroidery and plaster ceiling patterns into floral designs for the garden. The discipline imposed by a geometrical arrangement of beds and paths has its advantages: the plants are easy to reach for maintenance and harvest, their numerous and complementary shades and shapes are particularly suitable for combining in artistic patterns, and symmetry is satisfying for its own sake.

Designs can be simple and intimate: the familiar fan or cartwheel, for example, with wedge-shaped beds radiating from a common center, or a checkerboard arrangement of alternate paving slabs and square beds, perhaps with small vegetables and salad herbs to

Above: *Even a simple area of stone setts can be transformed into a miniature herb pavement when the joints are planted with prostrate mints, thymes, marjoram and similar mat-forming species.*

Left: *The clean classical outlines of dwarf hedges and evergreen topiary echo the restraint and balanced patterns of a formal herb garden.*

create a French-style *potager;* these are often the most effective, especially in small gardens. Where there is space, larger and more complex gardens are traditional, with beds of herbs surrounded by clipped dwarf hedges of germander, santolina, hyssop or box, either as strict frames for herb parterres or woven and intertwined to produce the classic knot garden.

Precision is essential for ambitious designs to succeed, as is frequent maintenance to keep the hedges trim. Within the chosen framework, herbs can be planted informally in whatever way pleases the eye, arranging them systematically so that culinary herbs are kept separate from medicinal species, for example, or in traditional style, using large numbers of a few

compatible herbs to create a form of carpet bedding.

THE WILD HERB GARDEN

The opposite of the strict parterre, a wild herb garden combines informality with the pleasures of re-creating a natural environment and providing a haven for wildlife. The ground needs to be prepared in the same way as for conventional herb borders, because there will be room only for chosen plants and not for some of the more invasive wild species. Arrange naturally meandering paths, together with one or two places to sit in peace and, if possible, a pool for moisture-loving herbs and aquatic wildlife. There is no need to level the ground – in fact, banks, hollows and gentle undulations add to the garden's

Above: *Many herbs have a natural exuberance that makes them ideal for herbaceous borders and wild gardens. These informal beds border a cool turf path beside which a strategically placed pedestal fountain plays.*

charm. Choose seeds of herbal wild flowers, grasses and woodland herbs such as angelica, woodruff, campion and lovage (some specialist seedsmen will blend a mixture to your requirements), and sow at the appropriate time. Add ferns, and a few suitable shrubs and trees such as elder, crab apple or quince. The only maintenance necessary will be routine cutting back to restrain vigorous species, the removal of unwelcome species, and occasional propagation of older perennials.

The Ornamental Herb Garden

Although individual herbs may look their best when in flower or in early spring as the young foliage unfolds, a decorative herb garden can be expected to give pleasure at every season, and year-round interest should be taken into account when drawing up garden plans. Include some hardy evergreen species to balance the seasonal changes and to provide winter color and continuity from one year to the next: variegated and colored forms remain brilliant highlights on even the darkest days.

Bryonia cretica

Herbaceous herbs die down to the ground as the season closes, leaving areas of bare ground, so be sure to disperse evergreens to provide plenty of attractive ground cover in spite of winter gaps in your design.

Some perennial herbs take time to get started in spring, but early color is provided by groups and drifts of bulbs such as winter aconites, snowdrops and early crocuses. Hardy annuals sown in pots or in a frame in autumn flower earlier than those sown outdoors, and they can be hardened off for transplanting where there is space in the herb garden. Later sowings of annuals provide a succession of color throughout the season.

Height is an essential consideration in any design, for many herbs are small to medium-sized plants and on their own may give a herb garden a disappointing uniformity. A feature such as a sundial, statue or large urn can relieve the flatness, although you should always consider the scale of the garden and the suitability of any ornaments – they must neither dominate nor spoil the overall impact of the design. A central feature is traditional, or you could embellish corners and turns in paths with smaller features – but guard against triviality, for it is easy to destroy the elegance of a herb garden with banal additions.

Topiary is another classic means of providing height, and several herbal plants adapt readily to formal

Left: *An inspired choice of striking colors and leaf forms will produce a memorable display, and proves that herbs are not only useful and practical plants, but also as decorative as any summer bedding.*

clipping. Common yew, holly, rosemary and bay where hardy, lavender and larger forms of box are ideal for bold designs that will catch the eye all the year round. Trained plants such as honeysuckle on pillars and standard or weeping roses are all suitable for hedges, and need little attention apart from annual pruning and tying in to supporting frames. On a larger scale, arches clad with climbers, tunnels of trained fruit, vines or hops, and even substantial pergolas of brick and timber can be used to frame paths or

emphasize paved areas. For shade, some of the more ornamental trees with herbal connotations can be planted – elder, almond, cherry, quince, juniper or walnut, for example, according to the space available.

At least one seat is essential for prolonged peaceful enjoyment of the herb garden, especially in the evening when colors and scents are most intense. Position it where you are likely to sit most often, perhaps at the far end or facing your favorite view. There is a wide choice of styles and

materials for garden seats, from elegantly wrought iron to simple rustic timber, or you can construct a bank from mounded earth, covering it with turf, thyme or chamomile around a stone or timber slab for all-weather seating; add a few plants of heartsease (wild pansy) and primrose for Shakespearean authenticity. Plant one or two aromatic herbs nearby to scent the area, and for intimacy train fragrant roses and honeysuckle on a framework arching over the seat to form a secluded arbor.

BUILDING A HERB WHEEL

1 Mark out the planned area, using a peg and taut line to ensure a perfect circle, before removing the turf and some of the topsoil. Ideally, the subsoil should also be loosened.

2 Position the edging materials, here house bricks arranged at an oblique angle and tapped firmly into place, but special-purpose edging tiles would be more frost-resistant.

3 Quarter the circle with two courses of sound bricks to allow access and create four separate beds.

4 Break up the excavated topsoil and refill the four quadrants almost to the surface of the brick paths.

5 Plant pot-grown herbs of your choice, watering them beforehand and allowing enough room for expansion as they grow.

6 Water in the plants if necessary, and then mulch with gravel or chippings to retain moisture and suppress weeds.

Herbs for Color

It is sometimes claimed that herbs are not sufficiently varied to create an interesting garden by themselves, but this is not so. Even if only green varieties are used, rather than variegated forms, there are so many leaf shapes and contrasting plant habits in an infinity of green shades that a satisfying composition can be made from basic species alone.

Malva sylvestris

Green is, after all, a color like any other, and green forms are particularly welcome in winter when evergreen herbs supply color while all around seems dormant, as noted by Thomas Hyll in 1563 in *The Art of Gardening*, where he advised that knot gardens should be 'set with winter savory and thyme, for these endure all the winter through greene'.

Above: *Formal geometrical designs are best planted in blocks of contrasting colors and leaf shapes for the greatest impact, using sculptural highlights such as simple topiary to relieve any uniformity.*

Achieving a riot of brilliant color with herbs is not easy. Most are subtly colored, low-key plants, which helps explain the healing sense of refreshment and well-being in a herb garden. Vibrant, exciting colors are only found in a few flowers and leaves – peonies and poppies, nasturtiums, golden elders and the ruby Pasque flower, for example. Many variegated leaves have a brilliance of their own, however, especially if grown in full sun. Always assess plants before you buy them, because some forms, gold variations in particular, can be confused with normal plants suffering from a mosaic virus.

Color needs to be used with discretion in the herb garden, where strident exuberance is usually out of place. Carefully position single specimens of brightly colored plants as important accents or to mark entrances, exits and changes in the layout – remember that a dominant color only works by contrast with its surroundings, and the more subdued plants should predominate for maximum effect. They may be paler, for example a sea of silver santolinas, set off with a few bobbing red poppies; or more somber, such as the dark foliage of a yew hedge as a background for bright yellow mullein.

The low-toned colors of most herbs work best in simple designs, such as the contrast between woven green box and grey lavender hedges in a knot garden, or variations on monochrome planting made popular by the garden

NOTABLE HERB FLOWERS

- borage – rich blue, for salads and summer drinks
- lavender – soft purple, for scent and pot-pourri
- nasturtiums – vivid reds and yellows, for colored garnishes
- violets – purple, for medicines and crystallized as decoration
- elderflowers – white and fragrant, for wines, cordials, and

flavoring fruit dishes
- pot marigolds or calendulas – vivid orange, for salads, pot-pourri and food coloring
- rose petals – red roses of scented varieties, for color and fragrance, wines and perfume
- woodruff – tiny and white, imparts scent of hay and vanilla when warm

designer Gertrude Jekyll (1843-1932), who created cool blue and grey borders and sunny yellow gardens. True blues are hard to find among herbs, though there are blue-flowered species such as chicory, borage, flax, hyssop, lavender and sea holly. However, there are many subtle shades of lilac and violet which harmonize with the greys and silvers of lavender, artemisia and rue. Yellows and golds are easier to mass, for these colors form the majority of variegations. Most herbs have forms with white leaves or flowers (cultivar names such as 'Alba', 'Alba Plena' and 'Albovariegata' are indications of these), and a white garden, at the same time cool and reviving, is perhaps the most popular of single-color themes.

Herbs in the red, purple and brown part of the spectrum are hardest to use effectively. Depending on the quality of light and surrounding plants, they can look rich and sumptuous, or merely lackluster. Deep red forms make excellent groundwork and specimen plants: crimson or purple bugle, for example, beneath the soft green of lady's mantle, or red

Above left: *Planted in drifts, flowering herbs such as wall germander can erupt into a startling carpet of color that will be alive with bees in summer.*

Right: *A branch of wild marjoram in full bloom reveals an intensity of color to rival any decorative shrub.*

Above right: *Ornamental forms of edible herbs add a decorative bonus to the salad garden: French sorrel (*Rumex scutatus*), for example, has the same tangy flavor as ordinary sorrel, but also creates a carpet of ground-cover foliage.*

sage (*Salvia officinalis* 'Purpurescens') standing out against a carpet of pale golden marjoram. Remember, though, that reds change as the day progresses and in full sun can reach out towards you, whereas evening twilight makes them recede almost to the point of invisibility.

FOLIAGE BEDS

When designing herb beds and borders, do not sacrifice leaf shape to color, for the two qualities work together and can blend to make a stun-

ning impact. The many thistle-like herbs are spectacularly eye-catching, creating dramatic stands of green, grey or silver foliage and robust stems: holy thistles, cardoons, globe artichokes, sea holly and milk thistles are all plants of great presence. Ferns, too, form a group with wide design potential, especially as a number of them have intricately varied forms with ruffled, divided or filigree detail. Their shades vary, and they tolerate moist shade, offering scope for planting schemes in corners where little else will flourish.

Herbs for Fragrance

Until the reign of King George IV (1820-30) English monarchs appointed Strewers of Herbs to precede them in procession and scatter dried aromatic herbs such as rosemary, thyme and rue to ward off diseases. The appointment of these royal 'strewing ladies', as they were popularly known, was a legacy from the times of the medieval plagues, which were thought to be caused by foul air. Dried herbs and essential oils were incorporated into pot-pourris, snuff, fumigants and scented waters, in the belief that fragrance would deter both infections and insects; and judges still carry posies of sweet herbs to shield themselves from the rest of humanity in the courtroom.

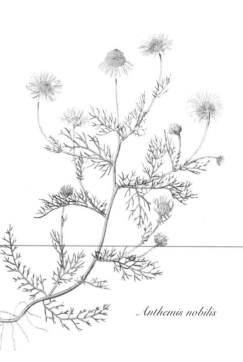

Anthemis nobilis

Research has shown that there is some substance to medieval ideas of hygiene. While most plants attract insects, others actively repel them. Others have an antiseptic effect, for example the gums exuded by some trees to heal wounds in their bark. These varied effects of fragrance have become part of the great tradition of herbal use, but in garden terms perfume is usually regarded as one of the pleasant qualities of desirable plants, especially herbs. Plant fragrances are hard to describe precisely. They are traditionally classified, simply by nose, in groups such as camphoraceous, fruity or hay-scented. Some scents, most notably those of open flowers (roses and gardenias, for example), are released as a reaction to sunshine – most of the Mediterranean herbs protect themselves from prolonged heat by surrounding their foliage with a defensive cloud of volatile oils.

Night-flowering plants often have heavy scents, and plants such as honeysuckle, nicotiana and evening primrose should be grown near an open window or beside a seat where you can enjoy their fragrance on a still evening. Plants that flower in winter also need planting close at hand for appreciation in all weathers. Disperse others according to the strength of their fragrance: the heady scent of *Lilium regale* can fill large areas and reach you from far away, whereas other plants need close approach to be enjoyed, and should therefore be placed within easy reach.

Left: *The smoky blue foliage of rue has a sharply resinous pungency, and a reputation for causing skin irritations if carelessly handled.*

WASTE FRAGRANCE

Although the fragrance of herbs is the main reason for their cultivation, in many cases the scent represents nothing more than the waste products of the plant's normal metabolism. Substances such as geraniol (the principal scent of roses), or the thymol and eucalyptol in thyme, are essential oils formed within the plant, and then stored in cells near the leaf surfaces. Pressure or movement, such as that of a browsing animal or of a strong breeze, or even the heat in sunlight, all cause the release of these chemicals to defend or shield the plant from injury. It is the release or evaporation of these waste materials that delights us when we walk on a thyme lawn or stand on a warm day downwind from a bush of rosemary.

***Drying lavender: 1** Heads of lavender flowers gathered at the peak of their perfection. Timing is important, and for full fragrance the flowers should be gathered when fully opened, whereas for medicinal use the critical time is often just before flowering.*

2 Spread out the complete flowering shoots to dry, in the sun or in shade according to species, or in warmth indoors in a cool season (lavender is best dried in a shady room). Turn the flowers frequently to ensure that all parts are dried.

3 The complete flowering shoots can be used intact, or individual blooms can be stripped off when dry for use in pot-pourri, herb bags and sachets. Keep different varieties separate, as their perfumes will be subtly different.

Leaf scents tend to be released when the foliage is bruised or brushed in passing, and most culinary herbs fall into this category, as well as aromatic trees and shrubs such as eucalyptus, rosemary, southernwood and the resinous conifers. Plant them strategically beside seats, at corners in paths or flanking gateways. Many of these species also make excellent hedges, and in earlier times it was the custom to spread freshly washed clothes on hedges to absorb a little of their fragrance while they dried.

Drying herbs often enhances their scent, sometimes releasing it from otherwise insignificant herbs – the delicious hayfield fragrance of sweet woodruff only reaches its full intensity days after the plant is cut and hung to dry, for example. Essential oils and tinctures are prepared from many herbs for use in aromatherapy or as Bach homeopathic flower remedies, where particular fragrances have been found to heal disorders and change moods. In the garden, plants can have the similar effect of raising your spirits or soothing tension, so be sure to plant your favorite scented herbs where they are accessible when needed.

Above: *The most important feature of pot-pourri is its fragrance, so ingredients such as thyme and lavender must be dried thoroughly to concentrate the volatile oils.*

Right: *Carpeting herbs such as chamomile, thyme and pennyroyal are ideal ground cover plants for informal lawns, which give off a heady scent when walked upon.*

Herbs for Clipping

Gratiola officinalis

The more you clip a woody perennial, the denser the foliage becomes: this is the principle behind hedge trimming, topiary and mowing lawns. Really a form of pruning, trimming off the end of a stem usually encourages the development of two or more side shoots, and the best species for hedges and lawns are those that respond to clipping by producing the densest regrowth.

Compact plants such as rosemary, lavender, santolina, southernwood, germander, hyssop, yew and, of course, box are traditional for herb garden hedges ranging in height from 6 in around small beds to 6 ft 6 in in grander schemes. Their chief function is to enclose, divide or define herb borders, conferring a sense of order and control, but they can be used to create the playful patterns of classic knot gardens and are often decorative in their own right, especially when kept neatly disciplined – this requires only one, perhaps two, trims a year in the case of box and yew, but vigorous plants such as privet and lonicera need clipping every month during the growing season.

Lavender is a particular favorite for a herb hedge and will yield a generous supply of flowers and leaves for dry-ing. Use a compact cultivar rather than the loose-growing English and trailing forms, and clip it to shape in spring without cutting into the old wood; leave it to flower and then trim it again, harvesting the fading blooms for use. In warm gardens, santolina's intricate silver foliage is a useful foil for green plants, and if it is trimmed close in mid-spring it will retain its neat shape, although the yellow button-shaped flowers will be sacrificed.

Frequently clipped hedges make special demands on the soil, and the site should therefore be well dug beforehand, at the same time adding plenty of compost or decayed manure to sustain fast growth. Clear perennial weeds as you work, for these are hard to remove afterwards, and always plant in single rather than staggered rows to allow access for weeding in the early years before the hedge is established. Water the hedge thoroughly in dry weather during its first year or two, and feed it annually because you want to encourage rapid development in both height and density, together with prompt revival after clipping, which must start at an early age.

Topiary needs the same kind of thoughtful preparation and care, for it is no more than a whimsical form of hedge training and clipping. Used for ornament since Roman times, it can have a dramatic impact, especially where specimens are given positions of prominence – a mop-head bay in the centre of a herb garden, box finials to embellish the corners of beds, or rosemary obelisks as sentinels beside gateways and paths, for example. Feed and water topiary regularly, and clip it frequently with scissors to maintain the shape. Use plants sparingly and with discretion: you are creating a herb garden, not an exhibition of topiary, and they should serve only as decorative highlights.

Herb lawns

Prostrate herbs are suitable for growing densely to create fragrant lawns that can be kept neat, preferably after flowering in most cases, by clipping with shears or mowing with the mower

Herbs for Potted Topiary

- germander
- mintbush (*Prostanthera rotundifolia*)
- rosemary
- scented-leaf pelargoniums (especially *P. crispum*)
- manuka (*Leptospermum scoparium*)
- myrtle – especially *Myrtus communis* 'Microphylla'
- santolina (including *S. virens*)
- Victorian rosemary

blades set high. They are not as hard-wearing as turf and therefore should be made in corners of their own or where traffic is not heavy, but they have a special timeless charm and surround you with fragrance when you tread on them.

A lawn made of chamomile is traditional – use a non-flowering clone such as 'Treneague' – and it has the advantage of remaining green long after drought has scorched ordinary turf. It can be difficult to keep weed-free, however, requires shearing rather than mowing, and after only a few years usually needs remaking; it is better planted in mortar joints between paving slabs where it is more easily maintained. Thyme (single or contrasting variegated cultivars) and mint-scented pennyroyal are far more satisfactory lawn herbs, producing thick mats of growth that once established suppress most weeds, and both bear heavy flushes of attractive flowers as a bonus.

To make a herb lawn, the ground needs thorough preparation in the same way as a seedbed, with a top dressing of general fertilizer raked in just before planting. Plant your lawn in

Above left: *Even while young and still growing, hedging herbs, such as santolina, need clipping to induce bushy growth.*

Above right: *A taut line acts as a guide and helps ensure consistent height and width along the hedge.*

spring or autumn, setting chamomile plants about 4 in apart, other species at 12 in spacings, and water it well until it is established. Chamomile spreads faster if it is occasionally rolled (Shakespeare's Falstaff noticed, 'The more it is trodden on the better it grows'). Remove any weeds promptly before they get a hold, especially in the early stages while there is still bare soil to colonize.

Above: *Many grey and silver herbs, such as santolina, can be kept neat and compact if clipped in spring and prevented from flowering by a further trim in summer.*

Left: *The traditional knot garden, with its contrasting threads of hedging plants, takes several seasons before it is established, and the small plants from which it develops need frequent clipping to transform them into dense hedges.*

Herbs as Flowering Plants

Visually the flowering season is a pinnacle of delight in the herb garden. Although herbs cannot compete with the gaudiness of summer bedding plants, their soft and subtle flower hues contribute a cottage garden innocence, altogether in keeping with their sensuous simplicity. Many of the flowers are useful in their own right, for their fragrance and color in pot-pourri, their medicinal uses in cosmetics and tisanes, or simply for eating in salads and adding to cool summer drinks.

Althaea officiualis

It is a mistake to assume that herbs are grown primarily for their leaves, and that allowing them to bloom exhausts their energies or dilutes their active properties. The removal of flowers is only occasionally necessary: strictly formal hedges lose their precise geometry if allowed to bloom, and annuals such as basil will deteriorate rapidly after flowering. Prolific self-seeders, such as fennel and angelica, need dead-heading for restraint, or you can cut out the flowering stems at an earlier stage.

Many herbs have a rich tradition of religious or national symbolism: the chrysanthemum in China and Japan, for example, and jasmine in Arab

ENCOURAGING HONEY BEES

If you keep honey bees yourself or find that large numbers regularly visit your garden, planting some of their favourite flowers (not necessarily the same as those frequented by bumble bees) will increase the honey flow or entice them to stay and fertilize your fruit and vegetable crops.

- basil
- borage
- clover
- crocus
- hollyhock
- ivy
- lemon balm
- marjoram
- mustard
- rosemary
- savory

- bergamot
- bugle
- comfrey
- dandelion
- hyssop
- lavender
- mallow
- mint
- pulmonaria
- sage
- thyme

cultures, and as early as the second century AD the Greek *Dream Book of Artimedorus* catalogued the meanings attached to flowers. A large number were sacred to the Virgin Mary – hence the profusion of common names prefixed with 'Mary', 'lady', and 'Our Lady's' – and these were often gathered in medieval St Mary Gardens.

Left: *Feverfew, like other members of the Compositae family such as chamomile and tansy, has pretty daisy-like flowers which are as medicinally useful as its leaves.*

Elizabethan floral alphabets and the Victorian love of creating bouquets of flowers to send floral messages are all part of this enduring tradition. Even herbal weeds and wild flowers had their significance: chickweed meant you wanted to make a rendezvous, buttercups promised prosperity and sorrel affection, while the course of love could be charted with foxglove for treachery and hops for injustice, followed inevitably by evening primrose for uncertainty, lily of the valley for restored joy and finally rosemary for remembrance.

Herbs for seeds

Flowering leads ultimately to seeding, an important part of the herbal calendar, as many plants are cultivated for their seeds, sometimes exclusively: caraway, coriander, cumin, dill, fenugreek, mustard, poppy and sesame are all staple seed producers. Where large quantities are needed, plants are best grown as utility crops in the kitchen garden, perennials gathered in a sunny corner and annuals sown in rows between the vegetables, for few seeding herbs look very decorative, and you will probably want to prevent accidental seeding among other herbs. Always choose a warm position for them, to help seeds ripen and dry on the plants.

Useful garden flowers

In addition to familiar herbs with attractive blooms, there are plants that are normally grown for ornament in flower beds and borders, but which have traditional herbal uses, and these provide valuable extra color in the herb garden. Larger species, such as eucalyptus, elder, broom, hollyhock and mullein, all contribute height as well as color. For the middle of borders, you can integrate blue cornflowers, sea holly, greater celandine (beware of self-seeding), peonies, columbines and hydrangeas, while the edges of beds are ideal for low-growing plants such as thrift, candytuft, violets and garden pinks.

Herb Tea

1 Many flowering herbs can be used to make herbal teas and tisanes. Collect the flowerheads in summer and allow them to dry. Store them in sealed containers so that they keep well. To make a tea, place 1 tbsp dried flowers or petals per person in a teapot or jug and fill with boiling water.

2 Leave the infusion to steep for 5-8 minutes. When the flavor is strong enough, pour slowly through a strainer.

Left: *The prolific heads of arching borage flowers self-seed freely and guarantee plenty of seedlings for the next year. The ample crop of blooms can also be floated in summer drinks, face-upwards to display their immaculate shape and intense violet-blue color.*

Salad Herbs

People have gathered herbs for thousands of years, not just in their search for natural remedies, but also to supplement their diet with nutritious wild plants. Lettuce, cabbage and carrots are all derived from wild ancestors that sometimes bear little obvious resemblance to their modern descendants. Few people today would want to depend on these primitive plants for their food, but numerous wild flowers, herbs and even weeds remain popular as salad ingredients, while some are still used occasionally as leaf vegetables or pot herbs for cooking.

Daucus carota

Early salads, or 'sallets' as they were known, seem wildly eclectic in comparison with today's cautious list of limited ingredients, and it is only recently that we are beginning once more to include the vast larder of herbal flavors. In the late seventeenth century, John Evelyn was already complaining about the impoverished imagination of contemporary cooks, compared with the Latin races 'who gather anything almost that is tender to the very tops of nettles, so as every Hedge affords a sallet (not una-greeable), and seasoned with Vinegar Salt and Oil, which gives it both the relish and the name of Salad…'.

It must be added that gathering wild herbs indiscriminately has its very real dangers, as Evelyn observed when he reminded us that 'Sad experience shows how many fatal mistakes have been made by those who took hemlock for aconite, cow weed for Chervil, Dog's Mercury for Spinach, whose dire effects have been many times sudden death and the cause of mortal accidents…'.

The best way to avoid 'mortal accidents' is to grow salad herbs in the garden where their identity is known. Even then it is wise to use only moderate amounts, for many are pungent or strongly flavored and are added sparingly for a hint of stimulating flavor, while the most benign herb can have unforeseen effects if taken in large

Above: *Sorrel is particularly welcome in early spring, when it supplies tasty and nutritious leaves long before conventional salad ingredients are ready. Lamb's lettuce is another useful hardy leaf herb.*

Left: *Garlic chives, like other alliums, are valuable members of the salad herb garden, combining culinary usefulness with all the charm of delicate wild flowers.*

quantities: over-consumption of parsley, for example, has been known to cause liver damage.

Nevertheless, a leaf taken from here and there, together with a few colored edible flowers, will add interest and piquancy to a plain salad, and there is every reason to revive the flair and variety of older traditions. Growing your favourite salad ingredients together in a separate bed will create an attractive miniature garden that can be harvested easily, for it need only take a few minutes to gather leaves of various lettuces, burnet, dandelion, fennel, lovage, lemon balm, common daisy and pulmonaria, together with flowers such as marigolds, cowslips, violets, nasturtiums and bugloss for a connoisseur's salad. Chinese cabbage is an ideal substitute for lettuce in oriental salads, especially when mixed with authentic herbs such as sesame seeds, ginger, lemon grass, mugwort and mallow.

NATURAL SEEDBEDS

Chervil and parsley, both popular salad herbs, can be grown as self-perpetuating crops, producing their own self-sown seedlings for subsequent use. Simply transfer a single parsley plant to a clear part of a nursery bed, where you can continue using its foliage until it flowers in its second year from sowing. Keep the soil clear around the base of the plant as the seeds ripen, and you will find these fall and produce a bed of seedlings to transplant for future supplies. Chervil behaves in the same way, although as an annual it self-seeds within a single season. It is best sown broadcast in patches, where later generations of seedlings can remain to form a constantly regenerating bed.

HOP SHOOTS

Apart from their important commercial use as a flavoring and preservative in brewing, hops have medicinal and culinary value, and are also grown as ornamental climbers where space allows. The twining annual stems can reach 20 ft or more on strong supports of posts and wires, their handsome foliage and decorative female 'cones' making them ideal companions for climbing roses to divide larger gardens. From the dormant crowns more shoots emerge in spring than will be needed, so thin them when they are about 6-8 in tall, leaving four to six of the strongest, and steam or poach the surplus shoots as an alternative to asparagus.

Above: *Many familiar flowering annuals make useful additions to a herb collection: nasturtiums not only add a bright splash of color to the garden, but their leaves are edible, the pleasantly flavored flowers can be used to brighten up salads, and the seeds, when pickled, taste very similar to capers.*

Herbs for Seasoning

National cuisines have evolved over many centuries and even now include strong echoes of former customs. The choice of seasoning herbs is no exception. Certain flavors are instantly attributable to regional cookery: sumac, cardamom and sesame in the Middle East, Mediterranean olives, garlic and dill in northern Europe, saffron in North Africa and chillies in Mexico, lemon grass in South-East Asia, ginger and star anise in China, and a multitude of Indian seasonings such as coriander, fenugreek, nigella and turmeric.

Coriandrum sativum

Modern cooks add herbs to a dish for flavoring rather than for medicinal or preservative purposes, but earlier generations used them from necessity. A medieval peasant, for example, often could not afford to feed his livestock through the winter and so would slaughter animals in autumn and keep the meat as best he could. In the days before refrigeration, stored produce gradually deteriorated, and strong flavors, easily provided by herbs, were needed to disguise stale ingredients in a dish.

Apart from the historical reasons for adding them, herbs all serve some further purpose, whether it is to stimulate the appetite, aid digestion or stop the food from going off.

Horseradish is a pungent seasoning with typical antibiotic properties, used for centuries in Europe to preserve meat and disguise 'off' flavors, although the sauce prepared from its roots is now more usually regarded as an optional condiment with roast beef. The plant, which resembles an over-enthusiastic dock, belongs in the safety of the kitchen garden, where it

can be grown as an annual root crop or as a perennial in a confined space to restrain its natural invasiveness. Here, too, you should grow coriander, whether for its seeds or spicy leaves; the sturdy annual fenugreek, undistinguished in appearance but essential for curries; and the various kinds of mustard with their medicinal, seasoning and carminative uses.

DIGESTIVE AIDS

Seasonings primarily satisfy the palate, while carminatives aid later digestion. Several herbs, all important candidates for the culinary herb garden, possess volatile oils that are helpful in preventing wind or stimulating the

MINT ROOT CUTTINGS

1 Mint beds need regular renewal, which is easily done by taking healthy young roots, trimming them into short sections and pressing these into trays of moist compost.

2 Cover the cuttings with a layer of compost, and they will soon start to grow – those prepared in early autumn can provide young shoots for winter use.

Above: *Many culinary herbs blend perfectly together; for bouquets garnis gather the various ingredients at the same time and mix together in small bunches, as they are easier to assemble while fresh.*

secretion of digestive juices, and many people like to include one or two of these at the table. Dill is perhaps best known because of its popularity in the form of dill water or 'gripe water', but caraway, coriander, fennel and aniseed are also effective carminatives, either separately or mixed in equal proportions. The seeds are the part used, so make a point of leaving them to flower for harvesting at the end of the season.

MAINTAINING SUPPLIES

Since gardeners tend to grow herbs mainly for seasoning, it is well worth trying to plan a continuous supply. Most culinary herbs can be preserved by drying or some other method, but in most cases the fresh product has a better flavor. Some kinds can be potted up in autumn or sown in late summer to reach their peak during the winter, and these will often provide useful crops on a kitchen window sill. A warm greenhouse or conservatory is a more congenial home out of season for potted herbs because they receive more light there, but you can also keep many hardy kinds growing in a cold frame by reserving a sequence of pots there until needed. A permanent collection of perennials may be planted in a soil-based frame, while a portable frame can be placed over a specially planted bed in the autumn. Protect individual plants with cloches or smaller covers, and wrap these with old mats or several sheets of bubble wrap in the event of frost.

HERB OILS

1 Herb oils can be used to add flavor to cooked dishes, salad dressings or marinades. Use one large bunch of herb leaves and 1³/₄ pints of olive oil. Take a large bunch of a leafy seasoning herb such as mint or basil and separate the leaves from the stems. Tear the leaves into rough strips and discard the stems.

2 Using a pestle and mortar, pound the leaves with a little of the olive oil to release the flavor, gradually adding more leaves as the first few begin to break up.

3 Half fill a sterilized bottle with olive oil and half of the herb leaves. Add a generous pinch of rock salt and fill the bottle with the remaining oil and leaves. Seal firmly and leave to stand for two weeks, tipping the bottle upside down occasionally to ensure the flavors mix.

Left: *Gather culinary herbs for preserving on a warm, dry day, selecting clean, healthy pieces which can then be tied for drying in bundles, on their own or combined in bouquets.*

Above: *Herbs gathered fresh from the garden provide an instant assortment of flavors. Short sprigs can be snipped using scissors or clippers; use quickly or keep in a jar of water on a window sill for a few hours.*

Right: *Seasoning herbs such as bay, chives, rosemary and parsley are easy to grow and have an excellent flavor when fresh. Try experimenting with different culinary combinations when planning a new herb bed.*

Herbs for Healing

Cedronella triphylla

Herbs have long held an important place in the treatment of ailments, and herbal remedies are still popular. Today, the pace of research is accelerating rapidly throughout the world, using various scientific skills to evaluate plants and native traditions in the search for new remedies.

Homer wrote of healing roots, one of the earliest records of the use of medicinal plants in Europe, but Chinese manuals and Indian Ayurvedic texts pre-date this by centuries. Much early herbal medicine was based on superstition: the 'Doctrine of Signatures', for example, stated that a herb would treat that part of the body which it most resembled. European settlers arriving in North America found that the Indian inhabitants had their own version of the doctrine, and would associate yellow herbs with jaundice or red ones with blood disorders.

Most herbal remedies were compounds extracted and blended by apothecaries from several plants, each of which was known on its own as a 'simple'. Apothecaries realized that there were differences in purity and potency between substances found in similar species, and that the effects also depended on factors such as the site where they were gathered, or the time of the month or year. In an attempt to standardize quality, the first secular gardens of simples were established in Pisa, Padua, and thereafter throughout Europe and elsewhere – the first such garden in North America was planted by Dr John Bartram in Philadelphia in 1782. They were organized along the lines of earlier monastic hospital gardens, and were generally known as 'Physic Gardens'. It was here that systematic study of plants began in earnest, combining the disciplines of botany and medicine.

Very often scientific discoveries are based on established local use. Romanies, peasants and rainforest tribesmen alike have needed to be accurate botanists for their very survival. These people have understood the healing capabilities of plants in skilled hands, but they have also appreciated the potential dangers of misuse: rue was chosen by Mohammed, for example, as the most blessed of all herbs and it is central to many Arab and Chinese therapies, but it contains a number of active princi-

Left: *In the herbal pharmacy, fresh or dried herbs have been prepared for medicinal use for centuries, drawing on the accumulated wisdom and experience of generations of herbalists. Diagnosis and prescription are still best left to a qualified practitioner, although simple remedies can be prepared at home.*

HERB BALM

1 A herb balm can soothe aching muscles and so aid relaxation. Weigh out 1 oz fresh lavender and rosemary stems, mixed.

2 Place the herbs in a small pan set over a bain-marie. Add 1 pint olive or sunflower oil. Cover with a light lid and simmer for 2 hours, adding more water as necessary.

3 Allow to cool slightly then strain the liquid into a clean bowl.

4 Leave the liquid to cool and then pour into a sterilized jar or bottle and seal. Apply sparingly.

ples which often cause sensitivity to light, and people often develop skin rashes after contact with the plant.

Herbs interact in complex ways with our body chemistry, and their power to heal is formidable. Compared with synthetic drugs their actions may seem very mild, but you should not underestimate the dangers of self-medication on the assumption that herbs are harmless. Many traditional remedies are based on fantasy, guesswork and suggestion, while even the most reputable herbs are selective in their effects, working for one patient but not another.

Only a trained practitioner is qualified to diagnose an ailment, and then to suggest a personal prescription after fully assessing your individual needs. The medical benefits of herbs are no longer in doubt, and many are generally quite safe, provided that they are not misused or taken in circumstances

Right: *It is not just the visible flowers and leaves of herbs that are valuable. Very often the fresh or dried roots, such as those of comfrey, contain the highest concentrations of active ingredients.*

where allergic reactions or side effects are possible – even garlic, widely regarded as an infallible panacea, may reduce blood pressure and so cancel the impact of drugs taken for cardiac disorders. All the plants are complex factories producing diverse chemicals, some of them fragrances to attract pollinating insects, others toxins to deter predators, and any one of these substances may be harmful in particular circumstances.

NATURAL INSECTICIDES

Many plants produce natural insecticides as part of their defence systems, and some of these are widely used as prepared powders and liquids in the garden. Derris, or rotenone, a popular insecticide approved for organic use, is extracted from the powdered roots of a Malaysian shrub known as tuba root (*Derris elliptica*).

Sometimes particular species are grown as companion plants to protect crops nearby from attack.

Various *Tagetes* species have been found to repel whitefly and other pests when grown in greenhouses, and scientific experiments now confirm that their flowers emit volatile chemicals into the surrounding air for protection. As these have proved toxic to the mosquitoes that carry malaria and yellow fever, it is hoped that a new generation of insecticides can be developed for their control.

Herbs for Dyeing

Urtica dioica

Anyone who has gathered wild blackberries in autumn or pinched out sideshoots from tomato plants will readily appreciate the possibilities of using plant stains to dye animal skins and woven material. Until chemical dyes were introduced, roots, bark, flowers and leaves were the chief sources of color, often made permanent by the addition of mordants – fixing chemicals – from mineral-rich earths and other sources. The shades obtained are rarely vivid, but mellow, subtle, and full of the lustrous beauty of the plants themselves.

Ancient China, India and other Asian countries developed sophisticated skills in dyeing, but similar techniques have always been used by tribespeople around the world, who adapted plant materials for painting on bark, to ornament clothing or decorate the skin in preparation for religious ceremonies or warfare, and even for disguise – Romanies once artificially tanned their faces with juices obtained from a favorite herb, *Lycopus europaeus* or gipsywort. The early Britons were described by Julius Caesar as 'blue and terrible' after they had dyed their skin with woad to make their appearance more alarming, while in ancient Egypt the plant was also used to color imperial garments.

Dyeing with herbs remains a popular and pleasant craft, although large amounts of material are often needed, and colors tend to fade gently unless made fast with chemical mordants such as alum, tin, iron or chrome. Results vary according to the strength of the dye, the length of time that the wool (the easiest material to color) is left immersed, and the parts of a plant that are used: the leaves of privet, for example, give yellow shades, whereas the berries impart a muted blue-green hue.

Some plants can be gathered from the wild, but in view of the amounts needed there is the risk of over-

Above: *Woad, or dyer's rocket, is cultivated in many countries for its distinctive blue dye.*

Left: *Manufacture of indigo dye paste from a species of* Indigofera *in southwest China.*

harvesting species that may not be abundant, and it is often better to grow your own supplies of the more useful kinds in a special dye border. This can be an attractive feature, for many of the plants are popular garden ornamentals whose flowers or fruits are the parts used, so that geraniums, dahlias, rudbeckia and mulberries can earn a place as dye plants in the herb garden. Experiment with various leaves after pruning or clipping shrubs and hedges, as many will impart various shades of yellow and green.

CLASSIC DYE CROPS

Traditional dye plants worth growing include the ancient woad (*Isatis tinctoria*), a leafy spinach-like plant whose use dwindled rapidly after the introduction of the more permanent blue dye from the indigo plant, *Indigofera tinctoria*, a subtropical species which needs to be grown in a warm greenhouse in temperate regions.

Dyer's madder (*Rubia tinctorum*) is a self-seeding perennial still cultivated

Above: *Woolen yarn dyed using homegrown* Polygonum tinctorum. *Shades are varied by the number of immersions in the vat.*

Right: *Indigo plants,* Strobilanthes flaccidifolius, *growing in a field in Guizhou Province, south-west China. Plants are cultivated annually from cuttings – the precursor of the dye is contained in the leaves.*

on a field scale in France and the Netherlands, and an important European source of strong red, while in North America bloodroot (*Sanguinaria canadensis*) was the main plant used by Indians for red body paint. Weld (*Reseda luteola*) (or dyer's greenweed, *Genista tinctoria*), a relative of broom, another dye source, is a traditional yellow dye plant with handsome flower spikes, and a tendency to colonize unless seedlings are kept in check.

The elder is guardian of all herbs according to folklore, and planting one of these will provide you with a green dye from the leaves and, from the berries, lilac (using alum mordant) or purple (using chrome).

SELECTED PLANTS FOR A DYE GARDEN

Part of the creative adventure of dyeing with plants is that the shades obtained can be varied considerably by using different mordants, so that madder, for example, can produce anything from light pink to dark brown.

- reds, pinks: bloodroot, chenopodium, madder, pokeberry, rose hips, sorrel
- yellows and orange: beetroot, coreopsis, dahlias, golden rod, heather, marigolds, Osage orange, pear leaves, rudbeckia, saffron, turmeric, weld, zinnias
- black: meadowsweet, walnut
- blues: blackberries, blueberries, dandelion root, elderberries, indigo, juniper berries, woad, yellow flag

- greens: bracken, dock, lily of the valley, nettles, weld
- browns: gipsywort, madder, sassafras, sumac, various barks (apple, birch, walnut), willow

Choosing Sites for Herbs

Choosing a suitable site for a herb needs preliminary assessment of factors such as the type of plant, the soil, the aspect, the exposure and the local temperature range. There are also practical considerations of space and appearance in relation to the rest of the garden. All this needs careful thought before starting to plant up sites.

Thymus vulgaris

Every form of gardening is artificial and depends for its success on matching as far as possible the natural environment of the plants. Herbs that you intend cultivating will be assembled in one place, and yet they come originally from all parts of the world and every kind of soil and climate.

Always find out where your herbs normally grow in the wild – it might be a sun-baked rocky hillside near the Mediterranean Sea or a well-watered rainforest where frost is unknown, a cool temperate woodland, or cold exposed cliff where wind keeps growth short and compact. Try to identify the warmest sheltered parts of the garden, the areas with the best drainage or dappled shade, corners where frost lingers or the sun arrives first in the morning, and allocate herbs according to their preferences. If you are planning a separate herb garden, assess its position at all times of the year and from all cultural aspects, and then choose the plants

Below: *A general mixed bed of herbs, combining, for example, borage, comfrey, lovage and lavender: this looks very effective against a backdrop of traditional wattle fencing.*

PLANNING A SMALL BORDER

Herbs for the back layer – 3 ft upwards
* *perennials: angelica, artemisia, bergamot, elecampane, fennel, liquorice, lovage, meadowsweet, rosemary, sea holly, shrub roses, European or American sweet cicely*
* *annuals and biennials: alexanders, foxglove, mullein*

Herbs for the middle section – 1 ft 6 in-3 ft
* *perennials: agrimony, balm, chicory, comfrey, costmary, curry plant, lavender, rampion, rue, sage, santolina, southernwood, St John's wort, tansy, tarragon, valerian, white horehound*
* *annuals and biennials: borage, bugloss, caraway, dill*

Herbs for the front edge – up to 1 ft 6 in
* *perennials: bistort, calamint, catmint, chamomile, chives, herb bennet, hyssop, lady's smock, marjoram, mint, sedum, sorrel, thyme, winter savory, wormwood, yarrow*
* *annuals and biennials: anise, basil, chervil, clary, coriander, cumin, marigold, parsley, summer savory*

that are most likely to succeed in its various beds.

Remember that the term 'herbs' is used as a broad and imprecise classification, and includes plants with very different life cycles. Annuals and biennials are short-term plants, the former completing their growth from germination to shedding seed within a single season (some such as chervil can manage more than one generation per year). This partly determines where they are grown, for they will change rapidly in appearance and leave gaps in a planting scheme when they have died down. Biennials germinate and make leafy growth during their first season, survive the winter on the stored nutrients in their roots, and then flower and set seed the following year; if they are grown for their foliage, you can treat them as annuals, but for flower and seed crops they will need space for two years.

Perennials, which may be hardy or tender according to their origin, provide the framework of any herb garden design, for they are permanent and maintain continuity from one year to the next.

Size varies widely, with some herbs low-growing but liable to expand sideways into broad ground-hugging mats of foliage, while others are tall and dominating. Ultimate height and spread should always be taken into account when planning beds and herb gardens, together with a plant's tolerance of pruning and clipping, for many bulky subjects such as evergreen shrubs can be cut back to manageable size. Site plants of various heights according to their probable impact on an overall design: the tallest species work best in the center of island beds viewed from all sides or at the back of borders, with the shortest plants at the

PLANTING A HEDGE

1 Mark out and excavate a shallow trench running the length of the proposed hedge, and thoroughly fork over the soil in the bottom to ensure good drainage.

2 Hedging plants need plenty of nourishment in their early years, so add a generous amount of garden compost to the trench and lightly fork in.

3 Mark the center line of the hedge with string and pegs, and space out the plants, using a length of cane or wooden batten to measure equal distances between them.

4 Planted, firmed and watered in the refilled trench, the hedge will soon begin to fill out, ready for its first trim to shape.

front, although positioning a large, attractive specimen where it is least expected (within a sea of contrasting short plants, perhaps, or on a bend in a path to conceal an alcove) can produce a satisfying impact.

Growing herbs in containers is the ideal solution where considerations of space, soil or climate suggest a plant might be difficult to grow. This is not a poor substitute for open-ground cultivation, but an attractive branch of gardening in its own right. Most herbs

adapt to pots and other containers, and when well tended can create satisfying collections to enhance otherwise barren areas of the garden – courtyards, flights of steps, entrances and exits, for example – and make herb growing a practical choice for window boxes, balconies and roof gardens. It is easy to supply container-grown plants with the kind of soil they prefer, and to move them under cover or to sunny spots if they are sensitive to cold or exposure.

Above: *Raised beds built within stone walls are convenient sites for herbs such as rosemary. They offer good drainage and ease of picking.*

Above: *Shady woodland spots suit many herbs which do not tolerate direct sun and dry soil. Herbs such as peppermint may provide useful ground cover for barer patches beneath trees in cultivated gardens.*

Planning the Herb Garden

Levisticum officiuale

Formal or relaxed, utilitarian or decorative, a herb garden must be satisfying to look at and work in, and manageable in terms of your time, needs, energy and commitment. A complex parterre, for example, must be kept clipped, weed-free and carefully aligned for success, whereas the cottage garden approach of profusion without confusion may be more appropriate if you want plentiful supplies of useful herbs combined with cheerful diversity and low maintenance.

Once you have explored the potential site and the chances of your chosen herbs liking the position, there is style to consider. This is an intangible but important matter, taking into account not only your personal tastes but the nature of the site, for any garden or border is intimately bonded to the house, and to the immediate and distant surroundings.

With a fairly clear vision of the garden you would like, you can draw together all the various elements in a final design. Measure the garden or plot, and mark its outline on graph

Above: *Design herb beds and borders to take advantage of contrasts between colors and shapes, but remember to match for height and impact.*

paper, together with existing assets such as shrubs and paths that are to be retained, and important nearby features – fences or hedges, large trees that might cast shade, and the house itself. Mark in with symbols the essential bones of the scheme, the new paths and beds, large plants, watercourses. The smaller the intended garden, the easier this planning stage will be, and for a simple bed of culinary herbs you might be able to omit drawing up a design altogether.

For larger plans always beware the illusion that you have more room in the garden than actually exists: it is easy on paper to draw a path or pack a large number of herbs into a given space, and then find that the result is hopelessly cramped or out of scale, or has unexpected visual effects on the rest of the garden. Look up the likely spread of trees and shrubs, mark this precisely on the plan, and then check frequently with the site itself; if necessary position stakes where significant plants and features are to go, or lay a garden hose on the ground to assess

Left: *Avoid mistakes and disappointment by making careful preliminary plans, drawing out the proposed design to scale to check its impact and feasibility.*

LAYING A PATH

1 Mark out and excavate the path, arranging stout boards along the sides with their upper edges at the finished surface level. Spread and compact a foundation of hardcore such as stones or broken brick.

2 Cover the base with a bed of sand, lightly tamped with the head of a rake to fill any gaps in the hardcore, and then rake a loose level surface in which to bed the bricks.

3 Arrange the bricks on the widest side in an attractive bond or pattern, firming them into place with the handle of a hammer and checking the surface in all directions with a spirit level as you go.

4 With all the bricks set out, spread more sand over the surface and brush repeatedly to fill all the joints; clear away any surplus sand.

5 Ease sand from the joints with a knife to create pockets for prostrate herbs which may be sown directly or, as here, planted as divisions from established specimens.

6 Tuck a little compost around the plants, firm into place and water if necessary; they will soon spread into mats and cushions of fragrant foliage.

the shape and course of a path or bed.

Work out planting schemes for individual beds and borders on separate sheets of paper only when you are satisfied with all this preliminary work make any necessary basic adjustments after trying out possible variations on the ground.

In addition to pictorial plans, you should also draw up a schedule of the work involved, because the various tasks are often best done in a particular order, perhaps at certain times of the year to ensure the least amount of disorder, mess and delay. Planting itself is almost the final operation and best timed for autumn in mild areas, or spring where winters are severe.

Before then you will need to repair or renovate existing hard structures such as paths, fences and walls, prune or move plants at the appropriate season, and remove turf or weeds to leave a clear site for marking out. Separate smaller beds can be prepared and planted piecemeal, but when planning a complete herb garden it is best to complete all these preliminary stages before transferring your design to the ground, using pegs driven in securely and joined with strings to mark the basic outlines. You can then dig over beds and borders to a suitable depth and condition, and set about constructing paths and hard edges.

Plant Requirements

Consideration should be given to the requirements of individual herbs for successful growth and yield; different surroundings are suitable for different herbs and a little time spent researching the ideal environment will help to produce a wonderful crop of pungent and decorative plants.

Lavandula spica

Although most of the well-known herbs are of Mediterranean origin and therefore prefer a sunny, free-draining position, re-creating the ecology they evolved in does not mean aiming deliberately for impoverished conditions. Only the nasturtium is recommended for hungry sites, because these encourage the production of flowers that might otherwise be usurped by lush leaf growth; but the result of improved flowering in the case of the nasturtium is often early death. It is worth remembering that most plants grown in gardens are often superior in form, size and performance to their relatives in the wild: the fact that they have adapted naturally to spartan surroundings is no reason to deny them care and nourishment.

It is fair to say, though, that aromatic herbs grown for flavoring or medicinal use are best grown in full sun, whereas those grown as pot herbs and leaf crops prefer moister conditions and some shelter from hot sunshine if they are to make plenty of growth. Arrange beds or the distribution of plants within a herb garden according to these needs, assembling leafy plants, for example, at the shady end of a border, in the shadow of shrubs, near hedges or beneath the canopy of open-pruned trees to provide them with a little dappled shade. Remember that variegated plants yield their best colors when exposed to morning and evening sunlight with a little shade at midday.

Similarly, free drainage is important for plants that are intolerant of damp conditions. These include plants with silver and grey foliage, which is usually produced by dense fine leaf hairs intended to trap moisture, developed as an adaptation to very dry conditions. Other plants of dubious hardiness may also succumb to prolonged damp around the stems. Raised beds or gravel mulches around stem bases can sometimes improve their chances of survival. Most woody-stemmed perennials need plenty of warm sunlight to ripen their growth and ensure

DIVIDING A BED

1 Segregate herbs with underground runners from other, more vulnerable plants with wide slates or pieces of durable paneling inserted vertically.

2 Replace the soil on both sides of the division, and firm into place with your heel or the handle of a trowel.

3 An invasive herb such as mint can then be planted a little distance from the inconspicuous division.

that they are well prepared to withstand winter temperatures.

Herbs that like damp, partially shaded sites, on the other hand, only thrive where their needs are met, both hot dry soil and gloomy waterlogged positions proving intolerable to them. Herbaceous perennial herbs, in particular, need to make maximum growth during the growing season to stock their roots with enough nutrients for survival and re-emergence the following spring.

Most herbs need shelter of some kind from the extremes of wind and frost. Though they might survive in the wild, their growth is often stunted by wind-pruning and frost injury, and you will do them a favor by enclosing beds and borders with windbreak hedges or fences that reduce their exposure. You will reap the benefits in summer, when the still sheltered air is heavy with the concentrated fragrance of volatile oils. Make sure, however, that the garden is not so enclosed that it becomes a frost pocket, without gateways or openings for cold air to drain away from susceptible plants.

SLOPING GROUND

Level ground is not essential unless you are planning an impressive parterre or knot garden, which really needs construction on a prepared platform in the same way as a bowling green or formal lawn. For most other herb schemes sloping ground, especially a dry bank, is ideal as a means of guaranteeing good drainage and, if it faces the sun for a large part of the day, plenty of warmth and light. There are enough prostrate and trailing herb varieties to ensure adequate ground cover and protection against soil erosion on a bank, but for larger specimens or where the incline is very steep,

making simple terraces or small level planting pockets will help with rapid establishment and any watering needed until plants are self-reliant. Paths can be cut as a series of steps, their outline perhaps softened by cascading thymes, ground-hugging Corsican mint, or tufts of chamomile and the creeping savory *Satureja spicigera*.

Above: *Herbs that need warm conditions do well when planted along the base of a brick wall facing the sun, which remains warm even after nightfall.*

Right: *A simple pit surrounded with firm walls of bricks or old wooden beams provides a useful bed for larger herbs, or (as here) a propagation and nursery frame that can be covered in cold weather.*

Above: *Stepping stones made from sawn log sections or paving slabs are a simple means of providing access for planting and maintenance in larger beds, and soon merge with the herbs as these grow and spread.*

HERBS FOR HEAVY SOILS

Although wet clays and other intractable soils will always benefit from some improvement to open their texture and speed drainage, the following herbs can usually cope well, especially if the surface is mulched in summer to prevent drought and cracking. Sunny or shaded sites are suitable, except where stated otherwise.

- alexanders
- borage (sun)
- chives (sun)
- fennel (sun)
- lovage
- nasturtium (sun)
- sorrel

- angelica
- calendula
- comfrey
- lemon balm (sun)
- mint
- sage
- sweet cicely

Structuring the Herb Garden

The design of a formal herb garden, whether it is a complex of knots or a simple wheel with radiating spokes dividing beds of culinary plants, allows plenty of scope for imagination. As William Lawson wrote in the seventeenth century, 'For special forms in squares, there are as many as there are devices in Gardeners' brains.' Simplicity is essential, for an elaborate layout will merely look confused once plants start to grow, and will only be comprehensible if viewed from above.

Gratiola officinalis

Graph paper is essential, as are accurate measurements. Sketch in the outlines of beds and borders as a rough guide, by all means, but decide first on the layout and dimensions of paths. Ornament is one thing, access at all seasons for harvesting and tending plants another, and all paths should be wide enough for comfortable passage (especially between shrubs after heavy rain) and must reach all parts of the garden. Main paths should be at least 2 ft wide, more if you use a wheelbarrow or need wheelchair access. You can make subsidiary paths narrower – 12 in might be enough – or you could use stepping stones instead of a continuous surface. Position the odd slab in large beds to stand on, or limit the beds' width to about 4 ft so that all herbs are within arm's reach.

While balance and good proportion are important in planning the layout of beds, there is no reason why an irregular herb garden cannot be as successful as a classically symmetrical one. Draw out several geometrical patterns of beds on tracing paper laid over the garden outline drawn to scale on squared paper, and check their measurements for practicality. Leave room for seats, statuary and other features, and remember that hedges occupy substantial space – allow a 12 in width for dwarf hedges, more for taller ones.

A series of small beds, each planted with a single type of herb, provides simple bold blocks of color and texture, but more comprehensive plant collections need larger beds, perhaps organized according to color, height or use. With elaborate designs, always measure the diagonals to make sure they are truly symmetrical, and take all measurements accurately, starting where possible from a base line – that is, the longest straight line that can be measured on the site – which can be used as a reference for all other

Left: *Herbs adapt to a number of styles and designs, not least to a relaxed cottage garden arrangement where the plants can grow and flower with their natural informality.*

Herb Spiral

1 Arrange bricks in a gradually increasing number of courses to create the outline of a spiral bed.

2 Spread a drainage layer of pea-sized gravel on the surface of lower levels, omitting areas where moisture-loving herbs are to grow.

3 Add garden compost to part of the lower level for hungry herbs such as parsley, basil and leaf coriander.

4 Partly fill the upper levels with broken bricks and rubble to ensure good drainage for herbs that like dry soil.

5 Fill between the parallel walls with good topsoil, and tamp into place or leave to settle.

6 Arrange the herbs for dry soil near the top and moisture- and nutrient-loving species at the base.

distances. Leave a string marking this line in position if possible to allow easy transfer of the design from paper to ground.

Raised beds

Early herb gardens comprised a series of beds, laid out as functional squares and rectangles or in decorative shapes; these were raised slightly above the level of intervening paths with the soil held in place by edging boards. Raised beds have several advantages over ground-level cultivation: their layout establishes a strong design pattern, and it is easier to improve individual beds than to change the nature of the soil on a large scale, and less bending is involved in cultivating the plants. A single layer of thick wooden planks or edging boards, or two or three courses of bricks, will considerably increase the rooting depth where soils are shallow, while the sides of beds can be raised as high as necessary for the comfort of disabled and elderly gardeners. Higher sides, though, may need foundations and footings for stability, together with a series of holes for drainage.

7 Finally, plant out the herbs and water thoroughly.

Preparing the Site

Teucrium chamaedrys

Many plants are site-specific, only growing well where conditions are perfect. Fortunately the commonest herbs tolerate a wide range of soils, although their performance may be less than ideal – silver and gray herbs, for example, thrive in light, sandy ground, but in the same place sage and winter savory soon develop bare stems and need frequent propagation, and leafy annual herbs quickly bolt to seed in a dry season.

Recreating a plant's preferred habitat is the ideal way to ensure success. Most of us, however, have to compromise by making the most of our garden soil. For positive health plants need enough moisture to maintain growth but not so much that their roots decay in airless surroundings; a balanced supply of nutrients and minerals in a soil that is not too acid or alkaline; sufficient warmth to sustain active growth, and freedom from weed competition. Any soil improvement must take all these factors into account.

Sandy soil is easy to work and warms up quickly, but soluble nutrients are easily leached out by rain, and drought may seriously check the growth of all but the toughest Mediterranean species. Adding plenty of garden compost before planting, together with annual mulches and occasional supplementary feeding to restore depleted fertility, helps to fortify the soil without destroying its naturally free drainage.

The tiny particles of clay readily stick together, producing wet, airless soil that sets hard and cracks in dry weather. Heavy ground with a large proportion of clay is potentially very fertile if you can improve its texture by digging in grit, coarse sand, leaf litter and bulky manure or compost to help aeration. A permanent mulch will protect the surface from being compacted by heavy rainfall and from drying out in hot sunshine.

Pools of water lingering on the surface of heavy waterlogged soils usually indicate poor drainage. Digging can relieve the problem if this is due to surface compaction, while deeper cultivation will break up a hard 'pan' – an impervious layer some distance below the surface. If saturation recurs, you may have to install a system of drainage pipes for permanent improvement unless you confine your herb collection to marshy species.

BEDS FOR WET GROUND

An alternative treatment for wet ground is to increase the depth of free-draining topsoil available for plants by creating raised beds. These are equally effective for coping with

HERBS FOR LIGHT, SANDY SOIL

Many herbs tolerate light, dry soils, but these are particularly suitable. Winter rain may remove large amounts of lime and nutrients each year, so be prepared to feed or compost the soil annually.

- alkanet
- arnica
- broom
- chervil
- coriander
- dianthus
- fennel
- hound's tongue
- lavender
- lemon verbena
- marjoram
- artemisia
- savory
- tarragon
- wormwood

- anise
- borage
- centaury
- chives
- cumin
- evening primrose
- foxglove
- hyssop
- lemon balm
- alfalfa
- sweet clover
- rosemary
- southernwood
- thyme

soils that are shallow, or too acid or alkaline to suit most species. Raised beds are not a modern innovation, but date back to medieval gardens. They may be enclosed by low walls of bricks, stone or timber boarding and their width is best limited to about 4 ft so that you can reach the center without walking on the soil.

Dig over the enclosed area thoroughly, work in as much organic material as you can to improve texture and drainage, and add 6 in of topsoil, perhaps saved from the making of paths, or bought. Finally cover the surface with an organic mulch that can be stirred in annually with a fork to maintain fertility.

CLEARING GROUND

The site for a herb garden is best prepared in autumn. Start by eliminating weeds, especially invasive perennial kinds that will be difficult to remove after planting; these can be forked out carefully or cleared with one or two applications of systemic weedkiller. If the area is under grass, skim this off

with a spade, stack neatly and cover with black plastic sheet until it decays into fibrous loam for potting.

Correct any drainage problems and dig the bed thoroughly. Dress with lime if the soil is too acid, and leave the surface rough over winter to be broken down by frost. In early spring treat any weeds that have appeared, and then fork in a good dressing of compost or decayed manure. Rake the

HERBS FOR CHALKY SOIL

- calamint
- chickweed
- cowslip
- elder
- juniper
- lemon balm
- lungwort
- mignonette
- Pasque flower
- rosemary
- sage
- Solomon's seal
- wormwood

- centaury
- chicory
- dianthus
- hound's tongue
- lavender
- lily of the valley
- marjoram
- mullein
- periwinkle
- roses
- salad burnet
- thyme
- yarrow

surface level, and leave the ground for a few weeks to settle before marking out the design.

Above: *A hand cultivator with prongs can be useful for clearing the site of weeds.*

COMFREY COMPOST

1 Recycling vigorous perennials such as comfrey returns precious minerals and nutrients to the soil. Cut the larger foliage, leaving the youngest leaves to provide further crops later.

2 Soak the leaves in water to make a liquid feed, or add them to the compost heap as this is built; there they will decompose and release their goodness.

Healthy Herbs

A good collection of herbs is an enduring asset and healthy herbs are essential for a functioning garden of plants. Sensible planting arrangements, soil types and the availability of light are all important considerations when beginning a new herb bed or renovating an existing one.

Mentha piperita

A herb garden is an enduring asset, so do not be over-hasty in getting started. With the site prepared, construct any edgings and paths, except for gravel which is best laid after planting to avoid depositing soil on it.

Although container-grown herbs can be planted at almost any time of the year, autumn is the perfect season (especially for bare-root plants) unless winters are very cold or the soil heavy, in which case wait until mid-spring. If you have to wait several months before planting, use the bed for a display of annual flowers or grow a 'green manure' crop of mustard, clover or vetch to dig in later as a soil improver.

Try to fill a whole bed at once, even if this means assembling a collection of herbs over a period of time. They can be kept in their containers, or transferred temporarily to a nursery bed where you might be able to take cuttings or divisions to supplement your stock. Bare-root plants must be heeled in to a piece of spare ground if they are not to be planted immediately.

Be generous with quantities; trees, shrubs and invasive herbs can be planted singly, but others, particularly small edging plants, are best ordered in quantity for an instant impression of lush establishment. Always choose young, short-jointed bushy plants with

PEST AND DISEASE CONTROL

Treating your herbs well by watering, feeding or propagating whenever necessary helps to maintain their vigor and so avoid disorders that normally affect ailing plants.

Any problems that do occur should be treated promptly. Aphids are perhaps the most common pests, and may be controlled by spraying with derris, or rotenone, which is harmless to their natural predators. Quassia is effective against caterpillars if there are too many to pick off by hand. Slugs and snails are also best controlled by picking off.

Diseases are occasionally more serious, especially fungal disorders such as rust, which commonly affects mint, as well as violets and other subjects. Cut down rusted growth to ground level for burning, and scorch the crown and surrounding soil with a flame gun; if all else fails use a commercial fungicide or alternatively transfer clean-rooted divisions to fresh soil.

Left: *Some herbs are attractive enough to mass on their own. Nepeta x faassenii, for example, is a favorite for planting as hedges, edgings and flowering borders.*

Right: *A healthy purple sage plant. For their strongest color such plants need full sunlight, though even in light shade the young tips will display their characteristic leaf colors.*

PLASTIC MULCHES

If you suspect the ground is still full of weed seeds or root fragments, or if the soil is very light and liable to dry out quickly, you can use a plastic mulch to suppress weed growth and retain moisture. Prepare the soil in the usual way when it is moist and rake the surface level, removing as many stones as possible. Spread a sheet of heavy-duty black plastic sheet or woven matting across the bed, and secure the edges by wedging them in the soil. Cut holes or crosses in the sheet through which to plant the herbs, and then cover the whole surface with a layer of gravel, or shredded bark or cocoa shells.

INVASIVE HERBS

Herbs such as mint, tarragon and woodruff are irrepressible colonizers, their creeping roots eventually taking over large areas of ground and infiltrating neighbouring plants. Restrain their invasiveness by planting them in containers, either above ground or buried in the soil. Large pots, bottomless buckets or thick plastic bags perforated with drainage holes are ideal. They can be filled with good garden soil, or a soil and compost mixture, which will sustain them for two or three years before the contents need division and replanting in fresh soil.

a good, healthy color, and make sure they are fully hardened off if bought in spring.

PLANTING

Choose a pleasant day for planting, and one on which you have the time to finish an area completely. Water plants well, whether they are in pots or the open ground, and then arrange them on the surface according to your ground plan – but mark the positions for bare-root plants with stakes or labels, rather than expose them to drying out. Check the overall effect and make sure everything has room to develop, although to avoid unsightly gaps you might prefer to space certain plants more densely and then sacrifice some later as others demand room.

Plant edgings first, together with strategic plants such as trees, shrubs or anything with a large rootball – stake these where necessary, and tread the soil firm around larger plants. Spread out the roots of bare-root specimens, working soil between them as you refill the hole, and make sure the

finished surface matches the soil mark on their stems. Re-level the intervening soil before planting the other herbs. Prune growing tips and side shoots of shrubby plants to encourage bushy growth. Label everything clearly, and then water the whole bed to settle the soil around the roots.

Looking after the Herb Garden

Herbs are relatively free from serious disorders, especially if you start with healthy plants in the first place. However, every plant depends for its welfare on the condition of the soil in which it grows, and the annual management routine in a herb garden should concentrate on building up and maintaining the soil's nutrients and vitality.

Origanum vulgare

WATERING AND FEEDING

Soils lose water through drainage or evaporation at different rates according to their type and condition: clay, for example, retains moisture for much longer than sandy soil, which in a hot dry season may need thorough watering at least every week. Plants can only absorb food in solution, so maintaining adequate moisture at the roots is essential for uninterrupted growth. The best way to ensure this is to add manure or compost to the soil to increase its content of humus, partly decomposed organic material that soaks up water like a sponge and releases it slowly, together with essential nutrients.

If the soil has been enriched with compost or decayed manure during initial preparations, it should be sufficient to spread a layer of compost annually over the surface of the moist soil in spring to maintain humus levels. Most aromatic herbs will then flourish without supplementary watering. Indeed, try not to be too generous when watering: too much water can dilute the essential oils, and may injure herbs that prefer relatively dry conditions.

Leafy herbs will need watering in a dry season to keep the soil constantly moist, while plants grown for their fruits or pods benefit most if watered when in flower and again while their crops are swelling. If you do water, soak plants thoroughly, and spread a further mulch afterwards to prevent evaporation. Plants in containers need regular watering, as will recently introduced herbs, especially if planted in summer. Be prepared to water new trees in dry weather for at least a season after planting.

As long as the soil is mulched annually with a light dressing of compost, most herbs will thrive without supplementary feeding. Too rich a soil, in fact, encourages soft rank growth with less flavor and perfume. Plants grown as bulky leaf crops sometimes benefit from an application of dried blood to supply extra nitrogen after a wet winter on light soils, and fruit quality is improved by a spring dressing of general fertilizer such as seaweed meal or blood, fish and bone. Avoid using artificial fertilizers, which may unbalance soil conditions and reduce the herbs' concentration of essential soils and active substances.

DIVIDING COMFREY

1 Vigorous clump-forming herbs such as bergamot, lovage and comfrey need dividing every few years to keep plants young and robust. Dig whole clumps for splitting, or use a spade to slice off outer portions from growing plants.

2 With a very sharp knife, cut these cleanly into small segments, each with a tuft of leaves or a dormant bud, and plenty of healthy roots. Replant immediately in good soil.

MULCHING

An essential part of soil care and plant health, mulching involves covering the

MAKING COMPOST

Apart from being a useful soil improver in the early stages of making a herb garden, animal manure is too rich for feeding all but the greediest plants. It can be used, however, as just one of the ingredients in a compost heap, where it will blend with plant waste to produce the ideal material for mulching and soil improvement. Site the compost heap on bare soil in a wire enclosure or commercial container, starting with a layer of plant stems and coarse material to let air penetrate the heap. Build the heap in layers, mixing organic household waste, manure, lawn mowings, weeds and discarded plants; avoid seeding and diseased plants, and pass any woody stems through a shredder first. Parts of herbs are particularly suitable ingredients, especially nettles, comfrey and yarrow, which all help the compost to ferment. Between the layers spread a thin dressing of garden lime, or gypsum if you do not want to increase the alkalinity of your soil. Cover the completed heap with plastic sheeting or old carpets. Leave it for a few months, then turn the contents to ensure even decomposition.

ground to protect it from erosion, rapid drying and structural deterioration after heavy rain or hot sun, and also to smother weeds.

An organic mulch of compost, pulverized bark or cocoa shells can be used for plants that like moist conditions, but herbs from hot dry habitats are better mulched with an inorganic material such as gravel or grit to prevent their stems from rotting – this is especially important on heavy soils that may remain wet for a large part of the year. Always spread a mulch when the soil is moist, and keep the material away from woody plant stems to ensure free drainage.

WEEDING

Although plants normally prefer to live in communities rather than alone, common weeds compete too energetically to allow them to grow

Above: *Herbs in constant use, as in this collection of culinary plants, need routine care if they are to prosper and stay in good condition: pruning or cutting back, watering, feeding and regular propagation all help maintain continuity.*

unchecked. A permanent mulch will suppress most annual weeds, which should otherwise be hoed or pulled by hand while still small. Perennial weeds such as buttercup, thistle and ground elder or goutweed are more tenacious and may be a problem even where the soil is mulched. Fork or pull them up with as much root as possible, or paint them individually with systemic weed-killer. Check when weeding, though, that you are not pulling up a potentially useful plant. Many herbs seed themselves and their seedlings can be transplanted to a nursery bed for growing on, while many weeds have

medicinal or culinary uses and so may be worth leaving or growing elsewhere.

The appearance and qualities of herbs change as the season progresses, but light pruning checks this by redirecting energy into new growth, keeping plants in good condition for longer. Dead-heading borage, pot marigolds and other annuals will prevent their setting seed and so prolong flowering for a few more weeks. This is also a useful precaution with prolific seed producers such as fennel and angelica, whose deep-rooted seedlings can take over a herb border – but leave a few heads to mature if you do need more seeds. Self-seeding may be a virtue, of course: you can have continuous supplies of chervil if this short-lived annual is left to seed itself in a permanent bed, while in its second year a parsley plant will sow a patch of seedlings for transplanting elsewhere.

Perennials grown for the soft tips of their shoots are best cut back once or twice as their stems start to age: mint and lemon balm, for example, will produce further flushes of young growth if pruned to ground level before their shoots reach full height. Shrubby perennials are best clipped lightly after flowering to keep the plants tidy and stimulate new side shoots, but if grown formally they will need more frequent trimming. Hedges of santolina, hyssop, rosemary and germander should be clipped in early summer and again two or three months later, and may be pruned hard in spring if they have grown too large.

Autumn care

As frost threatens, tender herbs such as basil, lemon verbena and scented pelargoniums should be dug up for potting and growing on indoors. Take cuttings from any of doubtful hardiness, or transplant a specimen to the cold frame as insurance against loss. Either leave dead stems on herbaceous perennials over winter to provide a little insulation against frost and wind, or cut them down for composting and insulate the crowns of cold-sensitive plants with a covering of bracken, leaves or straw held in place with wire netting. Remember that different varieties of the same herb may vary in hardiness, so check their individual needs. Always clear away fallen

FRESH CULINARY HERBS AVAILABLE IN WINTER

- burnet – outdoors or under cloches
- chives – under cloches or indoors in pots
- mint – in a cold frame or in large pots and boxes indoors
- rosemary – outdoors or in pots
- winter savory – outdoors or in pots indoors
- chervil – outdoors, in a cold frame or indoors in pots
- marjoram – outdoors or in pots indoors
- pelargoniums – indoors in pots
- sage – outdoors

leaves from prostrate herbs that might otherwise rot beneath them.

THE HERB GARDEN IN WINTER

With herbaceous plants now dormant, interest will focus on evergreen species. Not all these can withstand a bleak winter, so check their hardiness and if necessary arrange windbreaks of sacking or plastic mesh to filter cold winds. Shake off settled snow before its weight damages branches.

EXTENDING THE SEASON

To ensure a supply of basic herbs during winter, use some form of protection to keep them in active growth. Cloches and small covers set over parsley, chives and mint in autumn will prolong their usefulness for several extra weeks, or you can transfer a few plants to a cold frame where they will be available all winter if the frame is covered with matting in hard frost. Lettuce, coriander and chervil can be sown in cold frames to crop in winter. Many other herbs such as thyme, tarragon and sage may be dug up and potted for use indoors, with a few pots kept in reserve in a frame or greenhouse to take their place when they are exhausted. Some herbs respond to forcing, especially mint, whose roots can be dug up in late winter and buried in boxes of potting compost to make early growth in the greenhouse. Out of doors, cloches placed over dormant plants will revive them a little earlier than normal, while crops such as rhubarb, seakale and Good King Henry are usually forced into growth by covering them with boxes or blanching pots.

Right: *A sheltered area or potting shed is ideal for transplanting herbs and storing equipment.*

USING A COLD FRAME

1 A cold frame is a valuable accessory, both for growing plants out of season and for housing cuttings and young plants, such as these thyme seedlings, in their early stages.

2 Adequate humidity and protection from low temperatures or bright sunlight are essential, so cover the frame when necessary, but remember to admit ventilation whenever possible.

Propagating Herbs

*Seasoned professionals and amateur gardeners alike get immense satisfaction
from raising new plants. Your collection may start with a few bought herbs in
pots, but sooner or later you will probably want to grow your own from seed or
by rooting live parts of a plant. Some herbs can be started in more than one way
while others need a particular technique; whichever method is used, remember
always to start with healthy material or seeds from a reputable source to avoid
disappointment.*

Anagallis arvensis

GROWING FROM SEED

Most herb species can be raised from
seed, although this method takes the
longest to produce a mature plant and
is not recommended for named cultivars, especially variegated kinds, as
seedlings do not always resemble the
parent plant. Seed sowing is the quick-
est way to grow a particular plant in
large quantities, and the usual method
of raising annual and biennial herbs,
wild flowers, salad and vegetable
herbs, species from other countries
and easily germinated perennials such
as chives, fennel, feverfew, lovage, rue,
salad burnet, European and American
sweet cicely and winter savory.

Although a seed is a potential plant
just waiting to grow, it will only germinate when conditions are right.
For most, a combination of adequate
warmth, moisture and air is enough to
trigger them into life, but others have
special requirements which depend
on the kind of surroundings they normally meet in the wild.

The seeds of juniper, woodruff,
European sweet cicely and violets, for
example, are protected by a hard,
resistant coat against early germination when temperatures are too cold,
and they depend on frost to break this
down – a process called stratification.

SOWING

*1 Fill a sterilized tray with a moist seed
growing medium. Level and firm
lightly if this is soil-based; simply tap
the tray to settle soil-less composts.*

*2 Scatter small seeds evenly and thinly
over the whole surface of the compost;
larger seeds can be spaced at regular
intervals.*

*3 Some seeds need light for ger-
mination, but others prefer darkness
and must be covered with compost
that has been sifted to remove any
lumps or debris.*

*4 Sprinkle this fine compost evenly
over the seeds to the recommended
depth, label the tray and cover with
plastic or glass to conserve moisture.*

Sown in autumn, they may be left outdoors exposed to winter weather, or you can artificially break their dormancy by mixing the seeds with damp sand in a plastic bag, and leaving this in a refrigerator for about two months before sowing in warm conditions.

Hard-coated leguminous seeds need penetration by moisture before they will grow. This can be speeded up by scarification, a method that involves carefully nicking the coat with a sharp knife or gently thinning part of it with sandpaper; soaking overnight in warm water is an alternative way. Some ordinary seeds need light, others darkness, to trigger germination, so always follow the sowing instructions on seed packets carefully to make sure you have provided the right conditions.

SOWING OUTDOORS

The normal sowing time for the majority of plants is early to mid-spring, just as soon as the soil is warm enough to support active growth. Wait until new weed seedlings appear or the first hedgerow buds break as an indication of the best time.

Vegetables and herbs needed in quantity are sown in drills in the kitchen garden, others in shorter rows in a nursery bed; flowering herbs may be sown where they are to grow, either in short rows or in circular furrows made by pressing the rim of a pot into the soil surface. Wherever you are sowing, always fork, weed and rake the soil into a crumbly level seedbed first, and in cold weather warm the ground for a week or two beforehand by covering it with cloches.

Use a rake handle or garden stake to mark out a shallow depression in the soil for short drills, or draw the corner of the rake along a tight garden line for longer rows. Sow the

GROWING BASIL

1 Basil seeds may be sown individually in soil blocks to save pricking out later, or seedlings can be transferred from seed trays.

2 The richer compost mixture of the soil blocks combined with heat and regular watering encourage rapid early growth.

3 With two pairs of true leaves, these seedlings are well established and ready for potting up.

4 After hardening off, these young basil plants will soon be ready for transfer to the open garden.

seeds in the bottom of the drill, and then cover with a thin layer of soil and gently tamp with the back of the rake head to ensure good contact between soil and seeds. In very dry weather flood the open drill with water, allow to drain before sowing, and then cover with dry soil.

Keep the sown area well watered until seedlings appear. When large enough to handle these should be thinned to leave plants 2-4 in apart. Most annual herbs can be left to grow at this spacing, but biennials and perennials may need thinning again or transplanting to another patch of

ground until large enough to be moved to their permanent positions.

SOWING UNDER GLASS

This is the best method of raising half-hardy annuals and early crops, together with those herbs that need extra warmth or pot cultivation, and any that are particularly precious or expensive.

Use seed trays, pots or shallow pans according to the quantity of seeds, first cleaning and sterilizing the containers with soapy water and a little ammonia or disinfectant. Cover the drainage holes of earthenware pots with a few broken shards before filling with a moist seed compost; plastic containers can be filled without a drainage layer. Tap the pot sharply to settle the contents or gently firm with a flat board, and then scatter the seeds thinly and evenly over the surface.

Dust a thin layer of compost over them, as deep as the diameter of the seeds – but any that need light for germination should be simply pressed gently into the surface. Label and seal the pot and cover it with a clear plastic bag, or with a piece of glass and a sheet of opaque paper where darkness is required.

Stand the containers in a warm place, and keep the soil moist during germination, either misting it when dry or standing the container in shallow water until moist patches appear on the surface. Check frequently to see if seedlings are emerging - germination may take only a few days, or several weeks or more for slow growers such as parsley and bay. Once the first shoots appear, remove the covering and move them into the light, but avoid bright sunlight until they are stronger.

MOUNDING

Evergreen perennials such as sage can quickly develop into impressive mounds of shrubby growth.

1 When old woody herbs develop bare lower stems, they can be propagated by mounding.

2 Clear out any dead stems and leaves, and then heap soil in the center of the bush.

3 Leave for a few months. Each of the branches will have rooted and can be detached as a new plant.

LAYERING ROSEMARY

1 Choose a low, flexible branch, remove some of the leaves where it touches the soil, and cut a shallow notch to induce rooting.

2 Scoop out a shallow depression for the prepared section of branch, and hold it in place with a wire loop or clothes pin.

3 Cover the wounded section and peg with good topsoil, and firm gently. In dry weather water the layer (but not the parent plant) to hasten rooting.

STRIKING CUTTINGS

1 Prepare a gritty, free-draining rooting mixture by blending sharp sand with an equal volume of peat, peat substitute or seed compost.

2 Trim the cuttings to size, using a very sharp knife to cut through the stem just below a node. Remove the lowest pair of leaves.

3 Fill a pot with the mixture and insert a cutting in each. Water in the cuttings and enclose in a plastic bag supported on short canes.

When seedlings are large enough (usually when they have made true leaves in addition to their seed leaves), they will need pricking out (transplanting singly) except in the case of large seeds sown individually in small pots and those to be planted out or potted on intact. Replant the seedlings up to the base of their seed leaves in separate pots of moist potting medium or about 2 in apart in seed trays.

DIVISION

Division is used to multiply herbs that form clumps of rooted stems, and also to rejuvenate older specimens where the centre of the clump has died out, leaving a ring of young material. The whole crown of the plant is eased from the soil with a fork, during winter dormancy or in early spring as growth revives. Divide it into segments by plunging two forks back to back into the mass of growth and forcing them apart; smaller crowns can be split with a sharp knife or by tearing off rooted portions. Replant divisions firmly in fresh soil at the same depth as the original crown.

LAYERING

Layering is a slow but foolproof method of inducing the stem of a woody perennial such as sage, lavender or honeysuckle to make roots of its own while it is still nourished by the parent plant.

MOUNDING

When whole plants are layered to root large numbers of cuttings, or to restore a neglected herb that has become bare at the base, the technique is known as mounding or stooling. It is very useful for salvaging unpruned lavender bushes, but can be used on any woody herb; it is also the standard way to multiply rootstocks for fruit trees.

CUTTINGS

Cuttings are small portions of stem or root, trimmed off and induced to grow roots of their own. There are three main kinds of stem cutting: hardwood, taken in autumn from woody stems of trees and shrubs and rooted outdoors or in a cold frame over winter; semi-hardwood, taken in mid- to late summer from side shoots with a ripe base and often a 'heel' of old wood; and softwood cuttings taken in spring or summer, using the soft tips of the current year's growth. The differences are largely technical and most plants can be propagated by more than one method; clipping shrubby herbs and hedges to shape often yields plenty of cutting material.

Always use sturdy, healthy non-flowering shoots about 3-4 in long; hardwood cuttings rooted in the ground should be two or three times this length. Trim carefully just below a leaf joint with a razor blade or sharp knife. Strip the leaves from the lower half of the cutting using a knife or by pulling them away to leave a clean wound. The base of the cuttings can be dipped in a hormone rooting preparation as an insurance before inserting them firmly in a well-drained cuttings compost. Strike soft cuttings in pots in sealed plastic bags or a propagator, others in a cold frame or outdoors in a sheltered place. Shade from bright sunlight, and pot on or transplant to a nursery bed as soon as the cuttings are growing well.

Potted Herb Gardens

Lack of available ground need not stop you from making a collection of herbs, for most adapt readily to cultivation in pots and other containers. Even if most of your herbs grow in the open garden, growing some of your favorite kinds in pots adds a further dimension to herb gardening.

Origanum vulgare

Pots can be arranged near the house in decorative groups for easy access, their mobility allowing you to move them around to follow the sun as the season progresses or to shelter them from cold winds. You can bring them indoors in winter to maintain supplies or even for guests to help themselves to herbs at the table. Larger tubs or troughs provide room for several kinds to grow together as permanent miniature herb gardens, positioned where they get all the sun or shade they might need. In gardens on poor ground, container growing is the best way of providing perfect soil.

Almost any kind of container is suitable and the range is infinite, from wooden boxes, clay pots and stone urns, to used growing bags and large paint tins, cattle troughs and coal scuttles. Any you choose must be large enough to house plants comfortably – aim for a minimum 8 in diameter and depth - and should have adequate free drainage at the base to shift surplus water and so avoid sour, stagnant conditions at the roots. Provide several drainage holes in the base, together with a few more in the sides just above the base if the containers are not supported off the ground by small blocks or pieces of tile to let water drain away.

Try to match containers to their intended plants. Terracotta is an attractive material sympathetic to more decorative herbs such as a collection of colored sages (golden 'Icterina', cream and pink 'Tricolor' and red 'Purpurescens', for example) or the many kinds of scented-leaved geraniums. A larger tub would suit an informal arrangement of rosemary, hyssop, thyme and golden marjoram, and if mounted on castors could be moved to a greenhouse or conservatory for winter use. Utilitarian containers such as bottomless buckets or 2 gallon paint containers may be hidden behind more ornamental pots to house taller invasive herbs such as tarragon, sorrel, horseradish, comfrey and mint. Used growing bags are ideal for annual and biennial herbs such as basil, chervil and parsley, or for growing out-of-season supplies of mint in the greenhouse. Wooden 'Versailles' pots and similar large formal containers are best reserved for specimen bay trees, herb topiary, or perhaps a trained quince planted with annual nasturtiums, lettuce and trailing New Zealand spinach at the base.

POTTING ON

1 As plants develop they need to be moved on to increasingly large containers. Free drainage is essential and depends on a preliminary layer of small stones or gravel.

2 The pot is then part-filled with the appropriate growing medium, the plant is tapped from its old pot and centered in the new one, and the remaining space is filled with soil.

POTTING BAY

1 Leafy bushes of bay are reliable in containers, but be sure to plant in pots of adequate size; one such as this will sustain growth for several years before it is too small.

2 While there is still room in the container, smaller herbs such as parsley, thyme and marjoram planted around the base will transform the pot into a miniature garden.

Above: *Evergreen bay* (Laurus nobilis) *is a popular container shrub for formal situations, as here where a pyramid-trained specimen stands sentinel in a painted 'Versailles' box.*

PLANTING

The easiest way to start any potted collection is to buy pots of young herbs from a specialist nurseryman, and plant these straight into new containers. Cutting the tips of shoots for use will keep them compact for several months before they need potting on or exchanging for smaller plants. A stouter herb such as rosemary, lavender or sage can be started by rooting several cuttings together in a small pot and then transferring them as a single plant to the container until they become too large and need replacement.

At planting time check that drainage holes are clear and then cover them with a layer of gravel, stones or a few shards from broken clay pots. Over this spread a thin layer of peat or a moisture-retentive peat substitute before filling the pot with a soil-based potting mixture. Soil-less growing media can be difficult to moisten once completely dry, and as most contain fertilizers that are soon exhausted, supplementary feeding is often necessary after only a few weeks. They are easier to handle and lighter than soil-based mixes, but this may be a disadvantage outdoors where weight confers stability. John Innes No 2 or Cornell mix is a good commercial mixture, or you can blend your own from 7 parts good garden soil, 3 parts peat or leafmould, 2 parts horticultural sand, and a little seaweed fertilizer – but watch out for possible weed seedlings.

POT CARE

Herbs in pots need special attention, as they are totally dependent on the gardener for their welfare. Their greatest need is water: the toughest drought-loving herb cannot survive for long in bone-dry soil and you must therefore check regularly (daily or even twice daily in a hot summer) that the soil stays consistently moist. Leafy herbs will appreciate an occasional feed of houseplant fertilizer, but for others annual re-potting or top-dressing is enough to replenish their diet.

Young herbs in small pots need to be transferred to larger ones when their roots show through at the bottom of the pot. Once they are in their final containers, you need to replenish the nutrients annually in spring by gently knocking out the plants, and teasing away the soil from around the rootball before repotting them in fresh soil in the original container or one similar. Plants too large to repot in this way should have the top 2-3 in of soil replaced annually with a fresh supply.

Container Herb Gardens

Herbs are ideal subjects not only for conventional pots, but also containers of all kinds – wall pots, troughs, window boxes, and anything you have handy, from a battered old sink covered with 'hypertufa' to give it a new lease of life, to a beautiful terracotta chimney pot which can make a centerpiece in an informal cottage garden, especially if you put a few trailing plants around the edge. Containers have advantages of their own: they can be used to confine invasive herbs such as mint, or filled with ericaceous compost for lime-hating plants.

Ocimum basilicum "Anise"

WINDOW BOXES

A window box makes an ideal herb garden, accessible at all times and changing with the seasons if a supply of potted plants is kept in reserve. Make sure brackets are strong enough to support the weight of moist soil, and use a box about 10-12 in deep to allow a good root run for the plants.

Provide ample drainage in the same way as for other containers, and then fill with a moist soil-based potting mixture. Either plant young herbs directly into this or grow them in 4-5 in pots, burying these just below surface level in the box and replacing them as they are exhausted. Small herbs, especially ornamental varieties, are best but

HERBS FOR A SUNNY WINDOW BOX

- calendula
- dill
- lemon verbena – summer only
- nasturtium – in summer
- sage
- self-heal
- winter savory
- chives
- lemon thyme
- marjoram
- rosemary
- scented-leaved geraniums – summer only
- tarragon

Above: *A strawberry pot may be used not only for strawberries, but also for parsley or any other suitable herb. Always plant as you add the soil, firming each layer into place before filling the next hole.*

Left: *With regular watering and feeding, an ornamental pot on a wall can support alpine strawberries or an ever-bearing large variety that will fruit on trailing runners.*

space can be made for taller kinds such as bay and rosemary, started as cuttings and grown in the box until they are too large, when they may be transferred to the garden.

HANGING BASKETS

A hanging basket holds only a small volume of soil and is often exposed to wind and sun from various directions. It needs dedicated attention to watering in hot, dry weather. Nevertheless, many herbs will grow well in a deep basket – seasonal kinds such as basil, nasturtiums and parsley, or permanent decorative crops of pennyroyal, lady's mantle or golden lemon balm. Try growing small-leaved ivies to cascade and cover the sides of the basket, and add a little trailing lobelia or a basket tomato variety for extra flair.

PLANTING IN A STONE TROUGH

1 Protect drainage holes with large stones or curved shards of broken pot and then spread a layer of pebbles or gravel.

2 Fill the trough with a moist, nutritious soil mixture almost to the rim, and help this settle by repeatedly plunging in the trowel.

3 Arrange and plant a few chosen herbs in the trough, but not too many as they will soon fill the available space as they grow.

4 Complete the planting by covering the surface with a decorative mulch of fine gravel or chippings to conserve moisture.

Above: *Tall, emphatic containers such as chimney pots are perfect for displaying nasturtiums and other climbing or trailing herbs; fill the lower part of the pot with rubble for stability before topping up with soil or compost.*

To plant a hanging basket, mix a soil-based medium 50-50 with a soil-less type to reduce weight, and either add a slow-release fertilizer or make sure you feed twice weekly from mid-summer onwards. Suspend the basket out of the wind in a position where you can reach the herbs comfort-ably for picking and watering. In the autumn transfer the complete basket to a cool greenhouse to prolong the season of use and help plants to sur-vive the winter; the following spring you can take cuttings and remake the basket with fresh soil.

Right: *A stone trough is large enough to house a basic selection of useful herbs or a collection of dwarf species.*

HERBS FOR A LIGHTLY SHADED BOX

- bay
- catmint
- chervil
- corn salad
- mint
- lungwort
- violets
- French sorrel
- chamomile
- chives
- mignonette
- parsley
- salad burnet
- wild strawberry

Herbs Indoors

Herbs are not house plants, and all except the tenderest species need to spend most of their time out of doors if they are to thrive. But many kinds will stand some time indoors without permanent harm, and will add fragrance to your rooms. A pot of basil on an indoor window sill will, when the window is open, release its spicy odor every time the wind stirs the leaves. If you have a conservatory, of course, you can use it for a permanent collection of warmth-loving herbs of all shapes and sizes.

Origanum majorana

HERBS ON THE WINDOW SILL

Apart from shade-loving kinds and a few fleshy-leaved plants such as scented-leaved geraniums, most herbs remain in good condition only for a short time on domestic window sills, and soon suffer from lack of light. The best way to keep a supply of herbs near at hand is to grow several pots of each kind outdoors or in a cold frame or greenhouse, bringing them in one at a time to replace others as these are used up or become drawn and sickly. The superseded herbs are cut back and returned to the frame to revive, or may be planted outdoors after hardening off. All herbs thrive best in the open air, and even long-term pot plants are best moved outdoors in summer. With care, though, it is possible to keep a changing sequence of basic herbs on the window sill throughout the winter, supplemented by lettuce, coriander, and mustard and cress sown direct in pots to give two or three cuts of loose leaves for winter salads.

GROWING UNDER GLASS

In temperate climates a greenhouse or conservatory is essential for growing herbs from warmer parts of the world, and there is a wide enough variety of these to turn a fair-sized greenhouse into an indoor herb garden. Depending on their native habitat, some will be content with minimal frost protection, but tropical species

Above: *A greenhouse or conservatory admits plenty of light to keep plants healthy and compact; except for any in current use, keep potted herbs there where they will remain in good condition until needed.*

Left: *Although many herbs need preserving for out-of-season use, drying subtly alters their flavor and concentration. Parsley, basil, sage, mint and other fresh herbs grown in pots will supply an authentic and stimulating taste of summer.*

will need varying amounts of heat and humidity for good health all the year round. Check cultural needs and build your collection with compatible neighbours – the steamy conditions preferred by a vanilla orchid, for example, would prove lethal to a westringia or grapevine.

Use the walls and roof of the house for training climbers, especially fruiting kinds that will benefit from the good light and a long growing season: in a warm conservatory a fig tree can bear two or three crops of figs a year, compared with only one outdoors. These are best grown in deep containers or in a small soil border. Near the back of the bench arrange large pots of citrus fruit, tea and other greenhouse shrubs, filling the foreground with smaller herbs and trailing varieties to tumble down the front.

Like all pot plants these need regular watering and feeding while in active growth. During the summer paint the glass with shading to prevent sun-scorch and excessively high temperatures. Wetting down the staging and paths with a watering can helps

ESSENTIAL HERBS FOR WINDOW SILLS

- basil – sow a pinch in each pot, and prevent flowering for long life; sow again in midsummer for late supplies
- chives – pot up divisions from garden clumps, and keep well fed and watered
- parsley – choose a compact variety, sow in spring and again in late summer for winter cutting; use several pots in rotation
- thyme – start from seed or cuttings rooted direct in the pots; keep in full light and water sparingly

- chervil – sow in spring and again in late summer in quantity in a wide pan, and leave to seed itself when past its best
- marjoram – grow like thyme; choose sweet marjoram for warm rooms, or the hardier pot marjoram where it is cooler
- sage – strike cuttings and keep trimmed frequently; select a variegated kind for indoor color

maintain a healthy atmosphere, and occasionally misting the leaves with water deters red spider mite. If pests and diseases do appear, treat them promptly, as they multiply rapidly in a closed environment. Insect predators are available to control most common pests, while attention to greenhouse hygiene – removing dead flowers and leaves, ventilating freely whenever possible, and maintaining steady growth – will discourage most diseases.

Above: *Bunches of herbs can remain where they were dried, adding their pervasive scent to the room.*

DIVIDING CHIVES

1 To propagate fibrous-rooted herbs or multiplier onions such as chives, lift a healthy clump and shake off the surplus soil.

2 Gently pull the clump into several pieces; heavy clay soil might need washing off before roots can be disentangled safely.

3 Pot up the divisions in good growing medium, and keep on a warm sunny windowsill for a regular indoor supply.

Pruning and Training

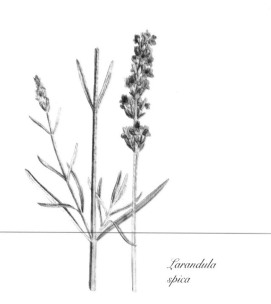

Annual and biennial herbs need little interference with their growth, apart from dead-heading to prolong their lives and seasonal tidying as top growth dies. Herbaceous perennials, too, are largely self-sufficient, although thinning congested growth and cutting their dead flowers to prevent unwanted seeding are often an essential part of their care.

Lavandula spica

Perennial woody herbs, usually need some kind of restraint if they are not to grow too large. In thoroughly prepared ground a contented perennial herb may grow vigorously, a reassuring sign that all is well – although this should not be an excuse for avoiding pruning. Left to their own devices, perennials will continue growing until they reach maximum size, often with unfortunate results such as limited flowering or fruiting and the development of bare stems at the base, while increased competition and overcrowding encourage disease.

Timely pruning will avoid all these complications and banish disorder from the herb garden.

UNDERSTANDING PRUNING

Plants grow upwards and outwards because growth hormones concentrate at the ends of shoots, suppressing the development of buds elsewhere. Cutting off a growing tip redirects the plant's energies to lower buds and stimulates them into growth as replacements for the lost leading shoot. Pinching out the tips of a citrus bush, clipping a lavender hedge and

mowing a thyme lawn to remove some of the top foliage are all forms of pruning to limit upward growth and encourage bushy side shoots.

Picking the tips of herb bushes in the course of normal use is a valuable form of basic pruning, but most perennial kinds need one or more overall trims each season to maintain a well-balanced plant. As a general rule, clipping with shears immediately after flowering will restore shapeliness, but this may be done earlier to prevent flowering and allow a longer period of regrowth before the end of the season. A mid-season trim of variegated herbs will provoke a flush of brightly colored new growth; at the same time cut out completely any shoots that revert to plain green. Herb hedges and topiary may need several trims a year, depending on the species used and the degree of strict formality intended.

RENOVATION

Plants such as rosemary, lavender and broom resent being pruned hard, but an annual trim after flowering is essential to maintain size and quality; confine cuts to young green growth, which regenerates freely, unlike older brown stems which may die after

CUTTING BACK

1 Once some herbs are past their best, often after flowering, it is a good idea to cut back their straggly stems almost to ground level.

2 With their long stems removed, young shoots at the base will be exposed to more light and will soon provide a fresh crop of usable leaves.

being pruned. Many other hedge and shrub species, on the other hand, can be cut back hard at the start of the growing season to restore their size. Always check first in a good handbook. Remember, the first rule of pruning is 'Think twice, cut once.'

The most conscientious pruning will not confer immortality on a plant, however, and once a woody perennial such as lavender or sage develops patches of bare stems, it is usually time to start again. Pruning should always be combined with taking cuttings to maintain a stock of available young plants; while these are growing, the older plants can be temporarily restored by hard pruning, layering side shoots of hedge plants to fill gaps, or tying adjacent branches together to disguise dead areas in an important specimen. Always cut out dead and diseased stems when starting pruning or before renovating a plant.

TRAINING

Training accompanies pruning to direct growth in a new direction. Knowing that the topmost bud of a pruned stem is usually the first to break and resume growth allows you to prune back to a bud facing a particular way in the knowledge that the plant will then grow in this direction. Pruning a lax species to upward-facing buds helps prevent it from sprawling too far sideways, while cutting vertical stems to outward-facing buds encourages bushiness.

This technique is particularly useful when training wall shrubs into decorative shapes, since rerouting growth in this way is often safer than attempt-

Right: *The sinuous curves of spiral topiary add a touch of whimsical artistry to a formally designed herb garden.*

ing to bend stubborn branches in a new direction. Some fruits and roses in trained forms need summer pruning to restrain growth and encourage the formation of productive buds, combined with winter pruning to maintain size and shape.

Climbing plants need careful training to prevent them from straggling. They need firm supports on which to climb, or trellis or horizontal wires so that the stems can be tied in evenly as they grow. The annual pruning of many climbers depends on the age of the wood on which flowers are borne – if they bloom on the current year's stems, prune hard in late winter to encourage plenty of young growth; thin this to retain the strongest stems for tying in. Climbers that flower on stems produced the previous year should be pruned immediately after flowering, cutting exhausted stems back to strong new shoots.

Right: *A young mop-head bay, its straight stem trained originally on a firm cane. The dense head of foliage is produced by repeatedly pruning or pinching off the tips of stems to encourage further side shoots.*

Above: *While many hedging and topiary evergreens can be clipped with shears, large-leaved species such as bay need pruning with secateurs or pruners to avoid leaving ugly wounds. Use the prunings as cuttings or for drying.*

Harvesting Herbs

For all their ornamental value, herbs are intended for use, and the dedication that you have put into growing them will be jeopardized by careless harvesting and storage. First establish which parts of the plant are normally used – in most cases it is the leaves and stems, but sometimes the flavor or medicinal value is most concentrated in the seeds, flowers, roots or even bark. Often the concentration is highest at a particular time of year, or even time of day.

Artemisia abrotanum

For routine culinary purposes leaves and sprigs can be picked fresh as needed and whenever available. However, many herbs are not evergreen or accessible all the year round, and it will be necessary at some point to gather larger quantities for preserving and subsequent storage for winter use. Top growth should be harvested when plants are in prime condition and active growth, normally during spring and summer. There is some evidence that oils and active principles are more concentrated in the morning before strong sunlight has affected them, so try to gather material early in the day – but after any dew has dispersed, because damp herbs soon turn moldy. Only gather as much as you can handle immediately from clean, healthy plants, keeping different species separate and clearly labelled.

DRYING LEAVES AND FLOWERS

Living parts of plants contain large amounts of water, as much as seven-eighths of their weight in many cases, and this must be removed before they can be safely stored. In a warm, dry climate, leaves and flowers may be tied loosely together in small bundles and hung in an airy, dust-free place out of the sun until brittle enough to break easily between your fingers (in dusty places enclose bundles in perforated bags). You can also spread them on a table or shelf between sheets of newspaper or muslin, and turn daily, or lay them on a mesh screen raised to allow air circulation beneath. The aim is to retain most of the color, flavor and aroma of the original, so avoid bright

Below: *Freshly gathered herbs in convenient bundles ready for tying and drying.*

sunlight which will bleach the color, and cool conditions that increase drying time with a resulting loss of quality – in most cases a week should be long enough.

In a cool or wet season when natural air drying is not practicable, an airing cupboard, shaded greenhouse, warm attic or dry ventilated shed is an acceptable place. Herbs may be dried in a domestic oven or dehydrator, provided that care is taken to keep the temperature no more than 90°F for the first day or two, after which it can be reduced to 75°F until the process is complete, usually after a further three to five days. Turn the material occasionally and complete one batch at a time – adding fresh material during drying will reduce the temperature and raise humidity. Bunching several herbs together for bouquets garnis will be easier before drying than afterwards.

DRYING SEEDS

Ripe seeds need careful handling because of their natural tendency to shed at the slightest touch. Gather them when they are dry, shaking them from open capsules into paper bags or snipping off complete seedheads, holding them steady as you do so to

GATHERING WILD HERBS – A WARNING

There are several reasons for taking extra care when harvesting wild herbs, a practice once part of everyday life but no longer easy or even advisable in some districts. Check first that there are no laws or local bylaws against removing plants from the wild (some laws prevent the digging of certain wild flower roots, for example), and as a matter of courtesy always obtain permission from the owner of the land. Pollution is an ever-present hazard, and plants should never be gathered from roadsides and near industrial sites, nor from agricultural land where chemical crop treatments are normally used.

There should be no doubt whatsoever as to the identification of the plants you intend using. Many well-known herbs are unmistakable in appearance or fragrance, but there are also a number of valuable wild herbs which are almost identical to useless or toxic near-relatives. Tasting is a risky identification test and not to be recommended. If you cannot distinguish a plant for certain by its appearance, leave it alone in case it is dangerous. Gather only from plants that are locally plentiful, taking just small amounts of material from any one plant so that its chances of survival are not diminished.

Hang up the open bags in an airy place under cover, or spread out seed-heads on paper, leaving them for two or three weeks to finish drying. When seed cases are quite crisp and papery, rub or shake the seeds from their capsules. Some kinds will inevitably be mixed with other plant remains such as broken pods or the aerial 'parachutes' typical of Compositae species, but these can be removed by shaking the seeds in a fine sieve, or simply by gently blowing away the debris.

HARVESTING ROOTS

In most cases roots are dried for storing with their skins intact, but a few such as liquorice, turmeric and marshmallow are best peeled. They are then cut into $1/2$ in slices, thicker roots being cut in two lengthwise. Whether peeled or not, roots take longer to dry than other parts of herbs, often several weeks with frequent turning, but the process can be accelerated in a warm oven set at 120°F. When the fragments are light and brittle, pack them in airtight tins or dark glass jars.

Where the roots of a permanent perennial such as angelica or comfrey are to be harvested, it is best to excavate the soil from one side of the plant and then cut off a few pieces of root with a sharp knife or spade (sometimes a few of these pieces can be used for propagation by potting or boxing them up in soil in the greenhouse). Rub them free of soil and fibrous lateral roots, before taking them indoors to scrub clean. A crop such as horseradish can be grown in a permanent bed, with a root or two being dug as required.

Below left: *Culinary herbs cut up small and packed in measured amounts with water in ice-cube trays lose little of their flavor when frozen, and are ready for almost immediate use.*

Below: *Herbs dried outdoors can be spread in layers if turned regularly, but in still conditions indoors it is better to arrange leaves separately on racks.*

avoid loss. Keep each variety separate and label the bags clearly. If you are saving seeds for sowing, always choose the best plants with typical growth and appearance; inferior plants yield seeds suitable for other uses as long as they are free from diseases. When dry, label and store in packets in airtight jars.

A-Z OF HERBS

———————— ❧ ————————

Achillea millefolium (Compositae)

Yarrow

milfoil, nosebleed, herb militaris, soldier's woundwort, thousand leaf, thousand seal, field hop

Description: hardy herbaceous pungent perennial, 6-24 in. Finely feathered, bright gray-green leaves and flat heads of small white, pink or red flowers midsummer to autumn. Grows in grassy places, including lawns.

Use: folk remedy for rheumatism, toothache, hemorrhage and fever; fresh young leaves used sparingly in salads; herbal tobacco and substitute for hops in brewing.

Cultivation: prefers full sun and well-drained ground; good for chalky and seaside gardens. Spreads readily, so segregate from other plants. Divide roots in spring or autumn, or sow seeds from spring until autumn; plant 6 in apart for lawns.

Parts used: top growth cut just before flowering. Dry outdoors in the shade or in gentle heat indoors.

Related species: *A. decolorans* (English mace): half-hardy perennial, 18-24 in, native to southern Europe. Feathery leaves; yellow flowers, summer. Light soil in full sun.

A. moschata (musk yarrow): rhizomatous perennial, 8 in, from European Alps. Ferny leaves; white flowers, summer. Needs good drain-age and full sun.

Agrimonia eupatoria (Rosaceae)

Common Agrimony

church steeples, liverwort, sticklewort, cockleburr

Description: wayside perennial often found on chalk, 6 in-2 ft. Attractive gray-green cinquefoil leaves, arranged in alternate large and small pairs, with pale yellow star-shaped flowers in summer on tapering spikes like a mullein; apricot scent, popular with bees. Seedheads are burrs which stick to clothes and fur.

Use: once regarded as a magic herb for healing jaundice; used as a spring tonic, as an astringent externally for treating wounds, and in oriental medicine to stop bleeding; a valuable yellow dye plant.

Cultivation: likes well-drained soil in full sun, but will also thrive in short grass. Sow in a seedbed outdoors in spring or autumn, or divide established roots in autumn.

Parts used: whole plant for dyeing; fresh leaves steeped in water to make an infusion; aerial parts except thick stems may be gathered just before flowering for drying gently in the dark; roots may be dried and grated to add to pot-pourri.

Related species: *A. odorata* (fragrant agrimony): highly aromatic plant with sticky, hairy leaves, larger in all parts than *A. eupatoria*. Often planted in wild and woodland gardens.

Ajuga reptans (Labiatae)

Common Bugle

creeping bugle, carpet bugle, carpenter's herb (note that North American bugle, bugleweed or gipsy wort refers to *Lycopus* spp.)

Description: short prostrate perennial, 6 in. Rosettes of coarse shining green leaves, and spires of blue, white or rose flowers in midsummer. Spreads freely by runners. Several cultivated forms including 'Atropurpurea', with metallic purple leaves, and 'Variegata', cream and green, grows best in shade.

Use: medicinally to treat bleeding from cuts and other wounds; popular ground cover among other herbs and for edging containers.

Cultivation: grows in moist, rich soils in shade or full sun; flourishes beneath hedges if compost is added. Sow in spring or autumn in trays and barely cover seed – germination is slow and erratic. Separate established roots and transplant divisions in spring or autumn.

Parts used: leaves picked as required and simmered to make an infusion; whole herb cut down to ground level in summer and dried in shade.

Related species: *A. chamaepitys* (ground-pine, arthritic ivy): short bushy annual with pine scent, 4-6 in. Red-spotted yellow flowers in summer. Whole herb used to treat bleeding and high pulse rate, and in Arab veterinary treatments.

Alchemilla vulgaris (Rosaceae)
Common Lady's Mantle

lion's foot, bear's foot, common alchemil

Description: an aggregate of closely related species, typically herbaceous perennials, 6-18 in. Leaves cloak-shaped and pleated. Small yellowish-green flowers in summer.

Use: used by alchemists in attempts to make gold; folk remedy for eye disorders and to stop bleeding; traditional treatment for menstrual disorders and in childbirth.

Cultivation: grows in sun or shade, in walls, as edging and as ground cover under trees and shrubs, where it self-seeds freely. Sow in trays in summer, and plant out in autumn; or divide clumps in early spring or autumn.

Parts used: leaves and flower shoots picked as required; aerial parts gathered in summer and dried outdoors.

Related species: *A. alpina* (alpine lady's mantle): evergreen dwarf perennial, grows to 8 in, for sinks, rock gardens and short grass in sun; soft furry, silvery leaves, tiny yellow flowers.

A. arvensis (parsley piert, field lady's mantle): similar to *A. vulgaris*, popular Romany tonic and remedy for bladder stone.

Allium (Liliaceae)

The various species all possess the familiar sulphurous smell, but individually they are valued as vegetables, herbs, medicines and decorative garden bulbs. Only the most important in herbal terms are described here.
Caution: some people are slightly allergic to all forms of onions.

Allium sativum
Garlic

Description: subterranean white-skinned bulb, subdivided into numerous 'cloves'. Short, flat upright leaves, 6-12 in, tall single flower stem bearing spherical head of pale pink or greenish-white blooms often mixed with tiny bulbils.

Uses: flavoring, vegetable and medicinal herb that has accumulated superstitions over the centuries. Used as an antibiotic, expectorant and digestive, and for treating high blood pressure.

Cultivation: cloves planted in autumn 2-4 in deep in rich soil, or in pots in a frame for planting out in spring in cold regions. Harvested in summer when foliage dies down, and dried in sunlight or warmth.

Parts used: bulbs, separated into cloves.

Related species: *A. oleraceum* (field garlic, wild garlic), *A. triquetrum* (three-cornered garlic), *A. scorodoprasum* (sand leek) and *A. rosea* (rosy garlic) used in various parts of the world as wild substitutes for garlic.

A. ursinum (wild garlic, ramsons): white-flowered wild onion, widespread in damp woodland; pungent garlic smell, but mild when cooked.

A. vineale (wild garlic, crow garlic): wiry version of cultivated garlic, widespread in temperate regions. Used by North American Indians.

Allium schoenoprasum
Chives

Description: small perennial bulb growing in clumps, with fine hollow dark green leaves, 8-12 in, and slightly taller flower stems bearing small clusters of mauve or purple blooms. Can be found wild in moist soils, but usually cultivated.

chives

Uses: mainly culinary for flavoring and garnishing where a mild onion flavor is required. Also a stimulant and digestive; high in vitamin C. Popular decorative herb for edging and for attracting bees. Chive tea is sometimes sprayed to prevent gooseberry mildew and apple scab. Chive flowers can be used in decorative dried flower arrangements.

Cultivation: sow seeds outdoors in spring, or divide clumps into small groups and plant in spring or autumn in moist rich soil. Lift and divide every 3-5 years according to growth. May be potted up in autumn for forcing winter supplies indoors.

(Continued)

Parts used: fresh leaves cut as needed. Chop and freeze in bags or ice-cube trays for use out of season.

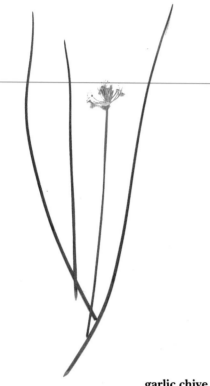

garlic chive

Related species: Larger-leaved forms available; also Chinese or garlic chives (*A. tuberosum*) and Siberian chives (*A. schoenoprasum sibiricum*).

Aloe vera, syn. *A. barbadensis* (Liliaceae)

Aloes

Cape aloes, socotrine, medicine plant, burn plant

Description: succulent drought-resistant tropical plant forming clumps of short-stemmed rosettes of fleshy evergreen leaves, up to 2 ft long, pointed and edged with teeth. Tall flower stem with spikes of yellow, orange or red tubular blooms. Often grown as a house plant in cool regions.

Uses: according to legend the sole survivor from the Garden of Eden. Gel-like sap from leaves used externally to heal wounds, burns and mastitis. **Caution:** traditional internal use as purgative bitters ill advised and may cause hemorrhage.

Cultivation: plants need sunny, arid conditions. May be started from seed in spring, or propagated from small offsets at base of parent plant. As house plants, best grown in gritty cactus mixtures in good light; minimum winter temperature of 41°F to ensure flowering, in summer may be stood outdoors. In frost-free gardens, ideal plants for sunny beds with fast drainage.

Parts used: broken leaves rubbed on affected part. Sap extracted from leaves and often dried to form a resin.

Related species: A. aristata: small relative with leaves 4-6 in long, white spines and orange flowers. Popular house plant and hardiest of the tropical aloes; may survive mild temperate winters out of doors.

Althaea officinalis (Malvaceae)

Marsh Mallow

guimauve, mortification plant, schloss tea, sweet weed, wymote

Description: tough-rooted herbaceous perennial, 4 ft. Velvety stems and leaves; white or pink flowers in leaf axils in late summer. Found in damp, often saline places.

Uses: valuable and handsome herb with a long tradition of use in medicine and cosmetics, and as a vegetable and confection. Cultivated by the Romans and promoted by Charlemagne. Soothing and mucilaginous; tops of young shoots added to salads (popular with Bedu); flowers and leaves infused to treat lung and bowel disorders; roots sliced and boiled to poultice external inflammation and relieve gastric ailments; root was made into traditional 'marshmallows' (now just sugar and gelatin).

Cultivation: sow seeds in spring indoors in warmth, or outdoors in summer, and transplant to permanent positions in autumn. Roots may be divided in spring or autumn. On light soils mulch freely in summer.

Parts used: flowers, leaves and young tips of shoots gathered fresh; roots at least 2 years old, dug up during winter dormancy when the active constituents are most concentrated, and used fresh or dried.

Althaea Rosea
🐛 **Hollyhock**

Description: biennial or perennial of waste places, and traditional cottage garden flower; grows up to 10 ft. Wide hairy leaves, up to 12 in across. Large flowers, often double, in summer; wild forms are white or pink; cultivated forms purple, red or yellow.

Uses: petals of purple-flowered variety once used to dye wine. Leaves used medicinally as a diuretic and to help some chest complaints. Provides relief for mouth ulcers; soothing to the face.

Cultivation: can be grown in any soil. Propagate from seed and prick out.

Parts used: flowers and leaves, fresh.

Anethum graveolens
(Umbelliferae)
🐛 **Dill**
dillseed, dillweed

Description: annual herb, 18-30 in, with finely feathered blue-green leaves and hollow stems. Small open umbels of creamy-yellow flowers in summer, followed by dark brown seeds. Grows wild in waste places, but can also be cultivated.

Uses: used as a condiment and flavoring and as a pickling spice. Often taken as 'dill water' to relieve digestive problems and flatulence. Occasionally used to perfume cosmetics; medicinal oil distilled from leaves, stems and seeds.

Cultivation: sow in rows or small patches in spring, and again in early summer for continuity, in a sunny, well-drained position. Grow well away from fennel, with which dill cross-pollinates readily. Choose right variety for seed or leaf production.

Parts used: young leaves gathered at any time for use fresh, also flowers for adding to soups; seeds harvested when dry for use whole or crushed. Leaves may be dried, but lose much of their flavor.

Related species: *A. sowa* (Indian dill, Japanese dill): similar in appearance and uses, popular in Asian cuisines.

Angelica archangelica
(Umbelliferae)
🐛 **Angelica**
garden angelica, Holy Ghost

Description: a robust biennial or short-lived perennial plant, 6 ft, of damp woodlands. Produces a few large, deeply indented leaves at ground level, followed by tall hollow stems bearing from their leaf sheaths heads of greenish-white flowers in midsummer.

Uses: all parts promote perspiration, stimulate appetite, and are used to treat ailments of the chest and digestion. Young leaves and shoots used to flavor wines and liqueurs, while the stout stems are candied as a cake decoration or cooked like rhubarb. Fresh or preserved roots have been added to snuff and used by Laplanders and North American Indians as tobacco.

Cultivation: sow fresh seeds outdoors in autumn for exposure to frost, or pre-chill in a refrigerator for a few weeks before sowing in spring. Transplant to a moist shady position as young as possible, before the roots become immovable.

Parts used: young leaves can be gathered any time during the growing season, the stems in the summer of the second year. Cut seedheads and ripen until seeds are dry enough to store. Roots are dug up just before flowering and dried slowly.

Related species: *A. atropurpurea*: a wild North American species used by Shakers as flavoring and medicine.

Anthriscus cerefolium
(Umbelliferae)
🐌 **Chervil**
salad chervil, garden beaked parsley

Description: decorative annual, sometimes grown as a biennial, 2 ft, with a tapering rootstock. A well-branched plant with sweet-scented and delicately cut pale foliage rather like parsley, and umbels of small white flowers in spring and summer, followed by large seedpods. Sometimes found wild as a garden escape, when it closely resembles young cow parsley (*A. sylvestris*). **Caution:** do not gather from the wild, as chervil may be confused with poisonous hemlock, fool's parsley and water dropwort.

Uses: leaves used in soups, salads and vinegars, and for garnishes. Medicinally the bruised plant is applied fresh or as poultices to wounds; an infusion aids digestion and encourages perspiration.

Cultivation: sow spring, summer or autumn *in situ* in rows or patches, in moisture-retentive soil in full sun or light shade. As plants often run to seed rapidly, sow little and often, or leave plants to self-seed. Sow in warmth for out-of-season supplies indoors.

Parts used: leaves gathered fresh as needed, and frozen or gently dried for storing. Roots sometimes dug and used in salad preparations.

Related species: *Chaerophyllum bulbosum* (bulbous chervil): a wild plant with tuberous roots; a close relative of *C. tenuilentum* (rough chervil).

Aquilegia vulgaris
(Ranunculaceae)
🐌 **Columbine**
granny's bonnets, European crowfoot

Description: tough-rooted herbaceous perennial with prettily cut leaves on wiry stems, 2 ft. Stout flowering stems in summer bear nodding spurred blooms in white, blue or pink. Found wild in meadows and waste places on chalky soils. Many garden forms with brilliant-colored flowers, often double or with extra-long spurs.

Uses: all parts have been used medicinally, but now usually grown only as a decorative plant for herb gardens. Roots, flowers and leaves have antiseptic properties, and roots were once used to treat ulcers. **Caution:** internal use is not recommended as aquilegias contain prussic acid, and all parts are poisonous, especially the seeds.

Cultivation: sow in rows in a nursery bed in late spring for transplanting in autumn; or sow early under glass, and plant out in summer after hardening off. Plant in moist soil in partially shady sites; dead-head garden forms promptly, as self-set seedlings tend to revert to wild form.

Arctium lappa (Compositae)
🐌 **Greater Burdock**
beggar's buttons, lappa, cuckoo button, flapper-bags, bardana, clotburr, gipsy's rhizome

Description: short biennial with strong vertical roots up to 3 ft long, and a rosette of large coarse white-backed leaves like rhubarb. In summer thick hairy stems, 6 ft, bear reddish-purple tubular flowers, followed by seedheads (burrs) with hooked spines, lasting all winter. A handsome wild plant of waste places and roadsides.

Uses: a plant of widespread and varied virtues, burdock is cultivated in Japan as a vegetable (*gobo*); used everywhere as a folk remedy for skin problems, especially psoriasis and eczema; grown in China for its seeds, used for throat and chest ailments. A wild vegetable used by North American Indians. The chopped root may be cooked, and the stalks treated like angelica (these contain inulin, a mildly sweet substance useful for diabetics). Roots used as flavoring.

Cultivation: usually gathered from the wild, but seeds may be sown *in situ* in rich, loamy soil in the wild garden.

Parts used: roots of 1-year-old plants, split and dried slowly; young shoots and peeled stalks (before flowering) for salads or as a cooked vegetable; dried seeds for medicinal use.

Related species: *A. minus* (common, lesser or small burdock): a similar plant, but with more pointed leaves and smaller seedheads.

Armeria maritima
(Plumbaginaceae)
Thrift
sea pink

Description: evergreen perennial forming mounds of narrow grassy leaves, 4-8 in, on woody rootstock. In early summer produces short-stemmed white or rose flowers with a strong scent of honey. Grows wild in sandy soil beside the sea, but often planted in gardens, sometimes in improved forms.

Uses: an infusion of fresh or dried flowers was formerly used as an antiseptic and to treat nervous disorders, but now thought to cause allergic reactions such as dermatitis. A valuable formal edging plant for herb gardens and for planting in paths; very popular with butterflies.

Cultivation: sow autumn or spring indoors in trays and plant out when hardened off. Tufts may be rooted as cuttings in a shaded frame in summer. Plant in full sun or light shade.

Related species: A. arenaria (Jersey thrift): plant of similar habit but altogether larger, with stout stems bearing deep pink flowers.

Armoracia rusticana, syn.
Cochlearia armoracia (Cruciferae)
Horseradish

Description: coarse herbaceous perennial. Long-stalked oval leaves, up to 3 ft long; umbels of off-white flowers in mid- to late summer. Pungent roots, up to 2 ft long.

Uses: used medicinally as a digestive, antiseptic and stimulant, and to make poultices for rheumatism, chest complaints and circulation problems. Young leaves may be used for flavoring in salads, or cooked; roots are often made into a sauce. **Caution:** use medicinally with care, as the roots may cause internal inflammation, affect the thyroid gland or, used externally, produce blisters.

Cultivation: although often grown as a perennial for occasional use, plants are invasive and virtually ineradicable, every fragment of bought-in root reviving to grow again. Better cultivated as an annual crop by burying 6 in long upper portions of bought-in roots about 12 in apart in ridges of rich soil in early spring. Water well in

dry weather, and in late autumn dig out all the roots for storing in boxes of moist sand.

Parts used: young leaves gathered in spring; roots dug in autumn.

Arnica montana (Compositae)
Arnica
mountain arnica, mountain daisy, mountain tobacco, fall dandelion, leopard's bane

Description: pungent ornamental perennial with creeping rhizomes and prostrate rosettes of downy leaves. Hairy flower stems, 1-2 ft, bear bright yellow daisies in summer and autumn. Grows wild in hilly and highland districts, but also often grown as garden ornamental.

Uses: homeopathic treatment for epilepsy and blood pressure. A formerly popular Shaker salve; used in many countries to treat bruises and sprains, and also for throat infections, wounds and paralysis. Included in some French herbal smoking mixtures. **Caution:** poisonous and not for self-medication, as the plant may be toxic and cause skin irritations.

Cultivation: sow seeds in a cold frame in spring (germination may be slow) and plant out in autumn in sandy acid soils in full sun; divide mature roots in autumn or spring.

Parts used: whole top growth, especially flowers, either fresh or after drying slowly in shade; roots dug up in late spring or autumn and dried in artificial heat.

Artemisia (Compositae)

A large genus of aromatic shrubs and herbaceous perennials, some with finely cut ornamental foliage ranging in color from gray-green to bright silver. Most shrubby kinds are adapted to hot dry places in full sun, and, apart from their medicinal uses, provide valuable color and form in the herb garden. Only the commonest types are described here.

Artemisia abrotanum

Southernwood

lad's love, old man, Crusader herb

Description: graceful woody perennial shrub, up to 3 ft, with pungent feathery leaves, gray-green and downy. Inconspicuous yellow-green daisy-shaped flowers in late summer.

Uses: like all the artemisias, named after the Greek goddess Artemis, who had special care of women. Used medicinally as an infusion or tincture to regulate menstruation, but also as an antiseptic, insect repellent (in mothballs) and air freshener; used by medieval Crusaders to ward off plague. Has a reputation as a hair-wash and bitter stimulant, and even as an aphrodisiac. Stems yield a yellow dye.

Cultivation: prefers to be grown in sun, in well-drained soil. Propagate from soft cuttings in summer, or semi-ripe cuttings with a 'heel' in autumn. Cut back new growth of shrubs by half every spring, and disbud to prevent flowering. An ideal low hedge if trimmed in spring and again in summer.

Parts used: shoots and leaves, which may be dried slowly in the sun.

Artemisia dracunculus

French tarragon

estragon, serpentarian

Description: herbaceous perennial of shrubby growth, with slim woody branching stems 3 ft. Smooth, dark green pointed leaves, and woolly white or grey flowers in late summer. Spreads by creeping rootstocks, which may be invasive.

Uses: popular culinary herb for stimulating the appetite and flavoring sauces, preserves and cooked dishes. Historically used for toothache, and by the Romans to treat snakebite. Useful for catarrhal and digestive problems, while tarragon tea is used to cure insomnia. An ingredient of perfumes and liqueurs.

Cultivation: may only be propagated by dividing the roots in spring or autumn, or from soft cuttings taken in early summer. Grow in rich, well-drained soil and confine roots in the same way as for mint. Renew every three years or so, and mulch in winter to protect roots. Young roots may be potted up for winter supplies but benefit from a dormant period.

Parts used: growing tips gathered for fresh use; all top growth may be harvested at flowering time for drying slowly in gentle heat.

Related species: A. *dracunculoides* (Russian tarragon): a more robust, coarser plant that may be raised from seed, as well as by division and from cuttings. Tolerates a wider range of soil types, but markedly inferior in flavor. Similar uses, but does not dry successfully.

Artemisia vulgaris

Mugwort

felon herb, St John's herb, moxa

Description: herbaceous perennial with red-purple stems up to 6 ft. Long green ferny leaves with white undersides, and numerous reddish-brown flowers in late summer. Com-mon in built-up areas and roadsides.

Uses: one of the nine Saxon magic herbs, used to make a tea for gastritis and digestive ailments, and to treat menstrual disorders. Insect repellent, and ingredient for herbal tobaccos and Chinese treatments for rheumatism. Used in stuffings for fatty meats. Leaves have been used to make fumigant candle wicks, flowers to flavor beer before the advent of hops. **Caution:** may be harmful when taken internally in excessive doses.

Cultivation: may be grown from seeds sown *in situ* in spring and thinned to about 12 in apart, in sun and light shade. Allow plenty of room, as plants grow quickly to full height. Take cuttings in autumn, or divide roots in autumn or spring. Take care that plants do not become invasive.

Parts used: all parts of the plant, either fresh or dried slowly in the shade.

Related species: A. verlotiorum: an Asian wild species, used in Chinese medicine.

Asparagus officinalis (Liliaceae)
♣ **Asparagus**
sparrow grass, sperage

Description: herbaceous perennial, up to 6 ft. Young, scaly edible 'spears' in spring grow into tall branched stems bearing fine ferny green needles. Greenish-white flowers appear in summer, followed on female plants by red berries in autumn. Fern or 'bower' turns bright yellow as it dies. Found wild on coasts, and widespread in the Middle East; stems may be prostrate.

Uses: an ornamental plant and early summer vegetable. Medicinally used as a laxative, while a tea brewed from the mature fern has been used for rheumatic and urinary disorders, and by Shakers to treat dropsy.

Cultivation: seeds may be sown in rows in spring, the strongest seedlings thinned to 6 in apart; transplant 2 ft apart the following spring in beds or single rows in light rich well-drained soil (on heavy ground create raised beds of suitable soil). Alternatively plant bought 1- or 2-year-old crowns. Start cropping when plants are 3 years old, cutting the 6-8 in high spears just below ground level from spring until midsummer (in parts of Europe the spears are first blanched by earthing up plants). Use largest spears for eating, thinner ones ('sprue') medicinally. Cut down fern and top-dress beds every autumn with compost.

Parts used: young stems ('spears' or 'tips') and fern; roots sometimes dug up for medicinal purposes.

Atriplex hortensis
(Chenopodiaceae)
♣ **Orach(e)**
(red) mountain spinach

Description: an erect leafy annual, up to 2-3 ft or sometimes taller still. Triangular fleshy leaves are dark green, or red in the attractive form *A. hortensis rubra* (red mountain spinach). Thread-like spikes of green or red flowers appear in summer. Common wild on sandy waste land, shingle beaches and salty sites.

Uses: traditional wild herb, often cultivated as a vegetable and garden ornamental; used as a spring tonic and stimulant, and in infusions to treat tiredness or exhaustion.

Cultivation: sow *in situ* in spring in sunny positions, either in rows or broadcast in small patches. Pinch out growing tips once and harvest shoots before plants flower, as they self-seed prolifically.

Parts used: larger leaves and whole young shoots.

Related species: *A. patula* (common orach, ironroot): mealy gray leaves and often trailing stems; common wild on warm beaches, used as a green vegetable.

A. prostrata (hastate orach): similar wild species with much larger leaves.

Borago officinalis (Boraginaceae)
♣ **Borage**
burage, bugloss, bee bread, bee plant

Description: stout herb, with hollow, bristly stems growing to 2-3 ft. Broad oval leaves, also stiffly hairy, and heavy bent clusters of blue star-shaped flowers (white form occasionally found), popular with bees, followed by oval seed capsules. A cultivated herb, sometimes occurring on waste ground.

Uses: a popular reviver included in some drinks. Young leaves add the flavor of cucumber to salads, older ones can be used as a vegetable, while in France and Italy the flowers are often cooked in batter as fritters. An infusion of leaves and seeds was a folk method of increasing the milk supply of nursing mothers, and to treat coughs, cold and depression. The roots are used to flavor wine, and the seeds are a source of gamma-linoleic acid, an essential fatty acid thought to reduce the risk of arteriosclerosis.

Cultivation: sow in early spring (outdoors or in pots) for flowers the same year, or in late summer outdoors to produce larger biennial plants that flower early the following summer. Grow in well drained soil in full sun. Plants self-seed freely to produce seedlings that usually overwinter safely.

Parts used: leaves and stems (latter said to have greater stimulating properties); flowers used fresh, candied, or dried in moderate heat and kept well sealed; seeds dried for medicinal use; roots dug after flowering.

Buxus sempervirens (Buxaceae)

Common Box

boxwood, box tree

Description: a slow-growing evergreen shrub, occasionally small tree, up to 16 ft. Crowded oval leathery leaves, shiny and dark green above, paler beneath. Small greenish-white flowers in mid-spring, male and female blooms in separate groups. Grows wild on chalky commons, but widely cultivated as a garden ornamental, especially as formal hedges since the dense growth tolerates frequent clipping.

Uses: leaves yield a red dye, and are used homeopathically to treat fevers and rheumatism and to promote sweating. One of the best shrubs for topiary and hedges, the compact 'Suffruticosa' being the form grown as dwarf hedging around formal flower and herb beds. **Caution:** the foliage is too toxic for amateur medicinal use.

Cultivation: plant autumn or spring in rich, light soil, preferably in full sun although light shade is tolerated. Keep well watered and feed annually in spring. For hedging choose young plants and space them about 4 in apart, as older ones have very large rootballs and need more space when planted; trim in spring and again at midsummer for formal appearance. Propagate from cuttings outdoors in early autumn, or by layering lower branches.

Parts used: leaves at any time; bark and timber from larger pruned branches.

Related species: *B. macowanii* (Cape box): very similar species used for the same purposes in South Africa.

Calendula officinalis (Compositae)

(Pot) Marigold

common marigold, marybud, marygold, English marigold

Description: perennial herb, usually grown as an annual or biennial, with sticky angular stems up to 2 ft. Long oval leaves, hairy and fleshy, larger at the base; solitary yellow-orange flowers from early summer. Many cultivated forms in a range of yellow, orange and brown, often double.

Uses: apart from being popular old-fashioned cottage garden plants, pot marigolds have a long history of medicinal use. A tea made from the flowers is used for internal spasms and gastric disorders, but the main reputation is as an antiseptic and anti-inflammatory healer of wounds; a common ingredient of many proprietary salves and ointments. Used by Shakers to treat gangrene. Petals can be used as a hair rinse, a coloring agent for butter and cheese, and a substitute for the color of saffron. Also used in cooking and as a garnish.

Cultivation: sow *in situ* in full sun or light shade, in spring for late flowering, or (better) in autumn to overwinter and make bushy plants that flower over a long season the following year. Dead-head regularly to prolong flowering. Although plants thrive best on heavier ground, they tend to self-seed most on light soils.

Parts used: petals fresh or dried in the shade; young fresh leaves in salads; whole flowers boiled as a dye.

Campanula rapunculus (Campanulaceae)

Rampion

rampion bellflower

Description: herbaceous biennial with thick fleshy turnip-like taproot, and slim straight angular stems to 3 ft with milky sap. Slim, toothed leaves, oval near plant base; overwinters as a low rosette, producing in the second year pale blue or white star-shaped flowers in midsummer. A wild plant of meadows, fields and hedgerows.

Uses: an ornamental wild flower, whose leaves are used in winter salads. Popular enough in the sixteenth and seventeenth centuries to be cultivated as a root vegetable (but note that 'German rampion' is the root of evening primrose).

Cultivation: for leaves, sow in spring for autumn use, and in early summer for winter crops. For roots, sow in rich soil in a shady position in the kitchen garden, in rows 8 in apart and thin seedlings to the same distance; sow in spring, but if plants flower early in a hot season, sow again in summer.

Parts used: leaves gathered any time before flowering; roots dug from autumn onwards – may be stored in sand in a cool place.

Centaurium erythraea, syn. *Erythraea centaurium* (Gentianaceae)

❧ (Common) Centaury

bitterherb, centaury gentian, feverwort

Description: a delicate annual growing to 12 in, often less. From a rosette of elliptical gray-green pointed leaves, several stems produce branching umbels of tubular flowers in late summer, pink with yellow centers, arranged in clusters and closing when rain is imminent. Found wild in damp meadows and grassy woodlands.

Uses: an ancient Greek and Celtic medicinal herb, used to make a poultice for skin disorders; taken as a bitter tonic by North American Indians. A tea made from the whole plant treats digestive disorders including heartburn, while homeopathic preparation is prescribed for the liver and gall bladder. One of the aromatic ingredients of vermouth.

Cultivation: although growing wild in damp places, it will adapt to most garden soils, thriving and self-seeding in sun or semi-shade in rock gardens and near the sea. Sow in autumn or spring where plants are to grow, and barely cover the seeds.

Parts used: whole plant gathered at flowering time and dried quickly in shade outdoors or in a warm room.

Related species: C. littorale (seaside centaury): smaller, with narrower leaves, flower paler but larger. A plant found on sand dunes, with similar uses.

Sabatia stellaris (American centaury): a biennial of marshes and wet localities, with similar uses.

Centaurea nigra

❧ Knapweed

lesser knapweed, black knapweed

Description: tough perennial with sturdy ridged stems and dark green hairy leaves. Grows up to 3 ft. Tubular purple flowers in summer. Grows wild on wasteland, roadsides and as a cliff plant.

Uses: a medieval wound salve; used to soothe sore throats and bleeding gums. Also acts as a diuretic.

Cultivation: grows easily in any soil; needs no particular attention. Self-seeds freely. May need containment.

Chamaemelum nobile, syn. *Anthemis nobilis* (Compositae)

❧ Lawn Chamomile

Roman chamomile, double chamomile, common chamomile, perennial chamomile

Description: a vigorous hairy creeping perennial, up to 18 in, with ferny leaves and apple-scented white and yellow flowers in summer; non-flowering forms available for creating lawns. Grows wild in stony ground.

Uses: popular since early Egyptian times, a traditional strewing herb, and often used by Arabs in the form of the essential oil. Ingredient of a famous herb tea for settling nervous disorders, stimulating the appetite and cleansing the blood. Made into herb beers and tisanes, hair rinses and eye lotions, as well as being used in the preparation of cosmetics and perfumes. Essential oil is said to revive cut flowers. Plants often grown as herbal lawns and on ornamental seats.

lawn chamomile

(Continued)

*(**Lawn Chamomile** continued)*

Cultivation: sow seeds in spring out-doors or under cover, but do not cover as the seeds need light for ger-mination. Established plants may be divided in spring, the only way to propagate named forms. Plant in fertile, well-drained light soil, 18 in apart for specimen plants and 6 in for lawns, and be sure to water well in dry weather.

Parts used: whole plant for distillation; flowers for essential oil and teas, col-lected as petals begin to reflex in the sun; dried rapidly in shade.

double
chamomile

Related species: *A. arvensis* (corn chamomile), *A. cotula* (stinking chamomile), *Tripleurospermum inodo-rum* (scentless mayweed): all simi-lar-looking wild flowers with wholly or partly downy leaves, but without the characteristic pleasant subtle apple fragrance.

True wild chamomile is *Matricaria recutita*, q.v.

Chelidonium majus
(Papaveraceae)
🐌 Greater Celandine
swallow-wort, tetterwort

Description: herbaceous perennial with brittle fleshy branching stems up to 3 ft, with soft, finely hairy leaves, yellowish above and blue-green beneath, divided into toothed leaflets. Numerous small yellow flowers appear in summer (double form also avail-able), followed by erect green seed capsules. All parts contain an acrid bright orange sap that may be irritat-ing to the skin.

Uses: once widely grown as a decora-tive cottage garden herb, but now regarded as a weed of waste and culti-vated ground, and walls. Antispas-modic and mildly sedative, tradition-al-ly valued for its sap as a treatment for warts and source of an orange dye. Flowers are beneficial for thyroid con-ditions, while the roots have been used to treat liver and gall bladder dis-orders. **Caution:** in large doses may be poisonous, and an internal and exter-nal irritant.

Cultivation: sow seeds in autumn or divide roots in spring, and plant in dry chalky soils in sun or light shade. Plants normally seed freely but are rarely a nuisance.

Parts used: top growth at flowering time, fresh or dried slowly in darkness; sap at any time from top growth or dormant roots; roots dug in autumn.

Chenopodium bonus-henricus
(Chenopodiaceae)
🐌 Good King Henry
all-good, mercury, poor man's asparagus

Description: herbaceous perennial with smooth, slightly fluted stems up to 2 ft 6 in, and thick fleshy triangular leaves, gray and mealy at first. Small yellow-green flowers in clusters appear at midsummer. Found wild on light, rich soils, but often cultivated.

Uses: cultivated as an early green spinach-like crop, the first shoots sometimes blanched by earthing up for use like asparagus.

Cultivation: sow in spring *in situ* or in a seedbed, and thin or plant at 18 in dis-tances in light, fertile soil. Plants seed freely, so dead-head to prevent inva-siveness.

Parts used: young leaves and shoots.

Related species: *C. album* (fat hen, common pigweed, common lambs-quarter, white goosefoot): red-stemmed salad ingredient, tonic herb for livestock and source of a red dye; seeds once used for flour.

C. ambrosioides anthelmiticum (Ameri-can wormseed), Mexican tea): annu-al wild plant, source of chenopodi-um oil widely used for the treatment of internal worms. **Caution:** large doses may be poisonous.

C. quinoa (quinoa): Peruvian annual, widely cultivated in South America .

C. botrys (ambrosia), *C. leptophyllum*, *C. nuttaliae*: other sources of fatty and nutritious seeds.

Chrysanthemum balsamita

ঞ Alecost

costmary, bible leaf

Description: sharp-tasting herbaceous perennial, growing up to 2 ft. Finely haired creeping rootstock, pale green ridged stems and pointed oval leaves with a minty fragrance. Small yellow flowers often with outer white petals, late summer.

Uses: in medieval times used to ease childbirth; formerly used in brewing as a preservative. Medicinally, used in infusion to soothe colds and digestive disorders. Can be added in small quantities to salads, game, soups and cakes.

Cultivation: sow seed in warm climates, or divide roots and plant in rich, well-drained sunny position. Thin the roots each year. Can also be grown as a pot herb indoors.

Parts used: leaves and flowers; gather young leaves at any time, and flowers as they begin to open.

Cichorium intybus (Compositae)

ঞ Chicory

succory, witloof, blue sailors

Description: tough herbaceous perennial, sometimes grown as an annual crop, with a large deep taproot that exudes a milky sap, and a basal rosette of long smooth leaves, green and jagged like a dandelion (wild species) or grayish and oval (cultivated forms). Hairy flower stems up to 5 ft bearing bright blue daisies (occasionally white or pink) all summer. A common weed in parts of the USA.

Uses: a vegetable and salad ingredient with a bitter flavor; often forced and blanched (witloof or Belgian chicory) to reduce bitterness. Leaves yield a blue dye. Roots and seeds often roasted as a coffee substitute and additive. Chicory tea used to stimulate bile secretion and to treat gout, rheumatism, anaemia and liver complaints. **Caution:** excessive use can lead to digestive upsets, and handling may cause dermatitis.

Cultivation: sow in rows in late spring in rich soil, and thin to 8 in apart. Roots of witloof varieties are dug in autumn, trimmed to leave a stump of foliage and stored in sand until forced in heat and darkness to produce young buds ('chicons').

Parts used: roots and flowering stems, fresh or dried slowly in the sun; woody core of dried roots discarded before rest is shredded and roasted for coffee; seeds also roasted for drinks.

Related species: *C. endivia* (endive, escarole): a bitter salad vegetable, with numerous decorative forms, sometimes blanched to reduce bitterness.

Clinopodium calamintha, syn. *Calamintha ascendens* (Labiatae)

ঞ Common Calamint

mountain mint, mountain balm

Description: hairy herbaceous perennial, with creeping rootstock and bushy growth up to 2 ft. Square stems bear grayish oval, toothed leaves with a mint-like fragrance, and dense branched whorls of lilac or purple flowers in late summer. Found wild in dry waste places, usually on chalk.

Uses: a medicinal plant of ancient Greek and medieval physicians, used in infusions as a tonic and expectorant, and in pleasant mint-flavored tisanes. The whole crushed plant can be used to make poultices for bruises and sprains. Flowers attract butterflies and bees.

Cultivation: sow direct in early spring or autumn outdoors, or in seed trays in autumn to overwinter in a cold frame; germination may be slow and erratic. Alternatively divide mature roots in late spring, or take cuttings from side shoots in early summer. Plant in well drained soil in full sun; will tolerate poor soil.

common calamint

(Continued)

(Common Calamint continued)

Parts used: leaves gathered any time, and dried slowly in warmth.

lesser calamint

common calamint

Related species: *C. vulgare*, syn. *Calamintha clinopodium* (wild basil): similar plant with clusters of purple flowers and bristly bracts in summer, and a scent between those of thyme and basil.

C. grandiflorum, syn. *Calamintha grandiflora*: smaller plant, gray-leaved and decorative, with bright lilac flowers in summer.

C. calamintha calamintha, syn. *Calamintha nepeta* (lesser calamint): similar in appearance and uses to common calamint, with grayer leaves and almost white flowers.

Cnicus benedictus, syn. *Carduus benedictus* (Compositae)

ᴥ **Holy Thistle**

blessed thistle, spotted thistle, St Benedict thistle

Description: branching annual with a single taproot, hairy, reddish stems up to 2 ft, and long white-veined green leaves, deeply cut and spiny. In late summer thistle heads of yellow flowers and brown bracts appear, almost enclosed in a tuft of small leaves and followed in autumn by fat achenes (single seedpods).

Uses: ancient remedial herb used as digestive tonic, to treat liver and gall-bladder complaints, and to induce sweating. A poultice of the leaves relieves chilblains, wounds and burns. Roots used in aperitifs and may be boiled as a vegetable, flowerheads sometimes eaten like globe artichokes.

Cultivation: usually found wild, but may be sown in spring or autumn in patches *in situ*, or for transplanting to loose fertile soil in full sun. For crops sow in rows 18 in apart.

Parts used: roots dug just after flowering; leaves picked before flowering and dried slowly; flowers used whole; seeds gathered when dry.

Convolvulus arvensis (Convolvulaceae)

ᴥ **Field Bindweed**

lesser or pink bindweed, cornbine, devil's guts

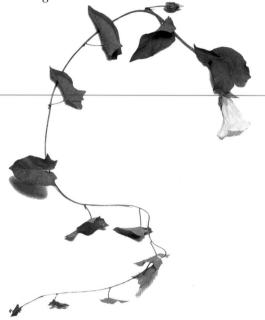

Description: climbing or scrambling herbaceous perennial, with twining stems up to 3 ft long and deep, often tightly coiled rhizomatous roots. Leaves neat and arrow-shaped with basal lobes, in summer and autumn white (or pink on soils rich in iron) funnel-shaped flowers. Difficult to eradicate.

Uses: a tonic and blood cleanser, sometimes used in infusion for fevers and constipation. The flowers may be added to salads.

Cultivation: rarely necessary, but may be propagated from stolons and planted in full sun.

Parts used: flowering top growth, fresh or dried.

Related species: *C. floridus*: North American species whose roots and stems are dried and ground into fragrant *bois de rose*.

Calystegia sepium, syn. *Convolvulus sepium* (hedge bindweed, bellbine): much stronger growing than field bindweed, up to 10 ft, with large white flowers.

Coriandrum sativum
(Umbelliferae)

Coriander

cilantro

Description: rigid, strong-smelling annual with pronounced taproot, and slender stems up to 2 ft. Ferny pinnate leaves, rounded and parsley-like at base, and umbels of small white or pink flowers in midsummer, followed by round red-brown seed capsules, aromatic when ripe. Many named forms selected for leaf or seed production; small-seeded varieties are usually grown in temperate regions, large-seeded kinds in warmer climates. Grows wild in bare places, usually as an escape from cultivation.

Uses: one of the oldest recorded spices, mentioned in ancient Sanskrit texts and in Exodus (coriander is one of the bitter Passover herbs). The leaves and shoots are added to salads, soups and stews, especially in India, South America and China (the leaf is sometimes known as 'Chinese parsley'). The seeds are a stimulant and digestive, often ground and included in curries and regional meat dishes. They are used as a flavoring for bread, and yield an essential oil for soaps and perfumes. They are sometimes added to pot-pourri, and to other herbs to disguise their unpalatability. The root supplies a stronger flavoring, and is often cooked as a vegetable in South-East Asia.

Cultivation: sow *in situ* in autumn or spring, and thin to 6 in apart. Grows fast in full sun, in well-drained soil with a little lime. Protect the brittle stems from wind. Plants usually self-seed freely. Several sowings are advisable for good leaf production.

Parts used: young leaves and shoots at any time; mature seeds dried, roasted and pulverized before use; roots dug after flowering.

Cymbopogon citratus (Gramineae)

Lemon Grass

oil grass, takrai, sereh

Description: coarse tufted tender perennial grass, lemon-scented, with strong roots and spear-shaped, brownish-green leaves up to 3 ft, growing from a tough, fibrous bulbous base.

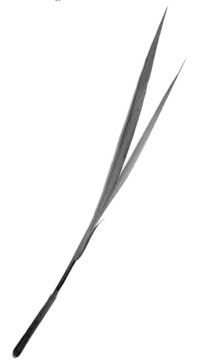

Uses: leaf buds and chopped stems are added to oriental dishes, and made into a tea for liver complaints. The plant yields lemon-grass oil, rich in vitamin A, which is used as a tonic and stimulant, antiseptic, and oily skin cleanser, as an ingredient of cosmetics, and as an aromatherapy oil.

Cultivation: divide clumps and plant offsets with their bottom 1 in buried in rich soil in a warm, sunny site sheltered from cold winds.

Parts used: leaf buds; stems fresh and finely chopped, or dried and ground.

Related species: *C. flexuosus* (Indian lemon grass): an alternative source of lemon-grass oil and an antiseptic.

C. martinii (ginger grass): a source of ginger-grass oil and palma-rosa oil.

C. nardus (citronella grass): yields Ceylon citronella oil for perfumery.

Cynara cardunculus

Cardoon

Description: a close relative of the thistle and globe artichoke, this short-lived perennial grows up to 6 ft. Impressive silvery leaves, ridged stems, often grown as an ornamental garden plant. Gray-blue thistle-like flowers appear in late summer.

Uses: an ornamental garden favorite, also an edible vegetable crop with a delicate flavor. Especially popular in Mediterranean countries. Best eaten in winter and spring.

Cultivation: from seed in almost any soil. To increase yield, cut down to ground level in early summer, feed and water copiously. New growth will be produced until well into autumn.

Parts used: stems, blanched, braised or fried; also added to sauces.

Cynoglossum officinale
(Boraginaceae)

Hound's Tongue

gipsy flower, rats-and-mice

Description: hairy gray-green herbaceous biennial, smelling of mice, with stems up to 3 ft. Leaves roughly hairy, large and oval or tongue-shaped near base of plant, upper ones much narrower. Clusters of hooded flowers, dull maroon or occasionally white, appear in midsummer, followed by hard, flat fruits covered with short-hooked spines. A wild plant of dry, grassy areas, especially near woods.

Uses: infusion from shaved root or crushed leaves used to bathe cuts, bruises, burns and eczema, and to treat coughs and bronchitis; leaves produce a potent poultice for external relief. A nectar-rich plant for bees and butterflies. **Caution:** self-medication is not recommended, as internal use can be dangerous, and external applications may cause dermatitis.

Cultivation: usually gathered from the wild, but seeds may be sown in late summer *in situ*: these need frost to stimulate germination and will not appear before the following spring. Grow in light, well-drained soils in full sun. Plants succeed in seaside gardens, and self-seed freely.

Parts used: flowers and leaves, fresh or dried in shade or a warm room; root fresh or dried.

Related species: *C. germanicum* (green hound's tongue): a similar plant, with leaves shiny and hairless, and lacking the distinctive odor of *C. officinale*.

Dianthus caryophyllus
(Caryophyllaceae)

(Clove) Pink

(clove) gillyflower, carnation, sops-in-wine, divine flower

Description: an evergreen perennial with gray-green branched stems 2-3 ft divided into sections by hard knuckles or nodes, from which long, thick gray-green waxy leaves, stiff and smooth-edged, arise in pairs often joined at their base. Showy, very fragrant flowers, rose-pink or white, appear in summer and early autumn. Found wild on walls and in chalky places in warm climates; cultivated in numerous forms and colors, especially as perpetual-flowering and border carnations.

Uses: an outstanding ornamental plant, whose fresh flowers are used in tonics, and to flavor drinks and syrups; dried petals are often added to pot-pourri.

Cultivation: easily grown on light, well-drained chalky soil in full sun. May be raised from seed sown under glass in spring, the seedlings potted on or transplanted outdoors to a nursery bed for planting in autumn. Propagate named forms from pipings in summer, or cuttings with a heel in early autumn.

Parts used: flowers, fresh or dried. Before culinary use remove the bitter petal base.

Related species: *D. plumarius* (cottage pink, grass pink): smaller plant with slender rough-edged leaves, and fringed flowers in white, pink or purple; one of the parents of the garden pink.

Dryopteris filix-mas

Male Fern

Description: a fern with large fronds which grow up to 4 ft. Veins on the underside of fronds are covered with sporangia. Grows in damp woodlands and in hilly and mountainous areas.

Uses: once used to expel tapeworms, and formerly believed to soothe wounds, cure rickets and ease rheumatism. **Caution:** recent research suggests many species of fern are carcinogenic; male fern should be avoided; it should never be taken internally, especially not by those suffering from cardiac problems or by pregnant women.

Cultivation: grows freely in damp areas and on hedge banks. Should be avoided in the herb garden because of possible health risks.

Echium vulgare (Boraginaceae)

Viper's Bugloss

blue weed, blue devil

Description: herbaceous biennial with an exceptionally long drought-resistant taproot and coarse, hairy stems up to 3 ft. Grayish freckled leaves, long and narrow with rounded tips near the base of the plant, shorter on the flowering stem. Plants flower at midsummer, the dense panicles of pink buds opening into bright blue flowers with long, conspicuous stamens. A wild plant of dry, stony or grassy places, often near the sea; cultivated blue or white forms grown in gardens.

Uses: an outstanding ornamental plant, originally used to treat snakebite (both the seeds and stem markings resemble the features of snakes), the whole plant being crushed and applied to the bite. Flowers are mildly tonic and antiseptic, and may be added to drinks or candied. Leaves may be cooked like spinach.

Cultivation: sow in late summer in any soil where plants are to flower, and thin seedlings to 18 in apart; transplant others to new sites while still young and their taproots undeveloped. Plants self-seed freely where happy.

Parts used: fresh young leaves and shoots before flowering; flowers when fully open.

Related species: E. lycopsis (purple viper's bugloss): more softly hairy, with larger red-purple flowers and fewer stamens. Similar uses.

Eruca vesicaria spp. *sativa* (Cruciferae)

(Garden or Sweet) Rocket

rocket-salad, rocket-gentle, rocquette

Description: fast-growing annual, with a rosette of smooth, dark green leaves, indented like a dandelion. Branched, leafy main stems, hairy and reddish, growing to 2 ft, producing sparse simple flowers of loose, floppy creamy-yellow petals with purple veins, followed by fat, crisp seedpods.

Uses: salad herb with pungent flavor, especially popular in Mediterranean countries. A tonic, mild stimulant and cough remedy. Crisp seedpods are edible, seeds used to treat bruises and supply mustard oils.

Cultivation: for succulent leaves grow in rich, moist soil in full sun or light shade; on hot, dry soils plants run to seed quickly and produce tough, bitter leaves. Sow in spring and again at midsummer (all year round in warm districts), and keep well watered. Plants usually self-seed.

Parts used: leaves gathered in succession as soon as plants are large enough; seedpods while young and juicy; seeds from ripe seedpods.

Eupatorium perfoliatum (Compositae)

Boneset

thoroughwort, agueweed

Description: perennial herbaceous herb, with branching rough stem up to 5 ft. Long narrow pointed leaves, dark green and shiny above, and white and downy beneath. Dense heads of small white, occasionally blue, flowers, followed by feathery seedheads.

Uses: a popular tonic and stimulant, best known as a hot infusion for treating coughs and colds, or as an ointment or syrup for muscular aches.

Cultivation: sow on the surface of seed trays in autumn or spring in a cold frame; divide mature plants in spring or autumn, and grow in damp or marshy soil in sun or light shade.

Parts used: whole plant as flowers open, fresh or dried quickly in warmth.

Related species: E. ayapana: Brazilian species, producing a stimulant and digestive tea.

E. cannabinum (hemp agrimony, water hemp): contains eupatorin, used to treat dropsy; flowering herb or root also used as a tonic and laxative.

E. purpureum (joe-pye weed, gravel-root, queen of the meadow): white- and purple-flowered plant up to 10 ft; North American Indian red dye plant; roots and seedheads used to treat rheumatism, backache and urinary disorders.

Filipendula ulmaria, syn. *Spiraea ulmaria* (Rosaceae)

🌿 **Meadowsweet**

queen of the meadows, meadsweet, meadwort

Description: herbaceous perennial with a pink aromatic creeping rootstock. Reddish stems, up to 4 ft, bear pinnate leaves. Dense panicles of fragrant, creamy-white flowers in late summer.

Uses: an early source of salicylic acid. Tea from the flowers reduces fever, and is used to treat stomach acidity, influenza and rheumatism. Flower buds produce oil for perfume, and the dried flowers are added to home-made wines. Leaves flavor drinks, especially beer and mead. Dyes made from the roots (black) and flowers (yellow).

Cultivation: sow in spring or autumn *in situ* or in trays of compost under glass, or divide roots in spring. Plant in moist, rich soil in sun or light shade.

Parts used: flowers fresh or dried gently in warmth; roots dried for homeopathic use; leaves for flavoring.

Related species: *F. vulgaris* (dropwort): smaller plant, up to 2 ft, with less dense flowerheads. Roots sometimes used as a vegetable.

F. rubra, syn. *F. magnifica* (queen of the prairie): similar North American species with pink flowers.

Foeniculum vulgare (Umbelliferae)

🌿 **Fennel**

spigel

Description: grayish-green, strong-smelling herbaceous perennial, with slim stems up to 6 ft, bearing soft lacy, dark green leaves with thread-like lobes and swollen bases. Creeping rootstock gradually extends plant into a sparse clump. Small mustard-yellow flowers appear in summer, followed by small egg-shaped seedpods. Grows

wild in waste places and damp sites; may become an invasive weed, as in Australia and New Zealand.

Uses: one of nine Anglo-Saxon sacred herbs; much used by ancient Greeks and throughout the Middle Ages. Roots once boiled as a vegetable, and used as an expectorant in cough mixtures. Dried stalks are an essential ingredient of Provençal cuisine. Soft growing tips are widely used to flavor and garnish fish dishes, soups and baked foods, and may be made into fennel tea to treat indigestion and colic. A popular flavoring for liqueurs and a scent for soaps and cosmetics. Oil produced from seeds is antibacterial. In warmer regions foliage attracts swallowtail butterflies. **Caution:** avoid large doses.

Cultivation: for lavish growth light, moist soils are best. Divide roots in spring and plant in a warm sunny place, or sow seeds in spring or summer, either in pots or *in situ* 20 in apart. Roots become long and tough,

so transplant while still young. Water well in dry weather. Fennel self-seeds freely, so dead-head if seeds not needed. Plants become congested and exhausted after 3-4 years, and are then best replaced. Do not grow near dill, as these two species cross-fertilize readily to produce useless hybrids.

Parts used: growing tips, fresh or dried in early summer (leaves and stems may be cropped several times before flowering); seeds, from seedheads cut in autumn before fully mature and dried in warmth; roots dug in autumn and dried slowly.

Related species: *F. vulgare* 'Dulce' (Florence fennel, finocchio, sweet fennel): annual cropped from the wild for its essential oil, and cultivated as a vegetable for its juicy, swollen stem base.

F. vulgare 'Piperitum' (carosella, cartucci): local Italian vegetable with blanched young stems.

Ferula foetida (asafoetida): perennial herb used as an Indian condiment and in sauces; medicinal resin extracted from the root.

Ferula galbaniflua (galbanum): Middle Eastern species, the stem and roots of which yield an aromatic gum used for incense.

Fragaria vesca (Rosaceae)
(Wild) Strawberry
wood strawberry

Description: deciduous herbaceous perennial, spreading by runners or stolons. Single white flowers on stems in summer, followed by red or white berries with numerous yellow seeds on the outside. Grows wild in woods and grassy places on dry soil.

Uses: mildly laxative fruits are a nerve tonic, rich in iron. Leaves can be made into a popular tea that is a diuretic and astringent; fresh leaves sometimes added to salads. **Caution:** excessive consumption sometimes leads to allergic reactions.

Cultivation: plant young runners in spring or autumn, or sow seeds under glass in spring (sow on the surface and keep moist – germination may be slow and erratic). Plant in sun or light shade, in any soil except clay.

Parts used: fruit when fully colored; leaves at any time; roots dug in winter.

Related species: *F. moschata* (hautbois strawberry, musk strawberry): wild species with larger flowers.

F. virginiana (wild strawberry): red-fruited wild species, an important North American Indian legendary and medicinal plant, and one parent of most large-fruited forms.

Galium odoratum, syn. *Asperula odorata* (Rubiaceae)
(Sweet) Woodruff
kiss-me-quick, master of the woods (Waldmeister)

Description: herbaceous perennial, often evergreen. Branched stems up to 12 in bear neat whorls of dark green leaves. Clusters of star-shaped flowers on long stalks appear in early summer.

Uses: flavors wines and other drinks, and scents linen, pot-pourri and perfumes. Medicinally used to poultice wounds and scabies, and to stimulate milk flow of nursing mothers. **Caution:** excessive use may produce dizziness and respiratory allergies.

Cultivation: divide roots at any time, or sow ripe seeds in late summer *in situ.* Grow in rich, alkaline soil in shade, and harvest from second year onwards.

Parts used: green plant cut at or just before flowering time, and dried slowly.

Related species: *G. verum* (lady's bed-straw): taller and with thinner leaves; sweet-scented yellow flowers used to curdle milk and color cheese; stems yield a red dye.

Asperula tinctoria (dyer's woodruff): white-flowered species, giving a yellow-orange dye.

Gaultheria procumbens (Ericaceae)
Wintergreen
partridge berry, tea berry, chequerberry

Description: evergreen perennial shrub with prostrate creeping stems from which erect branches grow to 6 in high. Top of each branch bears a few leathery, serrated oval leaves, shiny and paler beneath. Drooping white or pink flowers appear in midsummer, followed by pea-sized scarlet berries. A wild plant growing in woodlands on acid soils.

Uses: leaves made into aromatic infusion for use as a gargle. Leaves are pain-reducing, and when dried can be made into a tea. Oil distilled from the leaves rubbed in externally to treat muscular aches and pains, and also used to flavor dental preparations.

Cultivation: excellent ground-cover plant for moist, acid soils and rock gardens. Plant in autumn or spring in peaty soils in full sun or light shade. Propagate by seeds sown in a seedbed outdoors in autumn, or from rooted prostrate stems in spring.

Parts used: leaves fresh or dried in the sun, distilled for oil of wintergreen.

Related species: *G. antipoda*: New Zealand species, either prostrate or a medium-sized shrub, with edible red berries.

G. shallon (shallon, salal): vigorous, shrubby North American species, with purple berries.

Genista tinctoria (Leguminosae)

Dyer's Greenweed

dyer's broom

Description: dwarf deciduous broom-like shrub, sometimes prostrate or erect to 3 ft. Bright green branches and narrow pointed glossy leaves; long, leafy racemes of bright yellow pea-type flowers in summer. A wild plant of dry grassy places and heaths; numerous cultivated forms, including one with double flowers.

Uses: a decorative ground-cover plant to grow with heathers. Infusion made from young flowering shoots is diuretic and laxative, and used to treat dropsy and skin disorders. Young flower buds may be pickled like capers. Flowers yield a yellow dye, rich green if mixed with woad.

Cultivation: poor soil in an open, sunny position with good drainage is ideal. Plant autumn or spring, or sow seeds outdoors in autumn after rubbing them between sheets of sandpaper; named varieties may be grafted on to laburnum rootstocks in spring. Prune soft growth after flowering.

Parts used: flower buds; flowers for dye; young flowering shoots fresh or dried in shade.

Geranium maculatum (Geraniaceae)

American Cranesbill

spotted cranesbill, alum root, crowfoot

herb robert

American cranesbill

Description: hairy herbaceous perennial with stout rhizomatous root and stems up to 2 ft. Leaves elegant and downy, divided with scalloped edges and blotched with white as they age. Small pink-purple, occasionally white, flowers appear in late spring, followed by fruits with long barbs like the bill of a crane. A wild plant of hedgerows and woodlands.

Uses: a popular North American Indian herb; root is astringent, used in infusions or as a powder to treat diarrhoea, dysentery and bleeding, and ulcers, both internal and external.

Cultivation: divide mature plants in early spring, or sow in autumn or spring where plants are to grow after rubbing seeds between sheets of sandpaper. Grow in full sun or light shade in moist, leafy soil. Plants self-seed profusely and soon develop into thick clumps.

Parts used: roots gathered in autumn or winter, dried and powdered.

Related species: G. robertianum (herb robert, stinking cranesbill): annual with pink or white flowers; whole plant (including roots) is a powerful wound herb, used to stop bleeding and heal oral inflammations.

Geum urbanum (Rosaceae)

Herb Bennet

wood avens, clove root

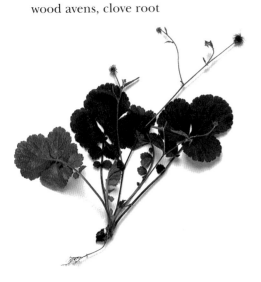

Description: downy herbaceous perennial with strong thick aromatic pink root and branched stems up to 2 ft. Grows as a rosette of dark green oval leaflets of unequal size, the terminal one largest, toothed or deeply lobed. In summer and autumn bears loose open panicles of yellow flowers. A wild plant of woods and shady fertile places, and 'weed' of cultivated soil.

Uses: spicy root, a medieval pot herb and substitute for cloves, can be made into an infusion for stomach and liver disorders, to increase appetite and stop bleeding, or into a strengthening tea to reduce fever; also used as a mouthwash. Young leaves can be eaten in salads.

Cultivation: sow in spring or autumn where flowers are to grow, and thin to 6 in apart. Grow in fertile soil in full or semi-shade.

Parts used: roots fresh or dried in shade or warmth; young leaves.

Related species: G. rivale (water avens, Indian chocolate): delicate perennial with trefoil leaves and nodding bell-shaped pink flowers, preferring damp shade or the margins of ponds. Similar uses, but milder in effect; also used to make chocolate-flavored drinks.

Glycyrrhiza glabra (Leguminosae)

Liquorice

licorice, sweet root

Description: vetch-like herbaceous perennial, with long yellow fibrous taproot, numerous subroots and creeping stolons. Stems to 5 ft, bearing pale green pinnate leaves with small oval leaflets in pairs. From the leaf axils loose, conical lilac-blue pea-type flowers appear in midsummer, followed by long brown seedpods.

Uses: cultivated for its sweet aromatic roots since the Middle Ages; used by Arab physicians as a laxative, and for treating stomach problems such as ulcers, and bladder and kidney complaints. Infusion given for bronchial catarrh and sore throats, and to reduce fever. Popular sweetener and flavoring for confectionery, beers and tobacco. Waste fibers after processing used to make wallboard. **Caution:** long-term use can raise blood pressure, lower potassium levels and lead to sodium retention.

Cultivation: grow in deep, well-drained soils in full sun. Divide roots in spring and plant 4 in deep and 18 in apart. Cut down foliage annually in autumn and remove any creeping stolons.

Parts used: roots from 3-4-year-old plants, dug in autumn or spring, peeled and dried; juice may be extracted from fresh roots.

Hamamelis virginiana (Hamamelidaceae)

(Common) Witch Hazel

winterbloom, spotted alder

Description: deciduous perennial shrub or small spreading tree with smooth pale bark, up to 13 ft. Small elliptical hazel-like leaves, downy when young, and ragged spidery bright yellow flowers on bare stems from late autumn onwards. A wild shrub of damp woods and watersides, widely grown as an ornamental and rootstock for cultivated witch hazels.

Uses: traditional astringent and cooling wound herb, sacred to North American Indians. Made into an infusion for treating bruises, sprains, varicose veins and bleeding, and an ointment for relieving piles. Commercial witch hazel is made from young flowering twigs. **Caution:** tinctures made from the leaves and bark may cause allergic reactions.

Cultivation: prefers lime-free soils in full sun or light shade, may be grown as a decorative lawn specimen or among other shrubs, or trained against walls. Sow seeds in spring in trays under glass or a seedbed outdoors, or layer branches in autumn. Cut out suckers annually; if rooted these may be transplanted for new plants.

Parts used: bark and leaves for tinctures; flowering twigs for distillation.

Hedera helix (Araliaceae)

🌿 **Ivy**

English ivy

Description: long-lived evergreen climber, with woody stems clinging by aerial roots, up to 100 ft. Dark green glossy leaves, often with paler veins; juvenile foliage pointed and lobed, often palmate. When stems reach full light they branch freely and bear smaller simple pointed oval leaves and globular heads of greenish fragrant flowers in autumn, followed by black berries. A wild plant growing in trees and hedges or prostrate on shaded soil; numerous ornamental forms.

Uses: once regarded as a protective magical plant, with numerous internal medicinal uses: berries were taken as a purgative, and leaves used to treat fevers and glandular disorders. They may safely be turned into an effective poultice for bruises and stiff joints. Plants produce a resin sometimes included in varnishes; flowers attract bees, and birds depend on the berries in winter. **Caution:** whole plant is poisonous and should be restricted to external use.

Cultivation: plants prefer rich, well-drained soil in full or semi-shade. Sow in autumn, exposing seed trays to frost over winter, or use pieces of stem bearing aerial roots as cuttings. Peg shoots to soil surface at first to encourage more rapid growth and coverage of walls. Prune in spring, trimming off old leaves and shortening or removing any unwanted straggly stems.

Parts used: young leaves, fresh or dried in shade.

Helichrysum italicum, syn. *H. angustifolium* (Compositae)

🌿 **Curry Plant**

everlasting flower, helichrysum

Description: evergreen aromatic bush with branched woody stems up to 2 ft. Fragrant narrow, silvery-white leaves; rich yellow daisies on long stalks in summer.

Uses: intensely aromatic herb for flavoring meat dishes, drinks and jellies, and effective as an insect repellent. Essential oil used in cosmetics, and for treating respiratory problems.

Cultivation: grow in poor soil in a sunny, well-drained position, protected from frost and cold winds in winter. Divide plants in spring, take cuttings from side shoots in summer, or sow under glass in spring. Plant in autumn or spring; in formal positions trim off flowering stems as these detract from the foliage, but never cut into old wood.

Parts used: leaves; flowers in bud dried for arrangements; flowerheads and shoots in summer for distillation.

Related species: *H. cochinchinense:* South-East Asian species, leaves used to flavor rice dishes.

H. serpyllifolium, syn. *Plecostachys serpyllifolia:* South African species, leaves made into tea.

H. stoechas (goldilocks): bright yellow-flowered dwarf shrub; leaves used as a vermifuge.

Humulus lupulus (Cannabinaceae)

🌿 **Hop(s)**

Description: hairy aggressive perennial climber, with long spreading stolons and twining stems ('bines'), often twisting around each other into ropes, up to 30 ft. Leaves heart-shaped or palmately lobed, with toothed edges. Clusters of greenish male and female flowers appear on separate plants in summer, female flowers ripening into large cones of overlapping bracts in autumn. Grows wild in hedges, cultivated commercially and grown as a garden ornamental.

Uses: common flavoring and antibacterial preservative in beer; female cones used to treat insomnia and nervous tension, and included for their hormonal content in skin creams and lotions. Hop poultices applied to boils and swellings. Young shoots and leaves cooked as vegetables; fibers from the stems are used in the textile industry.

Cultivation: grow from cuttings or divisions from the base of the plant in spring, or sow seeds in late summer and autumn in a cold frame. Plant in rich, moist soil in full sun or light shade, and grow up sturdy tall supports. Mulch in spring with rotted manure, thin young shoots to 5-6 per crown, and water freely in dry weather.

Parts used: female cones gathered in early autumn while still green, and dried until brown, sometimes powdered; young shoots 6-8 in long in spring.

Hypericum perforatum (Guttiferae)
(Perforate, or Common) St John's Wort

Description: low evergreen perennial, with long, wiry runners or stolons and branched stems up to 3 ft, woody at base and marked with two raised parallel lines. Small, pale green leaves arranged in opposite pairs and speckled with translucent dots, which are oil glands. Bright yellow flowers appear in late summer, petals edged with black dots. A wild plant of grassy and shady places, usually chalky.

Uses: leaves mildly sedative, and stimulate gastric and bile secretions. Sometimes used to treat poor blood circulation and irregular menstruation, but best known as an antibacterial remedy for slow-healing wounds and burns. Young leaves eaten in salads; flowers yield red and yellow dyes. **Caution:** avoid exposure to the sun during treatment, as the plant causes photosensitivity.

Cultivation: grow in sun or light shade in well-drained soil. Divide roots in spring, take cuttings in summer, or sow seeds in trays in spring. Plant in autumn or spring, and prune damaged stems after frosts.

Parts used: young leaves and flowers fresh or dried in shade.

Related species: H. androsaemum (all-heal, tutsan): larger, shade-loving plant with unspotted leaves and black berries in autumn; a noted wound herb.

Hyssopus officinalis (Labiatae)
Hyssop

Description: perennial evergreen shrub with branching stems up to 2 ft. Long narrow green fragrant leaves, hairy and dotted with oil-bearing glands; whorls of blue, pink, purple or white flowers on long narrow spikes in autumn, popular with bees. A wild plant of dry stony soils on chalk, and an ornamental herb, sometimes used for dwarf hedging.

Uses: a valuable expectorant; flowering tips infused in water used to treat coughs and sore throats, also to heal bites, burns and stings. Often added for flavoring to soups, stews and salads. Distilled oil used in liqueurs and perfumes.

Cultivation: grow in full sun in well-drained, light soil. Sow in spring under glass, take cuttings in early summer, or divide in spring or autumn. Plant 8 in apart for hedging and clip to shape in spring.

Parts used: leaves fresh at any time; flowering tips fresh or dried in sun.

Related species: Agastache foeniculum (anise hyssop): aromatic herbaceous perennial, dried leaves used for seasoning and teas.

A. urticifolia (nettle-leaved giant hyssop): herbaceous perennial, used by North American Indians medicinally and as flavoring.

Isatis tinctoria (Cruciferae)
Woad

dyer's weed

Description: biennial or short-lived perennial, with basal rosette of long-stalked, oval toothed leaves, blue-green and downy, with branched leafy stems up to 4 ft, stem leaves smaller, sessile and arrow-shaped. Graceful loose panicles of small yellow flowers in early summer, followed by pendulous black seeds. A wild plant of waste places on chalk, widely cultivated until this century.

Uses: an ancient dye and healing plant, fermented leaves producing a blue dye eventually superseded by indigo. Leaves were also traditionally used to stop bleeding and heal the wounds of battle. **Caution:** for external use only.

Cultivation: grow in full sun in well-drained, rich chalky soil. Sow *in situ* in late summer and thin seedlings to 12 in apart. Removing stems before they can flower extends the life of plants, which will otherwise seed themselves freely as biennials.

Parts used: leaves repeatedly fermented and dried in a complicated sequence of operations.

Below: Hyssop.

Juniperus communis
(Cupressaceae)
Juniper

Description: evergreen coniferous shrub or tree, prostrate or upright to 20 ft. Needle-like leaves, prickly and emitting scent of apples if bruised. Yellow-green flowers in early summer, followed by fleshy berries, green at first, turning blue-black with a white bloom in the second year.

Uses: Oil from unripe berries used in massaging rheumatic or gouty parts of the body. Ripe berries are added as a flavoring to drinks such as gin, and meat dishes, especially game. Wood of stem and roots is burned to smoke preserved meats. **Caution:** use internally only under medical supervision; may also be an external irritant.

Cultivation: plant in autumn or spring in good, well drained soil in an open position. Propagate from seeds sown in a cold frame in spring, or from cuttings in autumn.

Parts used: leafy shoots at any time; fruit gathered in late summer and dried in sun; woody stems and roots when available.

Related species: *J. sabina* (savin): poisonous shrubby species used under supervision as a veterinary herb.

J. oxycedrus (prickly juniper): oil of cade (juniper tar) distilled from the roots as a veterinary vermifuge.

J. virginiana (eastern red cedar): source of cedar oil for perfume and medications.

Laurus nobilis (Lauraceae)
(Sweet) Bay (Tree)
sweet laurel, bay laurel

Description: large dense evergreen shrub or ornamental tree up to 50 ft, with glossy dark green, oval pointed leaves. Small creamy-yellow flowers appear in early summer, followed in warm climates and on mature plants by black berries.

Uses: an ancient aromatic and antiseptic plant, used to weave a victorious Roman general's crown or 'laurels'. Leaves are a popular culinary flavoring, and stimulate the appetite; when pulped they can be applied as an astringent to burns and bruises. Berries are pressed to make oil for liqueurs, perfume and veterinary uses.

Cultivation: grow in rich, well-drained soil in full sun, sheltered from cold winds; sometimes scorched or cut back by severe frost especially while young. Plant in early autumn or spring, and trim to shape in summer; may be clipped into formal topiary. Propagate by layering shoots in autumn, or from cuttings of side shoots in a shaded cold frame in early autumn. Best grown in containers and moved to a cool greenhouse in areas with severe winters.

Parts used: leaves at any time, dried in darkness and lightly pressed flat; ripe berries pressed for oil.

Related species: *Umbellularia californica* (Californian laurel): similar shrub or tree, with more aromatic foliage.

Lavandula angustifolia, syn. *L. officinalis*, *L. spica* (Labiatae)
(English) Lavender
true lavender

Description: evergreen perennial woody shrub, dense and branching up to 3 ft. Long narrow, aromatic leaves, gray-green and downy, and intensely fragrant blue-mauve flowers in long spikes in midsummer. A wild plant of Mediterranean hillsides; numerous varieties widely cultivated as garden ornamentals and hedging.

Uses: an early strewing herb, often burnt on low fires to perfume rooms. As an essential oil and in infusion used as a cough suppressant, and to treat headaches and nervous disorders. As an embrocation an external stimulant and antiseptic. Flowers attract bees, and are gathered for perfume, potpourri and to scent clothing.

Lavandula 'Hidcote'

Cultivation: grow in light, dryish soils in full sun for maximum fragrance and color. Sow seeds in trays in late spring; take soft cuttings in spring or hardwood cuttings in late summer; or layer old plants by mounding soil
(Continued)

Lavandula 'Nana Alba'

French lavender

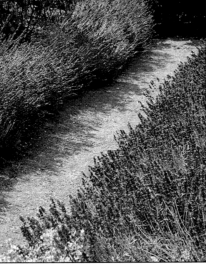

English lavender

around the stems. Prune annually to shape in spring to prevent straggly growth and bare stems, especially on hedges, but do avoid cutting back into old wood.

Parts used: flowers gathered just before fully opened and dried slowly; flowering shoots and leaves distilled for essential oil.

Related species: *L. a 'Hidcote':* slow-growing species, with low stems and deep purple flowers.

L. a. 'Nana Alba': pale flowers; a low-growing species.

L. stoechas (French lavender): slightly tender species, with a stronger scent than most.

Levisticum officinale, syn.
Ligusticum levisticum
(Umbelliferae)

Lovage

love parsley, lovage angelica, smallage

Description: pungent, clump-forming herbaceous perennial with rhizomatous roots and stout hollow ridged stems up to 8 ft. Broad glossy leaves, with large, dense umbels of greenish-yellow flowers in summer, followed by ridged golden-brown seedpods.

Uses: leaves can flavor soups and casseroles; stems are blanched like celery or candied like angelica; roots may be peeled and cooked as a vegetable; savory seeds are added to bread and other baked foods. Powdered root sometimes used as a condiment. Medicinally digestive and carminative. Essence of lovage used in perfumes. **Caution:** avoid taking large quantities.

Cultivation: mature plants are large and bulky, and so need plenty of room in deep rich moist soil, preferably in shade. Sow in spring outdoors in a seedbed or under glass, or divide roots in autumn or spring. Cut back once or twice during summer if a continuous supply of young leaves is needed.

Parts used: young leaves, avoiding the central flower stem; hollow main stems before flowering; roots of 2- or 3-year-old plants dug in autumn, sliced and dried; ripe seeds.

Related species: *Ligusticum scoticum* (Scots lovage): smaller wild plant of cliffs and seashores with milder flavor.

Levisticum chinensis: used in Chinese medicine for menstrual disorders.

Ligustrum vulgare (Oleaceae)

&c (Common) Privet

wild privet

Description: densely branched deciduous shrub up to 12 ft, with smooth leathery oval pointed leaves and short spikes of white strong-smelling flowers in early summer, followed by small black or yellow shiny berries. Grows wild in scrubland and open woods, especially on chalk, and often cultivated as a hedging plant; numerous attractive garden forms.

Uses: valuable hardwood timber for tools and charcoal; leaves once used by Shakers to make a mouthwash. Yellow dye made from the leaves. **Caution:** all parts are poisonous if ingested.

Cultivation: tolerant of most soils and positions. Sow seeds in autumn outdoors; put cuttings of young shoots in a cold frame in summer, or hardwood cuttings in a shady position outdoors in autumn. Plant and prune to shape in autumn.

Parts used: leaves at any time during the growing season; wood of larger pruned stems.

oval-leaved golden privet

common privet

Related species: *L. ibota* (ibota privet): small elegant shrub, grown in China where insect damage to the stems produces a wax with industrial uses.

L. japonicum (Japanese privet, wax-leaved privet): dense, large-flowered species, with seeds sometimes roasted as a coffee substitute.

L. lucidum (wax tree): handsome small Chinese tree, seeds made into an infusion for strengthening general metabolism.

L. ovalifolium (oval-leaved privet): best species for hedging, dense and semi-evergreen, with popular golden variety.

Linaria vulgaris (Scrophulariaceae)

&c (Common) Toadflax

yellow toadflax, butter and eggs

Description: herbaceous perennial with vigorous underground creeping rhizomes and numerous long slender grayish flax-like leaves. Stems up to 2 ft bear in summer and autumn dense spikes of long-spurred brilliant yellow flowers like those of antirrhinums, each with a bright orange spot on the lower lip, followed by capsules of numerous flat round black seeds. A wild plant growing on bare waste ground.

Uses: a highly ornamental plant, used in the Middle Ages for laundry starch. Used homeopathically to treat diarrhoea and cystitis, and by herbalists to treat jaundice. Has a folk reputation as a fly poison when boiled in milk. Flowers yield dyes: yellow, orange, green or brown depending on the mordant used.

Cultivation: best grown in the wild herb garden, in a confined space, or in mown grass to restrain the invasive stolons. Sow in spring or early autumn, either where plants are to flower or in trays of compost for transplanting; established roots may be divided in autumn or spring. Plant 2 ft apart in full sun. Plants self-seed liberally, so dead-head after flowering to restrain seeding.

Parts used: whole flowering herb, fresh or dried in shade.

Linum usitatissimum (Linaceae)
Flax
flaxseed, linseed

Description: slender annual with wiry stems to 3 ft. Linear pointed leaves; pale to bright blue flowers (best for fiber production) or white in summer, followed by pods of flat oval brown seeds, rich in oil. Grows wild in dry grasslands, usually as an escape from cultivation. A taller variety is grown for flax production in cool, moist regions, and a more compact type in warm climates for seed.

Uses: stem varieties are soaked ('retted') in water to release fibers for making linen cloth. Linseed oil from seed varieties is one of the most important commercial drying oils, used in paints, varnishes and putty. Oil used medicinally as a laxative and vermifuge; the seeds soaked overnight and strained can be used to treat gastritis, constipation and indigestion, and in poultices for cuts, bruises and other abrasions. **Caution:** large doses may be poisonous.

Cultivation: sow in late spring or early summer in dry, well-drained soil in sun.

Parts used: whole fresh flowering plant for medicinal purposes; stems of green plant for fiber; seeds used fresh or dried and powdered.

Related species: *L. catharticum* (purging flax): white-flowered annual with oval leaves; used homeopathically to treat bronchitis and piles.

Lippia citriodora, syn. *Aloysia triphylla* (Verbenaceae)
Lemon Verbena
sweet-scented verbena, herb luisa, Spanish thyme

Description: perennial evergreen shrub, almost small tree up to 10 ft in warm climates, with sparse, slender branches and long narrow pointed leaves, gray-green and downy in groups of 3 or 4 with oil-bearing glands forming dots on the underside, giving off a penetrating lemon scent. Long terminal racemes of tiny white or lavender flowers in late summer.

Uses: tea (sold in France as 'verveine') made from leaves is tonic, calming and sedative, and can be used to treat nausea, palpitations and flatulence. Essential oil ('Spanish verbena') distilled from leaves used as flavoring in cakes, drinks, stuffings and desserts, in pot-pourri, and formerly in perfumes – largely replaced by lemon-grass oil. Hot leaf pulp is effective against toothache. **Caution:** large doses or prolonged use can cause internal irritation.

Cultivation: grow in fertile, well-drained soil in full sun, under glass in temperate regions as plants are frost-shy; in warm gardens may be trained as a climber against a sunny wall. Sow seed under glass in early spring, or take cuttings in summer. Propagate every few years, as older plants become threadbare and more sensitive to cold.

Parts used: leaves any time, fresh or dried in shade; shoots picked just before flowering and distilled for essential oil.

Lonicera periclymenum (Caprifoliaceae)
(Wild) Honeysuckle
woodbine

Description: deciduous woody twining shrub or climber to 20 ft, with oval glossy leaves. Clusters of fragrant pink-cream flowers appear in summer, followed by bright red berries.

Uses: as perfume, and a traditional remedy for a number of ailments. Bruised leaves used to treat skin disorders; flaked and infused bark for rheumatism and painful joints; flowers raw or infused in a tea for asthma and as a heart tonic; inside of the root as a veterinary vermifuge. Today only external uses are recommended. **Caution:** the berries of all honeysuckles may be poisonous.

Cultivation: grow in any good soil, in sun or shade, and train up walls or as standards on pillars. Sow seeds in autumn in pots (germination may be slow) or take cuttings in summer. Prune and mulch with compost in spring.

Parts used: leaves and flowers fresh or dried in shade; fresh bark from prunings; roots dug in autumn and dried.

Related species: *L. caprifolium* (perfoliate honeysuckle): yellow-flowered species with orange berries, used as an expectorant and antiseptic.

L. japonica: rampant semi-evergreen climber, an invasive weed in USA; widely used in Chinese medicine.

L. nigra (black honeysuckle): hard-wooded shrub with orange flowers, and black berries used homeopathically to treat neuroses.

Lythrum salicaria (Lythraceae)
🐌 **Purple Loosestrife**

Description: herbaceous perennial with creeping rhizomes and square angled stems up to 5 ft. Narrow, pointed leaves without stalks, in opposite pairs or whorls of three, and long, dense spikes of bright mauve-pink flowers in midsummer, followed by ovoid seed capsules. A plant of river banks and damp places, with several cultivated garden forms.

Uses: high tannin content, so once often used in leather tanning, but now a mainly decorative and medicinal plant. Antibacterial, used as a gargle and eyewash.

Cultivation: sow on surface of pots of moist compost and stand in trays of water until seedlings emerge; divide mature plants in spring or take cuttings in summer in a moist cold frame. Plant in damp soil in light shade, or full sun where the plants will flower best. Be careful that it does not choke out native plants when naturalized.

Parts used: flowering herb, fresh or dried in shade.

Malva sylvestris (Malvaceae)
🐌 **Common Mallow**

Description: coarse herbaceous biennial, sprawling or bushy to 3 ft. Leaves hairy, crinkled and deeply veined, palmate but almost circular at base of plant and toothed with long stalks, sometimes marked with a distinct black spot. Flowers pink, white or mauve with purple veins, in pairs or groups, in summer and autumn, followed by flat green button-like seed capsules. A wild plant of banks and waste places, especially near the sea, but also cultivated as a flowering plant in gardens.

pink mallow

Uses: whole plant is mucilaginous and therefore soothing. Leaves used to reduce inflammations and ease bee stings, and in poultices to treat ulcers and hemorrhoids. Tea made from an infusion of the flowers given for colds and bronchitis. Leaves can be added to soups or cooked like spinach, seedpods eaten raw or boiled. **Caution:** large amounts may be purgative and cause indigestion.

Cultivation: grow in full sun in well-drained ordinary soil. Sow in spring or autumn where plants are to grow, and thin seedlings to 2 ft. Older plants have a tendency to develop severe rust, and will need to be sprayed with fungicide or replaced regularly with young stock.

Parts used: flowers repeatedly over the long season, picked when fully open and dried fast in warmth; young leaves

white mallow

used fresh, or the entire plant cut down at flowering time and dried; seedpods picked while still green.

Related species: *M. neglecta* (dwarf mallow): almost prostrate bushy annual with pink or white flowers; similarly used, especially by North American Indians.

M. parviflora (least mallow, little mallow): short annual with pale pink flowers and similar culinary uses.

Matricaria recutita, syn. *M. chamomilla, Chamomilla recutita* (Compositae)

Wild Chamomile

scented mayweed, German chamomile

Description: aromatic annual with branched stems up to 18 in. Sweetly fragrant small white daisies with prominent yellow flowers with central hollow cones appear in early summer. A wild plant found in fields and road-sides, and a cereal 'weed' on chalky soils.

Uses: popular herb with a wide range of applications. Chamomile tea is refreshing, digestive and mildly seda-tive. Flowers reduce inflammation; used to soothe teething pains and poultice wounds. Essential oil used to scent shampoos and soaps. **Caution:** may cause a severe reaction in those with ragweed allergies.

Cultivation: sow in autumn or spring where plants are to flower, and water seeds in gently (do not cover). Grow in dry, chalky soils in full sun. Plants self-seed freely and may spread weedi-ly unless checked.

Parts used: flowers, fresh or dried in shade.

Melilotus officinalis (Leguminosae)

(Common or Ribbed) Melilot

yellow sweet clover

Description: trailing or upright bienni-al with sturdy taproot and branched stems up to 4 ft. Leaves trefoil with long, toothed leaflets; flowers creamy-yellow and sweet-scented in loose stalked spikes in summer, followed by brown oval, wrinkled seedpods. Grows wild in pastures and bare waste places, and widely cultivated as a fodder and green manure crop.

Uses: the tea is tonic and anti-colic, used to treat sleeplessness, nervous tension, thrombosis and digestive dis-orders. Externally, often added to relaxing baths and made into a com-press for slow-healing wounds. Both flowers and seeds are used for flavor-ing. **Caution:** excessive consumption may cause vomiting and dizziness.

Cultivation: sow seeds in late spring where plants are to grow, in fertile well-drained soils in full sun.

Parts used: leaves and shoots of flower-ing plants, fresh or dried in shade.

Related species: *M. alba* (white melilot, white sweet clover): taller plant with fragrant white flowers; widely grown as a fodder crop ('Bokhara clover') and bee plant.

Melissa officinalis (Labiatae)

(Lemon) Balm

bee balm, melissa, sweet balm

Description: hairy clump-forming her-baceous perennial with creeping roots and erect square stems up to 3 ft. Lemon-scented leaves, heart-shaped, toothed and deeply veined; flowers white or pale pink, sparsely arranged in a loose terminal spike in late sum-mer. A wild plant of waste and derelict ground, widely grown in gardens, especially in golden and variegated forms.

Uses: vigorous and indestructible herb with a strong lemon fragrance. Young leaves used to flavor teas, soups, milk, custard, sauces, and added to liqueurs; pungent oil extracted from them is used in perfumery. Medici-nally, balm lowers blood pressure, and is used in infusion to treat colds and influenza, nervous tension, insomnia, indigestion and other stomach ail-ments. A notable bee plant. Leaves and stems are sometimes used to pol-ish and scent wooden furniture.

Cultivation: grow in rich, moist soil in full sun or light shade. Readily self-sows, or sow seeds in spring *in situ* or in trays under glass, or divide mature plants (advisable every 4-5 years to keep plants young and vigorous). Cut back in summer before flowering to encourage a further supply of young leaves.

Parts used: leaves and tips picked just before or after flowering, and used fresh or dried quickly in the shade (freezing retains more volatile oils than drying).

Mentha (Labiatae)

There are at least 18 species of mint and many more hybrids, most of them difficult to classify because of their variability and readiness to hybridize between each other. All are aromatic perennials, most containing menthol (essential mint oil) to some degree. **Caution:** handling mints may cause skin rashes and other allergic irritations; mint teas should not be drunk in large amounts over a long period.

Mentha x *piperita*
Peppermint

Description: hairy perennial with underground stolons and square pink or red stems up to 3 ft. Red-tinted oval, pointed leaves, deeply toothed and long-stalked, with mauve or white flowers on long spikes in midsummer. A hybrid between water mint and spearmint or corn mint (*M. arvensis*), found wild as an escape in hedgerows and rich moist soils; widely cultivated in gardens, and commercially for the essential oil.

Uses: the most medicinally valuable of all mints, with great cooling properties due to its high content of menthol. Used to treat gastric and digestive disorders, and nervous complaints such as tension and insomnia. Essential oil used to flavor confectionery, liqueurs and pharmaceutical products, and to scent cosmetics.

Cultivation: divide roots in autumn or spring, and plant in moist, fertile soil, cool in summer and with plenty of potash; cut back in summer to rejuvenate growth. Remake beds every 4-5 years, sooner if plants develop rust; or cultivate as an annual by containing the roots and replanting divisions every spring.

Parts used: leaves and stems, fresh or dried – gather before flowering for culinary use, in full flower for distillation of oil.

Mentha pulegium
Pennyroyal
pudding grass

Description: downy, bushy perennial with surface runners, and prostrate or erect stems up to 8 in. Small oval dark green leaves, hairy and slightly serrated, and mauve flowers in dense whorls in late summer. Grows wild on moist, light soils.

Uses: a very pungent herb, once used to disguise the flavor of putrid meat and still included in a few local dishes. Valued since Roman times as a flea repellent; also popular today as an aromatic ground-cover plant. Used medicinally to treat gastric ailments, headaches, colds, bites and minor abrasions.

Cultivation: sow in spring under glass, or divide plants in autumn or spring, and plant in light free-draining soil as edging or ground cover, or in the joints of paving stones.

Parts used: whole green plant, used fresh or dried.

Mentha x *rotundifolia*
Round-leaved Mint
apple mint

Description: sweetly aromatic perennial with shallow runners and slender, branched stems up to 3 ft. Oval, serrated leaves, soft green but paler and downy underneath, and slim spikes of white or pink flowers in late summer. Found wild as an escape on damp waste ground, and commonly grown in kitchen gardens, often in variegated or improved forms such as 'Bowles' Variety'.

Uses: the main culinary mint species in continental Europe, used to flavor both savory and sweet dishes, sauces and drinks.

Cultivation: as for *M.* x *piperita*.

Parts used: fresh leaves as required; can also be frozen or dried.

pennyroyal

peppermint

round-leaved mint

spearmint

Mentha spicata

Spearmint
garden mint

Description: branching perennial with underground runners and square stems up to 30 in. Short-stalked leaves are oval and sharply pointed, deeply veined and serrated, either smooth and bright green or sometimes grayish, downy and wrinkled. Slim pointed spikes of mauve flowers appear in late summer. Found wild in moist shade on waste ground.

Uses: the least pungent species, subtly fragrant; one of the main culinary mints, yielding an essential oil used for flavoring confectionery, and dental and pharmaceutical preparations.

Cultivation: as for *M.* x *piperita.*

Parts used: fresh, frozen or dried leaves.

Related species: *M. arvensis* (corn mint): coarse wild species, sometimes gathered for culinary flavoring.

M. arvensis var. *piperascens* (Japanese mint): cultivated widely in the Far East as the main commercial source of menthol.

M. x *gentilis* 'Variegata' (ginger mint): popular compact ornamental variety with gold variegation.

M. x *piperata* var. *citrata* (eau de Cologne mint, bergamot mint): highly aromatic form with predominantly citrus fragrance, used to perfume cosmetics.

M. requienii (Corsican mint): prostrate tiny-leaved species; occurs wild, cultivated as ground cover; peppermint fragrance used in preparation of crème de menthe.

M. x *smithiana*, syn. *M. rubra raripila* (rust-free mint): purplish leaves and stems, spearmint flavor; least prone to mint rust.

M. suaveolens, 'Variegata' (pineapple mint): a variegated species with a distinct fragrance. Often grown as a decorative border herb.

ginger mint

eau de Cologne mint

pineapple mint

Monarda didyma (Labiatae)

Bergamot
bee balm, Oswego tea, horsemint

Description: robust aromatic perennial with mat-like roots and runners that are sometimes invasive, and square stems up to 3 ft. Rough oval, serrated leaves, dark green or red-tinted, and large whorled heads of tubular red flowers in late summer, attractive to bees. Found wild, occasionally as an escape, in moist shaded woodland and on the banks of streams; more colorful but less fragrant varieties grown for ornament in gardens.

Uses: traditionally used to make a relaxing anti-depressant tea which can also be used to treat nausea and flatulence. An infusion is inhaled for colds, or used as an antiseptic for ulcers, wounds and acne. Included in potpourri mixtures and as a perfume in cosmetics. **Caution:** bergamot may cause photosensitivity in some people.

Cultivation: prefers rich moist light soil in sun or partial shade, mulched in dry seasons. Sow in spring, or divide mature plants every 2-3 years in spring.

Parts used: leaves and flowers, fresh or dried.

Related species: *M. fistulosa* (wild bergamot, purple bergamot): North American Indian tea and medicinal plant with purple (occasionally white or pink) flowers and a preference for drier soils.

Myrica gale (Myricaceae)
ꙮ **Bog Myrtle**
sweet gale, sweet willow

Description: deciduous shrub with shiny reddish, upright twiggy stems to 4 ft, and long narrow, gray-green leaves. Dense, yellow-brown catkins in spring are followed by orange, waxy berries. A rare wild plant of wet heaths, bogs and moorland.

Uses: tonic tea made from leaves, which are sometimes used with berries for flavoring cooked dishes and treating dysentery; dried leaves used as moth and flea repellent. Roots and bark give yellow dye.

Cultivation: grow in damp acid soils in shade, and prune in winter. Propagate in autumn from seeds sown outdoors, or from cuttings, layers or division.

Parts used: leaves, fresh or dried, or distilled for essential oil; berries fresh or dried; roots and bark.

Related species: M. *carolinensis* (bayberry): bushy shrub up to 8 ft, found on dry sandy soils; blue-gray waxy berries, used for candles.

M. *cerifera* (wax myrtle, candleberry): large shrub up to 30 ft; root bark used as circulatory stimulant and to treat diarrhoea; wax from berries made into candles.

M. *rubra*: oriental species, cultivated for edible seeds.

Myrrhis odorata (Umbelliferae)
ꙮ **(European) Sweet Cicely**
myrrh

Description: bushy herbaceous perennial with a thick taproot and stout hollow grooved stems branching to 5 ft. Hairy, sweetly scented bright green leaves, soft, thin and ferny; loose umbels of small white flowers in early summer, followed by dark brown seeds, ridged and sharp-tipped. Grows wild in hedgerows and grassy shade on high ground, and cultivated locally.

Uses: leaves and unripe seeds are eaten raw in salads, roots and leaves boiled as vegetables. One or two leaves at a time are included in conserves and tart fruit dishes to add sweetness and aniseed flavor; also added to brandy and liqueurs. Whole plant is tonic and gently laxative, and used in healing ointments. Dried seeds ground as a spice in Germany; leaves used to polish and scent oak furniture; horses are sometimes lured with a piece of the root.

Cultivation: divide roots in spring or autumn, or sow seeds in autumn in trays outside or where plants are to grow (frost is needed for germination). Transplant while young to deep, rich, shady soil in a moist location; plants self-seed freely and may be invasive in heavy soils.

Parts used: leaves fresh or dried, seeds, green and immature, or dried; roots dug in autumn; whole green plant for medicinal infusions.

Myrtus communis (Myrtaceae)
ꙮ **Myrtle**

Description: evergreen shrub, slow-growing in cool climates to 10 ft, stems with flaking red-brown bark. Long oval, leaves, dark green, shiny and dotted with oil glands. Scented flowers, white or rose-pink in late summer, followed by dark purple berries (some varieties white). Grows wild on Mediterranean scrubland and seashores.

Uses: The perfume *eau d'ange* is distilled from flowers and leaves to scent soaps and cosmetics; leaves added as flavoring to meat dishes; fruits fermented into alcoholic drinks. Medicinally, crushed leaves applied to external wounds, rashes and skin irritations; juice of berries good for stomach and digestive ailments. Dried buds and fruits used as a peppery condiment; roots and bark for tanning leather.

Cultivation: plants prefer fertile well-drained, acid soils, in full sun with good light; in cool regions the added warmth of a sunny wall is beneficial, or plants may be grown in large pots under glass. Prune to shape after flowering; dense foliage can be clipped into simple topiary. Propagate from cuttings under glass in summer, or seeds sown in greenhouse in spring.

Parts used: leaves fresh or dried; flower buds dried; flowers fully open; fruits fresh or dried; roots and bark.

Related species: M. *ugni*, syn. *Eugenia ugni*, *Ugni olinae* (Chilean guava, murtillo): small shrub with fragrant rose-pink flowers, and mahogany-red fruits used in jams and preserves.

Nasturtium officinale, syn.
Rorippa nasturtium-aquaticum
(Cruciferae)

Watercress

Description: lush aquatic or marginal
perennial, almost evergreen, spreading by hollow brittle fleshy stems that
root at each leaf joint. Leaves dark
green and silky, oval or pinnate, older
leaves burnished bronze. Racemes of
small white flowers in summer followed by short, fat pods containing
two rows of seeds (only one in some
species). Grows wild in ditches and
streams and widely cultivated in flood-
ed beds as a salad herb in two main
varieties: green or summer, and frost-
hardy brown or winter cress.

Uses: leaves, rich in minerals and vitamins C and A, prized since Roman
times for biting, rich flavor, raw or
cooked as a vegetable and in soups.
Also used as a cough remedy. Crushed
leaves are applied as poultice for
rheumatism and gout; raw seeds used
as vermifuge. **Caution:** do not con-
sume excessive quantities, and gather
wild plants only from clean running
water; plants in stagnant and polluted
water may be host to the dangerous
liver fluke.

Cultivation: sow in a moist, shady border in spring; divide plants, or root
pieces of stem in pans immersed in
water in spring. Plant in beds irrigated
with flowing water, in tubs of soil and
water, or in trenches of fertile moist
soil. Water frequently.

Parts used: older leafy stems, fresh or
dried; seeds when ripe.

Related species: *Rorippa palustris* (yellow cress): Australian wild herb with
crinkled leaves and yellow flowers.

Nepeta cataria (Labiatae)

Catmint

catnip, catnep

Description: pungent, hairy perennial
growing in a dense leafy mound. Long
branching leafy stems up to 3 ft bear
light gray, heart-shaped leaves, coarsely serrated and almost white beneath;
and from summer to autumn persis-
tent flowers, white with mauve markings, in whorls. Grows wild in open
spaces and roadsides on moist chalky
soils, and commonly cultivated in gardens.

Uses: well known for its popularity with
cats – volatile oil is a feline aphrodisiac
and also distilled for perfumes. Leaves
made into a mint-flavored tea for
colds, nervous tension, flatulence and
gastric disorders, or poultices for cuts
and bruises.

Cultivation: divide roots in spring or
autumn, or take cuttings in summer,
and grow in light, well-drained soil in
full sun. Also easily grown from seed.
Cut back after flowering.

Parts used: leaves and flowering stems,
fresh or dried in shade.

Nicotiana alata, syn. *N. affinis*
(Solanaceae)

Flowering Tobacco

sweet-scented tobacco

Description: tropical perennial, usually
grown as ornamental annual, with
fleshy roots and strong, simple stems
up to 6 ft. Long, tubular flowers, highly fragrant and white or pink, are followed by capsules of small seeds.
Numerous cultivated strains, some
dwarf, in various colors.

Uses: occasionally used as stimulant
for nervous system, but normally
grown as a handsome flowering plant
in herb gardens.

Cultivation: sow under glass in spring,
or outdoors in frost-free areas, and
transplant to flowering positions in
full sun. Water frequently in dry
weather.

Related species: *N. bigelovii, N. attentu-
ata, N. benthamiana* and numerous
other wild species have been used
by indigenous peoples in North
America and Australia as snuff and
ritual smoking tobacco.

N. rustica (nicotine tobacco) and *N.
tabaccum* (common tobacco) are
the main cultivated forms for commercial production of smoking
tobacco, nicotine insecticide and
citric acid.

Ocimum basilicum (Labiatae)

(Sweet) Basil

St Joseph wort

Description: bushy aromatic annual with brittle branched stems to 2 ft. Leaves oval, shiny, fleshy and fragile, dark green or red tinted, such as dark opal basil; flowers creamy white or mauve in whorls, in midsummer. Grows wild in hot, humid regions, and cultivated extensively in numerous forms such as Greek, lemon, red or ruffled basils.

Uses: popular culinary flavoring, typical of Mediterranean cuisines and used since ancient times (remains have been found in Egyptian burial chambers). Oil of basil used in perfumery, soaps, cosmetics and liqueurs. Plant is claimed to be an insect repellant, and can be used medicinally to soothe pain and treat vomiting, nervous stress and headaches.

Cultivation: sow under glass in spring or outside after risks of frost are past. Grow in rich, moist soil, with full sun and shelter from cold winds; or treat as a pot plant, sowing in small pots to avoid root disturbance. Pinch out flowering shoots to extend useful life of plants, and root non-flowering side shoots in pots during summer for winter use.

Parts used: leaves fresh or frozen, or dried in shade (flavor will change considerably).

Related species: *O. kilimandsharicum* (camphor basil): African hairy perennial used to treat coughs and colds.

O. minimum (bush basil): hardier small-leaved dwarf plant, 6 in, uses as for sweet basil; flavor bitter-resinous.

O. sanctum, syn. *O. tenuifolium* (holy basil): large, hairy plant with pink flowers; sacred in India, where it is known as *tulsi*.

O. viride (fever basil): West African species, used as a tea to treat fevers.

sweet basil

dark opal basil

purple ruffled basil

bush basil

Oenothera biennis (Onagraceae)

(Common) Evening Primrose

evening star, king's cure-all

Description: coarse biennial herb with thick fleshy taproot, and overwintering rosette of long, narrow willow-like leaves, bright green and wavy-edged with a reddish midrib. Robust flower stems to 6 ft bear large, sweet-scented pale yellow trumpets with red sepals in summer, individual blooms lasting only a single day, followed by elongated seed capsules. Grows wild in dry, sandy places; occasionally cultivated as a crop.

Uses: leaves are a winter pot herb, and may also be used to treat coughs and chest ailments. North American Indians have many uses for the plant, especially the roots, used in poultices for piles and boils; roots, sometimes known as German rampion, also eaten raw or cooked; ripe seeds used in bakery like poppy seeds. Medicinally the plant is an important source of gamma-linoleic acid, with other uses still under test.

Cultivation: sow in summer where plants are to grow, or in a seedbed for transplanting in autumn. Grow in full sun in light, well-drained soil.

Parts used: leaves, shoots and flowers for fresh culinary use; roots dug in autumn or early the following spring before growth resumes.

Related species: *O. erythrosepala* (large-flowered evening primrose): larger flowers with red stems, and edible shoots and roots.

Olea europaea (Oleaceae)
❧ Olive

Description: slow-growing evergreen tree with gnarled trunk and slender gray, fissured branches, to 30 ft. Leaves dark green, scaly and gray beneath, narrow oblong or pointed. White, fragrant flowers in panicles in summer are followed by hard ovoid fruits, green at first but later purple-black, with a single hard stone. Thorny wild form grows on stony hillsides in Mediterranean regions, cultivated forms widely grown in groves.

Uses: since ancient times the principal source of edible oil in the eastern Mediterranean area; biblical symbol of peace. An olive wreath was given to victors in the Olympic Games. Not only the fruits but also the leaves are edible. Oil pressed from the fruits is a major culinary and medicinal product, sometimes used as a laxative and in enemas, and in treatments for minor wounds.

Cultivation: trees only grow well away from frost and tropical heat. Grow in dry, well-drained warm soils, with winter protection in cool regions, or in large pots under glass. Prune where necessary in spring. Propagate from seeds sown in warmth in autumn, or from cuttings taken in summer and rooted under glass.

Parts used: leaves; fruits picked when green, pink or red, or fully ripe, sometimes cracked, fermented and soaked in brine, or pressed for oil.

Origanum vulgare (Labiatae)
❧ Oregano
wild marjoram, joy of the mountain, Mexican sage

Description: bushy, spicily aromatic perennial with horizontal woody rootstock and stems, often reddish, to 30 in. Downy gray-green leaves, oval pointed and toothed, and small tubular flowers in clusters, pink or mauve with darker bracts, in late summer. Found wild on dry, fertile hillsides, usually on chalk, and widely grown both as a crop and a garden plant, often in variegated forms.

Uses: tonic, digestive and expectorant herb, used to treat coughs and sore throats, indigestion and gastric upsets. Antiseptic leaves are chewed for toothache, and added to baths and poultices. Important culinary flavoring for meat dishes and salads, the leaves are also made into tea and beer, or distilled into an oil for perfumes and cosmetics.

Cultivation: sow in spring outdoors and thin or transplant to 12 in apart, or divide mature clumps in spring. Plant in light, well-drained soil in full sun (flavor more pungent in warmth), or grow in pots or a greenhouse border in cool regions.

Parts used: sprigs of leaves and flowers, or whole clump cut almost to ground

oregano

pot marjoram

level when in flower, for use fresh or dried in shade.

Related species: *O. dictamnus* (dittany of Crete): gray-leaved perennial with large, pink flowers; leaves have oregano flavor, used medicinally since Minoan times as painkiller and wound healer. *O. prismaticum* and *O. heracleoticum* (winter marjoram) have similar flavor, especially effective when dried.

O. majorana (sweet marjoram, knotted marjoram): sun-loving tender perennial often raised from seed each spring as an annual; mainly European culinary herb, with same medicinal uses as oregano.

O. onites (pot marjoram): tender perennial with white or pink flowers, for cooler gardens; ornamental plant also used like sweet marjoram.

Osmunda regalis (Osmundaceae)

Royal Fern

buckthorn brake

Description: dense, clump-forming perennial terrestrial fern, with heavy rootstock of tangled, matted fibrous roots, and elegant buff-pink fronds up to 6 ft, streaked with creamy yellow in spring, later vivid green and turning golden brown in autumn. Leaflets at tips of fronds have spore-bearing sori in late summer. Grows wild in wet shady meadows.

Uses: handsome ornamental fern with mucilaginous roots, often boiled in water to produce royal fern jelly, once given to invalids as a nutritious, easily digested food, and also used to treat dysentery, coughs and pulmonary disorders. Dried roots (osmunda fiber) are a traditional ingredient of orchid potting composts.

Cultivation: grow in rich, moist soil, in damp shade or semi-shade. Mulch with compost every spring; water freely in dry weather. Divide in autumn or spring, or sow spores on surface of moist compost under glass in spring.

Parts used: main roots, fresh or dried, for medicinal use; thinner fibrous roots dried for compost.

Pelargonium graveolens (Geraniaceae)

Rose Geranium

Description: tender perennial, green and succulent at first but later woody with light brown bark, growing up to 4 ft. Flowers small and pale pink in dense umbels in summer and autumn. Commercially grown for oil distillation; popular house plant in temperate regions.

Uses: rose-scented leaves used to scent desserts, cakes and teas, pot-pourri, drinks and fingerbowls. Oil distilled from the leaves is an insect repellent, used in perfumes.

Cultivation: sow seeds indoors in spring, or take cuttings in late summer and plant out the following summer in dry soils and full sun. Often grown as a house plant, best stood outdoors in summer to keep compact. May be grown permanently outdoors in warmer regions, cutting plants down in autumn and mulching with leaves or straw where light frost is possible.

Parts used: leaves, fresh or dried; all green parts, cut just before flowering for oil distillation.

Related species: *P. capitatum, P. radens*: alternative sources of rose-geranium fragrance. Other common species include *P. crispum* and *P. citriodorum* (lemon), *P. fragrans* (nutmeg), *P. nervosum* (lime), *P. odoratissimum* (apple), *P. parviflorum* (coconut), *P. tomentosum* (peppermint).

Petroselinum crispum (Umbelliferae)

(Wild) Parsley

Description: biennial or short-lived perennial with rosette of rich green leaflets (tightly curled in many cultivated forms). In early summer a glossy, solid sharp-edged leafy flower stem, up to 30 in, bears flat-topped umbels of yellow-green flowers, followed by capsules of brown seeds. Cultivated in gardens in numerous forms such as curly, plain 'Italian' and turnip-rooted Hamburg parsley.

Uses: tea made from leaves or roots used to treat jaundice, coughs and menstrual problems, rheumatism, kidney stones and urinary infections; juice expressed from them soothes conjunctivitis and eye inflammations. Both seeds and dried roots are used as spices; seeds, which contain poisonous apiol, are sometimes infused to produce an external vermifuge. **Caution:** avoid parsley during pregnancy or if suffering from kidney inflammation.

Cultivation: sow in spring in trays or outdoors in rich, moist soil – soak seeds for 24 hours in warm water or pour boiling water into seed drills immediately before sowing, as fluctuating temperatures hasten germination. Sow again in midsummer for winter use or for pots indoors.

Parts used: leaves, fresh, frozen or dried; roots dug in winter and dried; seeds when capsules are ripe.

Phlomis fruticosa (Labiatae)

Jerusalem Sage

Description: aromatic evergreen shrub with stout branching stems up to 10 ft. Silvery-green, wedge-shaped leaves are wrinkled and densely covered with yellow woolly hairs. Clear or rusty yellow tubular flowers appear in whorls in late summer. Grows wild in arid Mediterranean and Asian regions, and commonly grown as a shrub in herb and mixed borders.

Uses: mainly a handsome ornamental shrub; leaves sometimes made into an aromatic sage-flavored tea, especially in Greece and neighbouring Mediterranean countries.

Cultivation: sow seeds in spring, take cuttings in summer or divide in spring or autumn. Grow in dryish, well-drained soil in full sun.

Parts used: leaves, fresh or dried in the sun.

Plantago major (Plantaginaceae)

Greater Plantain

broadleaf plantain, rat's tail plantain, waybread, white man's footprint

Description: tough-rooted perennial with coarse basal rosette of long-stalked, elliptical leaves, pointed and deeply veined. Tall, dense cylindrical spikes of tiny greenish-yellow flowers appear in summer, up to 18 in, followed by a spike of seeds enclosed in sticky gelatinous pods. Found wild in cultivated land, waste ground, lawns and footpaths, where the spread of its sticky seeds is helped by passers-by. A local field crop in France, and also cultivated in gardens in improved forms.

Uses: an old herb, one of the nine sacred Saxon species and recovered from remains of Iron Age Tollund Man. The crushed leaves are cooling and pain-relieving, used in poultices and ointments for wounds and abrasions; an infusion of leaves or boiled roots is a useful gargle and eyewash; fresh leaves may be taken for both constipation and diarrhoea, according to the dosage. Very young leaves may be cooked like spinach; seeds are popular in Chinese and Malaysian drinks, and complete seedheads are fed to caged birds.

Cultivation: wild variety rarely grown deliberately, but seeds may be sown *in situ*, barely covered, in moist, fertile light soil or loam, in spring or autumn. Plants self-seed freely.

Parts used: leaves, fresh or dried quickly in sun or shade; roots, dug in winter and boiled; seed spikes, gathered in bags when they turn brown, and rubbed to free the seeds.

Related species: *P. coronopus* (crowfoot plantain, buckshorn plantain): biennial with dandelion-like leaves, used in salads while very young.

P. lanceolata (ribwort plantain): perennial with long, narrow leaves and short dense ribbed stem of yellow-brown flowers, used as cough remedy and wound healer.

P. media (hoary plantain): decorative perennial with scented, pink and white fluffy flowers, a great favourite with bees.

P. ovata (ispaghula): annual with medicinal seeds, producing a laxative and emollient oil.

P. psyllium (fleaseed), *P. indica* (branched plantain): annuals with branching globular heads of greenish flowers; known in Latin America as *llanten*, used in same way as ispaghula.

Portulaca oleracea (Portulacaceae)
‍ (Wild) Purslane
pigweed

Description: warm-climate annual, with fleshy pinkish stems, prostrate and branching to 12 in, bearing fleshy spatulate leaves, green or red-tinged. Small yellow flowers appear in the leaf axils in late summer, followed by seed capsules with opening lids and filled with numerous tiny black seeds. Grows wild in dry soils in vineyards and on hillsides in warm regions, a common weed in Australia, New Zealand and the United States; cultivated as an edible crop in the form var. *sativa* (kitchen-garden purslane), a larger erect plant with fleshy green or gold leaves.

Uses: ancient vegetable crop in India and Iran, still used as a salad herb and cooked vegetable. Infusion of the green plant is cooling and soothing, taken for fevers, headaches and chest complaints, and applied to skin rashes and abrasions. Seeds are an Australian Aboriginal wild condiment.

Cultivation: sow mid-spring in light, well-drained soil; water and feed regularly. Sow again for succession at monthly intervals until late summer.

Parts used: fresh leaves and stems, preferably before flowering, cut just above ground level.

Poterium sanguisorba, syn.
Sanguisorba minor (Rosaceae)
‍ Salad Burnet

Description: clump-forming perennial with strong woody rootstock, and red, furrowed stems branching to 2 ft. Gray-green pinnate leaves with rounded leaflets, each deeply indented, and small, bright red-brown petalless flowers in dense globular heads in early summer. Found wild in fields, woods and waste ground on dry chalk.

Uses: young leaves eaten as salad herb with cucumber-like flavor, and added to soups, sauces and cheeses. Leaves are digestive, and in infusions used to treat diarrhoea and haemorrhages. Decoction of root applied to cuts and burns; roots also produce a black dye and are used in tanning leather.

Cultivation: sow in spring in trays under glass, or divide roots in spring and plant in fertile soil in sun or light shade. Remove flowers to extend useful season for leaves. Plants self-seed very easily.

Parts used: young leaves before flowering; whole green plant, fresh or dried; roots dug in spring and dried.

Related species: *P. officinale*, syn. *Sanguisorba officinalis* (great burnet, bloodwort): taller herb with deep red, rectangular flowerheads; similar uses.

Prunella vulgaris (Labiatae)
‍ Selfheal
heal-all, woundwort, carpenter's herb

Description: downy perennial with creeping rhizome and square stems to 12 in. Long narrow oval leaves, bright green, pointed and toothed; flowers purple, pink or white in dense whorls in midsummer. Grows wild in moist meadows and pastures; many cultivated forms with larger flowers grown in gardens.

Uses: used in Middle Ages according to the 'Doctrine of Signatures' to treat throat conditions and internal bleeding, and regarded as a panacea by North American Indians and Chinese physicians, the latter using the seeds for nervous complaints. Flowering plant may be eaten in salads and cooked vegetable dishes, used to prepare a styptic for wounds, and made into gargles or mouthwashes for mouth ulcers and sore throats.

Cultivation: take cuttings or divide plants in spring, and plant out 8 in apart as ground cover in moist shade or full sun. In fertile soils plants are much larger than normal and may be invasive; growing in turf helps restrain unnatural growth.

Parts used: green flowering plant, fresh or dried in shade.

Pulmonaria officinalis
(Boraginaceae)

Lungwort

maple lungwort, spotted dog,
Jerusalem cowslip

Description: downy perennial with
creeping rootstock; stems hairy and
unbranched, up to 12 in. Rough
leaves in a rosette over winter, broadly
oval and pointed, green with gray
spots, stem leaves narrower. Flowers
bell-shaped in small, leafy sprays, pink
at first and later becoming blue, or
white or purple, in early spring. Grows
wild in woods and hedgerows on
chalk; often cultivated as ground
cover in shade.

Uses: ancient cure for lung disorders
according to 'Doctrine of Signatures'.
Young leaves used as spring pot herb
in soups, stews and salads; flowering
plant made into a tea for gastro-
intestinal and pulmonary ailments;
homeopathically used for bronchitis
and colds. Powdered roots and lower
leaves are wound-healing.

Cultivation: divide in autumn or after
flowering, and plant in light soils, not
too dry, in shade or semi-shade. Lift,
divide and replant every 4-5 years.

Parts used: young fresh leaves gathered; green flowering plant, fresh or
dried; roots dug in winter, cut, dried
and powdered.

Related species: *P. saccharata*
(Bethlehem sage): larger plant,
with leaves heavily marked with silver, flowers appear as lilac, white or
blue; grown as a foliage plant; similar uses to *P. officinalis*.

Reseda luteola (Resedaceae)

Weld

dyer's rocket

Description: coarse unbranched biennial with an overwintering rosette of
long, narrow wavy-edged leaves. In
summer stout leafy stem, 5 ft, termi-
nates in long, slim spike of small
bright yellow or yellow-green flowers.
Found growing wild in dry disturbed
soils in chalky areas.

Uses: traditional dye plant, once widely cultivated or gathered from the wild
for brilliant yellow or reddish-yellow
color extracted from leaves, flowers
and stems.

Cultivation: sow seeds where plants are
to flower, in late summer in well-
drained, fertile soil with a little lime.
Seedlings appear in spring and should
be thinned to 18 in apart.

Parts used: whole green plant gathered
at flowering time.

Related species: *R. lutea* (wild
mignonette): similar to weld, but
shorter with divided, wrinkled
leaves; popular and decorative bee
and butterfly plant.

R. odorata (common mignonette):
perennial normally grown as an
annual, both outdoors and in pots,
for its intensely fragrant tiny yellow
and white flowers, from which oil is
extracted for perfume; a soothing
herb for calming nerves, healing
wounds, and treating asthma and
hayfever; once used to stuff pillows
as a remedy for insomnia.

Rosmarinus officinalis (Labiatae)

Rosemary

Description: dense, woody evergreen
perennial, up to 10 ft. Bushy stems
with cracked gray bark and downy
young shoots are covered with narrow
aromatic, hard leaves, dark and shiny
above, grayish beneath. Short racemes
of small blue flowers appear in early
summer. Grows wild on dry, rocky
slopes and cliffs in warm regions, and
widely cultivated both commercially
and in gardens in numerous forms.

Uses: ancient strewing herb and
Romany charm, hung up to ward off
evil; popular culinary flavoring added
to meat dishes, baked foods and
Mediterranean recipes. Leaves medicinally valuable and for treating depression, migraine, and disorders of the
liver and digestion. Leaves also made
into ointment for neuralgia, rheumatism, eczema and minor wounds, and
used in hair rinses and mouthwashes.
Caution: excessive quantities or frequent use may cause poisoning.

Cultivation: sow seeds in trays in
spring, take cuttings in summer in a
cold frame, or layer plants in autumn.
Plant in well-drained, alkaline soil,
in a sunny position sheltered from
winds. Some forms are slightly tender
and may need protection in winter.

Parts used: leaves gathered at flowering time, used fresh or dried in shade.

113

Rubia tinctorum (Rubiaceae)

Dyer's Madder

dyer's cleavers

Description: herbaceous perennial with long fleshy complex yellow rootstock and red fibrous roots, and stiff square, prickly climbing stems up to 3 ft, with whorls of pale green bristly leaves, long and pointed. Clusters of small greenish-yellow flowers appear in midsummer, followed by blue-black berries. Grows wild in hedges and thickets on chalk, often as an escape from former wide cultivation.

Uses: infusions of leaves and stems treat constipation, and liver and bladder disorders; powdered root is wound-healing, often used for skin ulcers. Homeopathically used to treat anaemia and ailments of the spleen. Most popular use of the roots is as a variable red to purple dye.

Cultivation: sow seeds or divide plants in spring or autumn, and plant in deep well-broken, alkaline soil in full sun or semi-shade.

Parts used: leaves and stems; roots peeled and dried quickly, and powdered or fermented.

Related species: R. peregrina (wild madder): similar plant, though coarser in appearance, producing a paler red dye.

Rumex rugosus, syn. *R. acetosa* (Polygonaceae)

Common Sorrel

common sorrel

French sorrel

Description: leafy perennial with thin vertical rootstock, and basal clumps of thick shiny, arrow-shaped leaves. Leafy slender flower stems in early summer, slightly branching to 4 ft, bear loose spikes of small red-brown flowers. Grows wild in damp fields and waste land.

Uses: popular, sharply flavored pot herb since ancient Egyptian times, widely used by medieval apothecaries. Cooling and blood-cleansing, often taken as a spring tonic tea. Leaves made into poultices for acne and other skin complaints, and if picked very young can be eaten raw or cooked, notably in sorrel soup; juice of leaves will curdle milk and has also been used as a stain remover ('salts of sorrel'). Roots make a bitter tonic and a treatment for diarrhoea. **Caution:** leaves are high in oxalic acid and should be eaten sparingly; handling them may cause skin irritations.

Cultivation: sow in spring, thinning seedlings to 12 in apart, or divide roots in autumn. Grow in rich, moist soil, and keep well watered. Gather leaves frequently and remove flower stems to extend cropping.

Parts used: young leaves and buds, picked before flowering, and used fresh or frozen; roots fresh in summer.

Related species: R. acetosella (sheep sorrel, red sorrel): small smooth arrow-shaped leaves, piquant in salads or less sour cooked.

R. alpinus (monk's rhubarb): broad leaves, and thick creeping rhizome used in infusion as a treatment for constipation.

R. crispus (curled dock, yellow dock): tall with large, wavy leaves, used for skin complaints; root is laxative, powdered to make mouthwash and gargle; stems stewed like rhubarb; seeds ground and used in baking.

R. patientia (herb patience, sorrel-dock): tall and branched, leaves with low acidity, can be used as spinach substitute.

R. scutatus (French sorrel, round-leaved sorrel): short leafy plant, low in oxalic acid, used as a salad ingredient and pot herb.

R. vesicarius (ruby dock, wild hops): thick broad leaves and tall, bright red flowers; leaves popular vegetable with Bedu, young shoots can be added to salads.

Ruta graveolens (Rutaceae)

❧ **Rue**

herb of grace

Description: semi-evergreen perennial shrub with woody base and branching stems up to 3 ft. Powerfully aromatic green or blue-green leaves divided into a number of spatulate leaflets, dotted with shiny oil glands. Loose racemes of small pungent yellow or yellowish-green flowers appear in summer. Found wild on dry, rocky limestone soils; cultivated in gardens as an ornamental shrub, often in blue, gold or variegated forms.

Uses: ancient medicinal herb, formerly used as an antidote to poisoning and a talisman against witchcraft. A favourite Arab herb, the only one to be blessed by Mohammed; leaves used homeopathically to treat phlebitis and varicose veins, and herbally for epilepsy, nervous complaints and uterine disorders. Essential oil used in perfumery and cosmetics; small amounts of the pungent foliage used for flavoring foods and alcoholic drinks. **Caution:** to be taken internally only under medical supervision, and used externally with care as allergic skin reactions are possible.

Cultivation: sow in a seedbed outdoors in spring, or take cuttings in late summer, and plant in full sun in well-drained soil with a little lime.

Parts used: leaves from flowering plant, fresh or dried in shade.

Salvia officinalis (Labiatae)

❧ **Sage**

Description: variable evergreen perennial shrub, with strong taproot, and square woody, branching stems up to 2 ft 6 in, gray and woolly when young. Gray-green, pebbly-textured soft leaves are oblong or lanceolate, and finely toothed. Whorls of violet-blue flowers appear in spikes in summer. Found wild on hillsides and grassland on chalk in warm regions; widely cultivated as a pot herb in Mediterranean countries; popular herb garden shrub with numerous forms and decorative varieties, some gold or variegated. Best culinary sages are the plain narrow-leaved and non-flowering broad-leaved types.

Uses: an ancient herb, popular as a potent condiment for meat, fish, Mediterranean dishes, English Sage Derby cheese, and as a basis for sage tea, taken to counteract sweating. Infusion used to treat depression, nervous anxiety and liver disorders; homeopathic preparations given for circulation and menopausal problems. Leaves are also antiseptic, used in gargles for laryngitis and tonsillitis,

common sage

variegated sage

and as a mouth freshener and tooth cleanser. Essential oil used in perfumery.

Cultivation: grow in well-drained, rich soil, in full sun and with shelter from cold winds. Propagate from cuttings in spring and summer, or by layering (mounding for older bushes). Nip off points of shoots to induce bushy growth, and renew every 4-5 years as shrubs become leggy.

Parts used: leaves fresh, or dried in shade, picked before flowering for herbal use or when in flower for oil distillation.

clary sage

(Continued)

(Sage continued)

Related species: *S. azurea*: large blue-flowered perennial shrub, used in Mexico as a herbal panacea.

S. sclarea (clary sage): biennial with white, blue or pink flowers; leaves infused as a gargle and skin healer; source of muscatel oil for flavoring and perfumery.

S. viridis, syn. *S. horminum* (clary): annual, very similar to clary sage and similar uses; often grown as a flowering bedding plant.

S. horminoides (wild clary), *S. verbenaca*: purple-flowered species with jagged, toothed leaves and red stems; uses similar to clary sage.

S. fruticosa, syn. *S. triloba* (three-lobed sage): large perennial with lobed leaves, grown in Mediterranean countries for making the popular sage tea.

S. rutilans (pineapple sage): tender perennial with scarlet flowers in autumn and winter; fresh leaves add strong pineapple flavoring to desserts and drinks.

Sambucus nigra (Caprifoliaceae)

(Common) Elder (Berry)

Description: deciduous shrub or small tree with roughly fissured bark and numerous straight branches, up to about 30 ft. Leaves pungent and dull green, with 5-7 elliptical leaflets; red flowering stems bear broad, flat-topped heads of small white, fragrant flowers in midsummer, followed by numerous edible purple-black berries. Found wild in hedgerows, woods and built-up areas; commercially cultivated on a local scale; ornamental varieties (white, gold, cut-leaf) frequently grown in gardens.

Uses: legendary tree, long held to be guardian over all other herbs, with numerous virtues according to the part used. Leaves are an effective insect repellent, and soothing in ointments for skin complaints. Flowers soothe the eyes, are added to cosmetics, make a calming tea, and are popular for their sweet fragrance in drinks and fruit dishes. Fruits are used in cordials, syrups and preserves; medicinally to induce sweating and to treat coughs, colds, catarrh and throat infections; and as a blue-purple dye. Bark is an old treatment for epilepsy, and (together with the leaves) is laxative; root used for kidney ailments.

Cultivation: usually harvested as a wild plant, but may be grown in almost any soil and position (variegated forms best positioned in full sun for maximum color). Propagate by hardwood cuttings, easily rooted outdoors in autumn, or by suckers.

Parts used: leaves, flowers and fruits, fresh or dried; root and bark gathered as needed.

Related species: *S. canadensis* (American elder): smaller North American species with similar appearance and uses.

S. ebulus (dwarf elder, danewort): dwarf, strong-smelling perennial with creeping rhizomes, otherwise similar to common elder; used homeopathically for dropsy; berries give a blue dye; bark and flowers purgative (berries dangerously so).

S. racemosa (red-berries elder): small tree with more pointed leaves, flowers in early dense clusters, and scarlet berries in summer; purgative oil extracted from the seeds.

Santolina chamaecyparissus, syn.
S. incana (Compositae)

❧ **Santolina**

cotton lavender

Description: pungent evergreen perennial shrub with branched white stems up to 20 in, silver-gray filamentous leaves, toothed along the edges. Fragrant small, bright yellow flowers like hard round buttons appear in midsummer. Grows wild in dry rocky places and warm soils; popular in gardens as an ornamental shrub and dwarf hedging plant.

Uses: grown and used since classical Greek times as a vermifuge and moth repellent. Infusion of leaves used as a rub for rheumatism and painful joints; flowers make a tonic tea. Perhaps most popular today as a decorative hedging plant for parterres and knot gardens.

Cultivation: grow in well-drained, light soil in full sun. Propagate by layering, or root cuttings with a heel in autumn or spring outdoors or in a cold frame. Clip hedges to shape in spring, and again at flowering time if only foliage is important.

Parts used: leaves before flowering, dried and stripped from stalks; flowers.

Related species: *S. neapolitana* (Italian lavender): taller plant with very feathery gray foliage and pale lemon-yellow flowers; similar uses.

Satureja hortensis (Labiatae)

❧ **Summer Savory**

bean herb

Description: hairy aromatic annual with tough straggly or erect stems, up to 18 in. Long, dark green leaves, leathery and pointed, and lilac-pink or white flowers in small spikes from the leaf axils in late summer. Grows wild in dry, light soils and on rocky hillsides on chalk; locally cultivated for commercial use; popular garden herb.

summer savory

Uses: culinary herb whose use dates back to the early Romans; potent flavoring enhances all others in the same way as salt. Used sparingly in meat dishes and stuffings, with peas, beans and cabbage to improve their digestibility, and liqueurs. Infusion of leaves treats gastric upsets, indigestion and loss of appetite; tea is tonic. Spreading flowering shoots between clothing repels moths.

Cultivation: sow seeds in spring where plants are to grow, in well-drained soil in full sun. Species is sensitive to cold: delay sowing until the worst frosts are past, or grow the hardier winter savory. Plants self-seed freely.

Parts used: leaves gathered before flowering, fresh or dried in shade; flowering shoots fresh or dried.

winter savory

Related species: *S. montana* (winter savory): semi-evergreen bushy and woody perennial shrub, with smaller pink or white flowers and a slightly stronger flavor; commercially cropped for essential oil; other uses similar.

Scabiosa arvensis, syn. *Knautia arvensis* (Dipsaceae)

Field Scabious

blue buttons, pincushion flower

Description: evergreen perennial, with short rootstock and creeping stolons, long indented leaves. Bristly stem, up to 3 ft, bears flat heads of mauve flowers in late summer, followed by densely hairy seedheads.

Uses: infusion of roots treats cuts, sores, abrasions and itching; whole herb used as a remedy for dandruff. Homeopathically used for eczema and skin disorders.

Cultivation: sow in trays in autumn or spring, divide roots in spring or take cuttings of short side shoots. Grow in full sun in fertile, well-drained soil.

Parts used: whole flowering herb including roots, fresh or dried; roots dug in autumn, fresh or dried.

Related species: Succisa pratensis, syn. *Scabiosa pratensis* (devil's bit, daisy fleabane): perennial with purple, blue or white flowers; root used for wounds and diarrhoea; leaves eaten raw or cooked like spinach.

Scutellaria galericulata (Labiatae)

(Common) Skullcap

helmet flower

Description: downy perennial with creeping rhizome; short-stalked oval pointed leaves, bluntly toothed and dark green, with red veins on underside. Stems, up to 12 in, in summer bear large slender tubular bright violet-blue flowers in pairs. Found wild in moist lowlands, especially wet meadows.

Uses: bitter tonic and digestive herb; powerful nerve tonic, used in infusion to treat depression, headaches, insomnia, irritability and similar disorders. (Out of flower, skullcap is easily confused with wood sage, *Teucrium scorodonia*.)

Cultivation: sow seeds outdoors in spring, or divide roots in spring, and grow in good moist soil in an open, sunny position.

Parts used: all green parts during flowering, fresh or dried.

Sedum acre (Crassulaceae)

Biting Stonecrop

wall pepper, golden-carpet, gold moss

Description: succulent mat-forming perennial shrub with sprawling stems, and erect branches up to 8 in crowded with overlapping cylindrical short green fleshy leaves, hot and peppery to the taste. Leafy stems extend in midsummer and produce bright yellow flowers, 5-petalled and star-shaped, in loose clusters. Grows wild on walls and roofs and in dry stony soils, often on lime; and in gardens as a wall, rock garden and edging plant.

Uses: plants were often grown deliberately on roofs as charms against lightning. Homeopathically used to treat piles; bruised leaves, fresh or in ointments, are soothing for wounds, abcesses, bruises and minor burns. **Caution:** slightly poisonous; internal use may cause dizziness and nausea.

Cultivation: grow in full sun in dryish, sandy soil with a little lime. Sow seeds outdoors or divide roots in spring, or scatter some of the cylindrical leaves which root freely where they fall.

Parts used: leaves, fresh or dried in warmth.

Related species: S. reflexum (reflexed stonecrop): long-stemmed robust perennial, with long cylindrical leaves and golden-yellow 7-petalled flowers. Fresh non-flowering shoots are often added to soups and salads, or cooked as a tangy vegetable.

Sempervivum tectorum
(Crassulaceae)

Houseleek

hen-and-chickens

Description: fleshy perennial with short-stemmed rosette of tightly packed fleshy gray-green leaves, sometimes red-tipped, arranged in a spiral. Stem elongates in summer to form a thick leafy flower stem, 8 in high, with clusters of small rose-pink star-like blooms. Grows wild on walls, roofs and rocky mountain sites; often cultivated in pots, sinks and rock gardens.

Uses: ancient magical herb, planted on roofs as an insurance against fire and lightning. Sliced or crushed leaves used to poultice stings, burns, rashes and itching skin, and to cure warts and corns. Sometimes used as a skin lotion. In some parts of Europe young leaves and shoots are eaten as a vegetable.

Cultivation: grow in full sun in crevices and mortar joints packed with a little ordinary soil, or in sinks and pots filled with gritty compost. Propagate from seeds or leaves in trays at any time.

Parts used: leaves, sliced or pulped, as needed.

Silybum marianum (Compositae)

Milk Thistle

variegated thistle, Our Lady's milk thistle, spotted thistle

Description: prickly annual or biennial, with a thick taproot and downy white, furrowed stems up to 4 ft. Leaves oblong, wavy and spiny-edged, glossy dark green with clear white veins, and flowers red-purple and thistle-like above a collar of spiny bracts in mid-summer.

Uses: the herb has had a reputation for treating liver disorders since classical Roman times, and is included in several proprietary medicines for this purpose. Used in herbal infusions and homeopathic preparations for liver and abdominal ailments. Young shoots and leaves are edible and an Arab delicacy; roots may be cooked like parsnips, and base of flowerheads in the same way as artichokes; stems can be peeled and boiled as a vegetable; seedlings eaten raw in salads.

Cultivation: sow in spring in a sunny bed where plants are to grow, and thin seedlings to 2 ft apart.

Parts used: seedlings; young leaves and shoots; flower stems just before flowering; roots after flowering; flowerheads for medicinal use, fresh or dried in thin layers in warmth.

Smyrnium olusatrum
(Umbelliferae)

Alexanders

black lovage, horse parsley

Description: pungent biennial with solid ridged stems up to 5 ft, and large shiny, dark green leaves divided into several trefoil toothed leaflets. Flowers yellow-green and glistening with nectar, in small round umbels in midsummer, followed by globular capsules of aromatic black seeds. Grows wild on rocky banks and sea cliffs.

Uses: bitter herb cultivated since early Greek times; root is diuretic, seeds a condiment, crushed leaves or their juice a soothing and healing treatment for cuts and minor abrasions. Grown as a salad and pot herb before celery became popular, with the leaves, stems, shoots and flower buds all used, sometimes after blanching, in soups and fish dishes.

Cultivation: grow in full sun in moist soil. Sow in spring and grow as an annual leaf crop, or in autumn to overwinter and produce larger stems the following year.

Parts used: young leaves; young stems, after blanching with soil or straw if preferred; roots fresh or dried; ripe seeds.

Solidago virgaurea (Compositae)
Golden Rod

Description: herbaceous perennial with a stout knotted rhizome, and downy slender leafy stems occasionally branched, up to 5 ft. Leaves narow oval or lanceolate, and toothed; flowers tiny, bright yellow and powdery, in panicles on branched spikes in late summer. Found wild in woods, hedges and the edges of fields; commonly grown as an ornamental plant in several cultivated forms.

Uses: a medieval Arab healing herb, also used by North American Indians; made into poultices for external wounds, and infusions for fevers and digestive upsets. Occurs in several proprietary medicines for kidney and bladder ailments, and used homeopathically to treat these, as well as arthritis and rheumatism.

Cultivation: sow in spring outdoors, or divide in autumn or spring, and grow in light soils in full sun or light shade. Lift, divide and replant every 3-4 years.

Parts used: green flowering plant before flowerheads fully opened, fresh or dried in shade.

Stellaria media
Common Chickweed

Description: variable fast-growing clump-forming or sprawling annual, with weak branching straggling stems, up to 18 in long, each with a single line of longitudinal hairs. Small soft, oval fleshy leaves, long-stalked and yellowish-green, and tiny white flowers with separate thin petals, at any time. A common 'weed', forming dense mats on moist, cultivated and waste ground.

Uses: an ancient pot herb; seeds found in Neolithic burial sites. Traditionally fed to domesticated birds and fowls; a bitter salad and pot herb; homeopathic remedy for rheumatism. Poultice of stems and leaves used to ease arthritis and pains of the joints, cuts, skin irritations and inflammation.

Cultivation: seldom necessary. Plants self-seed themselves all too freely in all soils and positions, especially in dry weather.

Parts used: young stems and leaves, fresh or dried.

Symphytum officinale
(Boraginaceae)
Comfrey
knitbone

Description: stout rough perennial with thick brown, fleshy rootstock, and clumps of upright basal hairy leaves, long, oval and pointed. Branched stems up to 4 ft bear purple, pink or white bell-shaped flowers in forked, curled clusters in summer. Found wild in streams, ditches and other wet places; widely cultivated in selected forms for garden use.

Uses: root formerly a popular internal remedy for gastric disorders and a homeopathic treatment for ulcers. Leaves used in infusion for bronchitis, and in poultices for wounds, bruises and eczema. Young leaves and shoots were eaten as a vegetable, cooked with a change of water. Older leaves commonly used after wilting as an animal feed, for making compost and liquid fertilizer, and for mulching plants. **Caution:** absolutely not to be used internally under any circumstances – recent evidence suggests the plant is carcinogenic.

comfrey

Cultivation: divide roots in spring or autumn, or take root cuttings in spring. Plant in moist soil in sun or shade, and mulch annually with decayed manure for maximum leaf production. Lift, divide and replant every 3-4 years. May need containment.

Russian comfrey

**variegated
Russian
comfrey**

Parts used: leaves, fresh, wilted or dried; roots fresh or split lengthways and dried in sun.

Related species: *S.* x *uplandicum* (Russian comfrey): stiffly hairy, vigorous hybrid with larger leaves, cultivated for leaf production (up to 4-6 cuts per year); often found wild in dry places as an escape.

Tanacetum parthenium, syn.
Chrysanthemum parthenium,
Matricaria parthenium
(Compositae)

Feverfew

Description: robust downy perennial with branched stems up to 3 ft. Leaves yellow-green and pungent, divided into several smaller rounded leaflets. Flowers small white daisies with prominent yellow centers, in dense clusters in midsummer.

Uses: a bitter-flavored herb, long used as a tonic and to treat indigestion, but currently popular as a treatment for migraine. Leaves are made into pain-soothing poultices for limb and joint aches, and whole flowering stems are an insect repellant, keeping moths away from clothing. A popular bee plant. **Caution:** not to be taken during pregnancy; fresh leaves may cause mouth ulcers.

Cultivation: sow in spring outdoors on the surface and water in, or take cuttings in summer. Grow in dry, well-drained soil in full sun. Plants self-seed very easily.

Parts used: leaves or whole green flowering plant, fresh or dried in shade.

Related species: *T. vulgare,* syn. *Chrysanthemum vulgare* (tansy): pungent perennial, with feathery dark green leaves and flat heads of yellow button-like flowers; an old strewing herb, insect repellent (companion plant to ward off aphids) and vermifuge; crushed leaves used to treat bruises and varicose veins; leaves once added to lamb dishes and spring puddings.

Taraxacum officinale agg.
(Compositae)

Dandelion
blowball

Description: complex group of perennials with long, stout taproots, and milky sap. Flowers on hollow stems, often reddish and downy near the top, up to 18 in; large, sweet-scented and yellow, in late spring to early autumn, followed by fluffy heads of numerous seeds, each with a parasol of white hairs to aid wind distribution.

Uses: leaves are a diuretic; dried to make tonic teas; added to herbal beer; blanched for salads. Flowers used in wines, schnapps, pancakes and in Arab baking; inside surface of flower stems soothes burns and stings (also stains skin). Roots roasted as a coffee substitute, cooked in Japanese cuisines, and give a magenta dye (with the leaves they produce brown dyes). Medicinally, given for gall-bladder and liver complaints.

Cultivation: often gathered from the wild, but may be grown as an annual by sowing in full sun in spring, barely covering seeds.

Parts used: leaves fresh or dried in warmth; flowers when fully opened in sun; roots dug in summer for medicinal use, or autumn for drying and grinding for coffee.

Related species: *T. kok-saghyz* (Russian dandelion): similar Russian wild plant, with rich milky sap, producing latex, used together with roots of *Scorzonera tau-saghyz* to make rubber.

Microseris scapigera (Australian dandelion): similar plant with larger flowers and stout yam-like root used as a vegetable by Aborigines.

Teucrium chamaedrys (Labiatae)
🐌 **Wall Germander**

Description: semi-evergreen perennial with purplish stems, sprawling or upright to 12 in. Leaves oval with rounded teeth; flowers dark lilac-purple, pink or white, in summer.

Uses: leaves used in tonic teas, wines and liqueurs, and for treating digestive and gall-bladder disorders. Plants used for edging and hedges in herb and knot gardens.

Cultivation: sow seeds in spring outdoors, take cuttings in summer, or divide plants in autumn. Grow in well-drained soil with a little lime. Clip hedges in spring and again in midsummer.

Parts used: whole flowering plant, fresh or dried in shade.

Related species: *T. fruticans* (tall germander): larger plant with white stems, blue-green leaves and large blue flowers.

T. scorodonia (wood sage, wood germander): pebbly sage-like leaves and yellow flowers, smelling faintly of garlic, prefers acid soils in shade; leaves used to heal and dry wounds, and in teas inhaled for throat and sinus problems.

Thlaspi arvense (Cruciferae)
🐌 **Field Pennycress**

Description: strong-smelling annual with branched stem to 18 in, oval leaves, often clasping the stem. Small white flowers in spikes appear in spring and summer, followed by pods containing black seeds. Grows wild in waste places, and sometimes a troublesome 'weed' of arable ground.

Uses: finely chopped leaves have a spicy flavor like watercress, and are used in salads and cooked dishes. Seeds were once ground and used as a mustard.

Cultivated: rarely necessary, but may be sown *in situ* in spring in fertile soil.

Parts used: leaves and young shoots before flowering; seeds dried in the sun and ground.

Related species: *T. alliaceum* (garlic pennycress): similar plant, with earlier flowers, narrow seedpods and scent of garlic, similar uses.

Thymus vulgaris (Labiatae)
🐌 **Common Thyme**
garden thyme

Description: variable aromatic perennial evergreen shrub with gnarled thin, square stems, woody at the base, prostrate or upright to 12 in. Leaves small, elliptical and gray-green, paler beneath; small flowers in summer, lilac or white, fragrant and popular with bees. Found wild on warm, dry rocky banks and heaths; widely grown commercially for the leaves and essential oil; favourite culinary and hedging herb in gardens, with numerous decorative and variegated forms.

Uses: popular since classical times, thyme has a number of important uses. Leaves make a tonic and stimulating tea, used to treat digestive complaints and respiratory disorders, especially for loosening mucus. Antiseptic and vermifuge essential oil (thymol) added to disinfectants, toothpaste, perfumes, toiletries and liqueurs. A culinary herb with a powerful flavor, thyme is added sparingly to bouquets garnis, stuffings and savory dishes.

common thyme

Cultivation: sow seeds or take cuttings in summer; divide plants in spring, or layer older bushes by mounding. Plant in very well drained soil in full sun. Clip after flowering and again in autumn; replace every 4-5 years, and in cold climates protect in winter, grow in containers or as a hedge.

lemon thyme

caraway thyme

wild thyme

Parts used: leaves and flowering tips, fresh or dried in sun.

Related species: T. capitatus (cone-head thyme): large-flowered species, grown commercially for essential oil production.

T. x *citriodora* (lemon thyme): light green species with pink flowers and strong lemon scent.

T. herba-barona (caraway thyme); arching stems rooting at tips, bronze-green leaves, strong caraway flavor.

T. mastichinus: gray-green leaves and pink flowers; widely grown in Spain for flavoring, marinades and as essential accompaniment to olives.

T. serpyllum (wild thyme, mother of thyme): very hardy, mat-forming species with late red-purple flowers and mild flavor; ideal for herb lawns; reputation as a herb for women's ailments.

Trifolium pratense (Leguminosae)
Red Clover

Description: short-lived perennial often grown as an annual, with branching roots, and arching stems, up to 20 in. Leaves long-stemmed and trefoil. Flowers pink-mauve in summer and autumn.

Uses: dried flowers produce a volatile oil and a soothing tea for promoting sleep; taken medicinally as an expectorant for respiratory disorders, and to treat skin problems such as eczema and psoriasis. Externally, an infusion soothes burns and sores. Flowers also make a good wine and yield a yellow dye.

Cultivation: sow in spring (rub the seeds with sandpaper to improve germination) in free-draining, slightly alkaline soil in rows or patches.

Parts used: flowerheads, fresh or dried in shade.

Related species: T. alexandrinum (berseem, Egyptian clover): very tall white fodder crop grown in Egypt and Middle East.

T. amabile (Aztec clover): Mexican and South American species, eaten as a pot herb mixed with cereals.

T. hybridum (alsike clover): small white-flowered hybrid grown as fodder and green manure in cold regions and on wet acid soils.

T. repens (white clover, Dutch clover): creeping, drought-resistant perennial with larger leaves and fragrant white or pinkish flowers liked by bees; numerous cultivated forms.

Tropaeolum majus (Tropaeolaceae)
Nasturtium

Description: South American perennial grown in temperate climates as an annual, with creeping or climbing stems to 10 ft. Leaves bright green or blue-green. Flowers orange, sometimes red or yellow, in summer and autumn, followed by spherical fruits, first green and then brown, containing three large seeds.

Uses: antiseptic and digestive herb, also used to treat respiratory and urinary disorders; seeds are a vermifuge, and crushed for use in poultices for boils and sores. Leaves are edible and used in salads, the flowers as a garnish, and both seeds and flower buds are pickled for their pungent mustard-like flavor.

Cultivation: sow spring or early summer where plants are to grow, or in pots for transplanting after frosts cease. Grow in full sun with shelter from wind, in rich soil for leaf crops, poorer dry ground for flowers and seeds.

Parts used: leaves fresh or dried; flowers; seeds while green, or when ripe for grinding as seasoning.

Tussilago farfara (Compositae)
🐚 **Coltsfoot**
coughwort, horse-hoof

Description: robust herbaceous perennial with white, scaly creeping stolons, and pale red downy, scaly stems, up to 12 in, bearing golden-yellow dandelion-like flowers that open in sun in early spring. Sturdy long-stemmed fragrant leaves follow in late spring from basal clumps, rounded or heart-shaped, irregularly toothed and up to 12 in in diameter, pale beneath with a network of clear veins. A wild plant of ditches, moist banks, waste places and loamy soils.

Uses: leaves are an important cough remedy for bronchitis and laryngitis, commonly added to herbal smoking mixtures. Both leaves (after crushing the veins) and flowers can be used in poultices for sores and ulcers; root is boiled to make coltsfoot rock or candy. Flowers are made into wine, and mature leaves can be dried and burnt to an ash used as a salt substitute. **Caution:** roots contain similar substances to comfrey, and may be equally dangerous if taken internally.

Cultivation: usually gathered from the wild, but seeds may be sown in moist soil in summer, or plants divided in autumn or used for root cuttings in winter. Plant where exposed to sunlight for most of the day. In some soils may become invasive.

Parts used: flowers before fully open, fresh or dried in shade; leaves in summer, fresh or cut up and dried in shade.

Urtica dioica (Urticaceae)
🐚 **Stinging Nettle**

Description: stinging perennial with branching roots, and bristly stems sprawling or erect up to 6 ft. Leaves covered in stinging hairs; tiny yellow-green flowers, females hanging like catkins, males in spikes in summer and autumn.

Uses: young shoots and leaves widely used in spring soups and as a green vegetable, and added to beer. Older leaves laxative in infusion, expectorant and styptic. Made into hair restorers and used homeopathically to treat skin ailments. Stems fibers are strong enough for linen weaving, papermaking and spining into ropes. Foliage is a commercial source of chlorophyll and an effective compost activator. **Caution:** handle with care, as the formic acid injected by serious stings may cause recurrent 'nettle rash'.

Cultivation: rarely necessary, but seeds may be sown in summer in fertile soil, or roots can be divided in spring.

Parts used: leaves gathered before flowering, fresh or dried in sun.

Related species: *U. breweri, U. thunbergiana*: North American and Japanese species respectively.

U. urens (annual nettle, burning nettle): smaller plant with reddish stems and small oval deep green leaves; similar uses.

Valeriana officinalis
(Valerianaceae)
🐚 **Valerian**
garden heliotrope, cat's valerian

Description: deciduous perennial with strong-smelling branching roots, and stout tubular furrowed stems, up to 4 ft. Leaves bright green and pinnate, with 2-10 pairs of shiny oval leaflets, pointed and toothed. Small white or pink flowers in branching terminal clusters in summer. Grows wild in ditches, woods and fertile grassland.

Uses: mildly sedative and antispasmodic, used to treat tension, anxiety, insomnia, migraine and nervous ailments, as well as colic and cramp; externally in infusion for eye problems. Attractive to cats. An occasional culinary flavoring. **Caution:** large doses or extended use may lead to addiction.

Cultivation: sow in spring where plants are to grow, or separate stolons in autumn and plant in moist borders or beside pools. Tolerates full sun or deep shade; plants benefit from an annual dressing of manure.

Parts used: roots at least 2 years old and gathered after leaves fall, used fresh or dried in shade.

Related species: *V. celtica* (nard, spike): prostrate plant with brownish-yellow flowers, grown in rock gardens.

V. edulis: North American species with large tapering roots, occasionally cooked as a root vegetable.

V. phu (Cretan spikenard): white-flowered species with ornamental golden garden form; similar uses.

Veratrum viride (Liliaceae)

🌿 Green False Hellebore

American white hellebore, itchweed, Indian poke

Description: statuesque clump-forming perennial with strong, thick roots, rosette of broad elliptical pleated or ribbed leaves. Hairy, robust stems up to 5 ft bear branched spikes of pale green or greenish-white 6-petalled star-like flowers in summer. A wild plant of moist grassy places on hills and mountain pastures (not to be confused with *Helleborus viridis*, green hellebore).

Uses: handsome flowering plant for a prominent position, anti-parasitic; used by North American Indians as an arrow poison, and by the pharmaceutical industry in preparations for reducing blood pressure. **Caution:** highly toxic and not for home preparation.

Cultivation: divide roots in autumn or spring, or sow seeds in trays of peaty soil in a cool greenhouse in spring (seeds take several months to germinate). Grow in moist semi-shade.

Parts used: roots dug in autumn, cut in pieces and dried in sun or warmth.

Related species: V. album (white hellebore, langwort, false helleborine): similar plant with yellowish-green flowers with similar uses; roots dried and ground into 'hellebore powder', an insecticide.

Verbena officinalis (Verbenaceae)

🌿 Vervain

Description: hairy branching perennial with woody rootstock, and slender rough angular stems up to 3 ft, bearing long sparse 3-lobed leaves, dull grayish-green and toothed. Small lilac flowers in thin stiff spikes in late summer. Found wild in hedges, waysides and dry barren places; commonly cultivated in France and other European countries.

Uses: ancient herb popular with druids as a panacea, and used in the Middle Ages to ward off plague. Used homeopathically for dropsy; medicinally to treat rheumatism, and stomach and liver disorders. Tea is a stimulant, and relieves fevers and nervous tension. Externally used for sores and skin problems, and for eye complaints.

Cultivation: sow in spring or autumn on the surface of well-drained soil in full sun; lightly press or water in the seeds and thin seedlings to 12 in apart.

Parts used: green flowering plant, fresh or dried in sun or warmth.

Veronica officinalis (Scrophulariaceae)

🌿 (Heath) Speedwell

fluellen

Description: hairy prostrate mat-forming perennial, with stems creeping and rooting at nodes or erect to 12 in. Small rough leaves in opposite pairs, oval and finely toothed; flowering shoots from leaf axils, in summer bearing bright lilac-blue flowers with a white eye, in clusters. Grows wild in pastures and woods, and on dry slopes and heaths on acid soils.

Uses: a medieval healing herb, still used in a tonic tea ('Swiss tea') for liver, digestive and general intestinal complaints. Fresh juice used for skin ailments, for which there is also a homeopathic preparation. Cultivated as an ornamental ground-cover plant in the garden.

Cultivation: sow in spring or divide plants in early summer, and grow in rich, fertile soil in full sun. Water freely in dry weather, and replace plants every 4-5 years.

Parts used: whole green flowering plant, fresh or dried in shade or a warm room.

Related species: V. beccabunga (brooklime, water pimpernel): fleshy aquatic perennial with small, bright blue flowers found beside streams and in other wet places; popular salad plant high in vitamin C, and a very mild purgative.

Veronicastrum virginicum, syn. *Veronica virginica* (culver's root, bowman's root): very tall slender blue- or white-flowered perennial, once used by Shakers as a digestive. **Caution:** highly purgative.

Vinca minor (Apocynaceae)

Lesser Periwinkle

Description: evergreen perennial, with stems prostrate and rooting at leaf nodes, and leafy flowering stems erect to 2 ft. Leaves glossy and oval, flowers pale blue with lighter centers, or white, on hollow stalks in early summer.

Uses: used as a gargle for sore throats, as a styptic and astringent for wounds, sores and ulcers, and in a tea to reduce blood pressure and hypertension. **Caution:** large amounts may be toxic, leading to circulatory disorders.

Cultivation: divide in spring or take stem cuttings in autumn, and grow in fertile moist soils with a little lime.

Parts used: green flowering plant in spring, fresh or dried.

Related species: *Vinca major* (greater periwinkle, blue buttons): longer-stalked leaves and stems rooting only at the tips.

Viola tricolor (Violaceae)

Wild Pansy

heartsease, field pansy, johnny jump-up

Description: variable annual or short-lived perennial, almost evergreen, with hollow stems sprawling or erect to 8 in. Leaves oval and indented. Flowers yellow with purple and white markings, from spring to autumn, followed by capsules filled with shiny, light brown seeds, splitting into three segments when ripe.

Uses: renowned mild heart tonic, used to treat high blood pressure, indigestion and colds; cleanses blood and induces perspiration. Also used to treat dropsy and rheumatic conditions, and for skin disorders such as acne and eczema.

Cultivation: sow spring or summer where plants are to grow; press seeds into soil but leave uncovered. Surplus seedlings may be transplanted to any position in semi-shade. Plants self-seed freely. Cut back leggy plants to induce bushy growth and further flowers.

Parts used: green flowering herb and root, fresh or dried in shade.

Related species: *V. odorata* (sweet violet): trailing stoloniferous perennial with sweet-scented purple, white or pink flowers; ancient strewing herb and commercial crop for perfume industry; leaves and flowers used to treat coughs, catarrh and respiratory disorders; flowers crystallized.

V. sororia, syn. *V. papilionacea*: North American purple-flowered wild species with several cultivated forms; used by Indians for colds and headaches.

Vitex agnus-castus (Verbenaceae)

Chaste Berry

Indian spice, monk's pepper, chaste tree

Description: aromatic shrub or small tree up to 20 ft, with palmate leaves divided into narrow leaflets on gray, downy shoots. Small violet fragrant flowers in dense trusses growing up to 12 in long in autumn, followed in warm climates by purple-black berries. Found wild on light, stony soils in southern Europe; cultivated as a garden ornamental, sometimes with white flowers.

Uses: an ancient Greek herb thought to guarantee chastity, now used to regulate female hormonal activity. Also reputed to be a male anaphrodisiac; used as symbolic strewing herb in Italian monasteries. Seeds are used as a peppery condiment, slender branches in basketwork.

Cultivation: sow seeds in spring, layer in summer, or take cuttings under glass in autumn. Grow in well-drained, light soil, in full sun, and against a warm sheltered wall in temperate regions.

Parts used: fruits picked in autumn, fresh or dried in shade.

Related species: *Vitex negundo* (Chinese chaste tree): medium shrub with square stems and lavender flowers in late summer.

Right: *A fruitful, healthy herb garden – the results of only a little research and planning.*

BEE AND BUTTERFLY HERBS

- anise
- betony
- chicory
- comfrey
- evening primrose
- hyssop
- lemon balm
- mint
- sage
- thyme
- yarrow
- bergamot
- broom
- chives
- coltsfoot
- fennel
- lavender
- meadowsweet
- rosemary
- self-heal
- valerian

AN ESSENTIAL HERB COLLECTION

- basil – a tender annual
- bay – grown as a small trained specimen
- chives – for edging
- dill – an annual
- fennel – bulky and tall
- French tarragon – tall, best in a container
- lemon balm – a herbaceous perennial
- marjoram – shrubby
- mint – best in a pot
- parsley – ideal for edging
- rosemary – a bushy shrub
- sweet cicely – American (*Osmorrhiza longistylis*) or European (*Myrrhis odorata*)
- thyme – mats of evergreen foliage
- winter savory – short evergreen shrub

HERBS FOR FIRST AID

Part of the herb garden can be reserved for a selection of plants to provide help in emergencies; most can be used fresh in teas, compresses and infusions.

- aloe vera – grow as a pot plant and use a broken leaf to relieve sunburn
- lavender – use as an infusion for coughs, colds and headaches
- pot marigold – make a poultice from the flowers for burns and stings
- witch hazel – use in compresses for bruises and bleeding
- German chamomile – can be taken as a tea for insomnia
- lemon balm – infuse for digestive and menstrual upsets
- St John's wort – use as a compress for cuts and small wounds

PLANTS FOR FORMAL OUTDOOR TOPIARY

- box
- cephalotaxus
- *Cupressus sempervirens*
- holly
- *Ligustrum japonicum*
- *Thuja occidentalis*

- cassinia
- *Cryptomeria japonica*
- *Eugenia myrtifolia*
- ivy – on a wire frame
- *Phillyrea angustifolia*
- yew

PLANTS FOR A GRAY AND WHITE HERB BORDER

- *Acorus calamus* 'Variegatus'
- *Artemisia* 'Powis Castle'
- *Buxus sempervirens* 'Elegantissima'
- *Chrysanthemum balsamita*
- *Iris pallida* 'Variegata Argentea'
- *Mentha suaveolens* 'Variegata'
- *Nepeta cataria*
- *Ruta graveolens* 'Variegata'
- *Sambucus nigra* 'Albovariegata'
- *Thymus* 'Silver Posy'

- *Althaea officinalis*
- *Artemisia absinthium* 'Lambrook Silver'
- *Chamaemelum nobile* 'Flore Pleno'
- *Colchicum autumnale* 'Alboplenum'
- *Marrubium vulgare*
- *Myrtus communis* 'Variegata'
- *Primula vulgaris* 'Alba Plena'
- *Salvia sclarea*
- *Symphytum* x *uplandicum* 'Variegatum'
- *Vinca major* 'Variegata'

MARY FLOWERS

These are just a few of the numerous plants suitable for inclusion in a traditional St Mary Garden.

- *Alchemilla mollis*, lady's mantle
- *Cardamine pratensis*, lady's smock
- *Galium verum*, lady's bedstraw
- *Primula veris*, cowslip (Our Lady's keys)
- *Tanacetum balsamita*, costmary

- *Calendula officinalis*, marigold
- *Convallaria majalis*, lily of the valley (Our Lady's tears)
- *Lilium candidum*, Madonna lily
- *Silybum marianum*, Our Lady's milk thistle

Add to these any flowers that are white (for purity) and blue (the color of the Virgin Mary's robe), together with the monastic strewing herbs hyssop, tansy and meadowsweet as symbols of purity.

COOKING WITH HERBS

Herb and Chilli Gazpacho

Gazpacho is a lovely soup set off perfectly by the addition of a few herbs.

SERVES 6

2½ lb ripe tomatoes

8 oz onions

2 green peppers

1 green chilli

1 large cucumber

2 tbsp red wine vinegar

1 tbsp balsamic vinegar

2 tbsp olive oil

1 clove of garlic, peeled and crushed

1¼ cups tomato juice

2 tbsp tomato purée

salt and pepper

2 tbsp finely chopped mixed fresh herbs, plus some extra to garnish

1 Keep back about a quarter of all the fresh vegetables, except the green chilli, and place all the remaining ingredients in a food processor and season to taste. Process finely and chill in the refrigerator.

2 Chop all the remaining vegetables, and serve in a separate bowl to sprinkle over the soup. Crush some ice cubes and add to the center of each bowl and garnish with fresh herbs. Serve with bread rolls.

Pear and Watercress Soup with Stilton Croûtons

Pears and Stilton taste very good when you eat them together after the main course – here, for a change, they are served as a starter.

SERVES 6

1 bunch watercress

4 medium pears, sliced

3¾ cups chicken stock, preferably home-made

salt and pepper

½ cup double cream

juice of 1 lime

CROUTONS

1 oz butter

1 tbsp olive oil

3 cups cubed stale bread

1 cup chopped Stilton cheese

1 Keep back about a third of the watercress leaves. Place all the rest of the watercress leaves and stalks in a pan with the pears, stock and a little seasoning. Simmer for about 15-20 minutes. Reserving some watercress leaves for garnishing, add the rest of the leaves and immediately blend in a food processor until smooth.

2 Put the mixture into a bowl and stir in the cream and the lime juice to mix the flavors thoroughly. Season again to taste. Pour all the soup back into a pan and reheat, stirring gently until warmed through.

3 To make the croûtons, melt the butter and oil and fry the bread cubes until golden brown. Drain on paper towels. Put the cheese on top and heat under a hot grill until bubbling. Reheat the soup and pour into bowls. Divide the croûtons and remaining watercress between the bowls.

133

Warm Chicken Salad with Sesame and Coriander Dressing

This salad needs to be served warm to make the most of the wonderful sesame and coriander flavorings. It makes a simple starter or a delicious light lunch dish.

SERVES 6

4 medium chicken breasts, boned and skinned

8 oz snow peas

2 heads decorative lettuce such as lollo rosso or oak leaf

3 carrots, peeled and cut into small matchsticks

6 oz button mushrooms, sliced

6 rashers of bacon, fried and chopped

DRESSING

½ cup lemon juice

2 tbsp whole grain mustard

1 cup olive oil

⅓ cup sesame oil

1 tsp coriander seeds, crushed

1 tbsp fresh coriander leaves chopped, to garnish

1 Mix all the dressing ingredients in a bowl. Place the chicken breasts in a shallow dish and pour on half the dressing. Refrigerate overnight, and store the remaining dressing here.

2 Cook the snow peas for 2 minutes in boiling water, then cool under running cold water to stop them cooking any further. Tear the lettuces into small pieces and mix all the other salad ingredients and the bacon together. Arrange all these in individual serving dishes.

3 Grill the chicken breasts until cooked through, then slice them on the diagonal into quite thin pieces. Divide between the bowls of salad, and add some dressing to each dish. Combine quickly and scatter some fresh coriander over each bowl.

Spinach and Roquefort Crepes with Walnuts and Chervil

Crepes make a good starter or buffet dish as you can prepare them in advance. The pancakes can be frozen, but not the filling.

16 CREPES

1 cup plain flour

2 eggs

5 tbsp sunflower oil

a little salt

1 cup milk

3 tbsp butter for frying

FILLING

2 lb frozen spinach, thawed

1 cup cream cheese

1 packed cup Roquefort cheese, grated

2 tbsp chopped walnuts

2 tsp chopped chervil

SAUCE

4 tbsp butter

½ cup flour

2½ cups milk

1 tsp whole grain mustard

¾ packed cup Roquefort cheese, grated

1 tbsp finely chopped walnuts

1 tbsp fresh chopped chervil, to garnish

1 Process the flour, eggs, oil and salt, slowly adding milk until the mixture has the consistency of light cream. (You may not need to add all the milk.) Let the batter rest in the refrigerator for 1 hour. Put 1 tsp of the butter into a frying pan, and once it has melted swirl it around to coat the surface of the pan.

2 Drop a large tablespoonful of batter into the pan and tilt to spread it around evenly. Cook until golden brown on the bottom, then turn and cook briefly on the other side. Lay the crepe on a wire rack. Cook the others in the same way.

From top: *Spinach and Roquefort Crepes; Warm Chicken Salad with Sesame and Coriander Dressing*

3 Cook the spinach over a low heat for about 15 minutes. Strain off the water and let the spinach cool. Process in a food processor with the cream cheese and Roquefort until smooth. Turn into a bowl and add half the walnuts and chervil.

4 Preheat the oven to 375°F. Fill all the crepes and place in a shallow ovenproof dish, rolled tightly and in rows. Make the sauce by melting the butter, adding the flour and cooking for a minute or two. Add the milk and stir constantly until the sauce comes to the boil. Stir in all the other ingredients except the chervil. Pour the sauce over the crepes and bake for 20 minutes. Serve immediately, sprinkled with chopped chervil and the remaining walnuts.

Spinach, Cognac, Garlic and Chicken Pâté

Pâté is an easy starter, as it can be made well in advance. This smooth version is delicious with warm brown rolls and butter or garlic bread.

12 SERVINGS

12 slices lean bacon
2 tbsp butter
1 onion, peeled and chopped
1 clove garlic, peeled and crushed
10 oz frozen spinach, thawed
¾ cup finely crumbled whole wheat
  bread
2 tbsp Cognac
1 lb minced chicken (dark and light
  meat)
1 lb minced pork
2 eggs, beaten
2 tbsp chopped mixed fresh herbs,
  such as parsley, sage and dill
salt and pepper

1 Fry the bacon in a pan until it is only just done, then arrange it round the sides of a 1 quart ovenproof loaf pan, if possible leaving a couple of slices to garnish.

2 Melt the butter in a pan. Fry the onion and garlic until soft. Squeeze the spinach to remove as much water as possible, then add to the pan, stirring until the spinach is dry.

3 Preheat the oven to 350°F. Combine all the remaining ingredients, apart from any remaining bacon strips, in a bowl and mix well to blend. Spoon the pâté into the loaf pan and cover with any remaining bacon.

4 Cover the pan with a double thickness of foil and set it in a baking pan. Pour 1 in boiling water into the baking pan. Bake for about 1¼ hours. Remove the pâté and let it cool. Place a heavy weight on top of the pâté and refrigerate overnight.

Beef, Celeriac and Horseradish Pâté

This strongly flavored pâté would make a good lunch dish as well as a starter.

SERVES 4

1 lb topside of beef, cubed
1½ cups red wine
⅓ cup Madeira
1 cup home-made or canned beef
  or chicken stock
2 tbsp finely chopped celeriac
1 tbsp horseradish cream
salt and pepper
2 bay leaves
2 tbsp brandy
¾ cup butter, melted

1 Preheat the oven to 250°F. Place the beef in an ovenproof casserole. Mix all the other ingredients together except the brandy and butter, and pour them over the beef. Cover tightly and cook for 2 hours.

2 Remove and drain. Strain the liquid and reduce to about 3 tbsp. Slice and roughly chop the meat and put it with the reduced liquid in the food processor. Blend in bursts until fairly smooth. Add the brandy and a third of the butter. Turn into a pâté dish and leave to cool.

3 Melt the remaining butter, skim any foam off the top and pour over the top of the beef, leaving any residue at the bottom of the pan. Cover the pâté and refrigerate overnight.

Smoked Trout with Minted Grapefruit

Trout and grapefruit make a magical combination, especially with a slight hint of mint.

SERVES 4

1 lollo rosso lettuce

1 tbsp lemon juice

2 tbsp chopped fresh mint, and a few whole leaves for garnish

1 lb smoked trout, skinned, boned and sliced

2 grapefruit, peeled and segmented

½ cup store-bought whole mayonnaise

1 Toss the lettuce with the lemon juice and half the mint. Arrange on a plate and place the smoked trout among the leaves. Add the grapefruit segments as a decoration.

2 Mix the other half of the chopped mint with the mayonnaise and serve separately in a small bowl, garnished with a mint leaf or two.

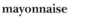

Potted Salmon with Lemon and Dill

This sophisticated starter would be ideal for a dinner party. Preparation is done well in advance, so you can concentrate on the main course.

SERVES 6

1³/₄ **cups cooked salmon, skinned and boned**

²/₃ **cup butter, softened**

rind and juice of 1 large lemon

2 tsp chopped fresh dill

salt and pepper

³/₄ **cup flaked almonds, roughly chopped**

1 Flake the salmon into a bowl and then place in a food processor together with two-thirds of the butter, the lemon rind and juice, half the dill, and the salt and pepper. Blend until quite smooth.

2 Mix in the flaked almonds. Check for seasoning and pack the mixture into small ramekins.

3 Scatter the other half of the dill over the top of each ramekin. Clarify the remaining butter, and pour over each ramekin to make a seal. Refrigerate before serving. Serve with crudités.

Herbed Halibut Mille-Feuille

The crisp puff pastry balances the creamy fish, and the herbs add their own special flavors.

SERVES 2

9 oz puff pastry

butter for cookie sheet

1 egg, beaten

1 small onion

1 tsp fresh ginger, grated

½ tbsp oil

⅔ cup fish stock

1 tbsp dry sherry

12 oz halibut, cooked and flaked

8 oz crab meat

salt and pepper

1 avocado

juice of 1 lime

1 mango

1 tablespoon chopped mixed parsley, thyme and chives, to garnish

1 Roll the pastry out into a square 10 x 10 in, trim the edges and place on a buttered cookie sheet. Prick with a fork, then rest it in the refrigerator for at least 30 minutes. Preheat the oven to 450°F. Brush the top with beaten egg, and bake for 10-15 minutes or until golden.

2 Let the pastry cool for a few minutes, then cut it twice across in one direction and once in the other to make six pieces. Leave to cool completely.

3 Fry the onion and ginger in the oil until tender. Add the fish stock and sherry, and simmer for 5 minutes. Add the halibut and crab meat, and season to taste. Peel and chop the avocado and toss in the lime juice. Peel and chop the mango reserving a few slices for garnishing. Add both to the fish.

4 Build up alternate layers of fish and pastry, starting and finishing with a piece of pastry. Serve garnished with herbs and mango slices.

Salmon and Ginger Pie, with Lemon Thyme and Lime

This exceptional pie is highly recommended. This recipe uses salmon's special flavor to the full.

SERVES 4-6

1¾ lb middle cut of salmon

3 tbsp walnut oil

1 tbsp lime juice

2 tsp chopped fresh lemon thyme

2 tbsp white wine

salt and pepper

14 oz puff pastry

½ cup flaked almonds

3-4 pieces ginger in syrup, chopped

1 Split the salmon in half, remove all the bones and skin, and divide into 4 fillets. Mix the oil, lime juice, thyme, wine and pepper, and pour over the fish. Leave to marinate overnight in the refrigerator.

2 Divide the pastry into two pieces, one slightly larger than the other, and roll out – the smaller piece should be large enough to take two of the salmon fillets and the second piece about 2 in larger all round. Drain the fillets and discard the marinade.

3 Preheat the oven to 350°F. Place two of the fillets on the smaller piece of pastry, and season. Add the almonds and ginger and cover with the other two fillets.

4 Season again, cover with the second piece of pastry and seal well. Brush with beaten egg and decorate with any leftover pastry. Bake for 40 minutes.

From top: *Herbed Halibut Mille-Feuille; Salmon and Ginger Pie*

Cod, Basil and Tomato with a Potato Crust

With a green salad, it makes an ideal dish for lunch or a family supper.

<u>SERVES 8</u>

2 lb smoked cod

2 lb white cod

2½ cups milk

2 sprigs basil

1 sprig lemon thyme

⅓ cup butter

1 onion, peeled and chopped

¾ cup flour

2 tbsp tomato paste

2 tbsp chopped basil

12 medium-sized potatoes

¼ cup butter

1¼ cups milk

salt and pepper

1 tbsp chopped parsley

1 Place both kinds of fish in a roasting pan with the milk, 1.2 litres/2 pints/5 cups water and herbs. Simmer for about 3-4 minutes. Leave to cool in the liquid for about 20 minutes. Drain the fish, reserving the liquid for use in the sauce. Flake the fish, taking care to remove any skin and bone.

2 Melt the butter in a pan, add the onion and cook for about 5 minutes until tender but not browned. Add the flour, tomato paste and half the basil. Gradually add the reserved fish stock, adding a little more milk if necessary to make a fairly thin sauce. Bring this to the boil, season with salt and pepper, and add the remaining basil. Add the fish carefully and stir gently. Pour into an ovenproof dish.

3 Preheat the oven to 350°F. Boil the potatoes until tender. Add the butter and milk, and mash well. Add salt and pepper to taste and cover the fish, forking to create a pattern. If you like, you can freeze the pie at this stage. Bake for 30 minutes. Serve with the chopped parsley.

Tiger Shrimp in Filo with Mint, Dill and Lime

Another wonderful combination – the mint, dill and lime blend together to make a magical concoction that will delight everyone who tries it.

SERVES 4

4 large sheets filo pastry

¹/₃ cup butter

16 large tiger shrimp, cooked and shelled

1 tbsp chopped fresh mint, plus a little more to garnish

1 tbsp chopped fresh dill

juice of 1 lime, plus another lime cut into wedges

1 Keep the sheets of filo pastry covered with a dry, clean cloth to keep them moist. Cut one sheet of filo pastry in half widthwise and brush both halves with melted butter. Place one half on top of the other.

2 Preheat the oven to 450°F. Cut eight of the tiger shrimp in half down the back of the shrimp and remove any black parts.

3 Place four prawns in the center of the filo pastry and sprinkle a quarter of the mint, dill and lime juice over the top. Fold over the sides, brush with butter and roll up to make a bundle.

4 Repeat with the other ingredients and place the bundles join side down, on a greased cookie sheet. Bake for 10 minutes or until golden. Serve with lime wedges, tiger shrimp and mint.

Camembert, Chervil and Plum Profiteroles

Most people are familiar with chocolate profiteroles, but this savory version is just as delicious and makes an attractive starter.

SERVES 8

1¼ cups water

⅔ cup butter, cubed

1½ cups plain flour

2 tsp mustard powder

1 tsp powdered cinnamon

4 eggs

¾ cup grated Cheddar

FILLING

1 packed cup Camembert

a little milk

1 tsp fresh chervil, chopped

6 fresh plums, stoned and finely
 chopped

SAUCE

10 oz can red plums

½ tsp powdered cinnamon

1 tsp chopped fresh chervil, plus a
 few sprigs to garnish

1 To make the profiteroles, put the water into a saucepan and add the butter. Gently melt the butter, then bring to the boil. As soon as this happens, sieve in the flour, mustard powder and cinnamon. Beat hard with a wooden spoon until the mixture comes away from the sides of the pan.

2 Leave to cool for 10 minutes, then beat in the eggs, one at a time. Add the grated Cheddar, and beat until glossy. Use a large nozzle to pipe blobs about 1 in across on a greased cookie sheet. Bake at 400°F for 20 minutes. Cool on a wire rack.

3 Chop the Camembert in small pieces and put in a food processor. Add a little milk and the chervil, and blend to a smooth paste. Remove from the food processor and add the fresh plums.

4 Also make the sauce while the pastries are cooling. Drain the canned plums and pit them if necessary. Add them to the cinnamon and chervil in the food processor and blend to a fairly smooth purée.

5 Assemble the profiteroles by halving them and placing some of the Camembert mixture inside. Place the profiteroles on individual plates and dust with a little cinnamon. Serve the sauce separately.

Pork, Thyme and Water Chestnut Filo Bundles

Filo pastry is easy to use and delicious – the light, crisp wrapping makes a simple recipe into a celebration.

MAKES 8

1 tbsp sunflower oil, plus more for
 frying

1 tsp fresh grated ginger

10 oz pork fillet, finely
 chopped

6 scallions, chopped

1 cup chopped mixed mush-
 rooms

½ cup chopped canned bamboo
 shoots

12 water chestnuts, finely chopped

2 tsp cornstarch

1 tbsp soy sauce

2 tsp anchovy paste

2 tsp fresh thyme, chopped

salt and pepper

8 large sheets filo pastry

scant 2 tbsp butter, melted

1 Heat the oil and fry the ginger for a few seconds and then add the pork. Stir well and cook until color changes. Add the scallions and mushrooms and cook until tender. Add the bamboo shoots and water chestnuts and cook quickly.

2 In a small bowl, mix the cornstarch with the soy sauce and anchovy paste. Add to the pan and stir well. Add the chopped thyme, season with salt and pepper, and cook until thickened.

3 Take a sheet of filo pastry and fold in half to make a square. Place two tablespoonfuls of filling across one corner and fold the corner over, then fold in the sides. Brush the folded sides lightly with a little melted butter to help the pastry stick. Complete the roll, and place it join side down on a cloth, then fold the cloth over the top to cover it. Finish all the rolls, putting each one in the cloth as it is made.

4 Heat some oil for semi-deep frying, and fry 2-3 rolls at a time until evenly browned. Drain on absorbent paper and serve hot.

From top: *Camembert, Chervil and Plum Profiteroles; Pork, Thyme and Water Chestnut Filo Bundles*

Lamb Pie, with Pear, Ginger and Mint Sauce

Cooking lamb with fruit is an idea taken from traditional Persian cuisine. The ginger and mint add bite to the mild flavors.

SERVES 6

1 boned mid-loin of lamb, 2 lb after boning

salt and pepper

8 large sheets filo pastry

scant 2 tbsp butter

STUFFING

1 tbsp butter

1 small onion, chopped

1 cup coarsely crumbled whole wheat bread

grated rind of 1 lemon

³⁄₄ cup drained canned pears from a 14 oz can, roughly chopped (rest of can, and juice, used for sauce)

¹⁄₄ tsp ground ginger

1 small egg, beaten

skewers, string and large needle to make roll

SAUCE

rest of can of pears, including juice

2 tsp finely chopped fresh mint

1 Prepare the stuffing: melt the butter in a pan and add the onion, cooking until soft. Preheat the oven to 350°F. Put the butter and onion into a mixing bowl and add the breadcrumbs, lemon rind, pears and ginger. Season lightly and add enough beaten egg to bind.

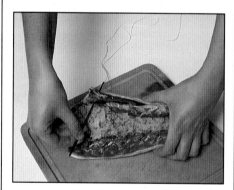

2 Spread the loin out flat, fat side down, and season. Place the stuffing along the middle of the loin and roll carefully, holding with skewers while you sew it together with string. Heat a large baking pan in the oven and brown the loin slowly on all sides. This will take 20-30 minutes. Leave to cool, and store in the refrigerator until needed.

3 Preheat the oven to 400°F. Take two sheets of filo pastry and brush with melted butter. Overlap by about 5 in to make a square. Place the next two sheets on top and brush with butter. Continue until all the pastry has been used.

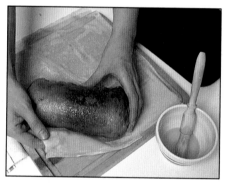

4 Place the roll of lamb diagonally across one corner of the pastry, without overlapping the sides. Fold the corner over the lamb, fold in the sides, and brush the pastry well with melted butter. Roll to the far corner of the sheet. Place join side down on a buttered baking sheet and brush all over with the rest of the melted butter. Bake for about 30 minutes or until golden brown.

5 Blend the remaining pears with their juice and the mint, and serve with the lamb.

Steak and Kidney Pie, with Mustard and Bay Gravy

This is a sharpened-up, bay-flavored version of a traditional favorite. The fragrant mustard, bay and parsley perfectly complement the flavor of the beef.

SERVES 4

1 lb puff pastry

2½ tbsp flour

salt and pepper

1½ lb rump steak, cubed

6 oz pork or lamb kidney

scant 2 tbsp butter

1 medium onion, chopped

1 tbsp made English mustard

2 bay leaves

1 tbsp chopped parsley

⅔ cup beef stock

1 egg, beaten

1 Roll out two-thirds of the pastry on a floured surface to about ⅛ in thick. Gently transfer to line a 1½ quart pie dish. Place a pie funnel in the middle.

2 Put the flour, salt and pepper in a bowl and toss the cubes of steak in the mixture. Remove all fat and skin from the kidneys, and slice thickly. Add to the steak cubes and toss well. Melt the butter in a pan and fry the onion until soft, then add the mustard, bay leaves, parsley and stock and stir well.

3 Preheat the oven to 375°F. Place the steak and kidney in the pie and add the stock mixture. Roll out the remaining pastry to a thickness of ⅛ in. Brush the edges of the pastry forming the lower half of the pie with beaten egg and cover with the second piece of pastry. Firmly press the pieces of pastry together to seal the edge, then trim. Use the trimmings to decorate the top in a leaf pattern.

4 Brush the whole pie with beaten egg and make a small hole over the top of the funnel. Bake for about 1 hour until the pastry is golden brown.

Turkey with Apples, Bay and Madeira

This casserole will win you many compliments without the worry of a complicated menu. The unusual apple garnish looks very attractive.

SERVES 4

1½ lb turkey breast fillets, cut into ¾ in slices

salt and pepper

4 tbsp unsalted butter, plus another 1 tbsp for the sliced apple garnish

4 tart apples, peeled and sliced

4 tbsp Madeira or cooking sherry, plus another 2 tbsp for the apple garnish

⅔ cup chicken stock

3 bay leaves

2 tsp cornstarch

⅔ cup heavy cream

1 Season the turkey, melt 2 tbsp of the butter in a pan and fry the meat to seal it. Transfer to an ovenproof casserole. Preheat the oven to 350°F. Add the remaining 2 tbsps butter to the pan with two sliced apples, and cook gently for 1-2 minutes.

2 Add the Madeira, stock and bay leaves to the turkey and stir in. Simmer for another couple of minutes. Cover the casserole and bake for about 40 minutes.

3 Blend the cornstarch with a little of the cream, then add the rest of the cream. Add this mixture to the casserole and return to the oven for 10 minutes to allow the sauce to thicken.

4 To make the garnish, melt 1 tbsp butter in a pan and gently fry the apple slices. Add the remaining Madeira and set it alight. Once the flames have died down continue to fry the apple until it is lightly browned, and garnish the casserole with it.

Beef with Orange Herbal Mustard

The orange herbal mustard is delicious with many different dishes, including cold ham and pork pies. It gives beef a fantastic flavor. This will become a firm favorite.

SERVES 4

3 tbsp oil

1½ lb braising steak, cubed

2 cups chopped onion

1 clove garlic, peeled and crushed

2 tbsp flour

1¼ cups beef stock

2 oranges, plus 1 more for garnish and herbal mustard

1 tbsp tomato paste

3 tbsp Grand Marnier

1 tbsp maple syrup

salt and pepper

1 cup sliced mushrooms

HERBAL MUSTARD

2 tbsp mixed fresh herbs, finely chopped, such as thyme and chives

juice and grated rind of half an orange

3 tbsp Dijon mustard

1 Heat the oil and fry the beef to seal it. Transfer to a casserole. Fry the onion and garlic, drain and add to the casserole. Add the flour to the pan and cook for 1 minute, then add the stock and bring to a boil.

2 Finely slice off the colored part of the rind of two oranges and chop into small pieces. Squeeze both oranges, and add the juice and the rind to the casserole. Add the tomato paste, Grand Marnier and maple syrup, and season to taste. Preheat the oven to 350°F.

3 Cover the casserole and cook in the oven for at least 1½ hours. Add the mushrooms and return to the oven for another 30 minutes. Serve garnished with slices from half the remaining orange and the herbal mustard described below (remember to grate the orange before cutting it up).

4 To make the herbal mustard, grate the orange rind and mix with the chopped fresh herbs. Then mix in the orange juice and the Dijon mustard. Serve with the beef in a separate dish.

Chicken Stew with Blackberries and Lemon Balm

This delicious stew combines some wonderful flavors, and the combination of red wine and blackberries gives it a dramatic appearance.

SERVES 4

4 chicken breasts, partly boned

salt and pepper

scant 2 tbsp butter

1 tbsp sunflower oil

4 tbsp flour

²⁄₃ cup red wine

²⁄₃ cup chicken stock

**grated rind of half an orange plus
  1 tbsp juice**

**3 sprigs lemon balm, finely chopped,
  plus 1 sprig to garnish**

²⁄₃ cup heavy cream

1 egg yolk

**²⁄₃ cup fresh blackberries,
  plus ¹⁄₃ cup to garnish**

1 Remove any skin from the chicken, and season the meat. Heat the butter and oil in a pan, fry the chicken to seal it, then transfer to a casserole dish. Stir the flour into the pan, then add wine and stock and bring to a boil. Add the orange rind and juice, and also the chopped lemon balm. Pour over the chicken.

2 Preheat the oven to 350°F. Cover the casserole and cook in the oven for about 40 minutes.

3 Blend the cream with the egg yolk, add some of the liquid from the casserole and stir back into the dish with the blackberries (reserving those for the garnish). Cover and cook for another 10-15 minutes. Serve garnished with the rest of the blackberries and lemon balm.

Pork and Mushrooms with Sage and Mango Chutney

The mango chutney and sage leaves add a special flavor to this traditional dish.

SERVES 4

scant 2 tbsp butter

1 tbsp sunflower oil

1½ lb cubed pork

**6 oz onion, peeled and
  chopped**

2 tbsp flour

1⁷⁄₈ cups stock

4 tbsp white wine

salt and pepper

8 oz mushrooms, sliced

6 fresh sage leaves, finely chopped

2 tbsp mango chutney

**1 fresh mango, peeled and sliced, to
  garnish**

1 Heat the butter and oil and fry the pork in a pan to seal it. Transfer to a casserole. Fry the onion in the pan, stir in the flour and cook for 1 minute.

2 Preheat the oven to 350°F. Gradually add the stock and white wine to the onion and bring to a boil. Season well with salt and pepper, then add the mushrooms, sage leaves and mango chutney.

3 Pour the sauce mixture over the pork and cover the casserole. Cook in the oven for about 1 hour, depending on the cut of pork, until tender. Check the seasoning, garnish with mango slices, and serve with rice.

From top: *Pork and Mushrooms with Sage and Mango Chutney; Chicken Stew with Blackberries and Lemon Balm*

Leek and Monkfish with Thyme Sauce

Monkfish is a well known fish now, thanks to its excellent flavor and firm texture.

SERVES 4

2 lb monkfish, cubed

salt and pepper

generous ⅓ cup butter

4 leeks, sliced

1 tbsp flour

⅔ cup fish or vegetable stock

2 tsp finely chopped fresh thyme, plus more to garnish

juice of 1 lemon

⅔ cup light cream

radicchio leaves, to garnish

1 Season the fish to taste. Melt about a third of the butter in a pan, and fry the fish for a short time. Put to one side. Fry the leeks in the pan with another third of the butter until they have softened. Put these to one side with the fish.

2 In a saucepan, melt the rest of the butter, add the remaining butter from the pan, stir in the flour, and add the stock. As the sauce begins to thicken, add the thyme and lemon juice.

3 Return the leeks and monkfish to the pan and cook gently for a few minutes. Add the cream and season to taste. Do not let the mixture boil again, or the cream will separate. Serve immediately garnished with thyme and radicchio leaves.

Fish Stew with Calvados, Parsley and Dill

This rustic stew harbors all sorts of interesting flavors and will please and intrigue. Many varieties of fish can be used, just choose the freshest and best.

SERVES 4

2 lb assorted white fish

1 tbsp chopped parsley, plus a few leaves to garnish

8 oz mushrooms

8 oz can of tomatoes

salt and pepper

2 tsp flour

1 tbsp butter

1⅞ cups cider

3 tbsp Calvados

1 large bunch fresh dill sprigs, reserving 4 fronds to garnish

1 Chop the fish roughly and place it in a casserole or stewing pot with the parsley, mushrooms, tomatoes and salt and pepper to taste.

2 Preheat the oven to 350°F. Work the flour into the butter to make a smooth paste. Heat the cider and stir in the flour and butter mixture a little at a time. Cook, stirring, until it has thickened slightly.

3 Add the cider mixture and the remaining ingredients to the fish and mix gently. Cover and bake for about 30 minutes. Serve garnished with sprigs of dill and parsley leaves.

Lamb and Leeks with Mint and Spring Onions

This is especially good with new season's lamb and organically grown leeks – best of all with leeks from your garden. If you have some home-made chicken stock it boosts the flavor tremendously; if not, use a good ready-made stock rather than a bouillon cube.

SERVES 6

2 tbsp sunflower oil

4 lb lamb (fillet or boned leg), cubed

10 scallions, thickly sliced

3 leeks, thickly sliced

1 tbsp flour

²⁄₃ cup white wine

1¼ cups chicken stock

1 tbsp tomato paste

1 tbsp sugar

salt and pepper

2 tbsp fresh mint leaves, finely chopped, plus a few more to garnish

²⁄₃ cup dried pears, chopped

2 lb potatoes, peeled and sliced

2 tbsp melted butter

1 Heat the oil and fry the lamb to seal it. Transfer to a casserole. Preheat the oven to 350°F.

2 Fry the onions and leeks for 1 minute, stir in the flour and cook for another minute. Add the wine and stock and bring to a boil. Add the tomato paste, sugar, salt and pepper with the mint and pears and pour into the casserole. Stir the mixture. Arrange the sliced potatoes on top and brush with the melted butter.

3 Cover and bake for 1½ hours. Then increase the temperature to 400°F, cook for a further 30 minutes, uncovered, to brown the potatoes. Garnish with mint leaves.

Stuffed Parsleyed Onions

Although devised as a vegetarian dish, these stuffed onions make a wonderful accompaniment to meat dishes, or an appetizing supper dish with crusty bread and a salad.

SERVES 4

4 large onions

4 tbsp cooked rice

4 tsp finely chopped fresh parsley, plus extra to garnish

4 tbsp strong Cheddar cheese, finely grated

salt and pepper

2 tbsp olive oil

1 tbsp white wine, to moisten

1 Cut a slice from the top of each onion and scoop out the center to leave a fairly thick shell. Combine all the remaining ingredients, moistening with enough wine to mix well. Preheat the oven to 350°F.

2 Fill the onions and bake in the oven for 45 minutes. Serve garnished with the extra parsley.

Herbed Chicken with Apricot and Pecan Potato Baskets

The potato baskets make a pretty addition to the chicken and could easily have different fillings when you feel the need for a change.

SERVES 8

8 chicken breast fillets

2 tbsp butter

6 mushrooms, chopped

1 tbsp chopped pecan nuts

½ cup chopped, Virginia-style boiled ham

½ cup coarse whole wheat breadcrumbs

1 tbsp chopped parsley, plus some whole leaves to garnish

salt and pepper

toothpicks to secure rolls

SAUCE

2 tsp cornstarch

½ cup white wine

¼ cup butter

¼ cup apricot chutney

POTATO BASKETS

4 large baking potatoes

6 oz pork sausage meat

1 x 8 oz can apricots in natural juice, drained and quartered

¼ tsp cinnamon

½ tsp grated orange peel

2 tbsp maple syrup

2 tbsp butter

¼ cup chopped pecan nuts, plus additional pecan halves to garnish

1 Place the chicken breasts between two sheets of waxed paper and flatten with a rolling pin or mallet. Melt the butter in a pan and sauté the mushrooms, pecans and ham. Stir in the breadcrumbs and parsley, and season to taste. Divide this mixture between the chicken breasts and roll up and secure each one with a toothpick. Refrigerate while making the sauce.

2 Put the potatoes in the oven to bake at 325°F while you prepare the sauce. Mix the cornstarch with a little of the wine to make a smooth paste. Put the remaining wine in a pan and add this paste. Simmer until smooth, and add the butter and the apricot chutney and cook for about 5 minutes, stirring constantly.

3 Place the chicken breasts in a shallow ovenproof dish and pour over the sauce. Bake in the oven (do not adjust the temperature) for 20 minutes, basting several times.

4 When the potatoes are cooked through, cut them in half and scoop out the inside, leaving a reasonable layer within the shell. Mash the potato and place in a mixing bowl.

5 Fry the sausage meat and remove some of the fat that comes off. Add the remaining ingredients and cook for 1 minute. Add the sausage meat mixture to the potato and blend gently. Fill the potato shells. Sprinkle the pecan halves over the top, put in the oven with the chicken and bake for another 30 minutes.

6 Remove the chicken breasts from the oven and then drain the sauce into a separate container. Slice the breasts, put on to individual plates and pour the sauce over the top. Serve with the potato baskets and garnish with parsley leaves.

Venison Steaks with Elderberry and Orange

Farmed venison is now widely available. The strong flavor of the meat is well matched by the sweet sauce.

SERVES 4

4 venison tenderloin steaks, 6-8 oz each

olive oil for basting

black pepper

salt

2 tbsp red wine

4 tbsp orange juice, plus slices of orange to garnish

2 tbsp elderberry jelly

sprigs of parsley, to garnish

3 In a pan, reduce the red wine, then add the orange juice and elderberry jelly and simmer for 10 minutes. Pour over the steaks and garnish with slices of orange and parsley sprigs.

1 Pound the venison steaks a little with a meat mallet to make the meat more tender. Preheat the broiler.

2 Brush with olive oil and season with freshly ground black pepper. Broil under a high heat until done to your taste. Sprinkle with a little salt.

From top: *Venison Steaks with Elderberry and Orange; Herbed Chicken with Apricot and Pecan Potato Baskets*

Chicken with Sloe Gin and Juniper

 Juniper is used in the manufacture of gin, and the reinforcement of the flavor by using both sloe gin and juniper is delicious. Sloe gin is easy to make, but can also be bought ready-made.

SERVES 8

2 tbsp butter
2 tbsp sunflower oil
8 chicken breast fillets
12 oz carrots, cooked
1 clove garlic, peeled and crushed
1 tbsp finely chopped parsley
¼ cup chicken stock
¼ cup red wine
¼ cup sloe gin
1 tsp crushed juniper berries
salt and pepper
1 bunch basil, to garnish

1 Melt the butter with the oil in a pan, and sauté the chicken until browned on all sides.

2 In a food processor, combine all the remaining ingredients except the watercress, and blend to a smooth purée. If the mixture seems too thick add a little more red wine or water until a thinner consistency is reached.

3 Put the chicken breasts in a pan, pour the sauce over the top and cook until the chicken is cooked through – about 15 minutes. Adjust the seasoning and serve garnished with chopped fresh basil.

Duck Breasts with Red Plums, Cinnamon and Coriander

Duck breasts can be bought separately, which makes this dish very easy to prepare.

SERVES 4

4 lean duck breasts, 6 oz each, skinned

salt

2 tsp stick cinnamon, crushed

¼ cup butter

1 tbsp plum brandy (or Cognac)

1 cup chicken stock

1 cup heavy cream

pepper

6 fresh red plums, pitted and sliced

6 sprigs coriander leaves, plus some extra to garnish

1 Preheat the oven to 375°F. Score the duck breasts and sprinkle with salt. Press the crushed cinnamon on to both sides of the duck breasts. Melt half the butter in a pan and fry them on both sides to seal, then place in an ovenproof dish with the butter and bake for 6-7 minutes.

2 Remove the dish from the oven and return the contents to the pan. Add the brandy and set it alight. When the flames have died down, remove from the pan and keep warm. Add the stock and cream to the pan and simmer gently until reduced and thick. Adjust the seasoning.

3 Reserve a few plum slices for garnishing. In a pan, melt the other half of the butter and fry the plums and coriander, just enough to cook the fruit through. Slice the duck breasts and pour some sauce around each one, then garnish with slices of plum and chopped coriander.

Turkey with Fig, Orange and Mint Marmalade

Turkey is a low-fat meat that should be used all the year round, not just at Christmas. This unusual sauce gives its rather bland flavor a tremendous lift.

SERVES 4

1 lb dried figs

½ bottle sweet, fruity white wine

4 turkey fillets, 6-8 oz each

1 tbsp butter

2 tbsp dark orange marmalade

10 mint leaves, finely chopped, plus a few more to garnish

juice of ½ lemon

salt and pepper

1 Place the figs in a pan with the wine and bring to a boil, then simmer very gently for about 1 hour. Leave to cool and refrigerate overnight.

2 Melt the butter in a pan and fry the turkey fillets until they are cooked through. Remove from the pan and keep warm. Drain any fat from the pan and pour in the juice from the figs. Bring to the boil and reduce until about ⅔ cup remains.

3 Add the marmalade, mint leaves and lemon juice, and simmer for a few minutes. Season to taste. When the sauce is thick and shiny, pour it over the meat and garnish with the figs and mint leaves.

Lamb with Mint and Lemon

Lamb has been served with mint for centuries – rightly, because it is a great combination.

SERVES 8

8 lamb steaks, 8 oz each

grated rind and juice of 1 lemon

2 cloves garlic, peeled and crushed

2 scallions, finely chopped

2 tsp finely chopped fresh mint leaves, plus some leaves for garnishing

4 tbsp extra virgin olive oil

salt and black pepper

1 Make a marinade for the lamb by mixing all the other ingredients and seasoning to taste. Place the lamb steaks in a shallow dish and cover with the marinade. Refrigerate overnight.

2 Preheat the broiler then broil the lamb under a high heat until just cooked, basting with the marinade occasionally. Turn once during cooking. Garnish with mint leaves.

Sirloin Steaks with Bloody Mary Sauce and Coriander

This cocktail of ingredients is just as successful as the well-known drink, but the alcohol evaporates in cooking, so you need not worry about a hangover.

SERVES 4

4 sirloin steaks, 8 oz each
MARINADE
2 tbsp soy sauce
4 tbsp balsamic vinegar
2 tbsp olive oil
SAUCE
2 lb very ripe tomatoes, peeled and chopped
tomato paste, if required
½ cup chopped onions
2 spring onions
1 tsp chopped fresh coriander
1 tsp ground cumin
1 tsp salt
1 tbsp fresh lime juice
½ cup beef consommé, fresh or canned
¼ cup vodka
1 tbsp Worcester sauce

1 Lay the steaks in a shallow dish, mix the marinade ingredients together in a bowl, pour over the steaks and leave for at least a couple of hours in the refrigerator, turning once or twice.

2 If the tomatoes are not quite ripe, add a little tomato paste. Place all the sauce ingredients in a food processor and blend to a fairly smooth texture. Put in a pan, bring to a boil and simmer for about 5 minutes.

3 Remove the steaks from the marinade and place under a hot broiler. Discard the marinade. Broil the steaks under a high heat until cooked. Serve with the sauce.

Roast Pork with Sage, Marjoram and Celery Leaves

Pork is an inexpensive choice which is equally suitable for a family dinner or a celebration meal. The fruity purée makes a delicious change from the more usual plain apple sauce.

SERVES 8

6 lb joint of pork
3 tbsp fresh sage
1 tbsp fresh marjoram
3 tbsp chopped celery leaves
salt and pepper
¼ cup cider
PURÉE
1 tbsp butter
2 eating apples
2 bananas
1 tbsp Calvados

1 Preheat the oven to 315°F. Cut a large piece of foil and place the pork in the center. In a bowl mix the sage, marjoram and celery leaves together. Cover the fatty part of the pork with the herb mixture, season to taste and wrap tightly. Roast for about 1 hour.

2 Fold back the foil and baste the joint with the cider. Continue cooking for another hour until a sharp knife pressed into the thickest part produces clear juices.

3 To make the purée, peel and slice the apples and bananas, put the butter in a pan and sauté the fruit. Add the Calvados and set it alight. When the flames have died down remove the mixture from the heat, put it in the food processor and purée. Serve the pork with the purée on the side.

From top: *Sirloin Steaks with Bloody Mary Sauce and Coriander; Roast Pork with Sage, Marjoram and Celery Leaves*

Corn on the Cob in a Garlic Butter Crust

Whether you are catering for vegetarians or serving this with other meat dishes, it will disappear in a flash. Even people who are not usually keen on corn on the cob have been won over by this recipe.

SERVES 6

6 ripe cobs of corn
1 cup butter
2 tbsp olive oil
2 cloves garlic, peeled and crushed
2 tsp freshly ground black pepper
1 cup finely crumbled whole wheat bread
1 tbsp chopped parsley

1 Boil the corn cobs in salted water until tender, then leave to cool.

2 Melt the butter, and add the oil, garlic and black pepper. Pour the mixture into a shallow dish. Mix the breadcrumbs and parsley in another shallow dish. Roll the corn cobs in the melted butter mixture and then in the breadcrumbs.

3 Grill the cobs under a high grill until the breadcrumbs are golden.

OTHER GARLIC BUTTER IDEAS

• Partially cut through a French loaf at regular intervals. Spread the garlic butter mixture between the slices and bake in a moderate oven for 30 minutes.

• To make garlic crôutons, melt the garlic butter in a pan and add cubes of bread. Toss frequently over a medium heat. When golden brown add to soups or salads.

• Drizzle over chicken breasts before roasting.

Vegetable and Herb Kebabs with Green Peppercorn Sauce

Other vegetables can be included in these kebabs, depending on what is available at the time. The green peppercorn sauce is also an excellent accompaniment to many other dishes.

SERVES 4

8 bamboo skewers soaked in water for 1 hour

24 mushrooms

16 cherry tomatoes

16 large basil leaves

16 thick slices of zucchini

16 large mint leaves

16 squares of red sweet pepper

TO BASTE

¹/₂ cup melted butter

1 clove garlic, peeled and crushed

1 tbsp crushed green peppercorns

salt

GREEN PEPPERCORN SAUCE

¹/₄ cup butter

3 tbsp brandy

1 cup double cream

1 tsp crushed green peppercorns

1 Thread the vegetables on to the bamboo skewers. Place the basil leaves immediately next to the tomatoes, and the mint leaves wrapped around the zucchini slices.

2 Mix the basting ingredients and baste the kebabs thoroughly. Place the skewers on a barbecue or under the broiler, turning and basting regularly until the vegetables are just cooked – about 5-7 minutes.

3 Heat the butter for the sauce in a frying pan, then add the brandy and light it. When the flames have died down, stir in the cream and the peppercorns. Cook for approximately 2 minutes, stirring all the time. Serve the kebabs with the green peppercorn sauce.

Garlic and Marjoram Mushrooms with Pumpkin Seed and Tomato Bread

Garlic mushrooms are always popular, and this unusual Italian-style bread makes a delicious accompaniment.

SERVES 6

GARLIC MUSHROOMS

12 oz mushrooms

3 tbsp olive oil

1 tbsp water

2 cloves garlic, peeled and crushed

4 tbsp chopped fresh marjoram

juice of 1 lemon

salt and pepper

TOMATO BREAD

¹⁄₃ cup sun-dried tomatoes preserved in olive oil

scant 1 cup boiling water

1 tsp chopped fresh basil

1 tsp chopped fresh marjoram

1 tsp chopped fresh rosemary

generous 3 tbsp butter

1 tsp salt

4 cups plain flour

1 package dried yeast

3 tbsp olive oil

1 egg

1 tbsp pumpkin seeds, hulled

1 To cook the mushrooms, put all the ingredients in a saucepan and bring the liquid to a boil, then turn down the heat and simmer for 10 minutes. Tip the mushrooms and liquid into a bowl. Refrigerate overnight.

From top: *Chicken Drumsticks in a Honey and Coriander Crust; Garlic and Marjoram Mushrooms with Tomato Bread*

2 To make the bread, drain the tomatoes and chop roughly. Put them in a bowl and pour on the boiling water. Add the herbs and leave to soak for 20-25 minutes.

3 Place the butter, salt and flour in a mixing bowl and rub the fat into the flour until the mixture resembles breadcrumbs. Stir in the yeast. Drain the liquid from the tomatoes, reserving the liquid, and heat this until lukewarm. Add the drained tomatoes.

4 Mix the tomato and herb liquid with the olive oil and egg. Make a well in the center of the flour mixture and pour in most of the liquid mixture. Mix well to form a fairly stiff dough. If it is too stiff, add more liquid.

5 Knead the dough until smooth, in the bowl or on a floured board or surface. Form into a round loaf shape and put this on a greased cookie sheet. Cover with a clean cloth and leave in a warm room until slightly risen – this will take about 30 minutes. Preheat the oven to 425°F.

6 Brush the loaf with a little water and gently press the pumpkin seeds into the top and sides. Bake for 15-20 minutes. Turn the loaf out on to a wire rack. Tap the upturned bottom. If the loaf is done it will sound hollow – if not, put it back in the oven for a few more minutes. Let it cool before slicing.

Chicken Drumsticks in a Honey and Coriander Crust

This delicious crunchy coating will be a hit with guests and family alike.

MAKES 8 DRUMSTICKS

8 chicken drumsticks

³⁄₄ cup butter

2 tbsp sunflower oil

5 tbsp clear honey

1 tbsp Dijon mustard

1 tsp roughly crushed coriander seeds

1 tsp freshly ground black pepper

4 cups breadcrumbs

coriander sprigs, to garnish

1 Preheat the broiler and broil the chicken for 6 minutes, turning several times. Place the butter, oil and honey in a small pan and warm until all three ingredients are combined.

2 Preheat the oven to 350°F. Add the mustard, coriander and pepper to the mixture. Stir well and brush on to the chicken. Roll the drumsticks in the breadcrumbs.

3 Bake in the oven for 20-25 minutes until fully cooked through. When cooked, the juices should run clear. Serve garnished with a sprig of coriander.

Lamb Steaks Marinated in Mint and Sherry

The marinade is the key to the success of this recipe. The sherry imparts a wonderful tang.

SERVES 6

6 large lamb steaks or 12 smaller
   chops

MARINADE

2 tbsp coarsely chopped fresh mint
   leaves

1 tbsp cracked black peppercorns

1 medium onion, chopped

½ cup sherry

¼ cup extra virgin olive oil

2 cloves garlic

1 Place the mint leaves and pepper-corns in a food processor and blend until very finely chopped. Add the chopped onion and process again until smooth. Add the rest of the marinade ingredients and process until completely mixed. The marinade should be of a fairly thick consistency.

2 Place the steaks or chops in a shallow dish and pour on the marinade. Cover with plastic wrap and refrigerate overnight.

3 Broil or barbecue the steaks on a very high heat until cooked, basting occasionally with the marinade.

Salmon Steaks with Oregano Salsa

This combination of salmon with piquant tomato works incredibly well. An ideal dish for a summer lunch.

SERVES 4

1 tbsp butter

4 salmon steaks, 8 oz each

½ cup white wine

½ tsp freshly ground black pepper

fresh oregano, to make 2 tsp chopped, plus sprigs to garnish

4 scallions, trimmed

8 oz ripe tomatoes, peeled

2 tbsp extra virgin olive oil

½ tsp superfine sugar

1 tbsp tomato paste

1 Preheat the oven to 275°F. Butter an ovenproof dish, put in the salmon steaks, and add the wine and black pepper. Cover with foil and bake for 15 minutes, until the fish is just cooked. Leave to cool.

2 Put the oregano in a food processor and chop it very finely. Add the scallions, tomatoes and all the remaining ingredients. Process in bursts until chopped but not a smooth purée.

3 Serve the salmon cold with the salsa, garnished with a sprig of fresh oregano.

Guacamole, Basil and Tomato Pita Breads

This is a favorite family recipe – the fresh basil and tomato are perfect partners for each other and for the spicy guacamole.

SERVES 6

6 large pita breads
1-2 large beefsteak tomatoes
12 basil leaves
2 large ripe avocados
1 tomato
½ red onion
1 clove garlic, peeled and crushed
1 tbsp lime juice
¼ tsp chilli powder
2 tbsp chopped coriander

1 Open the ends of the pita breads to make pockets and place a couple of slices of tomato and two basil leaves in each one.

2 Roughly chop the avocados, the remaining tomato and the red onion. Mix all the remaining ingredients briefly in a food processor.

3 Add the mixture from the food processor to the roughly chopped avocado, tomato and onions, and stir gently. Fill the pockets with the avocado mixture and serve immediately.

Brie and Grape Sandwiches with Mint

A slightly unusual sandwich combination, which works well judging by the speed with which the sandwiches disappear at family picnics or summer tea parties.

SERVES 4

8 slices whole wheat bread
butter for spreading
12 oz ripe Brie cheese
30-40 large grapes
16 fresh mint leaves

1 Butter the bread. Slice the Brie into thick slices, to be divided between the sandwiches.

2 Place the Brie slices on four slices of bread. Peel, halve and seed the grapes and put on top of the Brie. Chop the mint finely by hand or in a food processor, and sprinkle the mint over the Brie and grapes. Place the other four slices of bread over the top and cut each sandwich in half.

OTHER HERB SANDWICH IDEAS

- Feta cheese, black olives, lettuce, tomato and freshly chopped mint in pita bread
- Italian salami, cream cheese, tomato and fresh basil on peasant bread
- Sliced chicken breast, mayonnaise and dill sprigs on whole wheat bread
- Grilled mozzarella and sundried tomato focaccia bread sandwich, with black olives, fresh arugula and basil leaves
- Hummus, lettuce and freshly chopped coriander on French bread
- Dry cured prosciutto, green olives and arugula leaves on poppy-seeded white bread

From top: *Brie and Grape Sandwiches with Mint; Guacamole, Basil and Tomato Pita Breads*

Broccoli and Cauliflower with Cider and Apple Mint Sauce

The cider sauce made here is also ideal for other vegetables, such as celery or beans. It is flavored using tamari, a Japanese soy sauce and apple mint.

<small>SERVES 4</small>

1 large onion, chopped

2 large carrots, chopped

1 large clove garlic

1 tbsp dill seed

4 large sprigs apple mint

2 tbsp olive oil

2 tbsp plain flour

1¼ cups cider

1 lb broccoli florets

1 lb cauliflower florets

2 tbsp tamari

2 tsp mint jelly

1 Sauté the onions, carrots, garlic, dill seeds and apple mint leaves in the olive oil until nearly cooked. Stir in the flour and cook for half a minute or so. Pour in the cider and simmer until the sauce looks glossy.

2 Boil the broccoli and cauliflower in separate pots until just tender.

3 Pour the sauce into a food processor and add the tamari and the mint jelly. Blend until finely puréed. Pour over the broccoli and cauliflower.

Zucchini and Carrot Ribbons with Brie, Black Pepper and Parsley

This recipe produces a delicious vegetarian meal, or simply a new way of presenting colorful vegetables as an accompaniment to a main course.

SERVES 4

1 large green pepper, diced

1 tbsp sunflower oil

8 oz Brie cheese

2 tbsp crème fraîche or yogurt

1 tsp lemon juice

4 tbsp milk

2 tsp freshly ground black pepper

2 tbsp parsley, very finely chopped, plus extra to garnish

salt and pepper

6 large zucchini

6 large carrots

1 Sauté the green pepper in the sunflower oil until just tender. Place the remaining ingredients, apart from the carrots and zucchini, in a food processor and blend well. Place the mixture in a saucepan and add the green pepper.

2 Peel the zucchini. Use a potato peeler to slice them into long, thin strips. Do the same thing with the carrots. Put the zucchini and carrots in separate saucepans, cover with just enough water to cover, then simmer for 3 minutes until barely cooked.

3 Heat the sauce and pour into a shallow vegetable dish. Toss the zucchini and carrot strips together and arrange them in the sauce. Garnish with a little finely chopped parsley.

Smoked Salmon, Lemon and Dill Pasta

This has been tried and tested as both a main-dish salad and a starter, and the only preference stated was that as a main dish you got a larger portion, so that made it better.

<u>SERVES 2 AS A MAIN COURSE OR 4 AS A STARTER</u>

salt

3 cups pasta twists

6 large sprigs fresh dill, chopped, plus more sprigs to garnish

2 tbsp extra virgin olive oil

1 tbsp white wine vinegar

1¼ cups heavy cream

pepper

6 oz smoked salmon

1 Boil the pasta in salted water until it is just cooked. Drain and run under the cold tap until completely cooled.

2 Make the dressing by combining all the remaining ingredients, apart from the smoked salmon and reserved dill, in the bowl of a food processor and blend well. Season to taste.

3 Slice the salmon into small strips. Place the cooled pasta and the smoked salmon, in a mixing bowl. Pour on the dressing and toss carefully. Transfer to a serving bowl and garnish with the dill sprigs.

Avocado and Pasta Salad with Coriander

Served as one of a variety of salads or alone, this tasty combination is sure to please. The dressing is fairly sharp, yet tastes wonderfully fresh.

<u>SERVES 4</u>

1¼ cups pasta shells or bows

3¾ cups chicken stock

4 stalks celery, finely chopped

2 avocados, chopped

1 clove garlic, peeled and chopped

1 tbsp finely chopped fresh coriander, plus some whole leaves to garnish

1 cup grated sharp Cheddar cheese

DRESSING

⅔ cup extra virgin olive oil (cold pressed is best)

1 tbsp cider vinegar

2 tbsp lemon juice

grated rind of 1 lemon

1 tsp Dijon mustard

1 tbsp chopped fresh coriander

salt and pepper

1 Bring the chicken stock to the boil, add the pasta, and simmer for about 10 minutes until just cooked. Drain and cool under cold running water.

2 Mix the celery, avocados, garlic and chopped coriander in a bowl and add the cooled pasta. Sprinkle with the grated Cheddar.

3 To make the dressing place all the ingredients in a food processor and process until the coriander is finely chopped. Serve separately, or pour over the salad and toss before serving. Garnish with coriander leaves.

From top: Smoked Salmon, Lemon and Dill Pasta; Avocado and Pasta Salad with Coriander

Stuffed Tomatoes, with Wild Rice, Corn and Coriander

These tomatoes could be served as a light meal with crusty bread and a salad, or as an accompaniment to most meats or fish.

SERVES 4

8 medium tomatoes

⅓ cup corn kernels

2 tbsp white wine

¼ cup cooked wild rice

1 clove garlic

½ cup grated sharp Cheddar cheese

1 tbsp chopped fresh coriander

salt and pepper

1 tbsp olive oil

1 Cut the tops off the tomatoes and remove the seeds with a small teaspoon. Scoop out all the flesh and chop finely – also chop the tops.

2 Preheat the oven to 350°F. Put the chopped tomato in a pan. Add the corn and the white wine. Cover with a close-fitting lid and simmer until tender. Drain.

3 Mix together all the remaining ingredients except the olive oil, adding salt and pepper to taste. Carefully spoon the mixture into the tomatoes, piling it higher in the center. Sprinkle the oil over the top, arrange the tomatoes in an ovenproof dish, and bake at 350°F for 15-20 minutes until cooked through.

Spinach, Walnut and Gruyère Lasagne with Basil

This nutty lasagne is a delicious combination of flavors which easily equals the traditional meat and tomato version.

SERVES 8

12 oz spinach lasagne (quick cooking)

WALNUT AND TOMATO SAUCE

3 tbsp walnut oil

1 large onion, chopped

8 oz celeriac, finely chopped

1 x 14 oz can chopped tomatoes

1 large clove garlic, finely chopped

½ tsp sugar

⅔ cup chopped walnuts

⅔ cup Dubonnet

SPINACH AND GRUYERE SAUCE

⅓ cup butter

2 tbsp walnut oil

1 medium onion, chopped

⅔ cup flour

1 tsp mustard powder

5 cups milk

2 cups grated Gruyère or similar flavored cheese

salt and pepper

ground nutmeg

1 lb frozen spinach, thawed and puréed

2 tbsp basil, chopped

1 First make the walnut and tomato sauce. Heat the walnut oil and sauté the onion and celeriac. Cook for about 8-10 minutes. Meanwhile purée the tomatoes in a food processor. Add the garlic to the pan and cook for about 1 minute, then add the sugar, walnuts, tomatoes and Dubonnet. Season to taste. Simmer, uncovered, for 25 minutes.

2 To make the spinach and Gruyère sauce, melt the butter with the walnut oil and add the onion. Cook for 5 minutes, then stir in the flour. Cook for another minute and add the mustard powder and milk, stirring vigorously. When the sauce has come to a boil,

take off the heat and add three-quarters of the grated Gruyère. Season to taste with salt, pepper and nutmeg. Finally add the puréed spinach.

3 Preheat the oven to 350°F. Layer the lasagne in an ovenproof dish. Start with a layer of the spinach and Gruyère sauce, then add a little walnut and tomato sauce, then a layer of lasagne, and continue until the dish is full, ending with layer of either sauce.

4 Sprinkle the remaining Gruyère over the top of the dish, followed by the basil. Bake for 45 minutes.

Potato Salad with Curry Plant Mayonnaise

Potato salad can be made well in advance and is therefore a useful buffet dish. Its popularity means that there are very rarely any leftovers.

Serves 6

salt

2 lb new potatoes, in skins

1¼ cups good-quality store-bought
  mayonnaise

6 curry plant leaves, roughly chopped

black pepper

mixed lettuce or other salad greens,
  to serve

1 Place the potatoes in a pan of salted water and boil for 15 minutes or until tender. Drain and place in a large bowl to cool slightly.

2 Mix the mayonnaise with the curry plant leaves and black pepper. Stir these into the potatoes while they are still warm. Leave to cool, then serve on a bed of mixed lettuce or other assorted salad leaves.

Tomato, Savory and French Bean Salad

Savory and beans must have been invented for each other. This salad mixes them with ripe tomatoes, making a superb accompaniment for all cold meats or vegetable salads.

SERVES 4

1 lb string beans

2 lb ripe tomatoes

3 scallions, roughly sliced

1 tbsp pine nuts

4 sprigs fresh savory

FOR THE DRESSING

2 tbsp extra virgin olive oil

juice of 1 lime

3 oz soft blue cheese

1 clove garlic, peeled and crushed

salt and pepper

1 Prepare the dressing first so that it can stand a while before using. Place all the dressing ingredients in the bowl of a food processor, season to taste and blend until all the cheese has been finely chopped and you have a smooth dressing. Pour it into a pitcher.

2 Top and tail the beans, and boil in salted water until they are just cooked. Drain them and run cold water over them until they have completely cooled. Slice the tomatoes, or, if they are fairly small, quarter them.

3 Toss the salad ingredients together, except for the pine nuts and savory. Pour on the salad dressing. Sprinkle the pine nuts over the top, followed by the savory.

Summer Fruit Gâteau with Heartsease

No one could resist the appeal of little heartsease pansies. This cake would be lovely for a sentimental summer occasion in the garden.

SERVES 6-8

scant ½ cup soft margarine, plus more to grease mold
scant ½ cup sugar
2 tsp clear honey
1¼ cups self-rising flour
½ tsp baking powder
2 tbsp milk
2 eggs, plus white of one more for crystallizing
1 tbsp rosewater
1 tbsp Cointreau
16 heartsease pansy flowers
superfine sugar, as required, to crystallize
confectioners' sugar, to decorate
1 lb strawberries
strawberry leaves, to decorate

1 Preheat the oven to 375°F. Grease and lightly flour a ring mold. Take a large mixing bowl and add the soft margarine, sugar, honey, flour, baking powder, milk and 2 eggs to the mixing bowl and beat well for 1 minute. Add the rosewater and the Cointreau and mix well.

2 Pour the mixture into the pan and bake for 40 minutes. Allow to stand for a few minutes and then turn out onto the plate that you wish to serve it on.

3 Crystallize the heartsease pansies, by painting them with lightly beaten egg white and sprinkling with superfine sugar. Leave to dry.

4 Sift confectioners' sugar over the cake. Fill the center of the ring with strawberries – if they will not all fit, place some around the edge. Decorate with crystallized heartsease flowers and some strawberry leaves.

Borage, Mint and Lemon Balm Sorbet

Borage has such a pretty flower head that it is worth growing just to make this recipe, and to float the flowers in summer drinks. The sorbet itself has a very refreshing, delicate taste, perfect for a hot afternoon.

SERVES 6-8

2⅛ cups sugar
2⅛ cups water
6 sprigs mint, plus more to decorate
6 lemon balm leaves
1 cup white wine
2 tbsp lemon juice
borage sprigs, to decorate

1 Place the sugar and water in a saucepan with the washed herbs. Bring to a boil. Remove from the heat and add the wine. Cover and cool. Chill for several hours, then add the lemon juice. Freeze in a suitable container. As soon as the mixture begins to freeze, stir it briskly and replace in the freezer. Repeat every 15 minutes for at least 3 hours or until ready to serve.

2 To make the small ice bowls, pour about ½ in cold, boiled water into small freezer-proof bowls, about 1¼ pints in capacity, and arrange some herbs in the water. Place in the freezer. Once this has frozen add a little more water to cover the herbs and freeze.

3 Place a smaller freezer-proof bowl inside each larger bowl and put a heavy weight inside such as a metal weight from some scales. Fill with more cooled boiled water, float more herbs in this and freeze.

4 To release the ice bowls, warm the inner bowl with a small amount of very hot water and twist it out. Warm the outer bowl by standing it in very hot water for a few seconds, then tip out the ice bowl. Spoon the sorbet into the ice bowls, decorate with sprigs of mint and borage and serve.

From top: *Summer Fruit Gateau; Borage, Mint and Lemon Balm Sorbet*

Lemon Meringue Bombe with Mint Chocolate

This easy ice cream will cause a sensation at a dinner party – it is unusual but quite the most delicious combination of tastes that you can imagine.

SERVES 6-8

2 large lemons

²/₃ cup granulated sugar

3 small sprigs fresh mint

²/₃ cup heavy or whipping cream

2¹/₂ cups thick natural yogurt

2 large meringues

8 oz good-quality mint chocolate, grated

1 Slice the rind off the lemons with a potato peeler, then squeeze them for juice. Place the lemon rind and sugar in a food processor and blend finely. Add the cream, yogurt and lemon juice and process thoroughly. Pour the mixture into a mixing bowl and add the meringues, roughly crushed.

2 Reserve one of the mint sprigs and chop the rest finely. Add to the cream and lemon mixture. Pour into a 1¹/₄ quart glass bowl and freeze for 4 hours.

3 When the ice cream has frozen, scoop out the middle and pour in the grated mint chocolate, reserving a little for the garnish. Replace the ice cream to cover the chocolate and refreeze.

4 To turn out, dip the basin in very hot water for a few seconds to loosen the ice cream, then turn the basin upside down over the serving plate. Decorate with grated chocolate and a sprig of mint.

Apple Mint and Pink Grapefruit Fool

Apple mint can easily run riot in the herb garden; this is an excellent way of using up an abundant crop.

SERVES 4-6

1 lb tart apples, peeled, cored and sliced

8 oz pink grapefruit segments

3 tbsp clear honey

2 tbsp water

6 large sprigs apple mint, plus more to garnish

²⁄₃ cup heavy cream

1¼ cups custard

1 Place the apples, grapefruit, honey, water and apple mint in a pan, cover and simmer for 10 minutes until soft. Leave in the pan to cool, then discard the apple mint. Purée the mixture in a food processor.

2 Whip the heavy cream until it forms soft peaks, and fold into the custard, keeping 2 tablespoonfuls to decorate. Carefully fold the cream into the apple and grapefruit mixture. Serve in individual glasses, chilled and decorated with swirls of cream and small sprigs of apple mint.

Passion Fruit and Angelica Syllabub

Passion fruit have a unique fragrance and flavor which makes this syllabub quite irresistible.

SERVES 6

6 passion fruit

1 tbsp chopped crystallized angelica, plus more to decorate

grated rind and juice of 2 limes

¹⁄₂ cup white wine

¹⁄₃ cup confectioners' sugar

1¹⁄₄ cups heavy cream

²⁄₃ cup thick-set natural yogurt

1 Scoop out the flesh, seeds and juice of the passion fruit and divide between 6 serving dishes. Place the crystallized angelica in a food processor with the lime rind and juice, and blend to a purée.

2 In a large bowl, mix the lime pureé with the wine and sugar. Stir until the sugar is dissolved.

3 Whip the heavy cream until it begins to form soft peaks and then gradually beat in the wine mixture – the cream should thicken slightly. Whisk in the yogurt.

4 Spoon the cream mixture over the passion fruit, and refrigerate until ready to serve. Decorate with more crystallized angelica before serving.

Japanese Fruit Salad with Mint and Coffee

This dessert was served in a Japanese department store. Although it sounds a little strange, it works very well – the coffee flavor is excellent with the fruit.

SERVES 6

12 canned lychees and the juice from the can

1 small fresh pineapple

2 large ripe pears

2 fresh peaches

12 strawberries

6 small sprigs of mint plus 12 extra sprigs to decorate

1 tbsp instant coffee granules

2 tbsp boiling water

²/₃ cup heavy cream

1 Peel the fruit as necessary and chop into equal-sized pieces. Place all the fruit in a large glass bowl and pour on the lychee juice.

2 Put the mint, coffee granules and boiling water in a food processor. Blend until smooth. Add the cream and process again briefly.

3 Serve the fruit salad drained and chilled, with two small sprigs of mint on each plate, and the coffee sauce separately.

Clementines in Beaumes de Venise with Geranium

The fantastic bonus of using this recipe is that you have half a bottle of Beaumes de Venise left over, which simply has to be drunk as a digestif.

<u>SERVES 6</u>

10 whole clementines
12 scented geranium leaves
½ bottle Muscat de Beaumes de Venise or other dessert wine
orange leaves, to decorate

1 Peel the clementines and remove the pith.

2 Place the clementines in a glass dish and pour over the wine. Add the scented geranium leaves and refrigerate overnight. Discard leaves, then serve chilled and decorated with orange leaves. Any juice left over from this dessert can be served as a *digestif*.

Chocolate Mint Truffle Filo Parcels

These exquisite little parcels are utterly irresistible. There will be no leftovers.

18 PARCELS

1 tbsp very finely chopped mint

¾ cup ground almonds

2 oz plain chocolate, grated

2 apples, peeled and grated

4 oz crème fraîche or whole-milk ricotta cheese

9 large sheets filo pastry

⅓ cup butter, melted

1 tbsp confectioners' sugar

1 tbsp cocoa powder, to dust

1 Preheat the oven to 375°F. Mix the mint, almonds, chocolate, crème fraîche or ricotta and grated apple in a bowl. Cut the filo pastry sheets into 3 in squares, and cover with a cloth to stop them drying out.

2 Brush a square of filo with melted butter, lay on a second sheet, brush again, and place a spoonful of filling in the middle of the top sheet. Bring in all four corners and twist to form a purse shape. Repeat to make 18 parcels.

3 Place the filo parcels on a cookie sheet, well brushed with melted butter. Bake for approximately 10 minutes. Leave to cool and then dust with the confectioners' sugar, and then with the cocoa powder.

From left to right: *Clementines in Beaumes de Venise with Geranium; Chocolate Mint Truffle Filo Parcels*

Rosemary Vinegar

Flavored vinegars make a huge difference to the taste of a salad dressing. They are very simple to make, and the jars are a pretty windowsill decoration. Try the same recipe with nasturtium flowers, if you like.

ABOUT 2½ CUPS

fresh rosemary sprigs, to fill a 2½ cup measure, plus more to decorate
2½ cups white distilled vinegar

1 Fill a sterilized wide-necked bottle or jar with the sprigs of rosemary. Fill to the top with vinegar. Cover tightly and place in a sunny spot for around 4-6 weeks.

2 Filter the vinegar mixture through a coffee filter paper. Discard the rosemary. Heat the vinegar until it begins to simmer, but do not boil.

3 Wash the bottle or jar and its lid well in hot, soapy water, rinse thoroughly, and dry in a warm oven. Pour the vinegar back into it or other sterilized decorative bottles. You can add a fresh sprig or two of rosemary for decorative purposes if you wish, then seal. Store in a dark place. Use within one year.

Herb Garden Dressing

This dried mixture will keep through the winter until your herbs are growing again. It can be used to flavor salad dressings and to sprinkle over vegetables, casseroles and stews.

1 cup dried oregano

1 cup dried basil

½ cup dried marjoram

½ cup dried dill weed

½ cup dried mint leaves

½ cup onion powder

2 tbsp dry mustard

2 tsp salt

1 tbsp freshly ground black pepper

1 Mix the ingredients together and keep in a sealed jar to use as needed.

2 When making a batch of salad dressing, take 2 tbsp of the herb mixture and add it to 1½ cups of extra virgin olive oil and ½ cup cider vinegar. Mix thoroughly and allow to stand for 1 hour or so. Mix again and correct the seasoning before using.

Dill Pickles

A good pickle to have in your kitchen cupboard. It is excellent sliced onto a hamburger, served with cold meats, and in canapés and snacks. If you like, try varying the type of cucumbers used. The French are fond of tiny 'cornichons', while the traditional Northern American versions are much larger.

ABOUT 2½ QUARTS

6 small cucumbers

2 cups water

4 cups white wine vinegar

½ cup salt

3 bay leaves

3 tbsp dill seed

2 cloves garlic, slivered

dill flowerheads, to garnish

1 Slice the cucumbers into medium-thick slices. Put the water, vinegar and salt in a saucepan and boil, then remove immediately from the heat.

2 Layer the herbs and garlic between slices of cucumber in sterilized preserving jars until the jars are full, then cover with the warm salt and vinegar mixture. Leave on a sunny window sill for at least a week before using.

Parsley, Sage and Thyme Oil

Herb oils are an excellent ingredient for use in stir-fry cooking as well as salad dressings. This mixed herb combination is a good basic choice, but you can also be adventurous and try other, more exotic ingredients. Adding garlic and chillis to a herb oil produces a fiery condiment: try dribbling a tiny amount on to pasta for extra flavor.

ABOUT 2½ CUPS

2½ cups sunflower oil

½ cup chopped fresh parsley, curly or Italian

⅛ cup chopped fresh sage

¼ cup chopped fresh thyme

1 Pour the oil into a sterilized jar and add all the herbs. Cover and allow to stand at room temperature for about a week, no longer. Stir or shake occasionally during that time.

2 Then strain off the oil into a sterilized bottle and discard the used herbs. Add a fresh sprig or two for decorative purposes if you wish. Seal the jar carefully. Store, preferably in a cool place, for 6 months at the most.

Cranberry and Port Sauce with Lemon Thyme

Cranberry and port sauce is delicious served with turkey, chicken, pork or ham. Lemon thyme really sets off its unique flavor.

ABOUT 2½ CUPS

4 tbsp port

4 tbsp orange juice

½ cup sugar

8 oz fresh cranberries, picked over

1 tbsp finely grated orange rind

1 tbsp very finely chopped lemon thyme

1 Pour the port and orange juice into a saucepan and add the sugar. Place the pan over a low heat and stir frequently with a metal spoon to dissolve the sugar.

2 Transfer the mixture to a larger pan. Increase the heat a little and add the cranberries. Bring the mixture to the boil and simmer for 5 minutes, stirring occasionally, until the cranberries are just tender and the skins begin to burst.

3 Remove the pan from the heat and carefully mix in the orange rind and lemon thyme.

4 Leave the sauce to cool, then pour into sterilized glass jars and seal with waxed paper circles and cellophane lids secured with rubber bands. Add a label and decorate with short lengths of string tied around the top if you like.

Lemon and Mint Curd

Home-made lemon curd is infinitely tastier than the commercial variety. The addition of mint gives this version an interesting extra tang. Try experimenting with different types of mint. Lemon curd is best made using the freshest of ingredients. Buy fresh eggs, and try to find unwaxed lemons.

ABOUT 3 LB

6 fresh mint leaves

4 cups superfine sugar

1½ cups unsalted butter, cut into chunks

rind of 6 lemons, thinly pared, in large pieces, and their juice

8 eggs, beaten

1 Place the mint leaves and sugar in a food processor, and blend until the mint leaves are very finely chopped and combined with the sugar.

2 Put the mint sugar and all the other ingredients into a bowl and mix together.

3 Set the bowl over a pan of simmering water. Cook, whisking gently, until all the butter has melted and the sugar has dissolved. Remove the lemon rind.

4 Continue to cook in this way, stirring frequently, for 35-40 minutes or until the mixture thickens. Pour into sterilized glass jars, filling them up to the rim. Seal with waxed paper circles and cellophane lids secured with rubber bands. Add a label and tie short lengths of string around the top of the jars to decorate. This lemon curd should be used within 3 months.

From top: *Lemon and Mint Curd; Cranberry and Port Sauce with Lemon Thyme*

Rhubarb and Ginger Mint Preserve

Ginger mint is easily grown in the garden, and is just the thing to boost the flavor of rhubarb jam. Stewed rhubarb also tastes good with a little ginger mint added to the pan.

ABOUT 6 LB

4 lb rhubarb

1 cup water

juice of 1 lemon

2 in piece fresh ginger root, peeled

6 cups sugar

⅔ cup preserved ginger in syrup, drained and chopped

2-3 tbsp very finely chopped ginger mint leaves

1 Wash and trim the rhubarb, cutting it into small pieces about 1 in long. Place the rhubarb, water and lemon juice in a preserving pan and bring to the boil. Bruise the piece of fresh ginger root and add it to the pan. Simmer, stirring frequently, until the rhubarb is soft and then remove the ginger.

2 Add the sugar and stir until it has dissolved. Bring the mixture to a boil and boil rapidly for 10-15 minutes, or until setting point is reached. With a metal slotted spoon, remove any scum from the surface of the jam.

3 Add the preserved ginger and ginger mint leaves. Pour into sterilized glass jars, seal with waxed paper circles and cover with cellophane lids secured with rubber bands. Decorate with brown paper raffia.

Rose Petal Jelly

This subtle jelly is ideal for polite afternoon teas with thinly sliced pieces of bread and butter – it adds a real summer afternoon flavor to the bread.

About 2 lb

2½ cups red or pink
 rose petals

1⅞ cups water

generous 3 cups superfine
 sugar

scant ½ cup bottled white
 grape juice

scant ½ cup bottled red
 grape juice

2 oz package powdered
 fruit pectin

2 tbsp rosewater

1 Trim all the rose petals at the base to remove the white tips. Place the petals, water and about one-eighth of the sugar in a saucepan and bring to a boil. Reduce the heat and simmer for 5 minutes. Remove from the heat and leave to stand overnight for the rose fragrance to infuse.

2 Strain the flowers from the syrup, and put the syrup in a preserving pan or suitable saucepan. Add the grape juices and pectin. Boil hard for 1 minute. Add the rest of the sugar and stir well. Boil the mixture hard for 1 minute more. Remove from the heat.

3 Test for setting – it should make a soft jelly, not a thick jam. Do this by placing a teaspoonful of the hot mixture on a saucer. Leave it to cool: the surface should wrinkle when pushed with a finger. If it is still runny, return the pan to the heat and continue boiling and testing until the jelly sets.

4 Finally add the rosewater. Ladle the jelly into sterilized glass jars and seal with waxed paper circles and cellophane lids secured with rubber bands. Decorate the tops of the jars with circles of fabric held in place with lengths of ribbon.

Cheese and Marjoram Scones

A great success for a hearty tea. With savory toppings, these scones can make a good basis for a light lunch, served with a crunchy, green salad.

ABOUT 18 SCONES

1 cup whole wheat flour

1 cup self-rising flour

pinch salt

scant 3 tbsp butter

¼ tsp dry mustard

2 tsp dried marjoram

½ – ⅔ cup finely grated sharp Cheddar cheese

1 tsp sunflower oil (optional)

½ cup milk, or as required to make soft dough

⅓ cup pecan nuts or walnuts, chopped

1 Gently sift the two kinds of flour into a bowl and add the salt. Cut the butter into small pieces, and rub these into the flour until it resembles fine breadcrumbs.

2 Add the mustard, marjoram and grated cheese, and mix in sufficient milk to make a soft dough. Knead the dough lightly.

3 Preheat the oven to 425°F. Roll out the dough on a floured surface to about ¾ in thickness and cut it out with a 2 in square cutter. Grease some cookie sheets with the paper from the butter (or use a little sunflower oil), and place the scones on the sheets.

4 Brush the scones with a little milk and sprinkle the chopped pecans or walnuts over the top. Bake for 12 minutes. Serve warm.

Dill and Potato Cakes

Potato cakes are quite scrumptious and should be more widely made. Try this spendid combination and you are sure to be converted.

ABOUT 10 CAKES

2 cups self-rising flour

3 tbsp butter, softened

pinch of salt

1 tbsp finely chopped fresh dill

**scant 1 cup mashed potato,
  freshly made**

2-3 tbsp milk, as required

1 Preheat the oven to 450°F. Sift the flour into a bowl, and add the butter, salt and dill. Mix in the mashed potato and enough milk to make a soft, pliable dough.

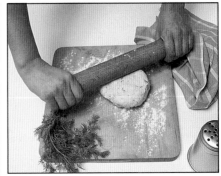

2 Roll out the dough on a well-floured surface until it is fairly thin. Cut into several neat rounds with a 3 in cutter.

3 Grease a cookie sheet, place the cakes on it, and bake for 20-25 minutes until risen and golden.

Rosemary Bread

Sliced thinly, this herb bread is delicious with cheese or soup for a light meal.

1 LOAF

1 x ¼ oz package dried fast-action yeast

1½ cups whole wheat flour

1½ cups self-rising flour

2 tbsp butter, plus more to grease bowl and pan

¼ cup warm water (110°F)

1 cup milk, whole or 2% (room temperature)

1 tbsp sugar

1 tsp salt

1 tbsp sesame seeds

1 tbsp dried chopped onion

1 tbsp fresh rosemary leaves, plus more to decorate

1 cup cubed Cheddar cheese

coarse salt, to decorate

1 Mix the fast-action yeast with the flours in a large mixing bowl. Melt the butter. Stir in the warm water, milk, sugar, butter, salt, sesame seeds, onion and rosemary. Knead thoroughly until quite smooth.

2 Flatten the dough, then add the cheese cubes. Quickly knead them in until they have been well combined.

3 Place the dough into a clean bowl greased with a little butter, turning it so that it becomes greased on all sides. Cover with a clean, dry cloth. Put the greased bowl and dough in a warm place for about 1½ hours, or until the dough has risen and doubled in size.

4 Grease a 9 x 5 in loaf pan with the remaining butter. Knock down the dough to remove some of the air, and shape it into a loaf. Put the loaf into the pan, cover with the clean cloth used earlier and leave for about 1 hour until doubled in size once again. Preheat the oven to 375°F.

5 Bake for 30 minutes. During the last 5-10 minutes of baking, cover the loaf with foil to prevent it from becoming too dark. Remove from the loaf pan and leave to cool on a wire rack. Decorate with rosemary leaves and coarse salt scattered on top.

Blackberry, Sloe Gin and Rosewater Muffins

Other berries can be substituted for the blackberries, such as elderberries or blueberries.

ABOUT 12 MUFFINS

2½ cups plain unbleached flour

generous ¼ cup light brown sugar

4 tsp baking powder

pinch of salt

generous ½ cup chopped blanched almonds

generous ½ cup fresh blackberries

2 eggs

⅞ cup milk

4 tbsp melted butter, plus a little more to grease cups, if using

1 tbsp sloe gin

1 tbsp rosewater

1 Mix the flour, sugar, baking powder and salt in a bowl and gently stir in the almonds and blackberries, mixing them well to coat with the flour mixture. Preheat the oven to 400°F.

2 In another bowl, mix the eggs with the milk, then gradually add the butter, sloe gin and rosewater. Make a well in the center of the bowl of dry ingredients and add the egg and milk mixture. Stir well.

3 Spoon the mixture into greased muffin cups or cases. Bake for 20-25 minutes or until browned. Turn out the muffins on to a wire rack to cool. Serve with butter.

Chocolate and Mint Fudge Cake

Chocolate and mint are popular partners and they blend well in this unusual recipe. The French have been using potato flour in cakes for years. Mashed potato works just as well.

1 CAKE

6-10 fresh mint leaves
¾ cup superfine sugar
½ cup butter, plus extra to grease pan
½ cup freshly made mashed potato
2 oz semi-sweet chocolate, melted
1½ cups self-rising flour
pinch of salt
2 eggs, beaten
FILLING
4 fresh mint leaves
½ cup butter
⅞ cup confectioners' sugar
2 tbsp chocolate mint liqueur
TOPPING
1 cup butter
¼ cup granulated sugar
2 tbsp chocolate mint liqueur
2 tbsp water
1½ cups confectioners' sugar
¼ cup cocoa powder
pecan halves, to decorate

1 Tear the mint leaves into small pieces and mix with the superfine sugar. Leave overnight. When you use the flavored sugar, remove the leaves and discard them.

Opposite: *Chocolate and Mint Fudge Cake; Strawberry Mint Sponge*

2 Preheat the oven to 400°F. Cream the butter and sugar with the mashed potato, then add the melted chocolate. Sift in half the flour with a pinch of salt and add half of the beaten eggs. Mix well, then add the remaining flour and the eggs.

3 Grease and line an 8 in pan and pile in the mixture. Bake for 25-30 minutes or until a skewer or pointed knife stuck into the center comes away clean. Turn out on to a wire rack to cool. When cool, split into two layers.

4 Chop the mint leaves in a food processor, then add the butter and sugar. Once the cake is cool, sprinkle the chocolate mint liqueur over both halves and sandwich together with the filling.

5 Put the butter, granulated sugar, liqueur and water into a small pan. Melt the butter and sugar, then boil for 5 minutes. Sieve the confectioners' sugar and cocoa and add the butter and liqueur mixture. Beat until cool and thick. Cover the cake with this mixture, and decorate with the pecan halves.

Strawberry Mint Cake

This combination of fruit, mint and ice cream is a real winner.

1 CAKE

6-10 fresh mint leaves, plus more to decorate
¾ cup superfine sugar
¾ cup butter, plus extra to grease pan
3 eggs
1½ cups self-rising flour
2½ pints strawberry ice cream
2½ cups heavy cream
2 tbsp mint liqueur
2 cups fresh strawberries

1 Tear the mint into pieces and mix with the superfine sugar. Leave overnight.

2 Grease and line a deep springform cake pan. Preheat the oven to 375°F. Remove the mint from the sugar. Mix the butter and sugar together and add the flour, then the eggs. Pile the mixture into the pan.

3 Bake for 20-25 minutes, or until a skewer or pointed knife inserted in the middle comes away clean. Turn out on to a wire rack to cool. When cool, carefully split horizontally into two equal halves.

4 Clean the cake pan and line it with plastic wrap. Put the bottom half of the cake back in the pan. Spread on the ice cream mixture and level the top. Put on the top half of the cake and freeze for 3-4 hours.

5 Whip the cream with the mint liqueur. Remove the cake from the freezer and quickly spread a layer of whipped cream all over it, leaving a rough finish. Put the cake back into the freezer until about 10 minutes before serving. Decorate the cake with the strawberries and place fresh mint leaves on the plate around the cake.

Carrot Cake with Geranium Cheese

At a pinch you can justify carrot cake as being good for you – at least this is an excuse for taking a good many calories on board. But the flavor is definitely worth it.

1 CAKE

2-3 scented geranium leaves (preferably with a lemon scent)
2 cups icing sugar
1 cup self-rising flour
1 tsp baking of soda
½ tsp ground cinnamon
½ tsp ground cloves
1 cup brown sugar
1½ cups grated carrot
½ cup sultanas
½ cup finely chopped preserved ginger
½ cup pecan nuts
⅔ cup sunflower oil
2 eggs, lightly beaten
butter to grease tin
CREAM CHEESE TOPPING
generous ¼ cup cream cheese
2 tbsp softened butter
1 tsp grated lemon rind

1 Put the geranium leaves, torn into small- to medium-sized pieces, in a small bowl and mix with the confectioners' sugar. Leave in a warm place overnight for the sugar to take up the scent of the leaves.

From left: *Lavender Cookies; Carrot Cake with Geranium Cheese*

2 Sift the flour, soda and spices together. Add the soft brown sugar, carrots, sultanas, ginger and pecans. Stir well then add the oil and beaten eggs. Mix with an electric beater for about 5 minutes, or 10-15 minutes longer by hand.

3 Preheat the oven to 350°F. Grease a 5 x 9 in loaf pan, line the base with waxed paper, and then grease the paper. Pour the mixture into the pan and bake for about 1 hour. Remove the cake from the oven, leave to stand for a few minutes, and then turn it out on to a wire rack until completely cool.

4 While the cake is cooling, make the cream cheese topping. Remove the pieces of geranium leaf from the confectioners' sugar and discard them. Place the cream cheese, butter and lemon rind in a bowl. Using an electric beater or a wire whisk, gradually add the confectioners' sugar, beating well until smooth.

5 Once the cake has cooled, cover the top with the cream cheese mixture.

Lavender Cookies

Instead of lavender you can use any other flavoring, such as cinnamon, lemon, orange or mint.

ABOUT 30

⅝ cup butter, plus more to grease baking sheets
½ cup granulated sugar
1 egg, beaten
1 tbsp dried lavender flowers
1½ cups self-rising flour
assorted leaves and flowers, to decorate

1 Preheat the oven to 350°F. Cream the butter and sugar together, then stir in the egg. Mix in the lavender flowers and the flour.

2 Grease two cookie sheets and drop spoonfuls of the mixture on them. Bake for about 15-20 minutes, until the cookies are golden. Serve with some fresh leaves and flowers to decorate.

Herbal Punch

A good party drink that will have people coming back for more, and a delightful non-alcoholic choice for drivers.

SERVES 30 PLUS

2 cups honey

8½ pints water

2 cups freshly squeezed lemon juice

3 tbsp fresh rosemary leaves, plus more to decorate

8 cups sliced strawberries

2 cups freshly squeezed lime juice

4 pints sparkling mineral water

ice cubes

3-4 scented geranium leaves

1 Combine the honey, 4½ cups water, one-eighth of the lemon juice, and the rosemary leaves in a saucepan. Bring to a boil, stirring until all the honey is dissolved. Remove from the heat and allow to stand for about 30 minutes. When cool, strain into a large punch bowl.

2 Press the strawberries through a fine sieve into the punch bowl, add the rest of the water and lemon juice, and the lime juice and sparkling water. Stir gently. Add the ice cubes 5 minutes before serving, and float the geranium and rosemary leaves on the surface.

Angelica Liqueur

This should be drunk in tiny glasses after a large meal. Not only will it help the digestive system, it tastes superb.

ABOUT 1¼ QUARTS

1 tsp fennel seeds

1 tsp aniseed

20 coriander seeds

2-3 cloves

2 tbsp crystallized angelica stems

1 cup superfine sugar

1 bottle vodka

1 Crush the fennel, aniseed and coriander seeds and cloves a little, and chop the crystallized angelica stems.

2 Put the seeds and angelica stems into a large preserving jar.

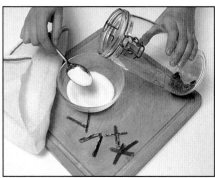

3 Add the sugar. Pour on the vodka and leave by a sunny window for 2 weeks, swirling the mixture daily.

4 Strain through fine muslin into a sterilized bottle and seal. Leave in a dark cupboard for at least 4 months. Drink in small quantities with a piece of angelica in each glass.

Strawberry and Mint Champagne

This is a simple concoction that makes a bottle of champagne go a lot further. It tastes very special on a hot summer's evening.

SERVES 4-6

1 lb strawberries

6-8 fresh mint leaves

1 bottle champagne or sparkling white wine

1 Purée the strawberries and mint leaves in a food processor.

2 Strain through a fine sieve into a bowl. Half fill a glass with the mixture and top up with champagne. Decorate with a sprig of mint.

Melon, Ginger and Borage Cup

Melon and ginger complement each other magnificently. If you prefer, you can leave out the powdered ginger – the result is milder but equally delicious.

SERVES 6-8

½ large honeydew melon

1 quart ginger beer

1 tsp powdered ginger (or to taste)

borage sprigs with flowers, to decorate

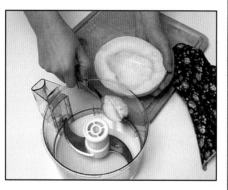

1 Discard the seeds from the half melon and scoop the flesh into a food processor. Blend to a thin purée.

2 Pour the purée into a large jug and top up with ginger beer. Add powdered ginger to taste. Pour into glasses and decorate with borage.

From left: *Melon, Ginger and Borage Cup; Strawberry and Mint Champagne*

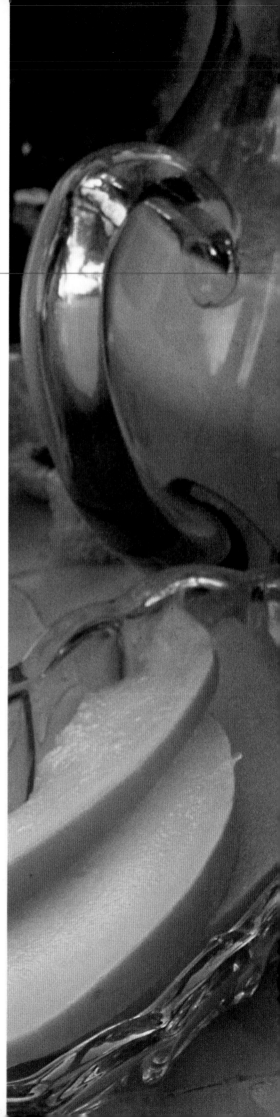

Mint Cup

Mint is a perennially popular flavor and this delicate cup is a wonderful mixture with an intriguing taste.

SERVES 1

4 sprigs fresh mint
½ tsp sugar
crushed ice
½ tsp lemon juice
2 tbsp grapefruit juice
½ cup chilled tonic water
lemon slices, to decorate

1 Crush two of the sprigs of mint with the sugar and put these into a glass. Fill the glass with crushed ice.

2 Add the lemon juice, grapefruit juice and tonic water. Stir gently and decorate with the remaining mint sprigs and slices of lemon.

Elderflower Sparkler

The flavor of elderflowers is becoming popular once again. This recipe produces one of the most delicious drinks ever concocted. Many prefer it to real French champagne because of its light and refreshing taste.

ABOUT 10 PINTS

3½ **cups superfine sugar**

2 **cups hot water**

4 **large fresh elderflower heads**

2 **tbsp white wine vinegar**

juice and pared rind of 1 lemon

8½ **pints water, heated almost to**
  boiling

1 Mix the sugar with the hot water. Pour the mixture into a large glass or plastic container. Add all the remaining ingredients. Stir well, cover and leave for about 5 days.

2 Strain off the liquid into sterilized screw-top bottles (glass or plastic). Leave for a further week or so. Serve very cold with slivers of lemon rind.

Chamomile Tea

The pretty yellow flowers that are used for brewing this tea give the infusion a delicate color.

SERVES 4

2½ cups boiling water

1 tbsp dried chamomile flower heads

superfine sugar or honey (optional)

1 Put the chamomile flowers into a teapot or directly into a cup or mug. Pour on the boiling water and leave to infuse for about 5 minutes, or longer if you prefer a stronger flavor.

2 Strain the tea and, if you wish, add a small amount of sugar or honey and stir to dissolve.

OTHER HERBAL TEAS

- Iced mint tea with fresh lemon verbena.
- Mint and lavender flower tea, serve iced in summer.
- Marigold and lemon balm.

210

Blackcurrant and Lemon Verbena Tisane

 A warm, comforting fruity drink that will revive you on a cold winter's night. It is also excellent served chilled on a hot summer's day.

SERVES 4

2½ cups boiling water

1 tbsp fresh or frozen blackcurrants

10 lemon verbena leaves

brown sugar (optional)

1 Pour the boiling water over the blackcurrants and lemon verbena leaves and leave to infuse for about 5 minutes, or longer to taste.

2 Strain the liquid into cups or tall glasses and decorate with a sprig of lemon verbena. If you prefer a sweeter drink, stir in 1 tsp of brown sugar.

HERBS IN THE HOME

Fresh Herbal Wreath

This ring looks very attractive hanging in the kitchen. If you choose culinary herbs to include in the design, it can act as a dried herb store as well, and you can snip pieces off the ring to include in recipes as they are needed. The example is purely decorative, as the herbs are not usually needed for cooking.

hot glue gun

silver rose wire

'twiggy' wreath ring, approximately
   10 in in diameter

small bunches of whichever herbs are
   handy – this example includes leaves
   and sprigs of golden sage,
   chamomile, lavender, santolina,
   scented geranium

scissors

2 yd co-ordinating ribbon,
   ³⁄₄ in wide

1 Use the hot glue gun or wire to attach a good covering of golden sage and anthemis leaves to the wreath ring.

2 Make small bunches of the lavender and santolina, binding them with wire on to the wreath ring.

3 Choose the point where you want to attach the ribbons, and put three medium-sized scented geranium leaves here to act as a backing for the ribbon. Make double loops and streamers with the ribbon of your choice, bind them with wire and glue or wire them on to the ring. Other small flowers or herbs could also be fixed on as an extra. Once the herbs start to dry, keep adding more so that the ring becomes fuller and fuller. It will then eventually dry to a beautiful decoration.

Lavender Nosegay Pot

Lavender smells wonderful in any room, and if you can use a deep blue variety it looks even better. Another suggestion is to use a selection of lavenders, perhaps pink, white and pale blue, together to make a different arrangement. It is better to use ready dried lavender than fresh, as the fresh wilts.

terracotta pot
1 block gray florist's foam for dried flowers
4-5 large bunches lavender
scissors
1 yd ribbon
thin florist's wire (optional)

1 Press the foam into the pot. Decide on the height you would like the lavender and trim the stalks to that length, plus about 2 in to go into the foam. Insert a small bunch into the center of the pot.

2 Continue filling the pot tightly with lavender. It takes quite a few bunches to fill even a small pot, so have plenty to hand.

3 Once the pot is completely full and you cannot get another stem into the arrangement, wrap the ribbon around the top of the pot and tie a large bow. The ribbon used here was wired with thin florist's wire, which makes it easier to produce an attractive bow.

Tussie-Mussie

This delightful herbal posy is easily made and would make a delightful alternative to a bottle of wine as a gift to take to a dinner party.

6 Minuet roses
1 bunch southernwood
florist's wire
hellebore leaves
few stems of asparagus fern
posy frill
florist's tape
scissors
ribbon, as preferred

1 Take one of the roses and wrap some southernwood around it. Bind well with wire. Make up and add small bunches of hellebore leaves.

2 Add small wired bunches of southernwood and asparagus fern.

3 Continue to bind in more roses and greenery, until you are happy with the size and composition of the posy. Push the flowers through the center of the posy frill, secure with florist's tape and tie ribbons around it to decorate.

Rose and Herb Basket

Fresh flowers and herbs make a perfect partnership. The scent of the roses and herbs together is subtle but wonderful, especially if you hang the arrangement so that you brush lightly against it as you pass – but do not place it so that the roses are likely to be crushed. If you do not have the herbs listed here, there are many alternatives, for example sage and rosemary, and the leaves of any evergreen shrub.

1 block green florist's foam
small flower basket with handle
plastic sheet
florist's tape
scissors
hellebore leaves
scented geranium leaves
12 small sprays golden oregano
12 cream roses

1 Soak the florist's foam well. Line the basket with the plastic sheet so that no water will seep through the basketwork. Put the foam brick inside the liner and hold it in with tape. Cover the foam completely with a mixture of hellebore leaves and scented geranium leaves.

2 Add the sprays of golden oregano, placing them so that there will be room between them for the roses. Place the roses evenly throughout the arrangement, putting six on each side of the handle so that the arrangement looks well balanced, but not too symmetrical. Top up the foam with water each day to prolong the life of the arrangement.

Front to back: *Tussie-Mussie; Rose and Herb Basket*

Herbal Tablepiece

Extremely strong-smelling herbs should be avoided for table centers, as their fragrance may overpower the flavor of the meal. However, gently scented herbs make a delightful table decoration.

shallow basket without handle

2 blocks gray florist's foam for dried flowers

florist's wire

florist's tape

scissors

2 bunches cardoon thistles

3 large ivory candles

bunches of dried herbs, where possible in flower, including oregano, lavender, marjoram, fennel

1 Fill the basket with foam, wedging it into position. Group the cardoon heads into three positions in the foam. Make hairpins from wires, and tape three hairpins around the base of each candle. Place the candles into the foam.

2 Wire small bunches of lavender and marjoram, and spread evenly around the arrangement.

3 Place the fennel flower heads in the arrangement singly or wired together in groups, depending upon the space you wish to fill.

Caution: make sure that this arrangement is never left unattended with the candles alight.

Dried Herbal Topiary Tree

Topiary trees are an attractive way of displaying flowers and natural objects. This design includes small terracotta pots, which add to the textural interest in the top of the tree.

1 large terracotta pot for the base
cement or plaster of paris
piece of tree branch for the trunk
5 in ball of gray florist's foam for
 dried flowers
small pieces of similar foam
2 large bunches of glycerined copper-
 beech foliage or other preserved
 foliage
scissors
heavy-gauge florist's wire
wire cutters
12 miniature terracotta pots
2 bunches golden rod
light florist's wire
hot glue gun, if necessary
2 bunches poppy heads

1 Cover the hole in the large terra-cotta pot and half fill with wet cement or plaster of paris. As the cement begins to harden, stand the branch in the pot to form the trunk. Leave to dry for at least 48 hours before proceeding to next step.

2 Press the foam ball on to the trunk, making sure it is firmly in place, but not so far down that the trunk comes out the other side of the ball. Cover the cement in the base with pieces of foam.

3 Cover the ball and the base with pieces of copper beech or other preserved foliage. Thread heavy-gauge wire through the holes in the small pots and twist to make a stem so that they can be attached to the tree and pressed into the foam at the base.

4 Arrange the pots throughout the tree and base, and fill with small wired bunches of golden rod, trimming with scissors where needed. These can be glued into position if necessary, using the hot glue gun. Finally, add the poppy heads.

Herbal Christmas Wreath

Orange slices can be dried on a wire rack in an oven at the lowest possible setting for several hours until crisp.
They should then be carefully varnished to prevent reabsorption of moisture.

a few stems fresh holly

2 sprays fresh conifer

scissors

hot glue gun

wreath ring, approximately
  9 in diameter

gold spray paint

2 in terracotta pot

broken pieces of terracotta
  pot

7 ears of wheat, sprayed gold

1 small bunch dried sage

1 small bunch oregano

florist's wire

3 dried orange slices

1 Attach the holly and conifer to the ring using the hot glue gun. Cover approximately half the ring.

2 In a well-ventilated area, spray a little gold paint on to the pot and pieces of pot and glue them to the design. Add the ears of wheat. Make small bunches of sage and tuck those among the pieces of broken pot.

3 Make a chunky bunch of the dried oregano, wiring it together. Glue into the main pot in the center of the design. Cut the orange slices into quarters and glue those into the arrangement. The fresh ingredients will dry on the wreath and look most attractive.

Dried Herbal Posy

This pretty posy could be given as a present or to say 'thank you'. It would also make a very pretty dressing table decoration. The ingredients are dried, so it can be made well in advance, or make a few to have to hand as gifts.

1 small bunch dried red roses

florist's wire

1 small bunch alchemilla

1 small bunch marjoram

cotton posy frill, deep pink

3 sprays dried bay

hot glue gun

florist's tape

scissors

ribbon, as preferred

1 Start with a small cluster of red roses, binding them with wire to form a center. Add some alchemilla, binding gently but firmly in the same spot.

2 Bind in some marjoram and then more red roses and alchemilla, until you are happy with the size of the posy. Push the stems of the posy through the center of the posy frill.

3 Separate the bay leaves from the stems and glue them in one at a time, through the arrangement and around the edge as a border.

4 Push the posy frill up towards the flowers and fasten with tape. Tie a length of ribbon around the stem of the posy and make a bow.

Scented and Decorated Candles

Candlelight is always a beautiful way of illuminating a room or dining table. Perfume can easily be added to candles by dropping a single drop of essential oil to the puddle of melted candle wax near the wick. These candles have been decorated with pressed herbs; the matching essential oil can be added later.

tall preserving jar, or other tall
  container
boiling water
large candles
pressed herbs, including geranium,
  lemon verbena, ivy, fennel flowers
essential oils of the herbs, as
  preferred

1 Fill the jar with boiling water. Decorating the candles one by one, dip a candle into the water, holding it by the wick, and keep it submerged for about one and a half minutes. Using tweezers, quickly press the leaves on to the softened wax.

2 Once the design is finished or the wax is no longer soft enough for the leaves to stick, immerse the candle in the boiling water again. This leaves a layer of wax over the design – the more you dip the candle, the further inwards the pressed leaves will move.

3 Make a set of several designs and display them in a group. Add one or more essential oils to the candles.

Herbal Pot-Pourri

Pot-pourri made at home bears no resemblance to the commercially manufactured variety. Using dried herbs you can quickly produce a mixture that smells wonderful and which will scent the room delightfully. Give it an occasional stir to release more fragrance.

1 handful dried mint leaves
2 handfuls dried marigold flowers
1 handful any other dried herbs, such
  as thyme, sage, marjoram
10 slices dried orange
6 cinnamon sticks
a few dried chillies
4 nutmegs
1 tsp mint essential oil
1 tbsp sweet orange
  essential oil
1 tbsp orris root
large metal or glass bowl
plastic bag

1 Mix all the ingredients, except for the orris root, together in the bowl – do not use a wooden or plastic one, as this will absorb the essential oils and will smell for a long time. Make sure the oils are well mixed with all the other ingredients.

2 Tip the mixture into a large plastic bag, add the orris root and shake well. Leave to mature for a week or two, shaking occasionally. Then tip the mixture into a suitable display bowl or dish. Remember that essential oils can damage a polished surface, so keep away from wooden table tops.

Front to back: *Herbal Pot-Pourri; Scented and Decorated Candles*

Herbal Moth Bags

Moths dislike any pungent herbal fragrance. Herbs such as tansy and southernwood work very effectively, but lavender is perhaps the most irritating to them, and the most pleasing to us.

2 cups dried lavender flowers

1 cup dried tansy leaves

2 cups dried southernwood

2 crushed cinnamon sticks

1 tsp orris root

small burlap bags

small rubber bands

ribbon or cord, as preferred

1 Mix all the ingredients together and bag them up in small hessian bags. Secure the necks with small rubber bands.

2 Decorate with cord or ribbons, and hang in wardrobes or place in drawers.

Herb Pillows and Cushions

Hop pillows have long been known for their sleep-inducing properties, but herbal mixtures are just as effective and can also be used to give a general fragrance to a room. This mixture is a useful basic recipe, but any dried herbs of your choice can be used.

1 cup dried mint

1 cup dried lavender

1 cup dried lemon verbena

1 cup dried lemon thyme

3 cups dried lemon scented geranium leaves

calico or muslin bags

rubber bands, or needle and thread

1 tsp orris root (optional)

1 tsp herbal essential oil (optional)

plastic bag

1 Mix all the ingredients together. Put them in the bags, and secure tightly with rubber bands or draw strings, or by sewing up the ends. Slip these herbal bags into pillows or cushions to give a gentle fragrance.

2 For a stronger smell, add 1 tsp of orris root and the same amount of any herbal essential oil. Leave the mixture to mature in a plastic bag for a week or two before using.

Lavender Sachets

Lavender sachets are always a welcome gift, and several sachets kept among the linen in the airing cupboard will impart a fragrance that makes clean sheets even more inviting.

small calico or muslin bags
lavender flowers
rubber bands
ribbon, as preferred
selection of dried flowers
hot glue gun
sprigs of dried herbs (optional)

1 Fill the bags with the dried lavender flowers, and secure with a rubber band. Do not overfill the bags, or they will be difficult to secure.

2 Tie the neck of the bag with a ribbon and decorate with a selection of dried flowers, attached with a hot glue gun. One of the most effective ways to decorate the bags is to use a couple of dried roses and perhaps a sprig of lavender or other herb.

Rosebud and Cardamom Pomander

These rosebud pomanders are fun to make and add a pretty touch to any room. They can be hung on a wall, or over a dressing-table mirror. When the color has faded they can be sprayed gold as a Christmas ornament.

ribbon or cord for hanging

medium florist's wire

3 in ball gray florist's foam for dried flowers

scissors

small rosebuds

general-purpose adhesive

green cardamom pods

1 Make a long loop with the ribbon or cord. Bind the base of the loop with wire. Leave a long end of wire, and push this through the center of the ball and out through the other side. Trim the wire to about 1 in long, and bend the end over to hide the end in the foam ball.

2 Stick the rosebuds into the foam by their stems. If they have no stems, use a little glue. Cover the entire ball with roses, pressing them close together to make sure that none of the foam is visible. Once the ball is completely covered, glue some green cardamom pods between the rosebuds to give a contrast in color and texture.

Scented Wooden Brushes

Wooden brushes and accessories can be given a delightful fragrance with a very tiny amount of essential oil. Varnish is damaged by essential oils, so do not get any oil on the shiny back of the brush.

wooden hairbrush, unvarnished
essential oil, such as lavender
wooden hair clip, unvarnished

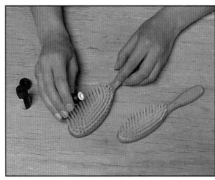

1 Take the wooden hairbrush and sprinkle two or three drops of your favorite essential oil on to the bristle side. The oil will be absorbed by the bristles and the wood, and will impart a fragrance for quite some time. When the scent fades, add a little more oil. As you brush your hair it will leave a lingering fragrance. Do not use too much oil, as this is messy and may also damage a polished surface.

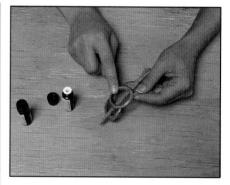

2 To add more fragrance to your hair, sprinkle a couple of drops of essential oil on the wooden hair clip. This should be an unvarnished one, which will absorb the oil and will not be damaged by it.

Herb Corsages

Making your own buttonhole or corsage is easy. Tiny posy frills are obtainable from specialist floral suppliers, or you could use the center of a paper doily.

1 medium-sized flower

1 sprig any herb with attractive leaves

thin florist's wire

miniature posy frill, or cut-down doily

florist's tape

1 For a centerpiece, you could use a rose or small spray carnation. Wrap some herb foliage around it – parsley would look good – and bind tightly with thin wire.

2 Push the stems through the center of the frill and tape them together, covering the stems all the way down. Other combinations could include rosemary, sage, lavender or box.

Scented Valentine Heart

Valentine gifts in the shape of a heart are always popular. This heart-shaped gift box with dried flower and herb decoration on the lid is accompanied by a matching wreath made with fresh leaves and flowers that remain attractive when they dry.

heart-shaped box

broad and narrow ribbon

hot glue gun

5 dried roses

dried bay leaves

1 bunch dried golden rod

heart-shaped wreath form

houttuynia leaves

Minuet roses

1 sprig fresh lavender

1 Start decorating the gift box by making a large bow with broad ribbon. Then stick the dried ingredients on to the box to resemble a bunch of flowers. Stick the bow on top.

2 Wrap some narrow ribbon around the wreath form and secure with glue. Add a few houttuynia leaves (this variety is *H. cordata*), some Minuet roses and fresh lavender. These could be attached with wire instead of glue if you prefer.

Herb-Decorated Crackers

Home-made touches are important at Christmas, as they add the final touch to a family celebration. These crackers are easy to decorate and could be made by adults and children together. Buy ready-decorated crackers and remove the commercial trimming.

crackers
narrow ribbon, as preferred
scissors
small sprigs of various herbs, as preferred
hot glue gun, or general-purpose adhesive

1 Tie the ends of the crackers with ribbon, making attractive bows.

2 Make small posies of herbs and glue them to the middle part of the crackers.

Scented Pressed Herb Diary

A notebook or diary can be scented by placing it in a box with a strong lavender sachet, or a cotton-wool ball sprinkled with a few drops of essential oil. Leave it in the sealed box for a month or so to impart a sweet lingering fragrance. Another idea is to wipe the inside of the covers lightly with a small amount of essential oil on a lint pad. Try to find a very plain diary or notebook which does not have lettering or decoration on the cover, as these would spoil the design. Use a plastic film made for covering books. Some types are ironed on, others cling by themselves.

pressed leaves and flowers, such as borage flowers, alchemilla flowers and small leaves, daisies, single roses, forget-me-nots
plain diary or notebook
tweezers
large tapestry needle
rubber cement
clear plastic film
iron and cloth pad, if required

1 Start by arranging a selection of pressed leaves on the front of the diary or notebook, using the tweezers for positioning.

2 Continue to build up your design by adding the pressed flower heads.

3 Once you are happy with the design stick it down, using a large tapestry needle and rubber cement. Slide the needle into the glue and then, without moving the design, place a small amount of glue under each leaf and petal so that they are secure. Cover with clear film. If the film needs heating, iron gently with a cloth pad between the film and the iron.

Pressed Herb Cards

A home-made card is always one that will be treasured long after the occasion has passed. Although it takes time and trouble to make your own cards, you could make a batch and keep them for a suitable occasion. It is always worth the effort to give someone something with your personal touch.

pressed herbs and flowers, such as blue cornflower, ivy, rosemary, borage
blank greeting card
large tapestry needle
rubber cement
clear plastic film
iron and cloth pad, if required

1 Arrange a selection of pressed herbs and flowers on the front of the card, using tweezers for positioning.

2 When the design is complete, stick it down, using a large tapestry needle and rubber cement. Using the needle, slide small dabs of adhesive beneath the herbs and flowers without altering their position. Cover with a clear film. If the film needs heating, iron gently with a cloth pad between the film and the iron.

Right: *assorted Pressed Herb Cards and Scented Pressed Herb Diaries*

Chamomile and Honey Mask

Although this mask makes you look a little strange while it is on your face, it smooths and softens skin beautifully.
Chamomile flowers are usually easy to obtain from a health food shop as they are often used for making chamomile tea.

1 tbsp dried chamomile flowers

¾ cup boiling water

2 tbsp bran

1 tsp clear honey, warmed

1 Pour the boiling water over the chamomile flowers and allow them to stand for 30 minutes. Then strain the infusion and discard the chamomile flowers.

2 Mix 3 tbsp of the liquid with the bran and honey and rub this mixture all over your face. It may be a little stiff at first but will smooth out over the skin. Leave the mixture on your skin for at least 10 minutes, then rinse off with warm water.

Tansy Skin Tonic

Tansy leaves smell fairly strong, but this tonic will invigorate your skin, especially if you keep the bottle in the refrigerator. Splash on this cool herbal liquid to start the day.

1 large handful tansy leaves

²/₃ cup water

²/₃ cup milk

1 Put the leaves, water and milk in a small pan and bring to a boil. Simmer for 15 minutes, then allow to cool in the pan.

2 Strain the tonic into a bottle. Keep the mixture in the refrigerator, and apply cold to the skin as a soothing toner or tonic.

Feverfew Complexion Milk

Feverfew grows prolifically in the garden, self-seeding all over the herb beds, and this is a welcome use for some of this over-enthusiastic plant. The milk will moisturize dry skin, help to fade blemishes, and discourage blackheads.

1 large handful feverfew leaves

1¼ cups milk

1 Put the leaves and milk in a small saucepan and simmer for 20 minutes.

2 Allow the mixture to cool in the pan then strain into a bottle. Keep it in the refrigerator.

FEVERFEW FLOWERS

- Feverfew can be cultivated easily; it is especially pretty grown in tubs and pots in the greenhouse or conservatory.

- Hang bunches of flowers upside down and leave to air-dry; use as a decorative addition to dried flower arrangements.

Fennel Cleanser

Fennel is another herb that self-seeds all over the garden, so once you have planted it supplies will be no problem. The leaves have an aniseed aroma. This mixture gently but thoroughly cleanses the day's grime away.

1 tbsp fennel seed
1 cup boiling water
1 tsp honey
2 tbsp buttermilk

1 Lightly crush the fennel seeds, pour on the boiling water and allow to infuse for about 30 minutes.

2 Strain the cooled liquid into a small bowl and add the honey and buttermilk. Transfer to a clean bottle and keep the mixture refrigerated.

FENNEL SEEDS

- The tall, graceful heads of fennel seeds add height to a cottage herb garden. The seeds are valued for their distinctive aroma. In Victorian times the seeds came to symbolize the virtue of strength.
- At one time, fennel seeds were combined with those of dill and caraway in little sacks or purses, to be chewed at prayer meetings to quell hunger pangs: they were known as 'meeting seeds'.

Parsley Hair Tonic

Parsley stimulates the scalp and gets the circulation going, which aids hair growth and adds shine.

1 large handful parsley sprigs
2 tbsp water

1 Place the parsley sprigs and water in a food processor.

2 Process until ground to a smooth purée. Apply the green lotion to the scalp, then wrap your head in a warm towel and leave for about 1 hour before shampooing as normal.

Lemon Verbena Hair Rinse

Add a delicious fragrance to your hair with this rinse. It will also stimulate the pores and circulation. Lemon verbena is worth growing in the garden, if only so that you can walk past and pick a wonderfully scented leaf.

1 handful lemon verbena leaves
1 cup boiling water

1 Pour the boiling water over the lemon verbena leaves and leave to soak for at least 1 hour.

2 Strain the mixture and discard the leaves. Pour this rinse over your hair after conditioning.

From left: *Lemon Verbena Hair Rinse; Parsley Hair Tonic*

Chamomile Conditioning Rinse

Chamomile flowers help to keep blonde hair a bright, clear color. They will not lift the color in hair that is medium to dark, but will help to brighten naturally fair hair, as well as leaving a pleasant fragrance.

½ cup freshly picked or dried
  chamomile flowers
2½ cups water
1 handful scented geranium leaves

1 Place the chamomile flowers and water in a saucepan and bring to a boil. Simmer for approximately 15 minutes.

2 While the liquid is still hot, strain on to the scented geranium leaves. Leave to soak for 30-40 minutes. Strain again, this time into a bottle. Use the mixture after shampooing.

Rosemary Hair Tonic

Rosemary is an excellent substitute for mildly medicated shampoos, and this tonic also helps control greasy hair and enhances the shine and natural color.

1 cup fresh rosemary leaves
5 cups non-carbonated bottled
  water

1 Put the ingredients in a saucepan and bring to the boil. Simmer for approximately 20 minutes, then allow to cool in the pan.

2 Strain the mixture and store it in a clean bottle. Use after shampooing the hair.

Herbal Bath Bags

These are much more fun than putting commercial bubble bath into the water. Tie them over the taps and make sure the hot running water is going through them – this will release lovely herbal scents that relax and comfort you.

9 in diameter circles of unbleached muslin

6 tbsp bran

1 tbsp lavender flowers

1 tbsp chamomile flowers

1 tbsp rosemary tips

3 small rubber bands

3 yd narrow ribbon or twine

1 Place 2 tbsp bran in the center of each circle of muslin. Add the lavender to one bag, the chamomile to a second and the rosemary to the third.

2 Gather each circle of material up and close with a rubber band. Then tie a reasonable length of ribbon or twine around each bag to make a loop so that the bag can be hung from the hot tap in the stream of water.

Rose Hand Cream

This is an excellent scented hand cream which softens and moisturizes.

1 tsp beeswax

¼ tsp honey

4 tbsp almond oil

4 tbsp rosewater

1 Put the beeswax, honey and almond oil in a glass jar standing in a small pan of hot water. Stir until melted and blended.

2 Stir vigorously while pouring in the rosewater. Take the jar out of the water, and continue to stir gently until the mixture has cooled.

Dill Aftershave

Most recipes are for fragrances for women, so here is one for men. It is best kept in the refrigerator so that the cool liquid has a bracing effect as well as smelling good.

¼ **cup dill seed**

1 **tbsp honey**

2½ **cups bottled water**

1 **tbsp distilled witch hazel**

1 Place the dill seed, honey and water in a small saucepan and bring to a boil. Simmer for about 20 minutes.

2 Allow to cool in the pan, then add the witch hazel. Strain the cooled mixture into a bottle and refrigerate.

Lavender Bubble Bath

There is no need to buy commercially made bubble baths again. This fragrance is quite delicious and so simple to make that you can make some spares as gifts for friends and family – you will be in great demand!

1 bunch lavender
clean wide-necked jar, with screw top
1 large bottle clear organic shampoo
5 drops oil of lavender

1 Place the bunch of lavender head downwards in the jar. If the stalks are longer than the jar cut them down, as it is the flowers that do the work. Add the shampoo and the lavender oil.

2 Close the jar and place on a sunny window sill for 2-3 weeks, shaking occasionally.

3 Strain the liquid and re-bottle. Use about 1 tbsp in a bath.

Dandelion Tea

Most warm herbal teas have a comforting effect. Dandelions are a diuretic, and can help to reduce water retention and bloated feelings. Many people find that this is a useful treatment for rheumatism. This tea also acts as a mild laxative so should not be drunk in large quantities.

5-6 dandelion leaves
boiling water
1 tsp honey (optional)

1 Remove any stems from the dandelion leaves. Break them into strips and place in the bottom of a mug. Pour on enough boiling water to fill the mug and leave to stand for 5-10 minutes.

2 Strain, discard most of the dandelion leaves, and drink. If you prefer a sweeter brew, add a scant teaspoonful of honey.

DANDELIONS

- Dandelion roots when dried can be used as a coffee substitute; they can also be added to beer and wine.
- Dandelion leaves are eaten as a salad vegetable in Mediterranean countries; they can also be blanched and served as a cooked accompaniment.

Thyme Tea

Thyme is excellent for treating chest infections and coughs. This tea is a comforting extra treatment, but do not rely on it to cure. However, it will help to combat sleeplessness and irritating coughs.

1 oz fresh thyme
2½ cups boiling water
honey

1 Take the fresh thyme and cover with the boiling water. Allow to infuse for at least 5-10 minutes, to taste.

2 Add a little honey, and drink while still piping hot.

DECORATIVE THYME

- Collect and air-dry bunches of thyme when in flower. The flowers can be used in dried floral arrangements.
- Alternatively, when the flowers are dry, crumble them between your fingertips and add to potpourri mixtures.

Lavender and Marjoram Bath

A long warm bath is an excellent way of relieving the stresses and strains of a busy day. This bath mixture has the added bonus of moisturizing the skin while it gently soothes away cares and troubles. The essential oils induce sleep. To enhance the effect, you could add a bath bag containing fresh lavender and marjoram to the water.

2 tbsp almond oil

7 drops lavender oil

3 drops marjoram oil

1 Measure out all the ingredients into a small dish or bowl.

2 Mix all the ingredients together and pour them into the bath while the water is running, then have a long, soothing soak.

Lemon Grass, Coriander and Clove Bath

If you are suffering from stiff limbs after excessive exercise, this bath will help stimulate the circulation and relieve suffering in joints and muscles.

2 tbsp almond oil

2 drops lemon grass oil

2 drops coriander oil

2 drops clove oil

1 Carefully measure the almond oil into a small dish.

2 Slowly drop in all the essential oils. Mix all the ingredients and pour into the bath while the water is running. Rinse the dish under the running tap to make sure all the oils have gone into the bath water. Take a long, relaxing bath.

Lavender Oil

Lavender oil is the most useful of all the essential oils, and perhaps the safest. Allergic reaction is virtually unknown and, unlike many of the other essential oils, it is safe to apply it directly to the skin.

It can help to promote sleep – sprinkle a few drops on to the pillow, or on to a handkerchief placed on the pillow, for adults and children to enjoy untroubled rest.

It is also excellent for treating burns, stings, scalds and minor wounds. Deter flying insects by rubbing the essential oil into uncovered parts of the body, such as hands and feet, on a warm evening when sitting outside.

Lavender oil can be added to bottled water (about 6 drops to 2½ cups) and sprinkled on to dry pillow cases or any other linen before ironing to leave a pleasant lingering fragrance.

From left: *Lemon Grass, Coriander and Clove Bath; Lavender and Marjoram Bath*

Comfrey Infusion

This is a useful lotion to make up to treat minor cuts and scrapes. It should be used at room temperature when not too cold, as it is more soothing used warm.

2 tsp fresh comfrey leaves (or 1 tsp dried comfrey)
1¼ cups boiling water

1 Shred the fresh comfrey leaves into small pieces and cover with the boiling water. Allow to steep for 10 minutes. Leave to cool.

2 Gently bathe cuts and abrasions with this lotion on a lint pad. It is also good for minor burns, scalds and sunburn.

Mint Footbath and Massage Oil

After a long day on your feet, try soaking them in this soothing footbath. Then rub the mint oil into your feet to smooth and soften before you go to bed. The mint essential oil also has a refreshing scent.

MINT BATH
12 large sprigs mint
½ cup cold water
10 cups boiling water
MASSAGE OIL
1 tbsp almond oil
1 drop mint essential oil

1 Place the mint in a food processor and add the cold water. Process well until it becomes a green purée. Pour this into a large bowl and add the boiling water. Once the mixture has cooled to a bearable temperature, soak both feet at once until the water is too cool to be comforting.

2 Gently rub your feet dry with a soft towel. Mix the almond oil and the mint essential oil and rub well into both feet.

251

Basil Water

This is a delicious herbal brew – some herbal teas are a little unpalatable, but this is very good. Basil relieves nausea and is thought to have mild antiseptic properties, but these should not be relied upon and the brew should only be used as an extra treatment for infections.

1 large sprig basil
1¼ cups boiling water
1 tsp fresh orange juice

1 Pour the boiling water over the sprig of basil, leave to infuse for about 5 minutes and then remove the basil.

2 Add the orange juice and stir. Drink while hot.

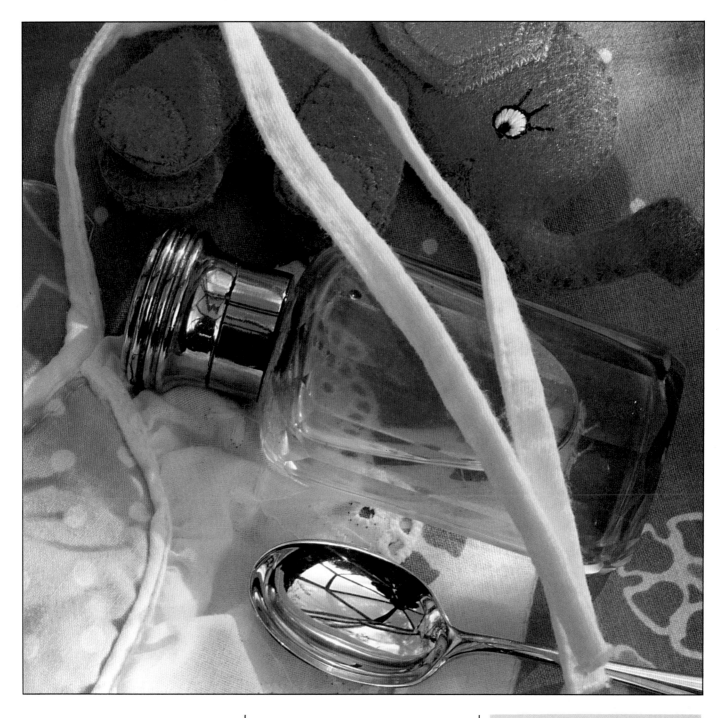

Fennel Gripe Water

Used occasionally to help digestion and to soothe colic, this gripe water can be gently effective. Although gripe water is usually associated with babies, it can also be useful for adults and children. Use 1 tsp fennel seeds to 1¼ cups water. For a small baby, after making, dilute the infusion with 2 parts water to 1 part gripe water. It may be drunk warm or cold.

1 tsp fennel seeds
1¼ cups boiling water

1 Crush the fennel seeds, cover with the boiling water and leave to steep for about 20 minutes.

2 Strain the brew, discarding the fennel seeds.

HERBAL PROJECTS FOR CHILDREN

- Lavender bags trimmed with sprigs of chamomile and bright ribbons.
- Pressed herb flower and leaf cards and stationery.
- Creating miniature dried gardens from lavender, marigolds and roses.

SPICES

SALLIE MORRIS AND LESLEY MACKLEY

Introduction

Spices have played a major influence in our lives and in the economic development of many countries for centuries. Exotic and aromatic spices give us pleasure in our enjoyment of food, they are invaluable in folk medicines and modern medications, they sweeten our rooms as well as our bodies and enliven our language with sayings like 'the spice of life' and 'spicing things up'. The spice trade has brought romance and drama into history, with the adventures of the sea captains and explorers who went in search of these sought-after and expensive prizes.

THE SPICE TRADE

As long ago as 3500 BC, the Ancient Egyptians were using spices for flavoring their food, in cosmetics and in lotions for embalming their dead. They believed that the spirit returned to the body of the deceased, so the bodies of their pharaohs, queens and nobility were mummified and entombed with their worldly treasures. From biblical references, we know that the Queen of Sheba traveled from her homeland, Ethiopia, to visit King Solomon in Jerusalem. His enormous wealth was due to the 'traffick of the spice merchants' and gifts of spices added to his treasure: 'All those who sought to hear him brought costly presents, including spices'. (1 Kings 10:25)

The story of Joseph, he with the coat of many colors, is also related to the spice trade. His jealous brothers resolved to kill him, 'but a company of Ishmaelites came down from Gilead with their camels bearing spicery, and balm and myrrh, going to carry it down to Egypt'. The brothers sold Joseph for twenty pieces of silver and returned to their father, Jacob, with the bloodstained coat. Jacob was consumed with grief. In reality, Joseph was sold to an officer of Pharaoh and he

Left: *Spices were once brought into the Middle East by camel caravans; today spices can easily be bought fresh in the marketplace.*

eventually became a high-ranking official at court. His ability to interpret Pharaoh's dreams saved his adopted country from famine. Later he had the enormous satisfaction of selling corn to his brothers, who did not recognize him. They brought appropriate gifts of balm, honey, spices, myrrh, nuts and almonds.

The spice trade, controlled by the Arabs for at least 5,000 years, grew through the Middle East to the Eastern Mediterranean and to Europe. Donkey or camel caravans, carrying precious cargoes of cinnamon, cassia, cardamom, ginger, turmeric, frankincense and jewels, traveled hazardous routes.

Below: *Brightly colored, fragrant spices tempt buyers in an Egyptian bazaar.*

Their journeys may have started in China, Indonesia, India or Ceylon (now Sri Lanka). Very often, enterprising Chinese merchants sailed to the Spice Islands (now Maluku, a group of islands in Indonesia), then brought their cargoes of spices and perfumes to the Indian or Sri Lankan coast, where they dealt with the Arab traders. The Arabs were anxious to conceal both the sources of their supplies and the overland spice routes. The classic route crossed the River Indus, through Pesharwar, over the Khyber Pass, through Afghanistan and Iran, then south to the city of Babylon on the Euphrates. From there the spices were taken to the most powerful city or town of the day. The Phoenicians, great seafarers and traders, thrived on the lucrative spice trade, and they set up their city of Tyre as a major distribution center, serving the whole of the Mediterranean from 1200 to 800 BC.

As seats of power switched from Egypt to Babylon and Assyria, the Arabs maintained their hold on the supply of spices from the East, throughout the development of the Greek and Roman civilizations. Clearly, the stories the Arabs related about the origins of the spices were impressive and believed: they told of cinnamon from deep snake-infested valleys and of cassia from shallow lakes protected by fierce and enormous

winged birds with nests built high on limestone cliffs. When the nests collapsed, the traders collected the cassia.

The Romans were prolific in their use of spices, and the demand increased the pressures to find a route to India so that they could break the Arab monopoly on the spice trade. Understanding the weather patterns and the monsoons provided the answer: soon Roman ships, laden with precious spices, were sailing into Alexandria, in Egypt, their chief port. The Romans were great gourmets and lovers of the good things of life, they used spices in cooking, scented their rooms with 'strewings' of spices and used the distilled spice oils for bathing and keeping their lamps alight. Wherever their legions marched they introduced a wealth of spices and herbs, and for the first time

the exotic flavorings were taken to Northern Europe. The fall of the Roman Empire in the 5th century and the dawning of the Dark Ages heralded a long period of cultural stagnation, including knowledge of spices.

Above: *A market seller in India sits surrounded by a vibrant array of spices.*

Mohammed, the prophet and founder of the Muslim faith, married the wealthy widow of a spice merchant. The missionary zeal in the spread of the faith through the East was inextricably linked with the trading of spices. Whilst Western Europe slept, the spice trade in the East expanded aggressively. The religious crusades from 1000 AD for three hundred years broadened the appreciation of spices from the East as the Christians tried to wrest power from the Muslims in the unholy trade. Venice and Genoa became trading centers, and ships traveling to the Holy Land with the crusaders returned with cargoes of spices, silks and jewels. Spices, because they were

continued. European seafarers became obsessed with the dream of finding the best sea route to India and the East. Vasco de Gama, the Portuguese navigator, was the first to discover the sea route to India by rounding the Cape of Good Hope, Africa's southernmost tip. He was not kindly received but he managed to load his ships with nutmegs, cloves, cinnamon, ginger and peppercorns. He was welcomed home as a hero in 1499 and, more importantly, he had a letter from the Indian rulers of Calicut agreeing to a trading partnership.

Lisbon took over the role of spice capital, a position so jealously guarded and enjoyed by Venice in the past. Prior to this, Christopher Columbus had a novel approach to the idea of sailing east: he sailed west. In 1492 he thought he had reached Japan but in fact it was San Salvador (now known as Watling Island), one of the islands near the Bahamas, Haiti and Cuba. He had discovered the New World and he was the first Westerner to taste the fiery chili. On his second voyage, Columbus left Spain with 1,500 men to establish Spanish power in the New World hoping that he would find gold and Oriental spices; instead he discovered allspice and vanilla, and, from the

scarce, became as precious as silver and gold and the trade began to flourish once more.

Marco Polo was born in 1256 AD into a family of jewel merchants who were fascinated with the East. They traveled as far as China, known as Cathay, staying at the court of the Mongol Emperor, the Great Khan, and, during a journey, which lasted twenty-four years, Marco traveled throughout China, Asia and India. His story *The Adventures of Marco Polo* was written on parchment while he was taken prisoner after a sea battle between Venice and Genoa. His book recalled the spices he had seen growing on his travels and dispelled the fearsome tales and myths told by the early Arab traders. He wrote poetically of Java: 'it abounds with rich commodities. Pepper, nutmeg ... cloves and all other valuable spices and drugs are the produce of the island which occasion it to be visited by many ships laden with merchandise, that yields to the owners considerable profit'. His book was to inspire the next and following generations of sailors and travelers who were keen to make their names and their fortunes.

The Age of Discovery (1400 AD) dawned and the epic history of spices

Above: *Cassia bark in a Cairo street bazaar.*
Below: *Dried red chili peppers available by the sackful.*

great South American continent, he introduced potatoes, chocolate, maize, peanuts and turkeys to Europe.

The Portuguese made a fundamental mistake in hiring the Dutch as their merchants in Europe, requesting them to sail to the Spice Islands to collect cloves, nutmegs and cinnamon. After a century of complete dominance, the Portuguese were overthrown by the Dutch. The Dutch East India Company was formed in 1602 in response to the formation of the British East India Company, which had been given a Royal Charter by Queen Elizabeth I in 1600. Meanwhile, Sir Francis Drake circumnavigated the world, sailing his ship, the *Golden Hind*, through the Magellan Straits and across the Pacific to the Spice Islands. These islands were the focus for the whole of Europe with each nation aiming for monopoly of the spice trade, which they knew to be the source of riches beyond compare. The Dutch approach was to restrict the growing of nutmegs and cloves to the islands of Amboyna and Banda in the Moluccas. This was foiled by a French missionary, Pierre Poivre, who found saplings on a nearby island, to which the seeds had been carried by birds, and he transported them to

Above: *Indonesian women offer a wide range of spices in the daily markets.*

Mauritius. The cloves were taken onto Zanzibar, which is still a major producer today, and the nutmegs to Grenada, in the West Indies, known as the 'Nutmeg Isle'. About the same time, the British were experimenting with the planting of nutmegs and cloves in Penang; later they cultivated spices in Singapore, under the direction of Sir Stamford Raffles, a famous employee of the East India Company and founder of Singapore.

The struggle between the British and the Dutch became very bitter and bloody and lasted almost two hundred years. The conflict was resolved when Britain took over India and Ceylon and the Dutch were left with Java and Sumatra, which remained under their jurisdiction until World War II. By this time, spices were more plentiful and cheaper than ever before.

The late 18th century brought another nation on to the spice stage, the United States of America. The clipper ships of New England were successful in tracking down peppercorns. Trading and bartering as they went, the clipper skippers returned to Salem in Massachusetts with bulging holds of the best Sumatran pepper. Salem became the center of the pepper trade and, with a potential profit of 700 per cent, the owners of the ships became the first millionaires. These journeys were not, however, without their difficulties: the round trip might take two to three years, the possibility of being killed by pirates or natives was extremely high, and the storms and tempests on the high seas were equally threatening.

Today we take the commonplace availability of exotic ingredients for

Below: *Spices cover every inch of space in this shop in Singapore.*

granted. It is difficult for us to imagine that a handful of cardamoms was the equivalent of a poor man's annual wage; that slaves were sold for a few handfuls of peppercorns; that a pound of mace could buy three sheep and a cow; or that a pound of ginger was

worth the same as a sheep. Dockers in London were made to sew up their pockets to discourage them from stealing even a single peppercorn.

Modern international travel has created a market for foods from all over the globe, and the principal spice markets are London, Hamburg, Rotterdam, Singapore and New York. Spices are inspected before being stored in huge warehouses, then they are sold and sent for processing and packaging. The spice trade is worth millions of dollars per annum: black pepper tops the list, followed by chilies and cardamom. India is the principal producer, followed by Indonesia, Brazil, Madagascar and Malaysia; spices are vital to the economies of all these countries. As cooks we depend on the spices they produce to enliven our daily meals and to bring fragrance to our lives. Empires have been won and lost in the historic battles for the seasoning on our kitchen shelves.

Spices in the Kitchen

Throughout the world, the cooking of every country is distinguished by the way in which spices are used to give it a unique character.

When we think of spices, it is often their imaginative use in Indian cooking that springs to mind. Up to fifteen spices may be combined in an elaborate Indian dish, used in different ways to produce the desired result. They may be added whole or ground, they may be fried or roasted to intensify the flavor, or they may be made into a paste.

India is a vast country and the style of cooking varies enormously from region to region, but the spices most often used include cumin, turmeric, black pepper, mustard seeds, fennel seeds, cardamom, cloves, garlic and ginger. Chilies are valued for both fire and flavor; some Indian dishes are extremely hot, but in others spices are used with rare subtlety.

Chinese cooks use liberal quantities of fresh ginger and garlic. They favor spices such as sesame seeds and star anise, which is the predominant flavor in their famous five spice blend. The spices in this blend are finely ground so that they release their flavor quickly in stir-fried dishes.

Thai food tends to be very hot, with the tiny – and fiery – Thai chilies appearing in many dishes. The heat, however, is tempered by the fresh light flavors of lemon grass and kaffir lime leaves and the soothing effect of coconut milk. In the recipes in this collection, some authentic Thai dishes, such as Hot and Sour Shrimp Soup, have been marginally modified for Western tastes; if your taste buds can take the heat, just add more chilies.

Mexican food is also characterized by the liberal use of chilies. Several different types are often combined in the same dish. Each chili contributes

Below: *An increasing range of formerly exotic spices and aromatics are becoming familiar to the Western cook.*

its own distinctive flavor as well as the fire for which they are famous.

Mexican chilies had already traveled to the Caribbean islands by the time Columbus arrived, and their use characterizes all island cooking. Allspice and cayenne are also widely used in Caribbean dishes. Traditional recipes such as Jerk Pork and Caribbean Fish Steaks typically combine these with a pungent fresh herb such as thyme.

Around the Mediterranean it is the warm spices such as cinnamon, coriander, saffron and cumin that create the typical flavors that so readily conjure up memories of holidays in Turkey, Greece or Morocco. These spices are frequently combined with fruit and nuts in dishes like Moroccan Harissa-spiced Roast Chicken or Lamb Tagine. In North Africa, harissa (an explosive chili sauce) is added to many dishes or handed separately, to add fire to fragrant spice combinations. A typical dish from the French Mediterranean is provençal fish soup, which is flavored with saffron and served spiked with a fiery rouille.

Many European dishes are flavored with spices like caraway, dill, cardamom and fennel. These spices are equally at home in sweet or savory dishes.

Although Europe has had a long tradition of using spices, particularly in preserves, pickles and sauces, their use in everyday cooking has been moderate until comparatively recently.

Only twenty years ago, although most kitchens probably had a spice rack on display, the ground spices in the jars would have been used sparingly – if at all – until they were so stale that they would have been of scant use as a flavoring. Cooks may have sprinkled a little ground nutmeg on a milk pudding, or added a clove or two to an apple pie, but that was a long way from the days of the 17th century, when expensive spices were used in Europe as a means of dis-

Above: *Chilies by the cupful in Brazil.*

playing wealth and food was heavily spiced and scented with ginger, pepper, cinnamon, cloves and nutmeg.

In recent years, however, we have been rediscovering the wealth of ways in which spices and aromatic flavorings can enhance all types of dishes from soups to sweetmeats. As we travel more and explore increasingly exotic locations, and as restaurants spring up in every town offering food from all over the world, we are becoming familiar with a wide variety of different cuisines. We are taking the tastes home, too, becoming more adventurous in what we attempt to re-create in our own kitchens.

Fortunately, it is no longer necessary to seek out ethnic shops for more unusual ingredients. Supermarkets and food stores now stock everything from turmeric to tamarind juice. Stale spices rapidly lose their flavor and can become musty, so it is important to buy small amounts from a shop with a rapid turnover, and use spices soon after purchase, particularly if they are ready ground.

Cooking, like other arts, is constantly evolving, and one of the most exciting developments that has followed the rediscovery of spices is the way in which classic dishes can be transformed by innovative use of familiar (and unfamiliar) flavorings. While many of the recipes in this book are entirely authentic, an equal number take a fresh look at old favorites by introducing new and sophisticated spice blends. For example, try Salmon Marinated with Thai Spices, a dish based on the traditional Scandinavian gravadlax, or enjoy pear tart Tatin, which owes its fragrance to the unusual addition of cardamom.

Do not be afraid of spices. This comprehensive collection will tell you all you will ever need to know about these fascinating flavorings, from advice on selection and storage to suggestions for making a wide range of powders and pastes. Mixing and blending spices is part of the pleasure. Quantities of spices given in recipes are only a guide, so experiment to discover the combinations you prefer. That way, you can personalize your own cooking – and prove that spices can make a world of a difference.

Above: *A bountiful display – spices as far as the eye can see.*

Choosing and Preparing Spices

What is a spice? Spices are the dried seeds (cumin, coriander, cardamom, mustard), buds (cloves), fruit or flower parts (peppercorns, allspice), bark and roots (cassia, cinnamon and ginger) or leaves (kaffir lime leaves, curry leaves) of plants. They are usually of tropical origin, and almost all are native to the Orient. There are exceptions: allspice, vanilla and chilies were originally found in tropical Central America and the West Indies.

CHOOSING SPICES

When buying spices, select whole seeds, berries, buds and bark, such as cumin seeds, cardamoms, peppercorns, allspice, cloves, cassia and cinnamon sticks, if you can, as these keep their flavor and pungency far longer than the powdered spices, and can be ground easily as needed. Fresh roots, such as ginger and galangal, and fresh lemon grass are essential for some dishes and have an entirely different flavor than the dried versions.

PREPARATION TECHNIQUES

Spices are prepared in many ways, depending on the form of the spice and the dish in which it is being used – the point though is always the same: to release the optimum amount of flavor and aroma.

Dry frying

This process, sometimes called dry-roasting, and often used in Indian cookery, increases the flavor of such spices as cumin, coriander, fennel, mustard and poppy seeds.

Heat a small heavy-based pan over a medium heat for about 1 minute, put in the whole spices and cook for 2-3 minutes, stirring or shaking the pan frequently to prevent the spices burning, or until the spices start to give off a warm, rich aroma.

Remove the pan from the heat and tip the spices into a bowl and grind finely in a mortar with a pestle.

Frying in Oil

Whole spices are sometimes fried in oil, either at the beginning of a recipe, before other ingredients are added, or simply to flavor the oil.

Grinding

Spices are frequently crushed or ground to release their flavor and aroma. Only a few, notably mace, dried ginger and turmeric, cinnamon and cassia, are hard to grind at home and are usually bought in powdered form. For the best flavor, grind spices as you need them. Do not grind them more than a day or two in advance.

For small, easily ground dried spices, such as cumin, fennel, ajowan and caraway seeds and cloves, use a china pestle and mortar. Grind only a small amount at a time – do not put more than a tablespoon or two in the bowl at a time, and grind in a circular motion.

Some harder spices, such as fenugreek, coriander seeds and allspice can be ground successfully in a pepper mill. Special nutmeg grinders, similar to pepper mills are also available and work fairly well.

An easier and quicker method of grinding these harder spices is to use an electric coffee grinder. Do not overfill the bowl and grind in short bursts.

Fresh ingredients, such as ginger and garlic, and larger spices, such as chilies, can be easily ground using pestles and mortars. Traditional Indian and Oriental mortars have pitted or ridged bowls and are good for making wet spice mixtures and pastes.

Wet spice mixtures can also be made in a food processor. Use the metal blade, add the ingredients and purée to a rough or smooth paste as required. Slicing the ingredients into small pieces before adding to the processor will result in a smoother paste. If the ingredients are all dry, add a little of the oil from the recipe to help the processing.

PREPARING CHILIES

Chilies need to be handled carefully. If you have sensitive skin, or are preparing a lot of chilies, it is worth wearing rubber gloves. Do not touch your eyes or mouth while you work, and always wash your hands and cooking implements after preparing chilies. It is easier to seed chilies before chopping: cut the chili in half and scrape out the seeds using the point of a knife.

Grating

Fresh root spices, such as horseradish and ginger, and whole nutmegs are grated before use.

To grate ginger or horseradish, peel the root, then grate it on the fine blade of a stainless steel grater.

Grate nutmegs on a special nutmeg grater or on the finest blade of a standard grater.

Bruising and Crushing

Some spices, such as cardamom, juniper, ginger and lemon grass, are often lightly crushed to release their aroma or, in the case of cardamom, to release the seeds for crushing. Garlic is often crushed rather than chopped.

Juniper berries and cardamoms are easily crushed using a pestle and mortar. (Alternatively, place them in a sturdy polythene bag and crush them with a rolling pin.)

Fresh ginger, galangal or lemon grass, which are to be added whole to a recipe during cooking for a subtle flavor and then removed before serving, can be bruised with one or two sharp blows, until the fibers are crushed, on a chopping board using the flat blade of a large knife, or a large pestle.

A simple and effective way of crushing garlic cloves is to trim off the root end and place the unpeeled clove cut end down in a garlic press. After the garlic is crushed, the skin can simply be removed, making cleaning the press very easy.

Shredding and Chopping

Some fresh spices, such as ginger, garlic and kaffir lime leaves, are cut into fine slices or pieces before use to maximize the flavor and aroma.

Kaffir lime leaves are usually shredded rather than chopped. Hold one or two leaves together on a chopping board and cut into fine strips using a small sharp knife.

To chop ginger, cut the peeled root lengthwise into fine slices then slice again into long strips. Hold a few strips together at a time and chop finely.

Infusing

One or two spices are always infused in a warm liquid before use. When saffron is infused it imparts not only a wonderful aroma, but also a vibrant yellow color. Tamarind is infused to produce a tangy juice that is used in a similar way to lemon juice or vinegar to add sharpness to a dish.

To infuse saffron strands, warm a little milk, water or liquid from the recipe. Add the saffron and leave to infuse for about 5 minutes. Do not strain the liquid, both strands and liquid are used in the recipe.

To infuse tamarind pulp, place a small piece of the pulp in a jug or bowl, add 4 tbsp warm water and leave to infuse for 10 minutes.

Mix with the fingers to loosen the purée from the seeds, then strain through a nylon sieve. Discard the pulp and seeds and use the juice as directed in the recipe.

PREPARING BLACHAN

Blachan, also called trassi or terasi, is not a spice, it is a strong-smelling, firm paste made of fermented shrimps that is used in South-east Asian cookery. It can be bought in Oriental shops. Unless it is to be fried as part of a recipe, blachan is always lightly cooked before use. If you have a gas cooker, simply mold the blachan onto the end of a metal skewer and rotate over a low to medium gas flame, or heat the piece of blachan under the grill of an electric cooker, until the outside begins to look crusty but not burnt. To avoid the strong smell filling the kitchen, wrap the blachan in foil and fry in a dry frying pan over a gentle heat for 4-5 minutes, turning from time to time.

Equipment for Preparing Spices

Spices are often ground, crushed, pounded or puréed to create powders and pastes. Although these processes are simple, there are a few useful items of equipment that make these tasks much easier.

Nutmeg graters come in a variety of shapes and sizes. They have very fine rough holes and produce a fine powder. The one on the left doubles as a storage container.

Smooth china pestles and mortars come in a variety of sizes and are excellent for grinding small amounts of dry spices.

Traditional Indian and Oriental granite or stone pestles and mortars are generally fairly large, with deep, pitted or ridged bowls. They are ideal for pounding fresh spices, such as ginger, galangal and lemon grass, as the rough surface seems to grip the pieces and prevents them flying out of the bowl as you pound the mixture.

Bigger, flat-bowled pestles and mortars are particularly good for making spice pastes that include large amounts of fresh spices, herbs, onion and garlic.

A simple garlic press makes quick work of crushing garlic cloves.

An electric coffee grinder is excellent for grinding dry spices. If you are going to do a lot of spice cooking, it is worth keeping a separate grinder purely for this purpose.

Electric food processors come into their own for making larger quantities of spice pastes and purées.

Nutmeg mills work by rotating the nutmeg over a blade – different models grate with varying degrees of success.

This small clear perspex mill can be used to grind both cinnamon and cassia bark.

Traditional wooden Japanese ginger graters make light work of grating ginger and are easy to clean. A stainless steel box grater works equally well – use the finest grating surface and work over a flat plate to catch the juices.

How to Store Spices

Very few cooks store spices correctly. Dried spices are usually displayed in glass jars on the kitchen shelf or in wall racks, and fresh spices, such as ginger or lemon grass, are often kept on a kitchen shelf or in a vegetable rack, sometimes in a sunny spot or under bright lights. Here are some tips on how to preserve the flavor and aroma of your spices.

STORING FRESH SPICES

Unless you are going to use fresh spices the day they are bought, they should be chilled rather than stored at room temperature. Lemon grass, kaffir lime leaves and curry leaves are best wrapped in a piece of paper towel and stored in the salad drawer of a fridge for up to 2 weeks. Fresh galangal, ginger and chilies will keep for up to 3 weeks in a sealed container, lined with paper towels, in the fridge. If you would like to keep them longer, fresh spices can be pounded to a paste, then put in small sealed containers and frozen for up to 6 months.

STORING DRIED SPICES

Both ground and whole dried spices should be stored in airtight containers in a cool, dark cupboard or drawer as light, heat and moisture lessen their quality. Whole spices will keep for 6 months or even longer, if stored carefully. However, most ground spices lose their color, flavor and aroma within 5 or 6 months. If you are unsure just how long the spices have been stored for, check the aroma – if the spice smells musty, or if there is little aroma, it is likely that the flavor will be impaired, too. It is a good idea to label new jars of spices with the date of purchase.

Opaque jars made of either china or metal do not need to be stored in a dark place, but they are still better kept in a cool cupboard out of the heat of the kitchen.

STORING OTHER SPICES

Bottles or tubes of spice pastes and purées, such as ginger and garlic paste, will keep unopened until the best-before date. However, once opened, they should be stored in the fridge and used within 6 weeks. Both dried and ready-made mustard will keep for up to a year even when opened. Dried tamarind and vanilla beans will keep in a cool dark place for up to 2 years.

This stainless steel spice container is ideal for storing dried spices. The individual pots are sealed when the inner lid is closed: a second lid ensures that no light or moisture gets into the tin.

Small glass jars with airtight seals or screw tops are perfectly good containers for storing dried spices, providing they are kept in a cool dark cupboard and not in a rack on the wall, or on a kitchen shelf.

THE SPICE INDEX

Garlic

BOTANICAL NAME: *Allium sativum* • FAMILY NAME: *Alliaceae*

FR. *ail*; G. *Knoblauch*; SP. *ajo*; IT. *aglio*

Garlic features in the mythology, religion and culture of many nations. For example, Arab legend has it that garlic grew from one of the Devil's footprints and onion from the other as he left the Garden of Eden, and there are many references to this noble plant in the Bible. Workers constructing the pyramids were given garlic, and it was found in the tomb of the young Pharaoh Tutankhamen. Roman labourers and soldiers chewed on garlic, the soldiers did so before battle, especially when they anticipated hand-to-hand fighting – it is little wonder they were so successful. In Chinese mythology, garlic has been considered capable of warding off the evil eye, the symbol of misfortune and ill fate. Culpeper, the famous herbalist, suggested chewing cumin or green beans to get rid of the smell of garlic on the breath; modern answers include drinking several glasses of red wine or, less drastically, eating fresh parsley, mint, thyme or celery leaves.

CULTIVATION

Garlic, a perennial of the lily family, grows like a leek to the height of about 2 feet. The name garlic comes from the Anglo-Saxon *garleac* in which *gar*, a spear, refers to the leaves and *leac* is a plant. A bulb or corm is made up of cloves of which there can be up to twenty but about twelve is the norm. Bulbs are ready for harvesting after 4-6 months, when they are dried in the sun before being plaited into a garlic string. Large quantities of garlic are grown in Spain, France, Egypt, Bulgaria, Hungary, USA, Mexico and Brazil.

purple garlic

There are many different types of garlic, the most common being the white papery-skinned variety. Pink- or purple-skinned garlic has a less papery outer skin and wonderfully fleshy, plump cloves. A giant variety comes from California, while in Southeast Asia there is a miniature type with only four to six cloves in each bulb.

Some gardeners believe that planting garlic under roses encourages the flowers to produce even more perfume, at the same time preventing black spot and greenfly.

AROMA AND FLAVOR

Garlic is indispensable in many cuisines. Before preparation, a whole clove has only a mild bouquet; it is only marginally stronger when sliced, but it has a very powerful flavor with a lingering aftertaste and aroma once chopped or crushed. The flavor is sharp, with a lot of punch for such a small ingredient. When frying, never allow the garlic to brown or else it will taste bitter.

garlic paste

PREPARATION TIPS

There are different schools of thought on how best to crush garlic; here are three suggestions.

Trim the root end from a garlic clove, place it in a mortar and give it one blow with a pestle to release the skin. Discard the skin, then crush the flesh with a tiny amount of salt to absorb the juices that might otherwise be lost. The salt also prevents the garlic from flying out of the mortar.

Place the unpeeled clove on a chopping board, cover with the flat blade of a knife and press hard. This releases the skin, which should be removed, then press again before finely chopping the flesh with a tiny amount of salt. Wash the chopping board and knife with hot soapy water to remove any odour.

If you have a garlic press, leave the garlic clove unpeeled and cut off the root end. Place the clove cut end down in the press.

Crush the garlic clove into a small bowl, or directly into the cooking pot. The garlic skin can be removed from the press in one neat piece, making the press easier to clean.

garlic granules

garlic
salt

smoked garlic

coarse garlic
granules

garlic flakes

minced garlic

white garlic

CULINARY USE

Garlic is an essential ingredient in thousands of dishes from around the globe. Along with ginger and onion it forms a 'trinity' of flavors that is familiar in Oriental and Asian cuisines.

Garlic is also widely used in Western cooking – roasted as whole cloves (up to forty may be used) or cut into slivers and inserted into meat, or cooked in sauces and casseroles. It flavors savory butters, dressings and sauces for pasta, fish, poultry, meat, game and vegetables.

Garlic butter is the classic accompaniment for snails, and it is served with shellfish or fish steaks. Alternatively, it can be spread on sliced French bread and baked in foil.

Raw garlic is used in salad dressings and some sauces, particularly in aïoli and rouille. For just a hint of garlic in a salad, rub the inside of the salad bowl with a cut clove of garlic.

Garlic products include paste, dried flakes and garlic salt, but it is best to use fresh garlic whenever possible.

MEDICINAL AND OTHER USE

Garlic is thought of as a wonderful tonic and is the subject of all manner of health-giving claims. It is said to purify the blood and lower blood pressure, which is enough encouragement for many people to take a garlic capsule on a daily basis. It is said to aid digestion and prevent flatulence. It is considered to be beneficial in the treatment of diabetes and to lower cholesterol. Garlic juice is used in cough medicines and it helps to alleviate asthma. An old country remedy for whooping cough was to put a clove of garlic in the shoe or the clog of the patient.

STORAGE

Peeled cloves should be a clean creamy white without blemish. Make sure that the bulbs are closely packed and firm; store them in a cool dry place, away from strong light.

Dill

BOTANICAL NAME: *Anethum graveolens* • FAMILY NAME: *Umbelliferae*

OTHER NAMES: *dill seed, garden dill;*
FR. *aneth;* G. *Dill;* SP. *eneldo;* IT. *aneto*

The name is believed to come from an ancient Norse word 'dilla' meaning to lull, refer-
ring to the calming effect an infusion of dill has on crying babies. Dill was widely used
in Greek and Roman times; in the Middle Ages it
was thought to have magical properties
and was used in witchcraft, love potions
and as an aphrodisiac.

fresh dill

CULTIVATION

Native to Southern Europe and Western Asia, dill grows wild in Spain, Portugal and Italy. It thrives in warmer
regions of the Northern hemisphere
and is particularly associated with
Scandinavian cuisine. It is now grown
in India and North and South America
as a commercial crop and much of
this is used to obtain dillweed oil. The
plant is an annual of the parsley family
and it grows to about 4 feet. It
has feathery, fern-like leaves with yellow flowers. The oval seeds are unusu-
ally convex on one side, with three
ridges, and flat on the reverse, with
two ridges.

AROMA AND FLAVOR

Dill has a sweet and aromatic bouquet;
the taste has a hint of caraway and is
slightly, but by no means unpleasantly,
bitter. Buy the whole seeds, which have
a long shelf life if kept away from
strong light. Indian or Japanese dill is
thinner and paler than its Western
counterpart.

CULINARY USE

Dill seeds are invariably found in jars
of pickled cucumbers. Crushed dill
seeds marry well with almost all fish
dishes: add a little to a creamy sauce
for a fish pie, or stir some into thick
yogurt with a teaspoon of chopped
chives and serve as a sauce with grilled
fresh salmon or cod fillet. Dill is also
good with egg dishes such as egg mayonnaise. Use dill vinegar or crushed
seeds to make a dressing for a mixed
seafood salad, coleslaw or potato
salad, adding a few feathery
leaves as a garnish.
Flavor homemade
bread with dill to
serve with vegetable
soups, such as carrot or tomato soup.

MEDICINAL AND OTHER USE

As well as its power to soothe crying
babies, dill is used widely as a
treatment for stomach and digestive
troubles, and to cure insomnia and hiccups. The Ancient Greeks believed
that carrying dill in the left hand could
prevent epilepsy.

COOKING TIP

Gravadlax (Scandinavian marinated
salmon) can be made successfully using
crushed dill seeds when dill leaves are
unavailable.

PREPARATION TIP

Dill vinegar is easy to make at home.

Place 2 tbsp dill seeds in a small
preserving jar. Top up with white wine
vinegar and close the lid. Leave the
vinegar in a cool dark place for 2-3
weeks, then strain and use in salad
dressings and sauces.

Indian or
Japanese dill seed

dill seed

dried dill

Celery

BOTANICAL NAME: *Apium graveolens* • FAMILY NAME: *Umbelliferae*

FR. *céleri*; G. *Stangensellerie*; SP. *apio*; IT. *sedano*

Celery was developed by Italian gardeners in the 17th century from the wild celery of the European salt marshes, a plant known as smallage. Celery seeds are small and gray-brown in color, with fine ridges.

CULTIVATION

Celery is a herbaceous biennial plant of the carrot, parsley and caraway family which throws up a flower head in the second year producing masses of seeds. Like caraway, the fruit of the celery plant consists of two joined carpels, which divide into single seeds when harvested.

AROMA AND FLAVOR

Celery seeds should be used with discretion as they have a fairly strong, and sometimes rather bitter, flavor. There is no mistaking their distinctive, celery aroma.

CULINARY USE

Whole celery seeds can be added to bread dough or when making cheese biscuits, and both may be served with soups and savory dishes. A few seeds can be sprinkled over lightly boiled carrots, grilled tomatoes or salads and they are especially complementary to egg and fish dishes. Celery salt and celery pepper are both made by grinding the seeds with either salt or peppercorns in the required proportions. Use these seasonings judiciously as their flavors are strong. Celery salt or pepper is best made when required.

MEDICINAL AND OTHER USE

The oil from the seeds is used medically to treat asthma, flatulence and bronchitic conditions.

celery sticks

ground celery seeds

celery seeds

celery leaves

Horseradish

BOTANICAL NAME: *Armoracia rusticana, syn Cochlearia armoracia, Armoracia lapathifolia* • FAMILY NAME: *Cruciferae*

FR. *cranson de Bretagne, raifort;* G. *Meerrettich;*
SP. *rábano picante;* IT. *rafano*

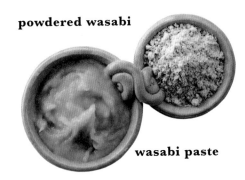

powdered wasabi

wasabi paste

dried horseradish

Horseradish has been used in the kitchens of Europe since the Middle Ages. It is said to have been one of the bitter herbs eaten by the Jews at Passover.

CULTIVATION

Horseradish is a perennial, a member of the mustard and, curiously, the wallflower family. The plant has large, long leaves with pronounced pale veins. It grows best in cool to moderate climates, flourishing in Northern and South-eastern Europe and in Scandinavia. Horseradish is an invasive plant and, if you do not take care to limit its growth, it will take over like a weed. Root sections are planted in the spring and harvested in autumn. The tubers can be stored for the winter, in the same way as potatoes, in a covering of sand.

horseradish cream

horseradish relish

WASABI

This is the Japanese answer to horseradish. Wasabi japonica by botanical name, it is also known as the mountain hollyhock. It is cultivated near fast-moving mountain streams. The peeled root reveals delicate, apple-green flesh, which is either grated, or dried and powdered. The dried powder is made into a cream with a little soy sauce or water.

AROMA AND FLAVOR

Horseradish is a long, rough, tapering root, not unlike a parsnip, with rings, and tiny roots sprouting from the main root. Its powerful smell and fiery taste put even mustard in the shade. The taste is very strong, very hot and very sharp.

fresh horseradish

CULINARY USE

There are no half measures associated with horseradish: it is a potent gastric stimulant and is the perfect accompaniment for rich or

horseradish sauce

rather fatty foods. It is richer in Vitamin C than lemons or oranges. Horseradish sauce with a creamy consistency varies in strength according to brand. Creamed horseradish, which is milder, can be used for the same purposes, as an accompaniment to beef, steaks and venison or served with a strong fish like mackerel, tuna or smoked trout.

STORAGE

To store horseradish, brush excess soil or dirt off the dry root, then wrap it in a paper bag (not polythene) and place in the vegetable box in the fridge. Commercial forms of horseradish, which are available widely and have a long shelf life, include the dried root, which can be used in the same way as the fresh root – but nothing ever quite matches the flavor of the fresh root.

Annatto

BOTANICAL NAME: *Bixa orellana* • FAMILY NAME: *Bixaceae*

OTHER NAMES: *achiote, anatta, annotto;* FR. *roucou, rocou;* G. *Annatto;* SP. *achiote achote;* IT. *anotto,* DU. *rocou;* FIL. *achuete*

The shrub, indigenous to both the Caribbean and tropical America, has heart-shaped, glossy leaves and spectacular, pink, rose-like flowers, which made it a favorite in colonial gardens, where it was planted to form a superior hedge. The plant produces a heart-shaped fruit capsule resembling a beech seed pod, with lots of spiky hairs that are its in-built protection from foraging animals. When ripe, the capsule splits exactly in half to reveal upwards of fifty seeds in a pulp. The Mayan Indians of Central America used the dye from the seeds, often described as 'the color of fire', as war paint.

annatto seeds

AROMA AND FLAVOR

Choose brick-red, triangular annatto seeds for a rich color, and for their slightly peppery flavor and bouquet, with just a hint of nutmeg in their aroma.

CULINARY USE

The seeds are washed and dried separately from the pulp for culinary use. An orange food coloring, made from the husk, is used as a coloring agent in dairy produce, such as Edam, Munster, Red Leicester and Red Cheshire cheeses. The famous Jamaican dish of salt cod and ackee is served in a vivid sauce, colored with annatto. The Spanish introduced the spice to the Filipinos and it is used widely in their cuisine.

COOKING TIPS

The seeds can be infused in hot water until the color is as intense as required. The water can be added to rice dishes and used as a substitute for saffron – but it lacks the beautiful aroma associated with saffron.

PREPARATION TIP

Annatto seeds impart a wonderful color to oil when fried for a few minutes, but have a lid ready to cover the pan as they splutter and jump out when hot.

Heat a little oil in a heavy-based saucepan, add the seeds and shake the pan over the heat for a few minutes.

Cool and strain the oil, which will keep indefinitely.

MEDICINAL AND OTHER USE

Annatto was once widely used in medicines, and in Africa it is used to control fevers and dysentery; however, it is now used principally as a dye. The pulp surrounding the seeds is the main commercial source of ox-blood red dye used in textile manufacture. The ripe seeds are soaked in water, the dye settles and it is then dried into cakes. As a natural coloring, annatto is also quite safe when used in cosmetics or in food. In India the pulp is used as an insect repellent.

Red Leicester cheese

Mustard

BOTANICAL NAME: *Brassica alba, B. juncea, B. nigra,*
syn Sinapsis alba • FAMILY NAME: *Cruciferae*

WHITE OR YELLOW MUSTARD (USA)

FR. *moutarde blanche;* G. *Senf, weisser Senf;*
SP. *mostaza silvestre;* IT. *senape bianca, mostarda*

BLACK OR BROWN MUSTARD (UK)

FR. *moutarde noire;* G. *schwarzer Senf;*
SP. *mostaza negra;* IT. *senape nera*

BROWN OR INDIAN MUSTARD

FR. *moutarde de Chine;* G. *indischer Senf;*
SP. *mostaza india;* IT. *senape indiana*

**yellow
mustard powder**

Mustard has featured in history and literature since early times. Pythagoras suggested a mustard paste as a treatment for scorpion stings, and Hippocrates, the father of medicine, recommended mustard for both internal and external use. Darius III of Persia was said to have sent Alexander the Great a bag of sesame seeds to indicate the numbers in his army and Alexander responded by sending mustard seeds to represent not only numbers but strength.

Mustard is mentioned many times in the Bible. From the New Testament: 'Another parable put he forth unto them saying, The kingdom of heaven is like to a grain of mustard seed, which a man took, and sowed in his field: Which indeed is the least of all seeds: but when it is grown, it is the greatest among herbs, and becometh a tree, so that the birds of the air come and lodge in the branches thereof'. (Matthew 13:31-32)

During the Middle Ages, mustard was introduced into Spain by Arab traders, and it was soon carried throughout Europe. The French mustard industry, in particular, has an impressive record, with Dijon, Meaux and Bordeaux all associated with mustard production and Dijon being referred to as the mustard capital of the world.

The word mustard comes from the Latin *mustum* or *must,* the name for the grape juice used to mix the ground seeds to a paste, which was known as *mustum ardens,* meaning the burning paste. There are three different types of mustard seed: white (*alba*), brown (*juncea*) and black (*nigra*). These are all part of the family of *cruciferae* (cross bearer) plants, which produce flowers in the shape of a cross.

American mustard

CULTIVATION

White mustard seeds are, in fact, sand or honey colored and are slightly larger than the other two varieties. The pale outer husk is removed before the seeds are used. This is the type of mustard grown in mixed punnets of mustard and cress, though rape seed is sometimes substituted for the mustard seed. *Brassica alba* is a native of the Mediterranean but it now grows throughout Europe and North America. It is a hairy, annual plant growing to nearly 2 feet. The bright yellow flowers form seed pods, which grow horizontally, each holding about six seeds.

Black mustard seeds *(Brassica nigra)* have been superseded in popularity by the brown seed for a very good reason: the black mustard seed plant grows tall and drops its seeds very easily when ripe. This makes harvesting by machine difficult so the plant is now grown only where harvesting by hand is the norm. The plant grows to over 3 feet tall; its bright yellow flowers are smaller than those of the white mustard plant and it forms erect pods close to the central stem, each containing twelve seeds.

Brown mustard seeds (*Brassica juncea*) have largely replaced the black seeds, though they are not as intensely pungent as the black seeds. Their color varies from light to darker brown. Native to, and grown throughout, India, the plant produces flowers, which are a pale yellow, and seed pods, which are larger than those on the other mustard plants.

brown mustard seeds

black mustard seeds

white mustard seeds

crushed yellow mustard

yellow mustard seeds

mustard oil

AROMA AND FLAVOR

Mustard seeds have little or no smell. The hot taste which gives mustard its 'bite' is released only when the seeds are crushed and mixed with water. Crushing and moistening the mustard, or mixing powdered mustard with water, activates an enzyme present in the seeds, and it reacts with other natural constituents to develop the essential oil, which gives the characteristic taste. The white seeds have an initial sweetness with a mild taste. Brown seeds have an initial bitterness to their flavor, from the outer husk, and then the sharp biting flavor comes through; black seeds share these same characteristics: they are sharp, biting and pungent.

PREPARATION TIPS

It is recommended that yellow mustard powder is mixed 10 minutes before it is required to allow the clean pungent flavors to develop. The mustard loses its pungency in a few hours, so fresh mustard should be made daily or as required. For hot results, mix mustard powder with milk or beer, never with boiling water or vinegar, as both kill the enzyme that gives the condiment its hot flavor, resulting in a mild, but bitter, mustard. Similarly when mustard powder is to be added to hot dishes such as sauces and stews, stir it in at the end of the cooking and heat gently on the lowest heat to retain its bite.

To make mustard, mix mustard powder with warm water, milk or beer.

French mustard

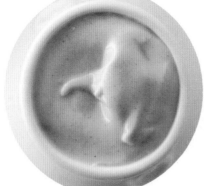

Dijon gray mustard

To bring out the flavor of mustard seeds, heat a little ghee or oil in a wide pan. Add the seeds and shake the pan over the heat, stirring occasionally, until the seeds start to change color.

Have a pan lid ready to prevent the mustard seeds popping out of the pan.

CULINARY USE

Mustard is an indispensable ingredient in cooking: the different whole seeds, powdered or ground seeds, prepared pastes and oil are all used. The white seeds are used in pickling, and the brown seeds are used throughout India in curry powders and in spiced ghee (baghar or tadka). The seeds are cooked in hot oil until they pop and turn gray and are then stirred into a variety of vegetable or dhal dishes. Whenever frying mustard seeds, always have a lid ready for when they start to pop, to prevent them from flying out of the pan. Mustard oil, available in Asian and Oriental stores, is used in many Indian recipes. Mustard is used in salad dressings and mayonnaise, where it helps the emulsification of the egg yolk and the oil. It is also added to cheese sauce and sauces for cabbage or cauliflower, Jerusalem artichokes or leeks.

MEDICINAL AND OTHER USE

A few spoonfuls of mustard powder in a footbath or bath are said to relieve and soothe muscular aches and pains. Mustard is a stimulant and it is used to relieve respiratory complaints and rheumatism. It also stimulates kidneys. Mustard used to be given as a laxative and emetic (to induce vomiting). A gargle of mustard seed in hot water is helpful in the relief of sore throats and bronchitis.

CLASSIC MUSTARDS OF THE WORLD

American Mustard: The obligatory accompaniment to hot dogs and burgers, this is made from mild white mustard seeds, vinegar, sugar, spices and turmeric. Mild with a hint of sweetness.

English Mustard: This hot mustard is made from yellow mustard powder and is sometimes mixed with wheat flour, for bulk, and turmeric, for color.

German Mustard: This is a smooth, dark mustard made from black seeds and vinegar to give a sweet and sour flavor with just a hint of sharpness, which complements the huge range of German sausages. There are also extra-strong German mustards.

Dijon Mustard: Traditionally prepared from only black seeds, Dijon mustard is now made from brown seeds. The seed husks are removed, resulting in a mustard with a pale blond color. The mustard is blended with wine or verjuice (the sour juice from unripe grapes or wild apples), salt and spices. This is the classic French mustard, which is eaten with steaks and grills. It is smooth, salty and sharp with a good mustardy flavor.

Bordeaux Mustard: Referred to as French mustard, this is darker than Dijon mustard. It is also made from a blend of

tarragon mustard

Provençal mustard

red grape mustard

honeycup mustard

old-style gray mustard

black and brown seeds and the husks are retained, which results in the darker color. Bordeaux mustard is mixed with vinegar and sugar, plenty of tarragon, plus other herbs and spices to give a mild sweet-sour taste, which goes best with cold meats and sausages.

Meaux Mustard: For this mustard, the black seeds are part crushed and part ground to give the typical crunchy texture. Mixed with vinegar and spices, this mustard is medium to hot in flavor with an interesting spiciness; it is good with cold meats, meat pies or sausages. Meaux mustard is often sold in stoneware jars with a sealed cork stopper.

Other Mustards: There are dozens of different mustards, such as French Maille mustard, from a company established in 1747, and Provençal mustard, which is flavored with garlic and red bell peppers. Tarragon, tomato, basil and honey are all examples of ingredients used to flavor mustard; for a touch of luxury, there is even a smooth, mild mustard blended with champagne.

COOKING TIP

To sprout mustard seeds, put about 2 tbsp of the seeds in a muslin-covered glass jar. Rinse and drain the seeds once or twice a day until they sprout.

mild whole-grain mustard

mustard seed sprouts

American mustard

German mustard

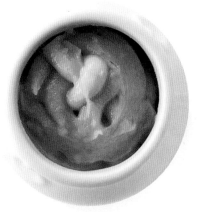

house neri karashi

Capers

BOTANICAL NAME: *Capparis rupestris, of which there are two types:*
C. spinos (spiny), C. inermis (no spines) • FAMILY NAME: *Capparidaceae*

FR. *câpre, câpre capucine, fabagelle;* G. *Kaper;*
SP. *alcaparra, tápana, tápara;* IT. *cappero*

*Capers are the flower buds of a low-growing bush with round, fairly thick leaves,
which is easily identified by its beautiful pink, dog-rose-type flowers that have long
tassels of purple stamens. The flowers open in the morning
and are dead by midday. The flower buds have been used
since biblical times.*

caper berries

nasturtium seeds

CULTIVATION

Capers grow in profusion all around
the Mediterranean, with its warm dry
climate. They have to be picked by
hand, which is labor intensive and
makes them expensive. The bushes are
checked each morning for small hard
buds that are just at the right stage for
harvesting. The capers are washed and
allowed to wilt for a day in the sun
before being put into jars and covered
with salted wine vinegar, brine or olive
oil. Alternatively they can be preserved
in salt alone.

AROMA AND FLAVOR

Some would describe the taste of the
pickled caper as like goat's milk cheese,
with sour and salt flavors coming
through when the bud is bitten.

CULINARY USE

Chopped capers are included in a huge
range of classic sauces, including
tartare, rémoulade and ravigote
sauces, and Italian tonnato sauce, used
in the famous dish of cold braised veal,
Vitello Tonnato. In Britain, hot caper

sauce is tradition-
ally served with boiled
mutton, but try it with salmon
or pan-fried or broiled fish with the
addition of a little grated lemon rind
to complement the distinctive flavor.

Capers are widely used in other
areas of Italian cooking, for example
as a flavoring in antipasti salads and as
a topping on pizza. They also feature
in fish and vegetable dishes from
Northern and Eastern Europe.

**dry-salted
capers**

STORAGE

Capers should always be submerged in
their pickling medium, otherwise they
will develop an off-flavor.

nasturtium flowers and leaves

capers in brine

COOKING TIP

*Nasturtium seeds, which have a sharper,
more mustard-like flavor, and the larger
caper fruits or berries can be used in
place of capers.*

Chilies

BOTANICAL NAME: *Capsicum annuum or C. frutescens*
FAMILY NAME: *Solanaceae*

OTHER NAMES: *chili pepper, chili;* FR. *piment, piment fort, piment rouge;* G. *roter Pfeffer, spanischer Pfeffer;* SP. *chile;* IT. *peperoncino*

Chili is the most popular spice and throughout history, wherever it was, chili transformed the previously bland cuisine. Latin American, Asian, African, Caribbean and certain regional Oriental cuisines make extensive use of this spice. The name chili is believed to be derived from an ancient Indian word txile. *Chilies are native to Mexico. Evidence of chili peppers is known from burial sites in pre-Colombian times in Peru. Christopher Columbus, who was searching the New World for pepper* (Piper nigrum), *came across these fruits, which, he discovered, were even hotter than peppercorns. He carried his prize to Europe and from there to Africa, India and the East where chili became an integral part of each cuisine. The long shelf life of the seeds (it can be 2-3 years) was a bonus in the days of sea travel.*

bird's eye chilies

Chilies have a chemical effect on our bodies which some of us enjoy more than others. Once you have got over the stage where the slightest hint of chili makes you cry and splutter, you may find that the flavor becomes pleasurable and even addictive. Chilies are rich in Vitamin C, they stimulate the appetite and cool the body, especially in hot climates, by making the person sweat. The cooling effect also creates a feeling of calm and benignity. To relieve the burning sensation in the mouth, drink yogurt or milk, not water or beer.

CULTIVATION

Chilies are part of the potato, tomato, eggplant and nightshade family of plants. The chili family is a minefield: there are at least 150 different types, so it is wise to assume that any unfamiliar chili is HOT! The plant, which is bushlike, grows up to about 2 feet and bears white flowers that produce fruits in a variety of sizes and shapes. Some chilies look like stout fingers (such as the cayenne), others are tiny (like the

bird's eye chili, which is very tiny, explosive and often used in Thai cooking), and some look deceptively like mini sweet bell peppers (for example, habanero, which is the hottest). The plants grow at altitudes from sea level to 6,000 feet in the tropics. Their pungency is influenced by several factors, such as high night temperatures and drought or over-watering. Green chilies are immature fruits and red chilies have been allowed to ripen for a further 4 weeks. Ripened chilies can also be orange-yellow, purple, dark brown or black.

India is the largest producer and exporter of chilies, with a significant part of the total crop used for home consumption. Travellers in Rajasthan and the south of India marvel at the acres of chilies, laid out to dry like a huge red carpet stretching as far as the eye can see.

Thailand, Mexico, Japan, Turkey, Nigeria, Ethiopia, Uganda, Kenya and Tanzania are also major producers, and they export chilies to other countries around the world.

The most common Mexican chilies, used in the cuisine to make fiery salsas, bean, fish and poultry dishes, are fresh green serrano, jalapeño and poblano chilies.

**small
green chilies**

caribe chilies

AROMA AND FLAVOR

The characteristic pungency of chilies is caused by the presence of capsaicin. Research has indicated that the components of capsaicin (capsaicinoids) promote different taste sensations when eaten, giving either a short fiery flavor or lingering hot taste. The hotness is said not to come from the seeds but rather the placenta. This is the pithy white part of the fruit to which the seeds are attached, and it contains the most capsaicin so removal of both seeds and placenta should reduce the pungency of chilies, if required.

The heat of chilies is measured in Scoville units, ranging from 0 (for sweet bell peppers) to 300,000 (for the habaneros). To provide a simple guide, the scale has been reduced to 0-10, with the habaneros having a scorching rating of 10.

CULINARY USE

The chili flavor revolutionized the cooking of tropical countries with bland staple foods, like cassava in South America, West and East Africa; rice in India and South-east Asia; and beans in Mexico and the Southern States of America. Famous Mexican moles, chili con carne and Tex-mex foods make extensive use of chilies. Curries from Thailand and Malaysia, and Indonesian sambals and satays all rely on chilies for their characteristic flavors. Many Szechuan dishes depend on the chili flavor. Countries which do not use chilies as extensively in everyday dishes also depend on their heat for certain traditional preparations; for example, piquant pasta dishes from Italy use fresh and dried chilies, and prudent use of chilies is made in many of the pickles, relishes and cooked chutneys of the more Northern European countries.

FRESH CHILIES

Fresh chilies are available almost everywhere, from independent green-grocers to Oriental stores and supermarkets. It is difficult to be specific about their heat: even fruits from the same plant can vary in strength.

Anaheim: These are about 4 in long, red or green and mild to medium in flavor.

PREPARATION TIPS FOR FRESH CHILIES

Cut away and discard the stalk end. Holding the chili under cold running water to prevent the oils from affecting your eyes and throat, slit it from the stalk end to the tip. Scrape out the placenta and seeds. Afterwards, wash your hands, knife and chopping board thoroughly to clean off the oils. Do not rub your eyes or lips – even after washing your hands. Those with sensitive skin should wear rubber gloves when preparing chilies.

cayenne chilies

anaheim chili

serrano chilies

small red chilies

Cayenne: Sometimes called finger chilies, these are slimmer than anaheim chilies, they are always red and hot.

Serrano: Slightly chunky, these red or green chilies can be hot or slightly milder.

Bird's Eye: These chilies are so hot that they taste explosive to the uninitiated. They can be green, red or orange in color.

DRIED MEXICAN CHILIES

New Mexico Red: HEATSCALE 2-4 This is a large red chili with a clean heat and earthy, fruity flavor. Great for red sauces.

Ancho or Dried Poblano: HEATSCALE 3 Sweet, fruity and mild, these can be stuffed, cut into strips or added to mole sauces (sauces enriched with bitter chocolate or cocoa).

Guajillo: HEATSCALE 3 These are mild, with a green-tea flavor. Used in many classic salsas.

Mulato: HEATSCALE 3 Similar to ancho, but with a more smoked taste, and a hint of licorice flavor. These can be stuffed, cut into strips or used in Mexican mole sauces.

Pasado: HEATSCALE 3 This crisp, roasted, peeled chili has a toasted flavor combined with apple, celery and citrus flavors. Use in soups and stews.

Cascabel or Little Rattle: HEATSCALE 4 Nutty and woody in flavor, with a medium 'rounded' heat, these thick-fleshed chilies are great in sauces, soups, stews and salsas.

Pasilla or Little Raisin: HEATSCALE 4 These medium-hot chilies taste of berries and licorice. Good with seafood and in mole sauces.

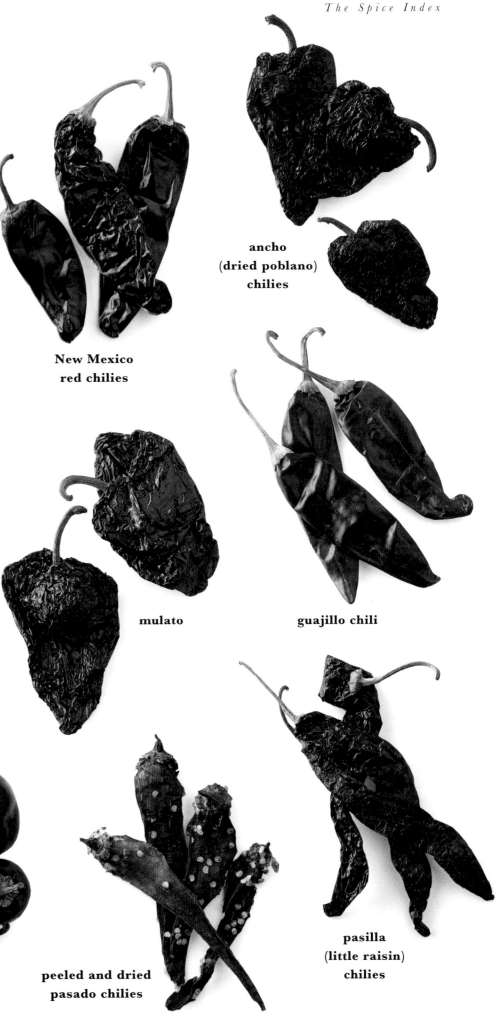

New Mexico red chilies

ancho (dried poblano) chilies

mulato

guajillo chili

cascabel (little rattle) chilies

peeled and dried pasado chilies

pasilla (little raisin) chilies

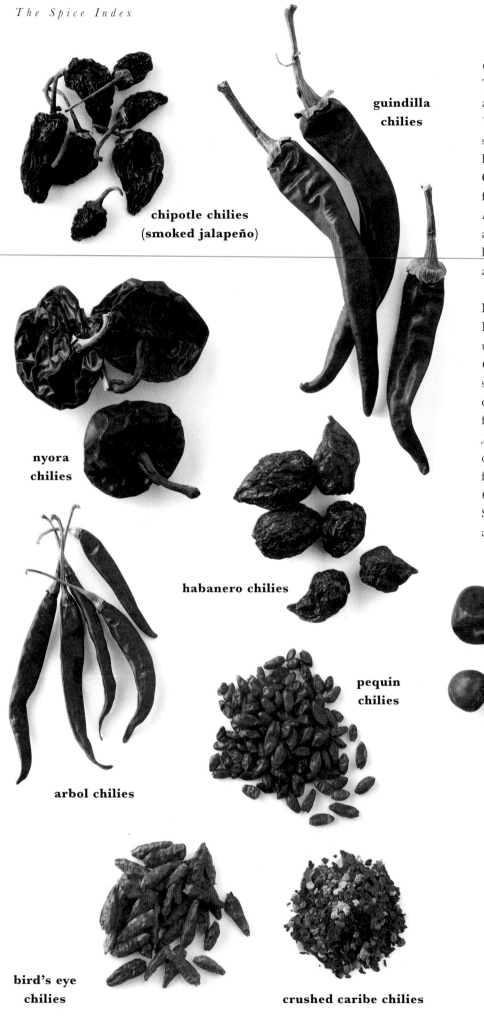

**chipotle chilies
(smoked jalapeño)**

**guindilla
chilies**

**nyora
chilies**

habanero chilies

arbol chilies

**pequin
chilies**

**bird's eye
chilies**

crushed caribe chilies

**cherry
chilies**

**Madras
chilies**

Chipotle or Smoked Jalapeño: HEATSCALE 6 This chili is smoky and nutty in flavor, and fairly hot.

Tepin or Flea Chili: HEATSCALE 8 This small, hand-picked chili has a searing heat and it tastes of corn and nuts. Crush the chili over food or use it to flavor bottles of vinegar or oils.

Habanero: HEATSCALE 10 With intense aroma and fiery taste, these are excellent in condiments, fish stews, curries and salsas.

DRIED SMOKED SPANISH CHILIES

Dried, mild-smoked chilies are widely used in Spanish cooking.

Choricero: HEATSCALE 0-1 An extremely sweet and mild Spanish chili, large enough to stuff or use to make well-flavored sauces, soups and stews.

Nyora: HEATSCALE 1-2 A dried Spanish chili with a sweet, fruity flavor; great for mild salsas, soups and stews.

Guindilla: HEATSCALE 3 A medium-hot Spanish chili with a sweet flavor, this adds 'zip' to fish.

kashmiri chilies

PREPARATION TIPS FOR DRIED CHILIES

Dried chilies can be soaked, then cut into thin strips and added to stir-fries, soups or other dishes. The strips can also be stored in a jar, covered with olive oil; herbs may be added to flavor the chili strips.

To make chili paste, remove the stem and seeds. Soak the chilies in boiling water for 20 minutes, then purée them with some of the soaking liquid. Strain the purée to make a smooth sauce. Add to taste when cooking. Pastes can be stored in a covered jar in the fridge for up to a week or frozen for up to a year.

COOKING TIPS FOR DRIED CHILIES

To make chili vinegar, fill a bottle with chilies, top up with vinegar and leave for two weeks before using.

Dry-roasting heightens the flavor of chilies. Heat a heavy frying pan without adding oil. Press the chilies onto the surface of the pan to roast them. Do not allow the chilies to burn, or their flavor will be bitter. When roasted, remove the chilies from the pan and grind them.

Larger, thick-fleshed and thin-skinned dried chilies (such as anchos or mulatos) can be stuffed with meat, rice or vegetable fillings. Make a small lengthwise split in the chili and remove the seeds. Leave the stem intact. Soak the chili, then drain and pat it dry on paper towels. Stuff carefully and bake until heated through.

CHILI PRODUCTS
Cayenne Pepper

This is a very fine ground powder from the *Capsicum frutescens* variety of chili. The placenta and seeds are included in the powder, making it very hot, so it must be used judiciously. This is named on account of its origins in the Cayenne region of French Guyana but the chilies used in its preparation now come from India, Japan and East Africa. Cayenne is widely used as a seasoning (in tiny amounts), for example in savory crackers and cheese and egg dishes, and it is also added to some curries.

cayenne pepper

pickled sweet cherry peppers

pickled hot chili peppers

pickled jalepeño peppers

pickled hot banana wax peppers

chili powder

ancho powder

pimentón de la vera

chimayo powder

pasilla powder

mulato powder

hot chili paste

Chili Powder

Milder than cayenne pepper and more coarsely ground, this is prepared from a variety of mild to hot chilies. Check the ingredients list, as some chili powders (especially those of American type) contain a variety of other flavors, such as garlic, onion, cumin and oregano. They are added for convenience for use in chili con carne. If the chili powder is dark in color, it may contain the rich-rust-colored ancho chili.

For best results make your own chili powder. Seed dried chilies, then dry fry them and grind them to the required fineness.

Chili Sauce

Tabasco sauce is a North American seasoning made from extremely hot tabasco or cone chilies, which are mixed with salt and vinegar and then matured in white oak casks for several years. Many of the islands of the Caribbean have their own style of chili sauce. Most are, like Tabasco, made from steeping the chilies in vinegar and all are very hot indeed. Chili sauces are widely used in small quantities as a general seasoning. Tabasco is served with tomato juice and used to flavor Bloody Mary cocktails.

Chili Paste

Ready-made chili paste is sold in small jars. However, it is easy to make at home. Simply seed fresh chilies, then purée them in a food processor to make a smooth paste. An onion can be added to the processor to add bulk to the paste. Store small amounts in the fridge for up to 1 week, or spoon into small containers, cover and freeze for up to 6 months.

Crushed Chilies

These dried chili flakes contain both the flesh and seeds from red chilies and can be used in place of some or all of the chili powder in a dish.

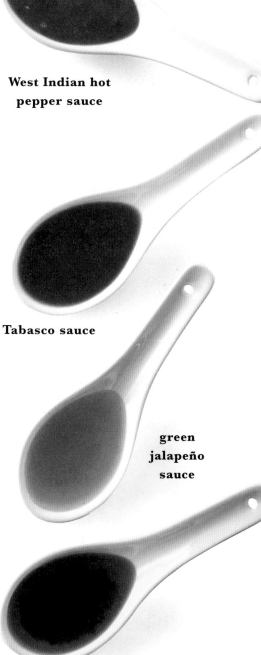

crushed chilies

chili sauce

West Indian hot pepper sauce

Tabasco sauce

green jalapeño sauce

chili oil

Paprika

BOTANICAL NAME: *Capsicum annuum* • FAMILY NAME: *Solanaceae*

OTHER NAMES: *Hungarian pepper,
sweet paprika, rose paprika, pimento pepper;*
FR. *piment;* G. *Paprika;* SP. *pimentón,
pimiento colorado;* IT. *paprica*

**Hungarian
paprika**

**Spanish
paprika**

A fine powder made from specially mild varieties of pepper, the fruit from the Capsicum
annuum, *which were originally taken to Hungary by the Turks. The core and seeds are
removed, then the flesh is dried and powdered, which results in the characteristic rich red
color. Paprika is mild to pungent and sweet with a hint of bitterness: always check the
label, which will give a guide to its pungency.*

Hungarians have adopted this as their national spice, using it generously in their famous goulashes, stews and chicken dishes. Paprika also has an affinity with Spanish and Portuguese cuisines. Crops are grown in Andalucía and Extremadura in Spain, and in Portugal. About half the Spanish crop, which can often be quite pungent, is exported to the USA.

If you find the true fresh paprika peppers, which are very like ordinary or sweet red bell peppers, but more pointed, try stuffing them with minced lamb seasoned with oregano or thyme, cooked in a tomato sauce – they are excellent.

Papaya Seeds

BOTANICAL NAME: *Carica papaya, syn Papaya carica*
FAMILY NAME: *Caricaceae*

OTHER NAMES: *pawpaw, papaw;* FR. *papaye;* G. *Melonenbaum
Papaia;* SP. *papaya;* IT. *papaia*

*The jet-black or gray-black seeds from papaya look like giant caviar when the fruit is
first cut open. The color of the seeds depends on the tree; white seeds indicate an unripe
fruit. The tree now grows in most tropical and sub-tropical countries worldwide.*

fresh papaya

CULTIVATION

The tree, a fast-growing herbaceous perennial, is found in the tropics, but not above 5,000 feet. The stem or trunk is straight, with a cluster of large, maple-shaped leaves on top. The fruits, which are called berries, can weigh up to 20 lb each. They are ovoid in shape and are attached to the trunk just under the leaves. The seeds are enclosed in the hollow center of the fruit, arranged in five rows.

AROMA AND FLAVOR

Papaya seeds are slightly aromatic when fresh but their aroma is less pronounced as they dry. Fresh seeds have a sparky taste, strongly resembling that of mustard and cress. They can be used fresh or allowed to dry in the sun, when their smell and taste are somewhat diminished.

CULINARY USE

The plant sap, which is tapped from the trees like rubber, is rich in the enzyme papain which is an efficient

**crushed
papaya seeds**

**fresh
papaya seeds**

meat tenderizer of commercial value. Both fruit and seeds also contain papain. Rub tough meat with the seeds and the skin of the fruit, or wrap it in papaya leaves (if available) and leave to marinate for several hours. Remove the papaya leaf wrapping before cooking. Crushed papaya seeds can be added to minced meat for koftas (spicy meatballs) or to a marinade for meat. Some of the pounded flesh of the fruit can also be added. When cooked, the meat will be tender, with an interesting, peppery flavor.

Crushed papaya seeds can be added to salad dressings or sauces to serve with fish. They also add texture and flavor to a fruit salad. The fresh fruit can be served in slim wedges with the seeds still intact. Next time you cut a papaya, remember the many interesting ways in which the seeds can be used before you discard them.

MEDICINAL AND OTHER USE

In India, papaya seeds are chewed to freshen the breath, and they are widely used as pessaries, also as a medicine for flatulence and piles. Australian aborigines have a more romantic approach to the seeds, and consider them to be of value as an aphrodisiac.

Ajowan

BOTANICAL NAME: *Carum ajowan, Ptychotis ajowan, Carum copticum* • FAMILY NAME: *Umbelliferae*

OTHER NAMES: *carom, bishop's weed, ajwain, omum, ajwan;* FR. *ajowan;* G. *Ajowan;* SP. *ajowan;* IT. *ajowan;* ETH. *cumin*

The celery-type, striped seeds (similar to caraway and cumin seeds in appearance) are used as the spice. They are sold whole – when crushed, they have a rather strong and distinctive thyme-like bouquet; indeed, they can be used as a substitute for thyme, but add them sparingly as they are stronger in flavour than thyme. In some Indian recipes ajowan is referred to as lovage.

CULTIVATION

Part of the *Umbelliferae* family, ajowan (pronounced aj'owen) looks like wild parsley. A native Indian plant, and usually a cool-weather crop, it is also grown in Pakistan, Afghanistan, Iran and Egypt. It is grown mainly for export, for the extraction of its oil, which contains a high percentage of thymol.

PREPARATION TIP

Before using ajowan seeds, crush them to release the aroma by rubbing between your fingertips.

Bombay mix

CULINARY USE

Ajowan is particularly popular in savory Indian recipes: savory pastries, snacks (including Bombay mix) and breads (especially parathas), bean and pulse recipes, all of which illustrates the affinity ajowan has for starchy foods. Ajowan can be crushed in the hand, which releases a powerful thyme aroma and flavor.

MEDICINAL AND OTHER USE

The medicinal properties of ajowan are numerous. In India, the seeds are used to ease asthma and indigestion. A liquid product of ajowan is widely used to treat diarrhoea and wind; ajowan seeds are popular in recipes for beans and lentils due to their properties in relieving flatulence. Its thymol content makes ajowan a potent fungicide.

ajowan seeds

ground ajowan

Caraway

BOTANICAL NAME: *Carum carvi*
FAMILY NAME: *Umbelliferae*

OTHER NAMES: *caraway fruit or seed, carvies (Scottish), wild cumin, Roman cumin, Persian caraway;* FR. *carvi, graines de carvi;* G. *Cumich, Kümmel;* SP. *alcaravea;* IT. *caro, carvi;* AR. *karawya*

This is one of the world's oldest culinary spices, with evidence of seeds found in the remains of food from the Mesolithic age, about 5,000 years ago. Caraway was used to flavor bread eaten by Roman soldiers and its popularity spread as their empire grew. The Ancient Egyptians always placed a container of caraway in tombs to ward off evil spirits. It was later considered to be an important ingredient in love potions, to prevent fickleness. In 16th-century Britain, caraway was used in breads, pastries and cakes.

caraway seeds

ground caraway

CULTIVATION

A member of the parsley family, caraway has feathery leaves. It grows to about 2 feet in height and blooms every two years to produce large creamy flowers. Caraway is widely grown in Europe, but principally in Holland, where this hollow-stemmed biennial thrives particularly well in the heavy clay soil and humid conditions. The oil extracted from Dutch caraway is said to be superior because the crops are grown quite close to the sea. It is also grown in Russia and India.

Caraway seeds are mericarps, that is, they split into two on harvesting. Each single seed, or carpel, is slightly crescent shaped and pale to dark brown, with five ribs. They are best harvested early in the morning when the seeds are less likely to fall off the flower head. The cut plants are stacked to dry and ripen for over a week and then the seeds are threshed.

AROMA AND FLAVOR

Caraway seeds have a warm, sweet and slightly peppery aroma. Their distinct flavor has a hint of fennel or aniseed. Caraway seeds have a slight eucalyptus-like tang to their flavor and are chewed to sweeten the breath.

CULINARY USE

Caraway is used extensively in Eastern European, German and Austrian cooking. It features in savory, as well as sweet, dishes, including sauerkraut, cabbage soups, coleslaw, goulash, potato- and cheese-based dishes. Caraway flavors breads, especially rye bread, cakes, including old-fashioned British seed cake, and cookies. Caraway seed cake was traditionally baked by farmers' wives to celebrate the end of planting and distributed among the farm workers. Caraway has also long been used to flavor cheese, with medieval recipes for caraway-flavored Dutch cheese still in use today. In Alsace, Munster cheese is always served with a saucer of caraway seeds to sprinkle on to slices before eating – a delicious combination of flavors.

Sausages and other meat preparations are seasoned with caraway. The leaves can be snipped into salads or used as a garnish. The carrot-shaped root has the same flavor as the seeds and it can be cooked in the same way as parsnips, either by baking or boiling.

Caraway is also a vital ingredient in the liqueur Kümmel, in Aquavit, a favorite tipple of the Scandinavians, and as an ingredient in gin and schnapps. To round off a meal, the seeds can be infused in water which is just off the boil and served as a tisane.

MEDICINAL AND OTHER USE

Oil of caraway was recommended as a tonic for pale girls by Dioscorides, a Greek physician in the 1st century: it was rubbed into the skin to improve the complexion. In more recent times, caraway in gripe water was used to settle babies with wind. It is used as a flavoring in children's medicines. Caraway is a useful antidote for flatulence and an aid to digestion. It is used in a multitude of ways for its flavor and aroma, for example in mouthwash and gargle preparations as well as in the perfume industry.

caraway cheese

Cassia

BOTANICAL NAME: *Cinnamomum cassia* • FAMILY NAME: *Lauraceae*

OTHER NAMES: *bastard cinnamon, canel, canton cassia, casia bark, Chinese cinnamon;* FR. *casse, canéfice;* G. *Kassia, Kaneel;* SP. *casia;* IT. *cassia*

This ancient spice was known to the Chinese as early as 3000 BC and mentioned in the early books of the Bible. Cassia was also mentioned in the Psalms and used by the Pharaohs. It came into Europe over the spice routes from the East.

CULTIVATION

Cassia is a native of Burma and it should not be confused with cinnamon, which originates from Sri Lanka. The bulk of the world's cassia comes from China, Indochina, Indonesia, the East and West Indies and Central America. Both cassia and cinnamon grow on small, evergreen laurel-like trees of the same family. Growing to 10 feet high in warm tropical conditions, the cassia tree has yellow flowers. The tree is cut down when the bark is ready to harvest and trimmed into workable lengths. Long slits are made in the grayish bark and inside this the pieces of cassia are a deep rust-brown color. The cassia curls slightly on drying, but not into the neat quills associated with cinnamon.

AROMA AND FLAVOR

The bouquet and the taste share similar characteristics. Cassia is coarser, more pungent and less fragrant than cinnamon; in America cassia is substituted for the finer-tasting cinnamon.

cassia bark

CULINARY USE

Cassia is generally used in savory dishes, while cinnamon is preferable in sweet and delicately flavored recipes. Cassia is an ingredient in mixed spice, pickling spices and Chinese five spices, and in Germany it is used as a flavoring for chocolate. Cassia is good with stewed fruits such as rhubarb and apple. Cassia buds resemble cloves and are used in the East for pickles, in curries and spicy meat dishes where they impart a warm aromatic flavor.

MEDICINAL AND OTHER USE

The volatile oil is used in some inhalants, in tonics and as a cure for flatulence, sickness and diarrhoea.

ground cassia

Cinnamon

BOTANICAL NAME: *Cinnamomum zeylanicum*
FAMILY NAME: *Lauraceae*

FR. *cannelle;* G. *Ceylonzimt, Kaneel, Zimt;* SP. *canela;* IT. *cannella;* SINH. *cinnamon*

Cinnamon and cassia, a relative spice, have long been associated with ancient rituals of sacrifice or pleasure. The Ancient Egyptians used the spice in embalming. Hieroglyphics discovered on a temple built around 1489 BC by Hatshepsut, a formidable Pharaoh queen, indicate that she sent ships to Punt, now Somalia, to bring back, among other things, cinnamon, frankincense and myrrh trees. Throughout the Old Testament in the Bible, references to cinnamon illustrate that it was more precious than gold. The Roman Emperor Nero is said to have murdered his wife in a fit of rage, then he ordered that a year's supply of cinnamon be burnt at her funeral as a sign of remorse.

ground cinnamon

The trade for cinnamon was first documented by the 13th-century Arab writer Kazwini. Waves of traders and merchants profited from this special aromatic crop: first the Portuguese in 1500, followed by the Dutch and then the British East India Company. When traders were taking European travelers to the island of Ceylon (Sri Lanka) they would spread cinnamon on the decks of their ships just before sighting the island and amuse their passengers by telling them, 'Now you can smell it, soon you will see it'. It was true, for the very best cinnamon grew at low altitudes on poor white sands. In the Victorian language of flowers, cinnamon is translated as meaning 'my fortune is yours'. In Austria lovers would exchange a posy containing cinnamon, reflecting warmth and love.

CULTIVATION

Cinnamon is native to Sri Lanka, Burma and the southern coastal strip of India. Sri Lanka still produces the best-quality spice. Cinnamon now thrives in South America and the West Indies. A substantial crop also grows in the Seychelles and Réunion, taken there from Sri Lanka by Pierre Poivre, an enterprising missionary.

Cinnamon is a bushy evergreen tree of the laurel family, cultivated as low bushes to ease the harvesting process. The bushes like shelter and moderate rainfall without extremes in temperature. Eight or ten lateral branches grow on each bush and, after three years, they are harvested in the rainy season, when the humidity makes the bark peel more easily. The slim branches are first peeled, then the inner bark is bruised with a brass rod to loosen it. Long incisions are made in the branch, the bark lifts off and the drying process begins. The quills of bark are rolled daily by hand until neat and compact, and any off-cuts are used to fill the longer quills.

cinnamon sticks

AROMA AND FLAVOR

The bouquet of cinnamon is delightfully exotic, sweet and fragrant, and its flavor is sweet and warm.

CULINARY USE

Cinnamon is appreciated in a multitude of dishes from around the world. The quills or cinnamon sticks are added whole to casseroles, rice dishes, mulled wines and punches, and to syrups for poaching fruit. In Mexico, they are used to stir mugs of hot steaming chocolate. Ground cinnamon is used in cakes, pastries and cookies.

MEDICINAL AND OTHER USE

Cinnamon is a stimulant, astringent and carminative, used as an antidote for diarrhoea and stomach upsets. It is also given to women in labour as a sedative. Oil is extracted from the leaves, which are long, dark, glossy and beautifully aromatic. Oil from the leaves is used as a substitute for clove oil; oil from the broken bark is used in the manufacture of perfume. In Mexico, cinnamon is added as a flavoring in the manufacture of chocolate.

STORAGE

Store cinnamon in an airtight jar, in a cool dark cupboard. Buy little and often for the best flavor.

COOKING TIPS

Cinnamon sticks and ground cinnamon are widely used in all kinds of sweet and savory dishes.

To make mulled wine add one or two cinnamon sticks to other flavoring ingredients and heat gently.

Sprinkle prepared fruit, such as peaches, nectarines, pears and apples, with cinnamon-flavored sugar and broil until the sugar is golden. Serve hot, with chilled sour cream.

To make cinnamon toast, toast bread on one side, then butter the untoasted side, sprinkle it with cinnamon sugar and toast it until golden.

Add cinnamon to bread dough to make savory buns to serve with tomato or pumpkin soup.

Stir a cup of hot, sweet, fresh coffee with a cinnamon stick or sprinkle ground cinnamon over frothy, milky cappuccino coffee.

Mexican chocolate

Kaffir Lime Leaves

BOTANICAL NAME: *Citrus hystrix* • FAMILY NAME: *Makrut, Magrut*

IND. *daun jeruk purut;* THAI *bai makrut*

The leaves of this member of the citrus family are responsible for the distinctive lime-lemon aroma and flavor that are an indispensable part of Thai and, to a lesser extent, Indonesian cooking. These dark green, glossy leaves grow in pairs and look like a figure of eight. The citrus fruit from this bush looks like a gnarled lime or lemon.

fresh kaffir lime leaves

kaffir limes

CULINARY USE

Apart from the leaves of the bush, only the fruit rind is used, finely grated, in Thai dishes. The bushes are grown in Thai homes, where the kaffir lime juice or the juice of the fruit may be used instead of lime juice. The leaves are torn or shredded and used in soups and curries.

MEDICINAL AND OTHER USE

The citrus juice used to be included in Thai ointments and shampoo, and in tonics in Malaysia.

AROMA AND FLAVOR

The haunting bouquet is unmistakably citrus and scented. The full citrus flavor is imparted when the leaves are torn or shredded.

STORAGE

Buy fresh lime leaves in Oriental stores and freeze them for future use. Dried lime leaves are now available.

dried kaffir lime leaves

grated kaffir lime peel

Coriander (Cilantro)

BOTANICAL NAME: *Coriandrum sativum* • FAMILY NAME: *Umbelliferae*

OTHER NAMES: *Chinese parsley, cilantro;* FR. *coriandre;* G. *Koriander;* SP. *coriandro, culantro;* IT. *coriandolo*

Coriander has been used as a flavoring and medicine since ancient times. Seeds have been found in the tombs of the Pharaohs, and the Roman legions carried coriander as they progressed through Europe, using it to flavor their bread. The origin of the name is rather off-putting – it comes from koris, *the Greek word for a bed bug, so given because of the similarity between the smell of cilantro leaves and the offending bug.*

CULTIVATION

Cilantro is a slender, solid-stemmed plant, growing to 2 feet high, with branching stems, compound leaves and small white flowers, which have a pink tinge. It is part of the parsley and carrot family, native to the Mediterranean and Middle East.

The seeds are tiny globes, about the size of peppercorns, and they are a pale, creamy-brown color. Cilantro grows wherever there is warmth. It needs a sunny position in well-drained soil and grows easily in boxes and pots. It is grown extensively as a crop in India, Russia, Brazil, South America, North Africa and Holland.

AROMA AND FLAVOR

Dry fried seeds have a heady, slightly 'burnt orange' aroma, which is very appealing. The ground seeds give a pleasing, mild and sweet taste. The seeds have a long shelf life and are easily ground to a powder: the freshly ground spice is to be recommended because it has a more pronounced flavor than ready ground coriander. The latter loses flavor and aroma quite quickly.

CULINARY USE

Every Indian household uses huge quantities of ground coriander in curry powders, garam masala and other spice mixes. Coriander seeds are frequently combined with cumin seeds, the two spices being dry fried together before being ground. This combination is common in Middle Eastern dishes too. Whole coriander may be added to chicken and pork casseroles, and it is one of the ingredients in pickling spice. Whole or ground coriander may be used in chutneys, particularly with green tomatoes. Whole or coarsely ground coriander may be used in dishes 'à la Grecque'.

MEDICINAL AND OTHER USE

Coriander seed oil has myriad medicinal uses. It has antibacterial properties and is also included in treatments for colic, neuralgia and rheumatism. The oil also counteracts unpleasant odours in pharmaceutical preparations and tobacco; and it is used in perfumes, liqueurs and gin. The seeds are ground into a paste for application to skin and mouth ulcers. Before toothpaste was commonly used, coriander seeds were chewed as a breath sweetener.

COOKING TIPS

Add freshly ground coriander to homemade tomato or béchamel sauces or include it as a seasoning in carrot, parsnip or pumpkin soups. Try adding ground coriander to savory bread dough with sun-dried tomatoes or olives.

coriander seeds

PREPARATION TIP

The flavor of the seeds is greatly enhanced by dry frying. Heat the frying pan without oil, add the seeds and toss them over a gentle heat until they begin to give off a rich aroma. Cool the seeds slightly before grinding them.

roasted coriander flakes

cilantro roots

ground coriander

fresh cilantro

Saffron

BOTANICAL NAME: *Crocus sativus*
FAMILY NAME: *Iridaceae*

FR. *safran*; G. *Safran*; SP. *azafrán*;
IT. *zafferano*; IN. *kesar, khesa, kesram*

saffron strands

The name saffron comes from the Arabic za'faran, *which means yellow — a sacred color chosen by Buddhist monks for their robes. Saffron is hugely expensive: consider that 200,000 flowers have to be harvested by hand to obtain 1 lb saffron and no further explanation for cost is necessary.*

Saffron has been highly prized as a dye, medication and culinary spice since Greek and Roman times. One of the more extravagant Roman Emperors, Heliogabalus, is said to have bathed in saffron-scented water. Arab traders introduced saffron to Spain, where its richness of color and flavor were appreciated, then rapidly assimilated in the cuisines all along the Mediterranean. From there saffron spread to Britain, where it was extensively grown in Essex, with the town of Saffron Walden as a center for cultivation. Early British saffron growers were known as 'crokers'.

Buy true saffron in fine, bright orange-red ragged strands for preference, as they are less likely to have been adulterated. Look out for telltale light patches on the strands. Ready ground (powdered) saffron is also a candidate for adulteration, so buy from a reputable source.

CULTIVATION

The *Crocus sativus* is a bulbous, fall-flowering perennial of the iris family. The flowers have three bright, orange-red stigmas which are the true saffron. These are toasted, or dried, in sieves over a very low heat. Nowadays, the very best saffron comes from Valencia or La Mancha in Spain; however, it is grown also in Greece, Turkey, Iran, Morocco and Kashmir.

AROMA AND FLAVOR

Saffron has a distinctive and lasting aroma with a certain warmth. Use saffron sparingly to avoid a medicinal flavor. The spice is so expensive that cheating is quite common.

CULINARY USE

Appreciated for its delicate, yet distinctive, flavor and striking color, saffron is added to special dishes in many cuisines. Celebration pilaus from India are scented with saffron, as are rice dishes from the Mediterranean, particularly Spanish paella and Italian risotto milanese. Bouilabaisse, the famous seafood soup-stew, is laced with saffron.

This spice is also widely used in sweet recipes: milky rice or vermicelli puddings and sweet custard-like desserts from India. Baked goods flavored with saffron

Chartreuse

include yeasted breads as well as cakes. It is one of the ingredients in the liqueur Chartreuse.

MEDICINAL AND OTHER USE

Saffron is used in sedatives, as an antispasmodic and for flatulence. It is also used in perfumes and dyes and, being so expensive, it is considered to be an aphrodisiac in some cultures.

PREPARATION TIP

Saffron strands can be infused in a little warm water or milk until the color of the liquid is even. Add the liquid and strands to the dish, usually towards the end of the cooking process. The powder can be added direct to food without soaking.

STORAGE

Store saffron, wrapped in its cellophane or paper sachet, in airtight tins, to keep it away from strong light.

SUBSTITUTES FOR SAFFRON

There are a number of substitutes for saffron: in India turmeric is often referred to as saffron. Turmeric does not have the fine flavor or bright color of true saffron. Safflower, known as Mexican or bastard saffron, is another saffron look-alike: the same comments apply, it can be used but does not compare well with the real thing.

saffron powder

Cumin

BOTANICAL NAME: *Cuminum cyminum*
FAMILY NAME: *Umbelliferae*

FR. *cumin*; G. *römischer Kreuzkümmel*;
SP. *comino*; IT. *cumino*; IN. *jeera, jira, zeera,
jeera safed (white), jeera kala (black)*

Cumin has a long and fascinating history. Evidence shows that it was known to the Egyptians 5,000 years ago and it was found in the pyramids. There are biblical references to threshing cumin with a rod, and this practice is still carried out today in remote regions of the Eastern Mediterranean. Theophrasatus, a Greek philosopher and celebrated botanist, was of the opinion that 'cumin must be cursed and abused while sowing if the crop is to be fair and abundant'. In ancient times cumin was a symbol of greed and meanness. Curiously, by the Middle Ages this derogatory reputation had changed and cumin was regarded as a symbol of faithfulness. For example, in Germany, where cumin is still a popular spice, a bride and groom would carry a little of the seed to represent their commitment to being faithful.

black cumin seeds

white cumin seeds

CULTIVATION

Cumin is a small, annual herbaceous plant of the parsley family, growing to a height of about 10 in. It is a native of Eastern Mediterranean countries and upper Egypt, but it is now cultivated in Morocco, Iran, Turkey, India, China and the Americas. Cumin flourishes best in sunny climes with some rainfall. The small white or pink flowers grow on small compound umbels, like many of the plants in the *Umbelliferae* family.

Harvesting takes place about 4 months after planting. The small, boat-shaped seed has nine ridges, and it is brown-yellow in color. Cumin seeds are sometimes confused with caraway, but the cumin seeds are lighter in color. There is a type of black cumin,

ground cumin

which grows in Iran. The seeds are smaller and they have a sweeter aroma. Black cumin is occasionally confused with nigella, which is sometimes called black caraway in Indian cooking.

AROMA AND FLAVOR

Cumin has a strong, spicy, sweet aroma with a slightly bitter and pungent taste. The pungency and bitterness are particularly noticeable in the ground spice; however, as it is frequently used with coriander, the bitterness is counteracted. Dry frying before grinding brings out a toasted, nutty flavor, making the spice less harsh. Buy the seeds and grind them as required for superb flavor. Black cumin seeds have a slightly sweeter, more delicate, flavor than the white seeds.

CULINARY USE

On account of its strong flavor, ground cumin is most popular in cuisines which are generally highly spiced; for example in Indian, Middle Eastern, North African and Mexican cooking. Cumin is an essential ingredient in most Indian curry powders and garam masala. It is added to soups and stews, especially Moroccan lamb dishes and Mexican meat dishes, such as chili con carne. Cumin seed contributes a lighter flavor, without the distinctive bitterness, and it is valued in Indian vegetable, rice and dhal recipes. Black cumin is particularly associated with Indian rice preparations.

Cumin features widely in German cookery, in classics like sauerkraut, pickles, sausages and Munster cheese. It is also used in Dutch cheese, based on an old medieval recipe.

MEDICINAL AND OTHER USE

Cumin is regarded as an appetite stimulant, and it is widely used to ease stomach disorders, flatulence, colic and diarrhoea. It is also used in veterinary medicines. Cumin oil is used in perfumes.

COOKING TIP

Dry fry cumin seeds in a heavy-based pan for a few minutes to bring out the flavor before using them whole or grinding them.

Turmeric

BOTANICAL NAME: *Curcuma domestica, syn C. longa*
FAMILY NAME: *Zingiberaceae*

FR. *curcuma*; G. *Gelbwurz*; SP. *cúrcuma*;
IT. *curcuma*; IN. *haldi*

The name turmeric is believed to have come from the Latin terra merita, *merit of the earth. Marco Polo was intrigued by the turmeric he found in Southern China: 'There is also a vegetable which has all the properties of true saffron, as well the smell and the color, and yet it is not really saffron'. Turmeric is much revered by Hindus and associated with fertility. During Hindu wedding ceremonies, a sacred thread dipped in turmeric paste is tied around the bride's neck by the bridegroom. In Malaysia, a paste of turmeric is spread on the mother's abdomen and on the umbilical cord after childbirth, not only to warn off evil spirits, but also for its medicinal value, as turmeric is known to be antiseptic.*

Fresh turmeric is available from some Oriental stores. Peel it in the same way as ginger, with a sharp knife. The vibrant color will stain heavily, so it is a good idea to wear rubber gloves. Once peeled, the fresh turmeric can be sliced, grated, chopped or ground to a paste with other ingredients and cooked in the same way as fresh ginger root. Fresh turmeric is superb in fish curries.

**fresh turmeric
root slices**

CULTIVATION

Turmeric is a robust, bright, deep yellow rhizome, similar in size and form to ginger, and it belongs to the same family of plants, which thrive in hot, moist tropical conditions. Huge quantities are grown and consumed in, as well as being exported from, India, the world's greatest source of supply. Today, turmeric crops are also harvested in China, Taiwan, Indonesia, Sri Lanka, Australia, Africa, Peru and the West Indies.

The spice is propagated by planting pieces of the previous season's rhizome, which grow to form plants of about 3 feet, with long-stemmed hosta- or lily-like leaves and pale yellow flowers. Turmeric is ready for harvesting after about 9 months, when the whole underground system of rhizomes is carefully lifted. The rhizomes are boiled, peeled and dried for a week in the sun before they are graded for quality. The superior grade is referred to as 'fingers', then there are 'rounds' and 'splits'. The rhizome loses about three-quarters of its original weight during drying. Almost all the turmeric crop is ground and sold as powder.

ground turmeric

fresh turmeric root

curry powder

**dried
turmeric root**

AROMA AND FLAVOR

Turmeric has a peppery aroma and flavor with a hint of wood. It has a warm, musky flavor with a slightly bitter aftertaste.

CULINARY USE

Where a recipe calls for saffron some might suggest substituting turmeric, but it is a misconception that turmeric is regarded only as a second-rate alternative to the most expensive of spices. In Indian cooking, turmeric is often used as an everyday alternative to saffron. It may be added to dishes usually spiced with saffron for its color, but not for the flavor, and it is sometimes referred to as saffron in this context. Using turmeric in place of saffron is in the interest of economy; saffron would be reserved for celebration dishes: pilaus for weddings, for example.

Turmeric is, perhaps, best appreciated as an ingredient in curries (especially fish curries) and curry powders, contributing flavor as well as the characteristic yellow color. It is also used in chutneys and pickles, particularly piccalilli, kedgeree and many Indian rice, vegetable and dhal dishes. Turmeric is popular in many North African dishes to spice lamb and vegetables.

MEDICINAL AND OTHER USE

Turmeric is aromatic and a mild digestive, and in Asian countries it is taken to ease liver complaints and stomach ulcers. Boiled with milk and sugar, it is said to be a cure for colds. The role of turmeric as a dye was mentioned in an ancient Assyrian herbal recipe from 600 BC, and it is still used as a dye for cotton and silk. It is widely used in the food industry as an edible coloring in mustards, butter, cheese and liqueurs.

STORAGE

The powder should be bought in small quantities and stored in an airtight container away from strong light to preserve its color and flavor. Whole pieces of dried turmeric are sometimes used in pickling. It is difficult to grind the dried spice and therefore best to buy ready ground turmeric.

Zedoary

BOTANICAL NAME: *Curcuma zedoaria, C. zerumbet*
FAMILY NAME: *Zingiberaceae*

> OTHER NAMES: *wild turmeric;* FR. *zedoaire;*
> G. *Zitwer;* SP. *cedoaria;* IT. *zedoaria*
> IND. *kentjur;* IN. *amb halad, garndhmul*

Native to India and China, zedoary was transported to Europe in the Middle Ages by Arab traders, but over the years its popularity waned and it is now used mainly in countries where it is grown.

CULTIVATION

A member of the ginger and turmeric family of plants, like turmeric, it is bright yellow in color and propagated in the same way, by planting pieces of the rhizome. Zedoary takes two years to mature before it can be harvested, which possibly has some bearing on its decline in popularity. The plant grows well in wet tropical forest areas. The rhizomes are similar in size to turmeric and ginger, and the leaves are similar to turmeric, but larger, growing to about 3 feet. The plant bears yellow flowers with red and green bracts. Powdered or dried zedoary is occasionally available from Oriental food stores under its Indonesian name of kentjur.

AROMA AND FLAVOR

Zedoary has a musky aroma with a hint of camphor. It has a ginger-like flavor but a bitter aftertaste.

CULINARY USE

Although its use is primarily medicinal, the peeled and chopped root might be pounded with turmeric and ginger to make a spice paste for goat, lamb or chicken curries.

MEDICINAL AND OTHER USE

Used as an aid to digestion, to relieve flatulence and colic. The starch, *shoti*, obtained from the root is easily digested and nutritious, and it is therefore used as a food in the East for the sick and young. Zedoary is also used as a dye.

chopped dried zedoary root

Lemon Grass

BOTANICAL NAME: *Cymbopogon citratus, syn Andropogon schoenanthus* • FAMILY NAME: *Gramineae*

OTHER NAMES: *citronella;* FR. *herbe de citron;* G. *Zitronengras;* SP. *hierba de limón;* IT. *erba di limone;* IND. *sereh;* MAL. *serai*

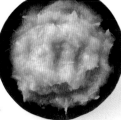

lemon grass paste

Trim and discard the root end, then cut the low bulbous end to 3 in long and slice it finely.

This tropical and subtropical scented grass flourishes all over South-east Asia. It was described by Tennant on Ceylon in 1860: 'These sunny expanses … are covered with tall lemon grass'.

chopped dried lemon grass

CULTIVATION

Lemon grass is a perennial tufted plant with long, sharp-edged leaves. It grows in dense clumps in sunny climates with some rainfall. Propagation is by dividing the root stock. The mother plant will grow for 3-4 years and the bulbous stems are cut three times a year. Lemon grass is cultivated on a commercial scale in South-east Asia, Southern India, Africa, Brazil, Guatemala, the USA and the West Indies. The cut stems are about 8 in long, and they look like thick scallions.

Lemon grass can be grown as an ornamental houseplant in colder regions. Fresh stems from an Oriental supermarket sometimes have little buds at the root: place them in water until roots begin to sprout. Dust the developing growth with rooting powder, place in a pot of compost and keep in a sunny place.

AROMA AND FLAVOR

Lemon grass stems do not have an identifiable aroma until they are cut, then they have a distinctive citrus bouquet. Lemon grass contributes a 'bright' lemon flavor to dishes – lemon rind is sometimes recommended as an alternative, but it does not match the lively flavor of the grass.

CULINARY USE

Lemon grass features in many dishes, including soups, marinades, stir-fries, curries, salads and pickles. It is a perfect partner for coconut milk, especially in those dishes using fish, seafood and chicken. Sereh powder (ground dried lemon grass) can be used in place of fresh – 1 tsp is equivalent to one stalk. In South America, a refreshing tea is made by infusing the leaves in water.

MEDICINAL AND OTHER USE

The medicinal and cosmetic value of lemon grass was recognized centuries ago by the Egyptians, Greeks and Romans. The essential oil from lemon grass is used in soaps and perfumes and for aromatherapy. An ointment containing the oil is said to be good for rheumatism, lumbago and sprains.

fresh lemon grass

Bruise the tough, top end of the stem in a pestle and mortar and add to gravies and soups for extra flavor but always remove before serving.

Alternatively, the stem end can be bruised at one end to make a brush, and used to baste meats with oil, marinade or coconut cream.

STORAGE

When wrapped in a paper bag, lemon grass stems will keep in the vegetable compartment of the fridge for 2-3 weeks. The lower part of the stem can be sliced or pounded and frozen along with the top half of the stems, tied in a separate bundle. Freeze the equivalent of two stems in separate portions and label them for future reference.

sereh powder

Cardamom

BOTANICAL NAME: *Elettaria cardamomum* • FAMILY NAME: *Zingiberaceae*

FR. *cardamome;* G. *Kardamome;* SP. *cardamomo;*
IT. *cardamomo, cardamone;* IN. *elachi*

It is said that cardamoms grew in the gardens of the King of Babylon in 720 BC. The Ancient Egyptians chewed cardamoms to whiten their teeth and simultaneously sweeten their breath. Even earlier, in 4 BC, Indian Ayurvedic medicine (of Hindu tradition) used the spice to 'remove fat' and as a cure for urinary and skin complaints. Cardamom was used in perfumes by ancient Greeks and Romans, and also recommended by Apicius, a famous Roman epicure, to counteract over-indulgence.

PREPARATION TIP

Bruise the pods in a pestle and mortar to open them, then dry fry over a gentle heat to heighten the flavor.

Although there are various similar types of cardamom-like spices, *Elettaria cardamomum* is the true spice. Buy unsplit pods from a reputable source to be sure of the best quality. Green cardamoms are the most common and useful; white cardamoms are the same type of pods which have been bleached (they are used in Indian desserts); and black cardamoms are quite different. The black spice is used in long-cooked, highly flavored, savory Indian dishes. The pods are large, hairy and brown-black, with a coarse, strong flavor. Black cardamoms are too crude for light dishes or sweet mixtures; it is best to use the green pods for all cooking.

CULTIVATION

Cardamom is a herbaceous perennial bush of the ginger family. It flourishes in areas which have a constant warm temperature with moderate rainfall, and grows wild in the forests of Southern India. Commercially, the bulk of the crop is grown in India. Unsuccessful attempts were made to grow the crop in Singapore and Penang late in the last century. India grows 80 per cent of the world's crop, exports half its production and makes domestic use of the remainder.

The bush bears fruit pods after three years and continues cropping for ten to fifteen years. The bush has elegant, long, oval leaves of 8-10 feet. The stalks which bear the seeds are near the base of the plant. The seed pods appear over a long period, and they do not ripen at the same time. They are triangular in cross-section and oval in shape. When opened the papery pod reveals three segments, each with a row of tiny, brownish-black seeds. The pods are removed carefully with scissors before they are ripe.

green cardamoms

cardamom seeds

black cardamoms

white cardamoms

If the pods ripen and split, the flavor and aroma are diminished. Hand picking is therefore essential to avoid damaging both pods and plants. This is very labor-intensive and it accounts for the fact that cardamom is one of the most expensive spices, along with saffron and vanilla. The pods are also dried slowly in the sun, in kilns or hot rooms to prevent them from splitting.

AROMA AND FLAVOR

The pungent and warm bouquet of cardamom seeds with their distinct aroma is unforgettable. Cardamoms have a pleasing, warm, slightly lemon-like flavor, with a distinct element of eucalyptus and camphor that will sweeten the breath if the seeds are chewed – the perfect antidote to garlic or alcohol.

CULINARY USE

Cardamom plays an essential role in both sweet and savory dishes, worldwide. It is essential in a wide range of Indian dishes: curries, pilaus, garam masala and other spice mixtures. It is also vital to the flavor of many Indian sweetmeats and desserts, such as the popular ice cream kulfi and milk puddings. Cardamom is used extensively in Scandinavian cooking, in pickles, with herrings, cakes and pastries. It also flavors Aquavit.

Arab traders became addicted to the cardamom-flavored coffee known as *gahwa*, and it is still served today, with much ceremony, as a symbol of Arab hospitality. The curved spout of the coffee pot is stuffed with a few opened cardamom pods which flavor the strong coffee as it is poured: good manners dictate that you must drink at least three cups.

MEDICINAL AND OTHER USE

The seeds and pods contain a volatile oil which is used in perfumes and as a stimulant. Cardamom features often in *The Arabian Nights*, where its aphrodisiac properties are extolled; that belief is still held in the Middle East today. Additionally it is held that cardamom is a stimulant, that it cools the body in extreme heat and that it aids digestion.

STORAGE

Always buy whole, unsplit pods in small quantities as they lose their flavor as they grow stale. Ready ground cardamom is rarely available,

ground cardamom

extremely costly and not to be recommended as the seeds lose their flavor very quickly once removed from the pods; also, the powder may well have been adulterated. Store the pods in a small, airtight jar in a cool dark place. They may be frozen.

Cloves

BOTANICAL NAME: *Eugenia caryophyllus* • FAMILY NAME: *Myrtaceae*

> FR. *clou de girofle*; G. *Gewürznelke*;
> SP. *clavo de especia*; IT. *chiodo di garofano*

The name clove is believed to be derived from the French word clou *meaning nail, which is an apt description of the appearance of this spice. There may be a lot of truth in the saying, 'nutmegs must be able to smell the sea but cloves must see it', as clove crops appear to flourish best on islands. The people of the Moluccas or Spice Islands (now Maluku, a group of islands in Indonesia) used to plant a clove tree to celebrate the birth of a child. If the tree flourished, this was a good omen for the child, who would wear a necklace of cloves as a protection from evil spirits and illness. Chinese physicians appreciated the medicinal benefits of cloves as early as 3 BC. Dignitaries visiting the emperor were expected to suck cloves to sweeten their breath; today eugenol, extracted from clove oil, is used in toothpastes and gargles.*

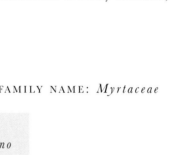

whole cloves

COOKING TIPS

Place an onion studded with cloves in the body cavity of a duck before roasting it. Alternatively, stud an orange with cloves and bake it briefly, then use it to flavor mulled wine.

tree is 6-8 years old. The crop can be sporadic: one year heavy and the next light.

The cloves are hand picked to avoid damaging the branches which would jeopardize subsequent crops. If the pink buds are not picked, small purple or crimson flowers develop. The buds change from a pale russet color to a darker brown as they dry slowly in the sun. This process cannot be hastened or the cloves become dry, brittle and withered, rather than plump.

AROMA AND FLAVOR

Approaching a clove tree is a heady experience, as the warm, pungent

CULTIVATION

The tree, part of the myrtle family, with fragrant, rich green leaves, is native to the Moluccas, part of the Indonesian archipelago. It was grown exclusively in the Moluccas until the early 18th century, when the French

ground cloves

decided to break the monopoly by asking Pierre Poivre, who had taken cinnamon to the Seychelles, to carry seedlings to Mauritius. The trees flourished in Mauritius, and subsequently further seedlings were taken to the islands of Zanzibar and Pemba on the East African coast, now the world's largest producer of cloves. The cloves, the unopened flower buds of this 40 foot tree, are harvested when the aroma drifts towards you. Cloves have a slightly astringent, sweetly pungent and strongly aromatic flavor.

CULINARY USE

Cloves are included in many classic spice mixtures, including Chinese five spice powder; Indian and Oriental curry powders; European whole pickling spices; spices for mulling wine; and ground mixed spice for baking.

Whole cloves are frequently used to flavor cooking liquids for simmering fish, poultry, game or meat. They feature in classic sauces and are a festive flavoring and garnish for baked hams.

Cloves have a particular association with apples and are added to apple sauce, tarts and pies or other apple puddings. Ground cloves are used to spice rich cakes, cookies, gingerbreads and satisfying puddings from all over the world.

MEDICINAL AND OTHER USE

Oil of cloves, which is distilled from the buds, leaves and stalks, is a valuable commodity: it is a strong antiseptic and preservative, and it is used in toothpastes, mouthwashes and gargle preparations. Additionally it is used to treat flatulence, colic, indigestion and nausea. A cotton bud soaked in oil of cloves eases toothache when applied to the tooth.

STORAGE

Buy whole cloves which have a long shelf life if kept in a cool place away from strong light. To make your own powder when just a small amount is required, grind the central bud at the top of the nail (this should still be intact if the cloves are reasonably fresh). Powdered cloves are available, but buy the powder in small quantities as required as the flavor and color soon dissipate.

Asafoetida

BOTANICAL NAME: *Ferula asafoetida* • FAMILY NAME: *Umbelliferae*

OTHER NAMES: *asafetida, assafoetida, devil's dung, food of the gods;* FR. *assa-foetida, férule périsque;* G. *Asafotida, stinkender Asant;* SP. *asafétida;* IT. *assafetida*

Early records mention that Alexander the Great carried this 'stink finger' west in 4 BC. Used as a flavoring in the kitchens of ancient Rome, this pungent, resinous gum is used widely in Indian vegetarian cooking.

asafoetida resin

CULTIVATION

Ferula asafoetida, a perennial of the carrot family, grows wild to 12 feet high in huge natural forests. The plant is indigenous to Iran, Afghanistan and in the north of India. There is a smaller species called *Ferula narthax*. The whole plant exudes the characteristic strong smell, described by some as a stink. The milky resin comes from both the thick stems and the root, and it dries into asafoetida.

AROMA AND FLAVOR

In its raw state, the resin or the powder has an unpleasant smell. This completely disappears when the spice is added to a variety of vegetable, fish, pulse and pickle ingredients.

CULINARY USE

Used mostly in Indian vegetarian cooking, in which the strong onion-garlic smell enhances many dishes, especially those of the Brahmin and Jain castes where onions and garlic are prohibited. Also used in curries, and pickles from the West and South of India. The lump of resin would only be acceptable to keen Indian cooks who use a very small piece at a time. For most of us, the powdered version is easier to handle. Buy asafoetida in small quantities. The powdered resin is usually mixed with flour to provide bulk and is often sold in a bright yellow tub.

asafoetida powder

asafoetida powder

MEDICINAL AND OTHER USE

Asafoetida is a useful antidote for flatulence, hence its popularity, with Indian vegetarian cooks, who make generous use of pulses. There are claims for it being used to cure bronchitis and even hysteria.

Fennel

BOTANICAL NAME: *Foeniculum vulgare*
FAMILY NAME: *Umbelliferae*

OTHER NAMES: *common fennel, sweet fennel, Florence fennel;* FR. *fenouil, aneth doux;* G. *Fenchel;* SP. *hinojo;* IT. *finocchio*

**fennel
flower heads**

The name comes from the Latin foenum, *a variety of fragrant hay. Fennel has been known to herbalists and doctors since time immemorial: it was believed to be the total cure and to have the power to make people young, strong and healthy. The American poet Longfellow summarized opinions about fennel in his poem* The Goblet of Life:

*Above the lowly plants it towers,
The fennel with its yellow flowers,
And in an earlier age than ours,
Was gifted with the wondrous powers,
Lost vision to restore.*

*It gave new strength, and fearless mood;
And gladiators, fierce and rude,
Mingled it in their daily food;
And he who battled and subdued,
A wreath of fennel wore.*

CULTIVATION

Fennel is a tall, leggy, aromatic perennial of the parsley family, native to Southern Europe and the Mediterranean, where it grows particularly well near the sea. It is extensively cultivated in India and Argentina, and grown throughout Europe, North Africa, Romania, Bulgaria, Russia, Japan and the USA. Fennel has fine feathery leaves and yellow flowers. The seeds are harvested when the fruits are mature and sage green in color.

The fruit splits into two seeds, which are oval in shape with five ridges. It is wise to avoid planting dill and fennel near each other to prevent cross-fertilization.

AROMA AND FLAVOR

Fennel has a delightfully sweet and warm aroma with a flavor of mild anise. Fennel is best bought in seed form and ground or dry fried as required.

CULINARY USE

Fennel has a great affinity with fish, especially oily fish like mackerel, herring and salmon. Dried stems of fennel may be burnt on the barbecue when broiling fish, to impart a unique flavor to the food. It also complements pork and lamb. The crushed seeds are used in salad dressings and in mayonnaise to serve with fish. Ground fennel is used in many curry powders and in Chinese five spice powder. Crushed seeds are used in savory and sweet

PREPARATION TIP

Dry frying and crushing fennel seeds before using them heightens the flavor.

Dry fry the seeds first in a heavy-based pan for 1-2 minutes until they release their aroma, then crush the seeds in a mortar with a pestle.

baking: in breads, doughs, cakes and cookies. Try sipping fennel tea for a jaded palate – infuse 1 tsp seeds in about $1\frac{1}{4}$ cups water that is just off the boil. Then strain the liquid into a tall glass.

MEDICINAL AND OTHER USE

Fennel is said to cure earache, toothache, asthma and rheumatism. It is meant to help stop hiccups and coughs, and improve eyesight. It has even been thought of as a good slimming agent. Fennel oil is used in cough medicine, liquorice sweets, perfumes and soaps.

fennel seeds

Licorice

BOTANICAL NAME: *Glycyrrhiza glabra*

FAMILY NAME: *Leguminosae*

OTHER NAMES: *liquorice (UK)*;
FR. *réglisse*; G. *Lakritze, Süssholz*;
SP. *regaliz*; IT. *liquirizia*

licorice powder

The name comes from the Greek glyks *or* glukus, *meaning sweet, and* rhiza, *meaning root. Licorice is particularly well known for its use in confectionery, particularly for the famous British sweets, Licorice Allsorts. It has been grown in the UK since the 16th century, when it was cultivated by Dominican monks in Pontefract, Yorkshire, where the confectionery trade began. Licorice was used in the famous Pontefract cakes before the children's sweets were manufactured.*

licorice allsorts

sliced licorice root

licorice sticks

CULTIVATION

Licorice, a perennial of the pea family, native to the Middle East and South-east Europe, grows to over 3 feet. Above ground, the plant has long stems with pinnate leaves, made up of nine to seventeen leaflets, and blue flowers, which produce pods containing three or four seeds. The root, which is the important part, sends out a deep and extensive network of rhizomes, which are grown for three to five years before they are harvested.

AROMA AND FLAVOR

When cut, the root is bright yellow and it smells sweet. It tastes strongly of anise, with a rather bitter-sweet flavor.

CULINARY USE

Licorice is best known as an ingredient in confectionery. It is also used in the making of the famous Irish ale Guinness and to flavor the Italian liqueur sambuca as well as other beers and soft drinks.

MEDICINAL AND OTHER USE

The strong smell and distinctive taste of licorice are often used in medicines to disguise other unpalatable flavors, for example in cough medicines and throat pastilles.

STORAGE

Dried sticks of licorice are sometimes available: store them in an airtight container in a cool dry place.

Pontefract cakes

The roots and rhizomes are cleaned, pulped, then boiled and the licorice extract is then concentrated by evaporation. Today licorice is cultivated in Russia and Southern Europe.

sambuca liqueur

Star Anise

BOTANICAL NAME: *Illicium verum, syn I. anisatum*
FAMILY NAME: *Magnoliaceae*

FR. *anis de la Chine*; G. *Sternanis*;
SP. *badiana, badián*; IT. *anice stellato*

CULTIVATION

Traditionally the Japanese used to burn the beautifully aromatic bark of the tree as incense. Star anise is the fruit of a small to medium, evergreen tree, native to South-west China and now grown in Indochina and Japan. Yellow, narcissus-like flowers yield fruits which open out into an eight-pointed star shape. The tree bears fruit after 6 years initially, but then it has a productive life of up to a hundred years. The fruits are harvested before they ripen. When ripe, they are rust-red and each point of the star-shaped husk contains an amber-colored seed. Both the seed and the husk are used for the ground spice.

star anise

star anise seeds

AROMA AND FLAVOR

Though star anise could not be more different from anise in appearance, both spices smell and taste very similar, with a distinct licorice-like aroma and flavor.

CULINARY USE

Star anise is one of the most important spices in Chinese cuisine, and it is the dominant flavor in Chinese five spice powder. More often the whole star or part of it is used whole as in the recipe, right, for Chinese Tea Eggs. Star anise is also used as a flavoring in alcoholic drinks, such as pastis and anisette and in confectionery.

ground star anise

MEDICINAL AND OTHER USE

Star anise is used in cough medicines. It is also added to pet foods. A point, the name given to one section of the star, is often sucked as a breath freshener by the Chinese.

STORAGE

The whole spice has a long shelf life. Buy the ground spice in small quantities and store it in an airtight container, away from strong light.

COOKING TIPS

Star anise goes well with duck or pork. The whole star anise, or part of it, can be used in long-cooked recipes. Try putting a whole star into the body cavity of a duck or chicken with an onion before roasting the bird to add a distinct Oriental-style flavor to the meal.

Chinese Tea Eggs

CH'A YEH TAN

MAKES 6

6 eggs
2 tbsp thick soy sauce
1 tsp salt
1 star anise
2 tbsp China tea
  or 2 tea bags

1 Cook the eggs in simmering water for 20 minutes, then leave them to cool in the cooking water.

2 Gently crack the shells to craze them, without actually removing any of the shell. Place the eggs in a saucepan of cold water. Add the soy sauce, salt, star anise and tea. Bring to a boil, cover and simmer for 1½-2 hours. Check the water level occasionally and top it up with more boiling water, as necessary, to keep the eggs covered. Leave the eggs to cool in the liquid overnight.

3 Remove the shells and the surface of the eggs will be crazed with fine lines. Cut the eggs into quarters and serve them with a selection of Chinese dishes, as part of a meal.

Juniper

BOTANICAL NAME: *Juniperus communis* • FAMILY NAME: *Cupressaceae*

FR. *genièvre;* G. *Wacholder;*
SP. *enebro, junipero, nebrini;* IT. *ginepro*

The juniper tree has long had a reputation for being a protector and friend to those in trouble. Old Testament biblical references mention juniper trees as places of refuge, and legend dictates that the baby Jesus was placed into the open branches of a juniper bush when the Holy Family were fleeing from Herod. The soldiers, intent on finding a couple with a baby, passed by Mary and Joseph. Juniper was subsequently dedicated to the Virgin Mary, and in Italy wreaths and branches of the tree are hung in stables and cow sheds. In the Middle Ages juniper branches were hung over doors as protection against witches, and when burnt the branches were thought to keep serpents and snakes at bay.

Juniper berries can be ground in a pepper mill for use in marinades or as a barbecue seasoning. Otherwise, crush the berries in a mortar using a pestle or by pressing them with the back of a teaspoon in a small cup.

CULTIVATION

The juniper is an evergreen coniferous tree of the cypress family, with sharp, pointed, awl-shaped evergreen leaves. It is a dioecious tree, having male and female counterparts, both of which must be cultivated close together in order that berries are formed. The male flowers are yellow and conical, the female are green and rounded. The berries are little globes, which ripen every two years but at different stages. Wear gloves to avoid being pricked by the spikes and pick only the blue berries which turn inky, blue-black and become slightly wrinkled when dried. The berries are harvested in September or October. The main producers of juniper are Hungary and Southern Europe, especially Italy; it is said that the further south the berries are grown the better their flavor.

AROMA AND FLAVOR

When bitten, a juniper berry tastes of gin first and then its flavor includes a touch of turpentine. If chewed, gin is

juniper berries

gin

crushed juniper berries

the primary flavor, with a slight bitterness that is not unpleasant. The aroma has the same characteristics: a smell of gin and turpentine.

CULINARY USE

Juniper is used in the production of gin, liqueurs, bitters and Swedish beer. It is a valued seasoning for game birds, venison, duck, rabbit, pork, ham and lamb. It is also widely appreciated as an excellent flavoring in meat pâtés and terrines.

MEDICINAL AND OTHER USE

Juniper is believed to help blood circulation and to restore youthful vigor to the aging. It is used in the treatment of colic, flatulence and rheumatism, and as an antidote for snake bites. It is a powerful antiseptic and is used in insecticides and perfumes.

COOKING TIPS

A little crushed juniper can be added to rich fruit cakes, such as Christmas cake and Christmas pudding. Juniper goes well with apples – try adding a hint to apple crumble or a fruit tart.

Galangal

GREATER GALANGAL

BOTANICAL NAME: *Languas galanga, syn Alpinia galanga*

FAMILY NAME: *Zingiberaceae*

OTHER NAMES: *galanga, Siamese ginger;* FR. *grand galanga;* G. *Galanga;* SP. *galanga;* IT. *galanga;* IND. *laos;* MAL. *lengkuas;* THAI *khaa*

LESSER GALANGAL

BOTANICAL NAME: *Languas officinarum, syn Alpinia officinarum*

FAMILY NAME: *Zingiberaceae*

OTHER NAMES: *aromatic ginger, Siamese ginger;* FR. *galanga de la Chine, galanga vrai;* G. *Galangawurzel;* SP. *galanga;* IT. *galanga;* THAI *krachai*

Fresh greater galangal should be thinly peeled, then sliced.

The spice may be pounded as part of a spice paste. Lesser galangal is more fibrous in texture and is prepared in the same way.

Used in the Middle Ages as a medicine, spice and an aphrodisiac, these members of the ginger family, Zingiberaceae, have only become widely available outside their countries of cultivation as fresh spices over the past few years.

CULTIVATION

The galangals are grown in India and South-east Asia where they are an essential ingredient in many dishes. In addition to greater and lesser galangal, there is another variety known as kaempferia galangal, which is quite different in appearance, looking like a clutch of fingers. Kaempferia galangal is only available in specialist shops.

Greater galangal grows to a height of 6 feet and it has long, elegant, blade-like leaves. The flowers are green and white with red tips. The root or rhizome is creamy white with brown rings at intervals along its knobbly length and occasionally, when really fresh, it has a few pink sprouts or knobs.

Lesser galangal is native to Southern China and, as its name implies, it is a smaller plant, growing to about half the height of the greater galangal. Although lesser galangal is grown in

India and South-east Asia, it is not as well known or widely used as the greater variety.

AROMA AND FLAVOR

Greater galangal has a pine-like aroma with a corresponding pungent flavor.

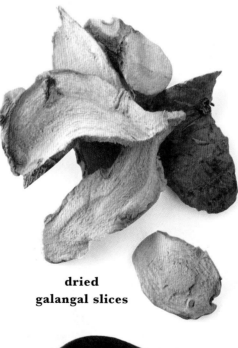

dried galangal slices

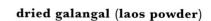

dried galangal (laos powder)

Lesser galangal is distinctly more aromatic with a stronger peppery taste, so when available it is used discreetly. It is well washed and cut into thin slices to add to earthy curries, which can accommodate its pungent aroma and strong taste.

CULINARY USE

Galangal is used in all the cuisines of South-east Asia, particularly in seafood and chicken dishes. It is frequently pounded with onion, garlic, chilies and ginger to make a spice paste. Slices are added to Thai soups with shreds of lemon grass and lime leaves.

**fresh
galangal root**

COOKING TIP

*Use 1 tsp laos powder instead of
1½ in fresh galangal root.*

STORAGE

Wrap the fresh root in a piece of paper
and store it in the vegetable compartment of the fridge for up to
two weeks. Dried slices and
powdered laos are available
from specialist shops. The
slices are added to curries
and stews and removed
before serving. Buy small
quantities of the powder
and store it in an air-
tight container away
from strong light.

kaempferia galangal

MEDICINAL AND OTHER USE

Galangal is used in medicines to treat
nausea, flatulence, stomach problems
and catarrh; in India it is also recommended as a cure for halitosis. It has
anti-bacterial properties and is used in
homeopathic medicines.

Bay Leaf

BOTANICAL NAME: *Laurus nobilis* • FAMILY NAME: *Lauraceae*

OTHER NAMES: *bay laurel, Apollo's bay leaf, Indian bay, wreath
laurel;* FR. *feuille de laurier, laurier franc;* G. *Lorbeerblatt;*
SP. *hoja de laurel;* IT. *foglia d'alloro*

*The bay is a tree of the sun under the
celestial sign of Leo. Culpeper, the
herbalist, regarded bay as a source of protection against 'all the evils of old Satan
to the body of man, and they are not
a few'. Parkinson, a 17th-century
botanist, was full of praise for the
virtues of the bay: 'The bay leaves are
of a necessary use as any other in the
garden or orchard, for they serve both for
pleasure and profit, both for ornament and
for use, both for honest civil uses and for
physic, yea, both for the sick and the sound,
both for the living and the dead; ... so that
from the cradle to the grave we still have
use of it, we still have need of it'.*

fresh bay leaves

Bay leaves were fashioned into laurel crowns to be worn by emperors
and heroes in ancient Rome as a sign
of great honor, and superstition indicated that the bay also gave protection
from lightning. Today, the Grand Prix
winner is decked with a laurel wreath
and the poet of the British Royal
Household is still given the title of poet
laureate after the laurel wreath
awarded to Greek and Roman poets.

CULTIVATION

The bay tree is native to Asia Minor,
but spread to all parts of the
Mediterranean in ancient times. The
flowers, yellow or greenish white, are
not very obvious and they produce a
dark-purple, one-seed berry. The true
bay tree must not be confused with the
cherry laurel, *Prunus lauro-cerasus*,
which bears poisonous leaves, or the
Caribbean bay *Pimenta acris*, the leaves
of which are used to make bay
rum. Bay trees can grow to over

50 feet in height, but they are most often pruned into neat bushes. They are also trained into ornamental shapes or cultivated as standard bushes.

AROMA AND FLAVOR
The leaves give off a pungent and warm bouquet and flavor when broken and added to a dish. When slightly wilted, they are strongly aromatic, so they should be used sparingly. Bay can be purchased as fresh or dried whole leaves or ground, but the latter rapidly loses its flavor.

CULINARY USE
Bay is always included in a bouquet garni and court bouillon. It is also an essential flavoring ingredient in many classic sauces, such as béchamel, bread sauce and tomato sauce. Bay leaves are used worldwide, in classic and contem-

porary cuisines, to flavor seafoods, poultry, meat, rice and vegetable dishes. They are added to soups, casseroles, marinades and sautéed foods; threaded on skewers of ingredients to be broiled, or laid in a roasting pan around foods to be baked or roasted. Bay leaves are also added to pickled foods. They are even used in certain sweet dishes, notably custards and creams. Remove bay leaves before serving as they are tough to eat and quite strongly flavored. You may have noticed bay leaves packed around dried figs: they are there to discourage weevils.

MEDICINAL AND OTHER USE
Medicinally, the properties of the bay leaf and berries are legendary: it has astringent,

PREPARATION TIP

Bay leaves add a warm pungent flavor to broiled or barbecued kebabs. Push one or two leaves onto each skewer between the chunks of meat.

diuretic and digestive qualities, and it is an appetite stimulant. The acid from the leaves is supposed to discourage moths. The bay oil from the West Indian bay tree is used in perfumery and in the production of bay rum.

STORAGE
The leaves should be picked and dried slowly, away from direct sunlight, in order to retain the volatile oils. If left on the branch, the leaves will curl attractively but, if they are to be stored in a jar or container, they should be dried between two sheets of paper to keep them flat. Pack and store away from strong light. The glossy, dark green leaves can be used fresh or dried, but are best after being allowed to wilt for a few days when their bitterness has gone but the leaves still retain their scent.

freeze-dried bay leaves

dried crushed bay leaves

dried ground bay leaves

dried bay leaves

Mango Powder

BOTANICAL NAME: *Mangifera indica* • FAMILY NAME: *Anacardiaceae*

FR. *mangue;* G. *Mango;* SP. *mango, manguey;* IT. *mango*
IN. *amchur, amchoor*

mango powder

dried mango

CULTIVATION

The mango tree is a member of the cashew and pistachio family, native to India, where the mango is known as the 'king of fruits'.

The name *amchur* comes from *am*, the Hindu word for mango, and *choor* or *chur*, meaning powder. The unripe mangos are sliced, sun-dried and ground to a powder, then mixed with a little ground turmeric.

AROMA AND FLAVOR

Mango powder has a sweet-and-sour bouquet and flavor, with just a hint of resin.

CULINARY USE

In the high temperatures of the Indian continent, mango powder keeps far better than fresh tamarind or lemons, other typical souring agents. It is used primarily in vegetarian dishes, where it is usually added towards the end of the cooking so that its astringent, yet slightly sweet-sour flavor is still detectable when the food is served. Mango powder is added to soups, marinades, curries and chutneys.

Curry Leaves

BOTANICAL NAME: *Murraya koenigii, syn Chalcas k, Bergara k*
FAMILY NAME: *Rutaceae*

OTHER NAMES: *nim leaf;* FR. *feuille de cari;*
G. *Curryblatt;* SP. *hoja;* IT. *foglia di cari;*
IN. *karipatta, kitha neem*

CULTIVATION

These leaves (in fact they are leaflets) come from a tropical tree of the citrus-rue family, which is native to Southern India and Sri Lanka. The long slender leaflets are dark green on top with a paler underside.

AROMA AND FLAVOR

The leaves have a strong, warm, curry aroma when bruised or rubbed and they add an aromatic curry flavor to dishes, which cannot be replaced by any other ingredient.

CULINARY USE

A classic way of using curry leaves is by frying mustard seeds in hot ghee, then adding a little asafoetida and several curry leaves for just a few seconds before stirring them into a plain dhal dish or dhal-based Indian soup. Alternatively, the leaves can be very finely chopped or minced before they are used in curries, added to marinades or omelets. They are widely used in Madras-style curry powders and pastes, and in shellfish dishes. If the leaves are added whole they should be removed before the dish is served.

STORAGE

The leaves can be bought fresh from Asian shops. They will keep in the vegetable compartment of the refrigerator for up to two weeks or they can be frozen. They are also available vacuum-dried, a process by which the leaves retain their color and flavor. If the leaves are allowed to dry naturally in the open air, they lose their pungency.

fresh curry leaves

dried curry leaves

Nutmeg and Mace

BOTANICAL NAME: *Myristica fragrans* • FAMILY NAME: *Myristicaceae*

FR. *noix de muscade*; G. *Muskatnuss*; SP. *nuez moscada*; IT. *noce moscata*

Nutmeg and mace are different parts of the same fruit of the nutmeg tree. These spices have been appreciated since Roman times – the Emperor Henry VI had the streets of Rome fumigated with nutmegs before his coronation. The Portuguese were able to keep the source of nutmeg and mace a close secret for a century, from early in the 16th century until they were driven out of the Spice Islands by the Dutch, who subsequently also jealously guarded the source of their spice treasures. By 1760 there were warehouses in Amsterdam full of these spices, but they were burnt in order to keep the price of the spice artificially high. The price of mace in London at that time was 85-90 shillings per pound. So determined were the Dutch to retain their monopoly, that they tried to restrict the growing of nutmeg trees to two islands; however, they had not considered the fruit pigeons that were responsible for the seedlings sprouting on nearby islands.

nutmeg and mace

Pierre Poivre (a Frenchman who, it is believed, is the Peter Piper in the tongue-twister nursery rhyme beginning with that name) was responsible for transporting the precious seedlings to Mauritius, where they flourished. This marked the end of the Dutch monopoly and the decline of their influence in the Spice Islands.

The British East India Company introduced the nutmeg tree to Penang, Singapore, India, Sri Lanka and the West Indies, especially to Grenada. Along with Indonesia, Grenada is the main source of nutmeg and mace.

CULTIVATION

The nutmeg tree is a large evergreen native to the Banda Islands in the Moluccas. It grows to about 60 feet and produces fruit fifteen to twenty years after planting. Once the tree begins to fruit, it crops for thirty to forty years, bearing 1,500-2,000 fruits per annum. The fruit of the nutmeg tree, which is about the size of an apricot and similar in color, splits when ripe to reveal brilliant red arils encasing the brown nut. The red arils are the mace, which turns to an orange color as the arils dry. The mace is removed from the nut and dried. The nut is also dried until the kernel inside rattles, and this is removed by tapping the end of the nutmeg shell – the kernel can be damaged if the shell is cracked on the side.

AROMA AND FLAVOR

Mace and nutmeg smell gloriously aromatic, sweet and warm. Both spices have a similar flavor, with the nutmeg being slightly sweeter than the mace.

CULINARY USE

Mace is sold either as whole blades or as the ground spice and it can be used in both forms. Mace is used in savory dishes, and nutmeg, though used in savory dishes, is especially complementary to puddings, cakes and drinks. In Malaysia the fleshy outer husk of the nutmeg is candied or pickled, then

whole nutmegs

ground nutmeg

whole nutmegs

ground mace

halved or sliced and sold in packs as a delicious snack.

Both spices have well-established roles in classic cuisines. Mace is used to flavor milk-based sauces, such as béchamel, and it is widely used in processed meats, such as sausages and charcuterie. It is also superb when added sparingly to delicate soups and sauces with fish, seafood, particularly potted shrimps, and eggs. Pickles and chutneys may be seasoned with mace. Try adding a little to milk-based puddings, cheesecakes and lemon curd tart.

Nutmeg is delicious with fillings for pasta, especially those using spinach and cheese, it may be added to risotto, tomato sauce or sauces for fish or chicken pies. It is excellent in cheese sauce for a cauliflower cheese or onion sauce to serve with lamb chops and in creamy mashed potatoes.

Nutmeg is a traditional flavoring for cakes, gingerbreads, cookies and fruit or milk puddings. A little grated or ground nutmeg added to a filling for cherry or apple pie introduces another flavor dimension. For a refreshing end to a meal, try sprinkling a little grated nutmeg and sugar onto slices of well-chilled orange. Mulled alcoholic drinks are enhanced by the addition of a little nutmeg, for example a sprinkling on an eggnog is delicious. It is also a warming addition to hot milk drinks.

MEDICINAL AND OTHER USE

Nutmeg is a narcotic, but not problematic when consumed in the quantities used in domestic recipes. It is astringent, a stimulant and an aphrodisiac; nutmeg oil is used in perfumes and ointments.

Nigella

BOTANICAL NAME: *Nigella sativa* • FAMILY NAME: *Ranunculaceae*

OTHER NAMES: *black caraway, black cumin, wild onion seed;*
FR. *cheveux de Venus, nigelle, poivrette;* G. *Schwarzkümmel;*
SP. *neguilla;* IT. *nigella;* IN. *kalonji*

nigella seeds

A plant from the same family as the pretty 'love in a mist' flower. The name nigella comes from the Latin nigellus, diminutive of niger, black. The seeds were used in Roman times and in India for cooking as well as by herbalists.

PREPARATION TIPS

Always dry fry nigella seeds before using them, to bring out their full flavor.

Nigella seeds are quite hard and difficult to grind by hand, better to grind them a few at a time in a coffee grinder or spice mill.

MEDICINAL AND OTHER USE

Used by Indian herbalists and doctors as a stimulant and in treatment of flatulence, indigestion and bowel disorders.

CULTIVATION

Nigella is a herbaceous annual of the buttercup family and it grows to a height of about 2 feet. It has gray-green wispy leaves and blue-white flowers. The bulk of the crop is grown in India. The seeds are held in a seed head similar to a poppy head: they are triangular in shape, matt black, with two flat sides and the other curved. They are similar to, and often confused with, onion seeds.

black onion seeds

Bengali five spices (panch phoron)

AROMA AND FLAVOR

The seeds have little aroma but when rubbed in the fingers they give off a peppery smell; they are sometimes used as a substitute for pepper. Additionally, they have a herb-like taste, similar to oregano or carrots.

CULINARY USE

Nigella is one of the five spices in Bengali five spices (panch phoron). It is widely used in Indian cooking, in dhal and vegetable dishes, pickles and chutneys. The seeds are often scattered on naan bread, where they give a distinctive peppery flavor. In Middle Eastern kitchens the seeds are scattered over breads and cakes, and the seeds are sometimes mixed with sesame seeds for the same purpose.

naan bread

Poppy Seeds

BOTANICAL NAME: *Papavera somniferum*

FAMILY NAME: *Papaveraceae*

white poppy seeds

OTHER NAMES: *opium poppy;* FR. *pavot somnifère, oeillette;* G. *Mohn;* SP. *adormidera, amapola;* IT. *papavero;* *kus-kus, khus-khus*

Relics from Ancient Greece have been found which clearly illustrate that people have long been aware of the medicinal and narcotic properties of the poppy. Through Arab traders and the spread of Islam to the East, the opium poppy was introduced to Persia, South-east Asia and India. When used in moderation, opium gave great relief from pain, but soon the trade was exploited as traders and merchants made their fortune from the addiction of countless thousands, bringing suffering and death to those caught in its trap.

black poppy seeds

Papavera somniferum means sleep-inducing poppy, referring to the opium in the latex that exudes when the unripe seed pod is cut. Poppy seeds bought for cooking are entirely free from any sinister side effects.

CULTIVATION

The poppy is a tall annual with blue-green stems. The seeds are planted in March and harvested in September. The best-quality blue-gray seeds are grown in Holland; crops are also grown in Poland, Iran, Romania, Russia, Turkey and Argentina.

AROMA AND FLAVOR

The seeds are sweet smelling and they give off a nutty aroma when cooked.

poppy seed sprouts

The taste is similar to the bouquet, but with a more highly developed, nutty sweetness.

CULINARY USE

The creamy colored poppy seeds are more common in India, where they are ground and used as a thickening agent in curries and sauces. They are also used in some Indian breads. The dark seeds are also popular as a crunchy topping for Western breads and biscuits, savory and sweet.

The dark seeds are used extensively as a filling or baking ingredient in German and Eastern European breads, cakes, cookies and pastries. Delicious pastries and a yeasted poppy seed roll are typical celebration treats baked for Christmas and other festive occasions. They are also sprinkled generously over cooked noodles, or sweetened with honey and made into a dessert dip or sauce.

Dry fried seeds are an interesting addition to salads and salad dressings, for example in potato, tomato, egg or pasta salads or coleslaw. Both white and black seeds can be sprouted to add to salads, sandwiches and in mixed vegetable dishes.

PREPARATION TIPS

Poppy seeds have a very tough outer husk. When adding them to the salads or pasta, dry fry them first. If the seeds are to be ground, then cover them with boiling water and leave to soak for 2-3 hours. Drain the seeds through a fine muslin cloth and they can be ground to a paste. The moist seeds are best reduced to a smooth paste by passing them through a mincer, using a fine blade, and repeating this for a smooth result. Alternatively, the dry, unsoaked, seeds can be ground in a coffee grinder.

MEDICINAL AND OTHER USE

Poppy seed oil is used by artists as a drying oil. The blue seeds are used in painkillers, cough mixtures and syrups and as an expectorant. An infusion of the seeds is said to relieve toothache and earache.

STORAGE

If the seeds are to be used in large quantities, for example as a filling in pastries and cakes, it is essential that they are bought from a source which has a high turnover and where they will be fresh. Stale poppy seeds are bitter and rancid in flavor. Delicatessens specializing in Eastern European ingredients usually sell fresh seeds: buy them as you need them. Store seeds in an airtight container in a cool, dark place for no more than a few weeks – they will not keep indefinitely.

COOKING TIPS

Fry 1–2 tbsp black poppy seeds in butter and add them to puréed pumpkin, squash or rutabaga. Scatter seeds over homemade breads, cookies and pastries. Mix ground poppy seeds with honey and use as a filling for pancakes.

Allspice

BOTANICAL NAME: *Pimenta dioica* • FAMILY NAME: *Myrtaceae*

OTHER NAMES: *English spice, Jamaican pepper, pimento;*
FR. *toute-épice, piment poivre de la Jamaïque;* G. *Jamaikapfeffer;*
SP. *pimiento de Jamaica;* IT. *pimento*

The Mayan Indians used allspice to embalm their dead long before the Spaniards arrived in the West Indies. Christopher Columbus is reported to have shown a handful of black peppercorns to natives on the Caribbean islands, which might account for the confusion in name: it is possible that they thought allspice berries and peppercorns (which the Spanish called pimienta) were one and the same spice.

The preservative properties of allspice were valued by 17th-century seafarers for keeping both fish and meat edible on long voyages. The spice is still used extensively in the fishing industry in Scandinavia, where barrels of fish are transported from market to market. At the end of the 19th century, the wood of allspice saplings was much in vogue for making walking sticks and umbrellas; however, legislation was introduced to prevent the young trees from being felled, avoiding the potential decimation of the allspice industry.

CULTIVATION

A member of the myrtle family, the allspice tree is an evergreen indigenous to the West Indies, Central and South America. In the early 19th century saplings were taken to Ceylon and Singapore but they did not flourish. The tree grows to an average height of 30-40 feet, except in the rain forests of South America where this can be doubled. Avenues of trees are charmingly called 'pimento walks'. Every part of the tree – bark, leaves, white flowers and later the berries – contributes the heady perfume that fills the air in allspice plantations.

The fully developed, but green, berries are harvested between July and

allspice berries

September, about three or four months after flowering. The berries change to purple, then brown as they are dried in the sun. Young trees start bearing fruit after five or six years, they are fully productive by their fifteenth year and can thrive for up to a hundred years, so they are a worthwhile investment. Jamaica produces two-thirds of the world's supply of the spice and exports it principally to Germany, the USA and the UK.

You may notice an allspice shrub in garden centers called Carolina, Japanese or wild allspice, or strawberry bush: this is an entirely different variety, the *Calycanthus*.

AROMA AND FLAVOR

Allspice is suitably named for its bouquet and flavor. The spice smells of cloves, nutmeg and cinnamon and some even detect a hint of mace and peppercorns in its aroma. When crushed or ground, allspice has quite a pungent flavor. Ideally, buy the whole spice and grind it when required as the ground spice soon loses its punch. The very best-quality allspice berries come

COOKING TIPS

Keep a pepper mill for grinding whole spices like allspice. Alternatively, add a few allspice berries to a mill of pepper-corns for a savory seasoning.

ground allspice

from Jamaica. The round berries have a rough surface because of tiny oil glands; inside, there are two hard, kidney-shaped seeds, but most of the flavor comes from the husk.

CULINARY USE

In Jamaica, a local drink, known as Jamaica dram, is made from allspice and rum. Allspice is also one of the ingredients in Benedictine and Chartreuse. The whole berries are a popular ingredient for mulled wine.

Allspice is widely used in European cooking as an ingredient in sweet recipes and festive baking, including Christmas puddings, cakes and cookies. The ground or whole spice may be used in preserves and chutneys as well as the Christmas mincemeat.

Many Scandinavian herring dishes are enhanced by the distinctive flavor of allspice, and German recipes often call for allspice.

MEDICINAL AND OTHER USE

The oil from berries and the leaves is used in antiseptics and medicines for flatulence. It is also used in perfumes.

Anise

BOTANICAL NAME: *Pimpinella anisum* • FAMILY NAME: *Umbelliferae*

OTHER NAMES: *aniseed, sweet cumin;*
FR. *anis;* G. *Anis;* SP. *anís;* IT. *anice*

anise seeds

Anise is indigenous to the Eastern Mediterranean and coastal countries of the area once referred to as The Levant, and it was well known to the Ancient Egyptians. Its ability to counteract indigestion was recognized by the Romans, who used to serve a special spice cake containing anise after gastronomic orgies.

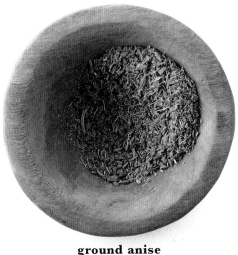

ground anise

CULTIVATION

A member of the parsley and carrot family, this feathery plant grows to about 2 feet in countries as far apart as Southern Russia, North Africa, India and South and Central America. The fruit consists of two united carpels, which are harvested when the fruit begins to ripen and left in stacks until ripening is complete. The seeds are separated from the flower heads by threshing. The seeds are tiny and ovoid, with fine lines marked against a green-gray background.

AROMA AND FLAVOR

They have a delicately sweet and aromatic bouquet with a distinctive licorice flavor. The spiciness of the seeds is similar to fennel. The flavor is heightened by dry frying the seeds. Buy the seeds in small quantities as they soon lose their flavor and, if necessary, grind them finely as required.

CULINARY USE

Anise is used in savory and sweet cooking, in spicy dishes from India as well

aniseed balls

anisette

Pernod

as lightly flavored cuisines. This spice flavors fish soups, sauces, breads (particularly rye bread), cakes, cookies and confectionery. Popular aniseed flavor drinks include French pastis, Pernod and Ricard, a liqueur called anisette, Spanish ojen, Turkish raki, Greek ouzo and Arab arrack.

MEDICINAL AND OTHER USE

Oil from the seeds is used in cough mixtures and lozenges as well as antiseptics. Anise is also used in perfumes and soaps. The seeds are chewed after a meal in India to sweeten the breath. As a simple cure for hiccups, chew a few seeds and wash them down with a glass of water. Dogs find the smell of anise attractive, so it is used to lay a trail in hound trailing.

anise sweets

315

Pepper

BOTANICAL NAME: *Piper nigrum* • FAMILY NAME: *Piperaceae*

OTHER NAMES: *black pepper, white pepper, green peppercorns;*
FR. *poivre (blanc – white, vert – green);* G. *Pfeffer (weisser –*
white, grüner – green); SP. *pimienta negra (blanca – white, verde –*
green); IT. *pepe (bianco – white, verde – green)*

white peppercorns

five peppercorn mixture

The king of spices, pepper is one of the oldest
and most popular spices in the world. It was
the search for the source of pepper more
than any other spice which led early
sailors eastward. At one time, pepper-
corns were more valuable than gold.
The Romans were the first to identify
the significance of the prevailing
winds and monsoons to sea voyages,
and they were able to guarantee
supplies of this precious spice from
Southern India. They made Alexan-
dria the chief port for trade between
Europe and Asia and built huge warehouses
to store the spice. One entrance to the city was
called Pepper Gate. At the siege of Rome, the King of the Goths demanded a ransom of
3,000 pounds of peppercorns, gold and silver; the Romans reluctantly paid them, but to
add insult to injury, the Goths ransacked the city anyway.

By the Middle Ages pepper was considered desirable currency: dowries, taxes and rents were frequently paid in peppercorns. The term 'peppercorn rent' was established in those days to indicate payment in full, which was often expensive due to the scarcity of the spice. Today it means a nominal sum. A Guild of Peppers was set up in London in 1180; similarly, France had *poivriers* and Germany *Pfeffersäcke* societies. Its value in the preservation of food and flavoring of tasteless and insipid meat, more than likely in the first stages of decay, kept the demand for pepper high. The race for the Spice Islands began with the great names of Marco Polo, Columbus, Vasco de Gama, Magellan and Drake searching the globe for pepper and the spices that were to make their fortunes.

CULTIVATION

The name pepper comes from the Sanskrit (ancient language of India) word *pippali* meaning berry. It originally referred to the Indian long pepper (*Piper longum*), which looked rather like a catkin and was familiar to the Greeks and Romans but is now difficult to find, even in its native India. *Piper nigrum* is a perennial vine indigenous to the Malabar coast of India, where, it is claimed, the best pepper is still grown. The Hindu colonists are believed to have taken pepper to Java, one of the Indonesian islands, which contributed to its gradual spread throughout the Far East, to Malaysia, Borneo, Sumatra, Sri Lanka, Penang and Singapore. Pepper grows best near the Equator:

today it is also grown in Thailand, tropical Africa, the South Sea islands and Brazil.

In the Malaysian state of Sarawak, the vines grow up frames resembling slim wigwams, tapering at the top. In other places, the vines are encouraged to grow around living trees. The vines are pruned to prevent them from growing too high, which makes harvesting difficult. The vine has leaves that are long, green and pointed. White flowers bloom on the peppercorn 'spikes', which look like slim clusters of redcurrants. The plant starts fruiting after three to five years and continues to do so every third year for up to forty years. Pickers move from vine to vine

fresh green
peppercorns

on tripod-type ladders, hand picking the spikes on which some of the berries are red but the bulk are still green. The peppercorns are then sorted and the stems discarded.

black peppercorns

**coarsely ground
black pepper**

ground black pepper

**green peppercorns
in brine**

crushed black pepper

ground white pepper

THE PEPPERS

Black Peppercorns: The green berries are dried on mats in the sun and raked several times a day for a week until they are wrinkled and black. Sometimes, the berries are scalded with boiling water before they are dried.

White Peppercorns: The red and orange berries are packed in sacks and soaked for a week under slowly running water. This process rots the outer husk of the berries so that it can then be removed by rubbing them between the hands over strainers. The husked berries are white peppercorns.

Green Peppercorns: These are occasionally available fresh, still on the long stem. Used particularly in Thai cooking, green peppercorns also complement game and duck dishes, terrines and creamy sauces. Green peppercorns are available pickled in brine or vinegar, or freeze dried. Remember to rinse pickled peppercorns well before using them.

Long Pepper: Though this was popular in Greek and Roman times, it is difficult to find now, even in its indigenous home in India. Part of the *Anacardiaceae* family, this takes the botanical name *Piper longum.*

Cubeb: Grown mostly in the wild, cubeb are the dried unripe fruits of a member of the vine family. They are similar in size to a peppercorn with a distinctive 'tail'. Cubeb can be used as a pepper substitute as it has similar characteristics. Buy it ground in health food and specialist shops.

long pepper

cubeb berries

PREPARATION TIPS

Peppercorns can be crushed by placing them in a plastic bag and pressing them with a rolling pin. The resulting coarsely crushed peppercorns are ideal for steaks or they can be pressed onto a duck breast before cooking. Peppercorns can also be crushed in a mortar, using a pestle, or in a coffee grinder. For everyday use it is best to keep a pepper mill full of the whole spice to be ground as required.

AROMA AND FLAVOR

Black peppercorns have a special, earthy, rich aroma and they taste highly pungent with a richness reflected in the aroma. White peppercorns are less earthy and not as pungent or rich as the black spice. The flavor of white pepper is cleaner, less rich and not as complex. Green peppercorns are lighter in flavor than the black spice, but just as hot. They do not smell or taste as complex as the other peppers.

CULINARY USE

Pepper is one of the most versatile spices, used in virtually all savory cooking. Both black and white pepper is used in cuisines worldwide, at all stages of the cooking process and as a table condiment. Not only does pep-per contribute its own special season-ing, it has the capacity to enhance other flavors.

This spice is also used in sweet cookery; black pepper is added to fruit cakes and gingerbreads, sometimes in quite considerable quantities, and it can be served as a light seasoning on fresh fruit. Try grinding pepper on slices of fresh pineapple, fry them in unsalted butter and flambé them with rum for a flavor sensation. Fresh straw-berries are excitingly different when topped with a light grinding of black pepper before the ubiquitous dollop of cream is added. Sweet, juicy figs accompanied by soft goats' cheese taste wonderful seasoned with pepper.

White pepper is milder than the black spice and has a distinguishably different flavor. It can be used in pale milk or cream sauces, where specks of black pepper would spoil the appear-ance; in some instances freshly ground white pepper is more complementary to the flavor of the food, for example with creamy mashed potatoes.

MEDICINAL AND OTHER USE

Pepper has long been recognized as an ingredient for stimulating the appetite as well as being an aid in the relief of nausea. In India it has been used as a medicine since time immemorial for the treatment of anything from paraly-sis to toothache. East Africans are said to believe that body odor produced after eating substantial amounts of pepper repels mosquitoes.

Szechuan Pepper

BOTANICAL NAME: *Zanthoxylum piperitum, syn Xanthoxylum piperitum*

FAMILY NAME: *Rutaceae*

OTHER NAMES: *anise pepper, fagara, Chinese brown pepper, Japanese pepper;* FR. *poivre anisé;* G. *Anispfeffer;* SP. *pimienta de anís;* IT. *pepe d'anis*

This spice is often wrongly assumed to be part of the pepper family when it is the berry of the prickly ash tree. The spice, which is the ground husks of the berries, is common in the Szechuan region of China, and spices from the leaves of the plant are also used in Japan. The ripe seed pods of the tree open out in a similar way to star anise, which is probably why they were named anise pepper.

Szechuan pepper

CULTIVATION

Anise pepper is the fruit of the tree of the prickly ash family. The rust-red berries contain bitter black seeds that are usually removed before the spice is sold.

AROMA AND FLAVOR

The bouquet is pungent, with a hint of citrus. Dry frying brings out the flavor, which is pleasantly peppery.

CULINARY USE

Sold whole or ground, Szechuan pepper is much used in Chinese cookery, especially with chicken and duck. It is one of the spices in Chinese five spice powder, and it is used in Japanese seven-flavor seasoning mix. The leaves are dried and ground to make sansho, a Japanese spice (see below).

MEDICINAL AND OTHER USE

The ground bark of the plant is an old-fashioned remedy for toothache in the USA. Both bark and berries are stimulants and they are used in traditional medicines and herbal cures to purify the blood, promote digestion and as an anti-rheumatic.

Pink Peppercorns

BOTANICAL NAME: *Schinus terebinthifolius*
FAMILY NAME: *Piperaceae*

> FR. *poivre rose;* G. *blassroter Pfeffer;*
> SP. *pimienta rosa;* IT. *pepe rosa*

These are not true peppercorns but they have a pungency associated with that spice and are similar in size to peppercorns.

dried pink peppercorns

CULTIVATION

Native to South America, pink peppercorns are grown in Réunion in the Indian Ocean. They are picked when ripe and dried or pickled in brine.

AROMA AND FLAVOR

Pink peppercorns do not have a strong aroma until they are crushed, when they give off a faintly sweet-peppery smell. Their flavor is sweet and slightly scented with only a peppery aftertaste.

CULINARY USE

Valued for their appearance and once the subject of a food fashion trend, dried pink peppercorns are frequently mixed with other peppercorns in a clear mill to make an attractive-looking table spice. Pink peppercorns should not be confused with true peppers (black, white and green) for culinary use: they are an interesting seasoning ingredient, but they are not hot pungent seeds to use instead of ordinary pepper. They are popular for seasoning fish and used in Mediterranean cooking.

When they were in vogue and added generously to all sorts of dishes, there were reports of the ill effects they caused when consumed in quantity. Therefore it is recommended that pink peppercorns be used in small quantities (for example, limit the use to twelve to fifteen peppercorns in any one dish) to avoid any likelihood of adverse reactions to them.

**pink
peppercorns
in brine**

SANSHO

Sometimes confusingly called Japanese pepper. Although it is not a true pepper, this is one of the few spices used in Japanese cooking. It is used mainly to counter fatty flavors, is usually sprinkled on cooked foods and is only available ground.

Salt

CHEMICAL NAME: *Sodium chloride*

FR. *sel de cuisine, gros sel, sel gris;* G. *Kochsalz;*
SP. *sal gema, sal de cocina;* IT. *sale di cucina*

We like salt, we need it and we cannot survive without it. Salt consists of two elements – sodium and chlorine, sodium being an essential trace element for maintaining animal and human life.

fine sea salt

coarse sea salt

black salt

Maldon salt

AROMA AND FLAVOR

Salt is the universal seasoning ingredient used to bring out the flavor in both sweet and savory dishes. Salt is odorless but strongly flavored: without it our meals would be dull and insipid.

CULINARY USE

Salt is used widely in preserving meat, fish and vegetables. An intriguing Chinese recipe envelops a chicken in hot salt. After one hour the sweet tender juicy chicken is ready, and the salt can be used again.

MEDICINAL AND OTHER USE

A salt water gargle is the traditional source of relief when a cold threatens or for a sore throat.

STORAGE

Store in an airtight container in a cool dry place. Do not keep salt in silver salt cellars or leave a silver spoon in salt. The chlorine in the salt reacts with the silver, causing it to turn green.

table salt

TYPES OF SALT

Rock salt, salt from the earth, comes from underground deposits formed over the millennia by the drying up of inland lakes and seas. Water is pumped into the salt caves and the brine is pumped to the surface. The brine is then boiled and allowed to crystallize.

From this we obtain kitchen salt or cooking salt, which used to be sold as block salt but is now sold as a fairly coarse, refined salt kept free flowing by the addition of magnesium carbonate to prevent it taking in moisture from the air.

Table salt is finer in texture. A few grains of rice used to be added to salt cellars; the rice absorbed moisture from the salt. This tip is still practised in some countries where salt tends to become damp.

Rock salt is the term usually given to the larger crystals produced by the process. Some believe it to be superior in flavor. The salt is either ground in a salt mill or pounded in a mortar with a pestle.

Sea salt is produced by the evaporation of sea water, either naturally or by artificial means. It is said that there is enough salt in the sea to cover the world's landmass to a depth of over 100 feet. Some find that the flavor of sea salt is the best for both cooking and for table use. It is sometimes called bay salt.

English sea salt comes mainly from Maldon in Essex. The characteristic flakes have an excellent 'salty' flavor and can be sprinkled on to bread rolls and savory crackers before baking.

Black salt is dark gray and it has a pinkish tinge when ground. It is used as both a seasoning and a spice in Indian cooking. It has a definite tang and hint of smokiness to its flavor.

Pomegranate Seeds

BOTANICAL NAME: *Punica granatum* • FAMILY NAME: *Punicaceae*

FR. *grenade*; G. *Granatapfel*; SP. *granada*; IT. *melograno*;
IN. *anardana, anar*

Romantics would say that the pomegranate was the apple in the garden of Eden; it was certainly known in the gardens of Babylon and mentioned frequently in the Bible. In Turkey, legend has it that a bride can predict the number of children she will have by the number of seeds that spill out of a pomegranate when she drops it on the floor.

CULTIVATION

Pomegranates are grown on small, lush bushes with red flowers, which look rather like those of the hibiscus. Some bushes have thorns. Native to Iran, pomegranates are also grown in Mediterranean countries, South America, the USA (particularly California) and parts of Africa. The bush flourishes best in climates that are cool in winter and hot in the summer. The smooth-skinned, golden to red fruit is about the size of a large apple. The plump red seeds are encased in individual compartments, each surrounded by a creamy colored, bitter membrane and pith. The seeds are extracted from the peel, pith and membranes, then dried. When dry, they are small and dark-red to black in color and slightly sticky.

AROMA AND FLAVOR

Pomegranate seeds have an astringent smell and sweet-sour taste.

CULINARY USE

Crushed pomegranate seeds are sprinkled on the popular Middle Eastern dip, hummus, and they are also used in sweet dishes and fruit salads from the region. In Indian cooking, pomegranate seeds are often used as a souring agent instead of lemon juice. Grenadine, a syrup made from the juice of the pomegranate, has a sweet, fresh flavor, while pomegranate syrup, used in Middle Eastern cooking, has an intense, concentrated flavor.

MEDICINAL AND OTHER USE

Pomegranate seeds are used in gargles, and they are said to ease fevers and assist in counteracting diarrhoea. They are widely used in Indian medicines.

PREPARATION TIPS

Fresh pomegranate seeds can be dried at home.

Cut off and discard a slice from the stem end of the fruit. Stand the fruit on a board and make five incisions from top to bottom. Use your fingers to prise open the fruit in wedge-shaped sections and scoop out the seeds, avoiding the bitter membrane. Spread out the seeds on a baking pan or ovenproof dish and dry them in the sun or in a cool oven, until they harden.

Use a pestle and mortar to crush the seeds, if necessary. A food processor or electric grinder is not suitable as the seeds are too sticky.

fresh pomegranates

dried pomegranate seeds

fresh pomegranate seeds

fresh pomegranate juice

grenadine

pomegranate syrup

Mahlebi

BOTANICAL NAME: *Prunus mahaleb*

FAMILY NAME: *Rosaceae*

OTHER NAMES: *Mahlab;* FR. *mahaleb;*
G. *Mahaleb;* SP. *mahaleb;* IT. *mahaleb*

mahlebi seeds

mahlebi powder

*Mahlebi is the dried kernel of a small cherry stone. It is an ancient
spice that is used principally in the Middle East and Turkey.*

CULTIVATION

The tree is usually found only in the
Middle East and Turkey. It is deciduous and it grows to a height of about
35 feet. The wide, outspreading
branches bear white flowers and fruit
that are small, oval and green at first,
turning black when they are picked.
The stone is creamy yellow when powdered.

AROMA AND FLAVOR

The bouquet is distinctly nutty, with
hints of almond and cherry. The taste
is slightly bitter but not unpleasant.

CULINARY USE

The ground spice is used in breads, cookies and pastries from the Middle East and
Turkey. It makes an unusual addition to
a pastry mixture for a fruit tart.

STORAGE

Ideally it is best to buy the mahlebi
whole and grind it to a powder in a
mortar, coffee grinder or food processor as required. The powdered version
soon loses its interesting flavor, even
after short periods of storage. Store
the seeds or powder in an airtight container in a cool drawer or cupboard
away from strong light.

Sumac

BOTANICAL NAME: *Rhus coriaria* • FAMILY NAME: *Anacardiaceae*

FR. *sumac;* G. *Sumach;* SP. *zumaque;* IT. *sommacco*

*The Romans used sumac berries as a souring agent as we would use lemon juice or vine-
gar, or tamarind in Eastern cooking. Buy sumac only from a specialist shop selling
Middle Eastern ingredients as some members of the
sumac family (found mostly in the USA) have
poisonous berries.*

CULTIVATION

The sumac bush grows to a modest
10 feet and its leaves turn a vibrant
rust-red in the fall. It grows wild and is
also cultivated around Southern Italy,
Sicily and throughout the Middle East.
It is said that the higher the altitude at
which the bush grows, the better the
quality of the fruit. The white flowers
produce spikes of red berries, which
are picked just before they ripen, then
they are dried and will keep indefinitely.

ground sumac

AROMA AND FLAVOR

Although it has little aroma, sumac has
a definite, astringent quality, with a
pleasing sour-fruit flavor.

CULINARY USE

Sumac is widely used in Lebanese,
Syrian, Turkish and Iranian cuisines.
Sometimes the berries are used whole,
with the small brown central seed
intact. They can be ground or cracked,
then soaked for about 15-20 minutes in
warm water and squeezed to release
their astringent juice. This is strained
and usually added to food towards the
end of the cooking process. Ground
sumac is available from specialist
Middle Eastern stores: it may be rubbed
on to fish, chicken, steaks or kebabs
before cooking or over potato, beetroot
or mixed bean salads to give just a hint
of its flavor. The juice can be used in
marinades and salad dressings.

MEDICINAL AND OTHER USE

In the Middle East sumac is used to
make a drink for anyone suffering from
an upset stomach, and to treat fevers
and bowel complaints.

Sesame

BOTANICAL NAME: *Sesamum indicum,*
syn S. orientale • FAMILY NAME: *Pedaliaceae*

FR. *sésame;* G. *Sesam;* SP. *sésamo, ajonjolí;*
IT. *sesamo;* JAP. *goma*

black sesame seeds

halva

**sesame
seeds**

The name sesame was listed as sesemt *in about 1500 BC in the* Ebers Papyrus, *a
65-feet-long scroll on ancient herbs and spices discovered by the famous German
Egyptologist, Ebers. It is not clear whether sesame originated in Africa or India, but t
his valuable crop soon reached China, where 5,000 years ago the Chinese were burning
sesame oil to make soot for their ink-blocks, and both seeds and oil have long been used
in cooking. Slaves from Africa took the sesame seed to America and the West Indies in
the belief that it would bring them luck.*

CULTIVATION

The sesame plant is a tall, tropical herbaceous annual growing to about 6 feet. It has pink or white foxglove-type flowers and hairy leaves, which are often used in folk medicine to make an eyebath for tired eyes. When ready for harvesting, the stems are cut and hung upside down over mats until the seeds are all disgorged from the pods. The seeds are small, flat and oblate; they may be red, brown, black or yellow. When they are husked they are a creamy color. Black sesame seeds are available, but the majority are sold as the husked, white type. They are also available ready roasted, when they are a darker beige color. Sesame grows in many countries: India, China, Burma, Mexico, Pakistan, Turkey, Uganda, Sudan and Nigeria; much of each country's crop is consumed at home, except for Sudan and Nigeria, the main exporters.

**air-dried
sesame seeds**

AROMA AND FLAVOR

In spite of their high oil content, sesame seeds have little aroma, but when they are dry fried their nutty aroma is very pronounced and their flavor heightened.

CULINARY USE

Sesame oil is used in margarines and as a cooking medium and a flavoring ingredient. The seeds are ground to an oily, beige-colored paste known as tahini, which is used in hummus, a Middle Eastern dip. Sometimes the tahini is mixed with lemon juice and garlic and used as a dip with hot pita bread as an appetizer or picnic food.

The Chinese are fond of sesame: sesame oil is widely used in Chinese cooking as a flavoring. The seeds are also used, for example sesame shrimp toasts are scattered with seeds before they are deep fried. They are also sprinkled over Chinese toffee apples, pieces of apple fried in a light batter and coated in caramel. Both oil and seeds are used in the cooking of other Far Eastern countries such as Singapore, Malaysia and Indonesia. Gomasio is a Japanese speciality using sesame seeds: a mixture of the ground seeds and salt used as a seasoning.

The seeds are popular scattered on bread, sweet and savory crackers, particularly in Greece and Turkey.

MEDICINAL AND OTHER USE

Sesame is used in laxatives, as an emollient and in poultices. Sesame oil, also called gingelly oil, is highly stable and it does not become rancid quickly in hot humid conditions; it is used in lubricants, soap, cosmetics and ointments. The mixture or 'cake' that remains after the pressing of the oil is full of protein and eaten as a subsistence food.

tahini

sesame oil

hummus

Tamarind

BOTANICAL NAME: *Tamarindus indica,*
syn T. officinalis • FAMILY NAME: *Leguminosae*

FR. *tamarin;* G. *Tamarinde;* SP. *tamarindo;*
IT. *tamarindo;* IN. *imli, amyli*

tamarind pods

The word tamarind literally means date of India, *which is an apt description.*
Believed to be native to East Africa, tamarind now grows extensively throughout India,
South-east Asia and the West Indies: all areas where its particular sour flavor is used in
the diverse cuisines.

CULTIVATION

A semi-evergreen, tropical tree, the tamarind grows to a magnificent 80 feet and it has long, drooping branches. The flowers are yellow, each with a red stripe. The dark brown fruit pods are 6-8 in long. The sticky pulp surrounding the seeds has a high tartaric acid content, which accounts for its wide use as a souring agent.

AROMA AND FLAVOR

Tamarind has little smell – perhaps a hint of sweet and sour to its aroma – but its flavor makes up for this, being particularly sour, yet fruity and refreshing, resembling sour prunes.

CULINARY USE

Recipes which have been adapted for Western kitchens may suggest substituting lemon juice for tamarind, but if you know the taste of tamarind, it alone will suffice. Tamarind is readily available in Oriental stores in slices, as a block or as a concentrate. Tamarind is a standard ingredient throughout India and South-east Asia in curries, chutneys, lentil and bean dishes as well as in the famous hot and sour soups. The juice is made into a refreshing drink in both the Middle East and the West Indies. Tamarind is also one of the ingredients in the famous Worcestershire sauce.

compressed tamarind block

dried tamarind slices

tamarind balls

tamarind concentrate

tamarind paste

compressed tamarind

PREPARATION TIPS

COMPRESSED BLOCK: Tear off the equivalent of 1 tbsp and soak it in $^2/_3$ cup warm water for 10 minutes. Swirl the tamarind with your fingers so that the pulp is released from the seeds.

Strain the juice through a nylon strainer: do not use a metal strainer which will react with the acid. Discard the pulp and seeds and use the liquid as required.

TAMARIND SLICES: Soak them in $^2/_3$ cup warm water for 30 minutes to extract their flavor. Squeeze with your fingers, then strain the juice and store it as above.

TAMARIND CONCENTRATE: Just mix 1 tbsp with 4-6 tbsp warm water and use as required. Once opened, it is best to keep the jar of concentrate in the fridge, with the top firmly secured.

MEDICINAL AND OTHER USE

Tamarind is used as a laxative and for tummy upsets. It is antiseptic, used in eye baths and for the treatment of ulcers. Over-ripe fruits can be used to clean copper and brass, a common practice in colonial times.

Fenugreek

BOTANICAL NAME: *Trigonella foenum-graecum*

FAMILY NAME: *Leguminosae*

FR. *fenugrec sénegré, trigonelle;* G. *Bockshornkraut, griechisches Heu;* SP. *alholva, fenogreco;* IT. *fieno greco;* IN. *methi*

The botanical name is easily explained: trigonella *refers to the angular seeds and* foenum graecum *translates as 'Greek hay', which explains its use as cattle fodder. Fenugreek was used by the Ancient Egyptians in embalming and for incense. The Romans grew it as fodder for their animals, which is still the practice in India today, with the benefit that it restores nitrogen to the soil and acts as a natural fertilizer.*

dried fenugreek leaves

CULTIVATION

Fenugreek is native to India and Southern Europe, and it grows wild all over North Africa. India, Pakistan, Lebanon, Egypt, France and Argentina all export the crop. The fenugreek plant is an annual, which grows to about 2 feet with light green leaves, not unlike clover, and white flowers. Between ten and twenty seeds are obtained from each fenugreek pod.

AROMA AND FLAVOR

Fenugreek is highly aromatic, smelling of curry – the whole plant exudes the characteristic, but mild, curry-powder aroma. The spice has a tangy flavor, rather like burnt sugar, and anyone who has tried old-fashioned or inexpensive curry powder will recognize the smell of fenugreek.

CULINARY USE

Commercially, fenugreek extract is used as a flavoring in imitation maple syrup and in mango chutney. Fenugreek is rich in protein, minerals and vitamins, which makes it an important ingredient in vegetable and dhal dishes eaten in the poorer areas of India. The leaves, called *methi*, are widely used, fresh or dried, in Indian cooking and are often combined with vegetables, such as spinach, potato and yam.

Fenugreek seeds are used in a wide range of home-made or commercial curry powders. The small seeds, which resemble tiny, irregular, beige stones, are extremely hard and difficult to grind at home. Used in spiced fish dishes and vegetable curries.

MEDICINAL AND OTHER USE

Used in the Middle Ages as a cure for baldness, fenugreek is still used in Indonesia as a hair tonic.

Fenugreek is traditionally used to stimulate the metabolism and to help control blood-sugar levels in cases of diabetes. It is also given to assist with stomach and digestive orders, and lowering blood pressure. Having a valuable iron content, fenugreek was also given in cases of anaemia. The powder is sometimes used as a dye.

fresh fenugreek leaves

PREPARATION TIPS

Always dry fry the seeds before grinding them: a light roast gives a mellow flavor, too dark and the flavor will be bitter. Sometimes the seeds are soaked overnight, when they become gelatinous and easier to combine into curry pastes.

STORAGE

If kept in an airtight container, in a cool, dark place, the whole seeds have a long shelf life. The powder should be bought in small quantities and stored away from strong light as it loses its flavor if stored for long periods.

The seeds can be sprouted very easily: put 2-3 tbsp in a jar, cover with muslin and secure with an elastic band. Rinse with water and drain once or twice a day until the seeds sprout. The sprouts add an intriguing flavor to salads or can be used in a sandwich filling, with avocado, tomato or cheese.

Add ground fenugreek judiciously in cooking because it has a strong penetrating flavor.

fenugreek seeds

fenugreek sprouts

ground fenugreek

fenugreek powder

Vanilla

BOTANICAL NAME: *Vanilla fragrans, syn V. planifolia*
FAMILY NAME: *Orchidaceae*

FR. *vanille*; G. *Vanille*; SP. *vainilla*; IT. *vaniglia*

The name vanilla comes from the Spanish vainilla, *meaning 'little pod'. A drink that combines chocolate and vanilla may seem to be a modern combination, but the Aztecs discovered this combination of exotic flavors centuries before the Spanish first set foot in Mexico in 1520. Vanilla was taken back to Spain and from there it quickly spread throughout Europe, where its magical flavor was much enjoyed by those who could afford to buy it.*

CULTIVATION

Vanilla is the seed bean of a tropical climbing orchid, a native of Mexico and exclusive to the country until the 19th century. Attempts were made to introduce the plant elsewhere but the flowers never produced beans. The flowers open only for one day and are naturally pollinated by the melipona bee

vanilla beans

and a particular long-beaked humming bird, both native to Mexico, which explained the lack of success in propagation elsewhere. The plant was artificially pollinated, and it now grows principally in Madagascar and the Seychelles, with some crops in Réunion, Mauritius, Indonesia, Puerto Rico, Mexico and the West Indies.

Being vine-like, the plant is encouraged to grow around the trunks of trees, the leaves of which provide the shade in which vanilla thrives. The plant bears fruit after three years and has a productive life of twelve years, after which time the vines are replaced. The unripe beans are harvested when they are 5-8 in long and yellow in color. At this stage the bean does not have the characteristic smell.

The drying process is somewhat lengthy, and it contributes to the high price of the spice. In Madagascar and Mexico, the beans are blanched briefly in boiling water and then sweated and dried over a period of weeks until they are dark brown and wrinkled, yet supple. The superior beans are coated in a white crystalline efflorescence which is the vanillin, the real vanilla flavor. The beans keep their flavor well.

AROMA AND FLAVOR

Real vanilla is highly fragrant, with an exotic and memorable aroma. The taste reflects the smell, with a soft, flowery mellowness.

CULINARY USE

One of the finest flavors, used almost exclusively in sweet cookery. Vanilla is added to cakes, cookies, puddings and desserts. It is used to flavor confectionery, and it has a special affinity for chocolate. Vanilla is one of the distinctive ingredients in crème de cacao and Galliano, two popular liqueurs.

MEDICINAL AND OTHER USE

Vanilla is used as a pick-me-up and an antidote to fevers. It is also attributed with aphrodisiac qualities, and it is used in perfume production.

STORAGE

Vanilla beans are usually sold singly or in pairs, packed in a long clear tube. Store one vanilla bean in a jar of sugar (usually superfine sugar), allowing three or four weeks for the flavor to permeate the sugar fully and just top up the jar with more sugar as required. This gloriously fragrant vanilla sugar is marvellous in cakes, cookies, sweet pies, ice creams and milk puddings. A good-quality bean, with plenty of vanillin crystals, will remain potent for as long as four years.

VANILLA FLAVORINGS

Natural vanilla flavoring extract is made by finely chopping the beans and infusing them by dripping alcohol on the pieces. Inferior beans are used; they may not be good enough for selling whole, but their flavor is fine. Madagascar bourbon is one example of a title given to superior vanilla flavoring.

Artificial vanilla extract or flavoring is light-years away from the true flavor of vanilla. The flavor is synthesized from wood pulp waste, coal tar or

Galliano

vanilla sugar

natural vanilla extract

vanilla extract

coumarin, which is banned in many countries. Substantial quantities of the artificial flavoring are sold and used each year. This type of vanilla extract has a harsh flavor with a definite aftertaste. Buy the vanilla bean or natural vanilla flavoring or extract and you will notice the difference in flavor.

Ginger

BOTANICAL NAME: *Zingiber officinale, syn Amoumum officinate*
FAMILY NAME: *Zingiberaceae*

OTHER NAMES: *Jamaican Ginger;* FR. *gingembre;*
G. *Ingwer;* SP. *jengibre;* IT. *zenzero*

fresh ginger root

The name is believed to come from the Sanskrit (an ancient Indo-Aryan language) singabera, *meaning 'shaped like a horn', evolving to the Greek* zingiberi *and subsequently the Latin* zingiber. *Ginger has a long respected history as a spice. Its origins lie either in India or China, where it was mentioned in 500 BC in the writings of the philosopher Confucius. Arab traders from the Orient introduced ginger to Greece and Rome, and it is quite likely that the invading Romans carried it to Britain. The ginger rhizome was easily transported, allowing the Arabs to introduce it to East Africa, and the Portuguese to take it to West Africa in the 13th century. The Spanish expanded the trade by taking ginger to Mexico and the West Indies, especially Jamaica, a country that still claims to produce the best-quality ginger. By the 14th century, ginger was the most common spice after pepper.*

CULTIVATION

The ginger plant is an upright tropical plant, which is propagated by dividing the rhizomes. It grows to about 3 feet, with elegant lance-shaped leaves and yellow flowers lightly tinged with purple. Harvesting takes place 9 or 10 months after planting, and in many parts of the world this is still done by hand. Much of the crop is washed, sun-dried and then ground to a powder for domestic and commercial use. The largest markets for ground ginger are the UK, Yemen, the USA, Middle East, Singapore and Malaysia. Large crops are grown in India, China, Taiwan, Nigeria, Jamaica, and Mauritius; Australia is also now a significant producer.

AROMA AND FLAVOR

The aroma when you cut into a piece of fresh ginger root has a hint of lemon, with a refreshing sharpness. Jamaica ginger is said to have the finest aroma, with the Kenyan spice being of good quality too. Other African and Indian gingers have a darker skin and a biting, less pleasant flavor.

CULINARY USE

The essential oil is used in commercial flavorings. Fresh ginger root is extremely popular in a huge variety of stir-fry or curry dishes. Authentically, fresh ginger root is used in a host of dishes from India and Oriental countries. It is incorporated by different techniques: slices may be added to marinades or in cooking, to be discarded on the side of the plate or bowl as the food is eaten. Grated, chopped or crushed ginger is used in pastes or braised dishes. Finely shredded ginger is added to fried and stir-fried dishes, or it may be used raw in salads. Pickled and preserved types are served as appetizers or used in savory cooking.

All these methods are employed to flavor fish and seafood, poultry, meat, vegetable and noodle dishes. Ginger is also widely appreciated in new cooking

PREPARATION TIPS

Thinly peel or scrape off the skin from a piece of fresh ginger root.

Grate the root, taking care not to graze your fingers at the end!

Peeled ginger can be ground to a paste with garlic, other spices and a little oil to make a smoother mixture.

Cut thin, peeled, slices into matchstick strips for use in stir-fries or similar dishes. The strips can be cut across to provide coarsely chopped ginger or the spice can be chopped in a food processor.

Bruise the root using the flat blade of a knife for use in dishes where it will be removed or not eaten.

styles, for example with chicken and game in casseroles.

Ginger is also essential in much Western baking, for example in traditional gingerbreads, cakes, cookies (such as ginger snaps), French pain *d'épice* and German *Pfefferkuchen*. The spice is also important in chutneys, pickles, jams and sweet preserves as well as drinks, such as ginger beer, ginger ale and ginger wine.

MEDICINAL AND OTHER USE

Henry VIII is said to have used ginger as a medicine for its qualities, as outlined by Culpeper, the herbalist, 150 years later: 'Ginger helps digestion, warms the stomach, clears the sight, and is profitable for old men; it heats the joints and is therefore useful against gout'. Ginger has an impressive record in treating all kinds of ailments: it is said to help poor circulation, and to cure flatulence and indigestion; it is taken as a drink for coughs, nausea and influenza. In the East ginger is chewed to ward off evil spirits. It is considered to be a cure for travel sickness. The essential oil is used in perfumery.

TYPES OF GINGER

Fresh Root or Green Ginger: the fresh spice. Look for plump, silvery skinned pieces, which are called a 'hand'. Young ginger has smoother, thin skin firmly clinging to the firm, quite heavy, root. Older ginger has thicker, papery skin, which sits more loosely on the root. The root itself is slightly lighter, more fibrous and, by comparison to the young budding ginger, it looks dead. Avoid ginger that is wrinkled, softening or very light in weight. Similarly, reject pieces where cut ends look dehydrated and coarsely fibrous or even slightly moldy! Fresh, young ginger is usually available only from Oriental stores – buy it when you find it to sample the smooth, juicy and tender texture, and the light, hot, citric flavor.

COOKING TIPS

Use a little crushed ginger in marinades for pork steaks or chops. Try adding a little finely grated fresh or chopped crystallized ginger to fruit puddings using rhubarb, plums or pears, to crumbles, Eve's pudding or pastry pies.

Dried Whole Ginger Root: a traditional pickling spice. It is placed in a muslin bag of spices for flavoring vinegar or other pickle mixtures. The dried root is rarely used where fresh ginger root is readily available.

Ground Ginger: pale sand-color spice widely used in baking, both domestic and commercial.

Pickled Ginger: a savory condiment used in Oriental cooking. There are different types: Chinese pickled ginger in sweetened vinegar is light, sweet-sour and quite hot in flavor. It is eaten as an appetizer or used in cooking. Sweet red pickled ginger is artificially colored and slightly tangy, but mainly sweet as it is candied. Japanese pickled ginger is more delicate than the Chinese pickles, and there are two different types: one red, one pale, both with traditional savory roles.

Preserved or Stem Ginger: traditionally packed into the decorative, bulbous Chinese ginger jars, the plump tender young ginger is peeled and preserved in syrup. This is sweet and fairly spicy.

Chopped Candied Ginger: a sweet ingredient. The ginger is preserved in a strong syrup, as for stem ginger, and chopped then packed in a small amount of heavy syrup.

Crystallized Ginger: preserved by cooking in syrup, then drying and rolling in sugar.

pickled ginger

ground ginger

crystallized ginger

stem ginger in syrup

dried ginger root

SPICE MIXTURES

Curry Powders

The name curry is a corruption of the Tamil word karhi. Throughout the days of the Raj, the word evolved as a loose description of any Indian food cooked in a sauce. The early aficionados of richly spiced Indian dishes, the merchants and soldiers who visited India, were keen to introduce the flavors to their home cooking when they returned. Demand for a commercial curry powder developed over decades, and such spice mixtures have slowly become more authentic, better in quality and less crude in terms of flavor. Today there are ready prepared curry spice mixtures for Oriental cuisines as well as Indian cooking in most supermarkets.

Curry powder is a blend of different spices, combined to indicate seasonings used in different regions. It is not a traditional, authentic ingredient in Indian cooking: in a huge subcontinent like India and in countries throughout the East, individual spices are mixed in particular styles of cooking. Curry powders reflect the availability of the spices and the climate of the region to which they are credited.

Spice blends from the hotter regions contain more fiery chili flavors; for example, Madras, Mysore and Goa (vindaloo) are all hot, while spice mixtures from cooler, northern climes usually concentrate on warmer and more fragrant flavors.

Achieving the right balance of ingredients for a curry powder is highly personal. The basic recipe with variations can be adapted to suit your taste and the main ingredients for any particular dish.

Curry Powder

MAKES 16 TBSP
6-8 dried red chilies
8 tbsp coriander seeds
4 tbsp cumin seeds
2 tsp fenugreek seeds
2 tsp black mustard seeds
2 tsp black peppercorns
1 tbsp ground turmeric
1 tsp ground ginger

1 Remove the stalks and seeds from chilies unless you like a fiery mixture, in which case leave a few seeds in the pods.

2 Roast or dry fry the chilies, coriander, cumin, fenugreek, mustard seeds and black peppercorns in a heavy-based pan over a medium heat until they give off a rich aroma. Shake the pan constantly so that the spices are evenly roasted.

3 Grind the roasted spices to a powder in a mortar or coffee grinder, then stir in the turmeric and ginger.

VARIATION

Dry fry 4 curry leaves and add them to the ground mixture; remove from the cooked dish before it is served as the curry leaves are not eaten.

For a milder result, halve the number of chilies, then add 1 cinnamon stick, 1 tbsp fennel seeds and 6 cloves to the spices before roasting or dry frying.

dried red chilies

black mustard seeds

coriander seeds

black peppercorns

cumin seeds

ground turmeric

fenugreek seeds

ground ginger

Sambaar Powder

Also known as sambar, this classic blend of spices is used extensively in South Indian dishes to flavor vegetable and lentil combinations, braised dishes and spicy broths so typical of Brahmin cooking. The powder has a pleasing nutty flavor, which comes from dry-roasting the dhal before grinding them. This also gives a smooth, velvet-like thickening to the finished sauce. The dhal are readily available in Asian stores and in some of the larger supermarkets.

MAKES 17 TBSP

8-10 dried red chilies
6 tbsp coriander seeds
2 tbsp cumin seeds
2 tsp black peppercorns
2 tsp fenugreek seeds
2 tsp urad dhal (white split gram beans)
2 tsp channa dhal (yellow split peas)
2 tsp mung dhal (yellow mung beans)
1½ tbsp ground turmeric

1 Discard the stalks and seeds from the chilies. Heat a heavy-based frying pan, add the chilies, coriander, cumin, black peppercorns and fenugreek. Toss all the spices together over a medium heat until they give off a rich aroma, then turn the mixture into a bowl.

2 Repeat the process with the pulses, tossing them over a medium heat continuously until they are toasted but do not allow them to burn.

3 Grind the spices and pulses to a fine powder and then mix in the turmeric.

dried red chilies

coriander seeds

channa dhal

black peppercorns

mung dhal

fenugreek seeds

ground turmeric

urad dhal

cumin seeds

COOK'S TIP

Authentically, spices would usually be prepared and mixed as required, on a daily basis, but the mixture can be made in advance and stored in an airtight jar for 3-4 months, away from strong light, or the spice mixture can be frozen.

Bengali Five Spices

In this spice mix of Bengali origin, also known as panch phoron, equal quantities of the whole spices are simply mixed together, without roasting or grinding. The mixture is used in either of two ways: the mixture may be fried in oil to impart flavor to the oil before adding the main ingredients or fried in ghee and stirred into cooked dhal or vegetable dishes just before they are served.

MAKES 10 TBSP

2 tbsp cumin seeds

2 tbsp fennel seeds

2 tbsp mustard seeds

2 tbsp fenugreek seeds

2 tbsp nigella seeds

1 Mix the spices and store them in an airtight jar away from strong light.

mustard seeds

cumin seeds

fenugreek seeds

fennel seeds

nigella seeds

Sri Lankan Curry Powder

This has quite different characteristics from Indian curry powders. The spices are highly roasted, the coriander, cumin, fennel and fenugreek separately, resulting in a gloriously rich, dark curry powder, which can be used for fish, poultry, meat or vegetable curries.

MAKES 12 TBSP

6 tbsp coriander seeds

3 tbsp cumin seeds

1 tbsp fennel seeds

1 tsp fenugreek seeds

2 in piece cinnamon stick

1 tsp cloves

8 green cardamoms

6 dried curry leaves

1-2 tsp chili powder

1 Dry fry or roast the coriander, cumin, fennel and fenugreek separately because they turn dark at different stages. Dry fry or roast the cinnamon stick, cloves and cardamoms together until they give off a spicy aroma.

2 Remove the seeds from the cardamom pods and grind all the ingredients, with curry leaves and chili powder, to a fine powder.

dried curry leaves

cinnamon stick

coriander seeds

green cardamoms

chili powder

cumin seeds

fenugreek seeds

cloves

Singapore-style Curry Powder

Singapore is a culinary melting pot of different cuisines and cooks who are all extraordinarily keen on their particular type of food, each creating a particular blend of spices. This basic recipe is suitable for both poultry and meat dishes.

MAKES 10 TBSP
3-4 dried red chilies
6 tbsp coriander seeds
1 tbsp cumin seeds
1 tbsp fennel seeds
2 tsp black peppercorns
1 in piece cinnamon stick
4 green cardamoms
6 cloves
2 tsp ground turmeric

1 Unless you like a fiery curry powder, discard the stalks and seeds from the chilies.

2 Dry fry or roast the chilies with all the remaining spices except the turmeric, stirring continuously, until they give off a rich aroma.

3 Break the cinnamon stick into small pieces and remove the seeds from the cardamom pods. Grind all the spices to a fine powder, then stir in the turmeric.

dried red chilies

black peppercorns

coriander seeds

cinnamon stick

cumin seeds

green cardamom and cloves

fennel seeds image

fennel seeds

ground turmeric image

ground turmeric

Singapore Seafood Curry Powder

MAKES 8 TBSP
2-3 dried red chilies
6 tbsp coriander seeds
1 tbsp cumin seeds

2 tbsp fennel seeds
1 tsp fenugreek seeds
1 tsp black peppercorns
2 tsp ground turmeric

1 Prepare as for the Singapore-style curry powder, add the ground turmeric last.

dried red chilies

coriander seeds

cumin seeds

fennel seeds

ground turmeric

fenugreek seeds image

fenugreek seeds

black peppercorns image

black peppercorns

Seven-seas Curry Powder

This milder blend of spices is much enjoyed in Indonesian and Malaysian cooking, for curries, sambals, casseroles and kebabs. The name is derived from the fact that seven seas, including the Andaman and South China Sea, converge on the shores of Malaysia and the thousands of islands that make up the archipelago of Indonesia.

MAKES 13 TBSP

6-8 white cardamoms
6 tbsp coriander seeds
3 tbsp cumin seeds
1½ tbsp celery seeds
2 in piece cinnamon stick or cassia
6-8 cloves
1 tbsp chili powder

1 Bruise the cardamom pods and place them in a heavy-based frying pan with all the other spices except the chili powder. Dry fry the mixture, stirring it and shaking the pan continuously, until the spices give off a rich, heady aroma.

2 Remove the cardamom seeds from their pods, then grind them with all the other roasted ingredients to a fine powder. Add the chili powder and mix well.

piece of cassia

white cardamoms

coriander seeds

cumin seeds

celery seeds

cloves

chili powder

Tadka

MAKES ENOUGH FOR 1 DISH

2 tbsp ghee
2 tsp black mustard seeds
½ tsp ground asafoetida
about 8 fresh or dried curry leaves

1 Assemble all the ingredients – more curry leaves can be added if liked.

2 Melt the ghee in a frying pan or large saucepan and have a lid ready to cover the pan. When the ghee is hot add the mustard seeds, which will jump when they pop so be ready to cover the pan with a lid.

3 Draw the pan off the heat and add the asafoetida and curry leaves. Stir and then add to a dhal, soup or stew.

black mustard seeds

ground asafoetida

curry leaves

ghee

Cilantro Baghar

A baghar or tadka is a mixture of spices and flavorings fried in hot ghee or mustard oil to release their flavors. They are then quickly poured over or stirred into Indian dishes of dhal, vegetables, yogurt, salads or pulse and vegetable combinations. Traditional regional mixtures are used; for example, garlic and dried red pepper are used in a baghar for lentils in North Indian cooking. The combination of spices below, fried in mustard oil, are also used in North Indian cooking as a topping for dhal; in the south, black mustard seeds, asafoetida and fresh or dried curry leaves are used.

MAKES ENOUGH FOR 1 DISH

4 tbsp mustard oil
3-4 tsp cumin seeds
1 small onion, finely chopped
4 tbsp finely chopped
  fresh cilantro

1 Assemble all the ingredients. Heat the mustard oil until it is just smoking. Turn off the heat and allow the oil to cool briefly.

2 Reheat the oil and fry the cumin seeds until they are changing color. Add the onion and cook until it is turning golden.

3 Finally, add the cilantro leaves and stir for only a few seconds, then pour the mixture over a dhal, soup or stew.

mustard oil

fresh cilantro

chopped onion

cumin seeds

Masalas

Masalas are a blend of spices which can be a dry mixture or a paste. The flavors can be mild and fragrant or more highly spiced. This depends largely on the cook and the dish in which the masala is to be used. The spices are usually dry fried before grinding, which greatly enhances the flavor.

Garam Masala

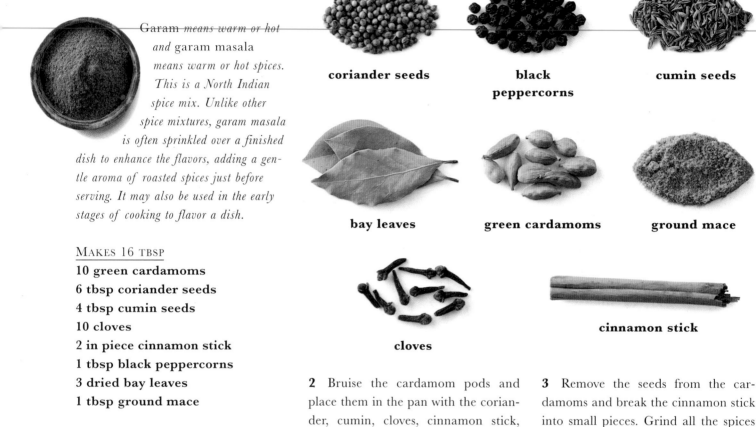

coriander seeds

black peppercorns

cumin seeds

bay leaves

green cardamoms

ground mace

cloves

cinnamon stick

Garam *means warm or hot and* garam masala *means warm or hot spices. This is a North Indian spice mix. Unlike other spice mixtures, garam masala is often sprinkled over a finished dish to enhance the flavors, adding a gentle aroma of roasted spices just before serving. It may also be used in the early stages of cooking to flavor a dish.*

MAKES 16 TBSP

10 green cardamoms
6 tbsp coriander seeds
4 tbsp cumin seeds
10 cloves
2 in piece cinnamon stick
1 tbsp black peppercorns
3 dried bay leaves
1 tbsp ground mace

1   Gently warm a dry heavy-based pan.

2   Bruise the cardamom pods and place them in the pan with the coriander, cumin, cloves, cinnamon stick, peppercorns and bay leaves. Keep tossing the spices over a gentle heat until they give off a rich aroma.

3   Remove the seeds from the cardamoms and break the cinnamon stick into small pieces. Grind all the spices to a fine powder, then mix in the ground mace.

Kashmiri Masala

This masala is particularly good with prawn and lamb dishes.

MAKES 4½ TBSP

12 green cardamoms
2in piece cinnamon stick
1 tbsp cloves
1 tbsp black peppercorns
1 tbsp black cumin seeds
2 tsp caraway seeds
1 tsp ground nutmeg

cinnamon stick

black peppercorns

cloves

1 Split the cardamom pods and break the cinnamon stick.

2 Warm a heavy-based frying pan and then dry fry all the spices except the nutmeg, tossing them continuously, until they give off a rich aroma.

3 Remove the cardamom seeds from their pods and grind all the spices to a fine powder. Mix in the nutmeg.

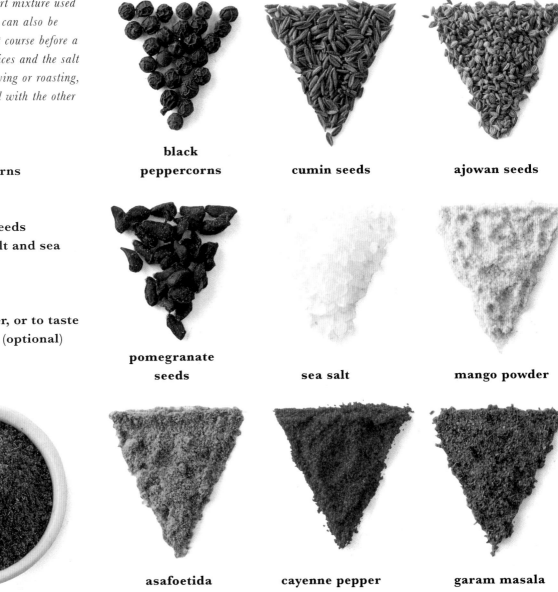

green cardamoms

caraway seeds

ground nutmeg

cumin seeds

Chat Masala

Chat is an Indian salad snack sold on street stalls or by food hawkers – it might consist of banana, papaya, guavas and chikoo or apples. The following recipe is for the spicy and rather tart mixture used to flavor the salad, which can also be served as a refreshing first course before a main meal. The whole spices and the salt are ground without dry frying or roasting, and then thoroughly mixed with the other ingredients.

MAKES 2¹/₂ TBSP

1 tsp black peppercorns
1 tsp cumin seeds
1 tsp ajowan seeds
1 tsp pomegranate seeds
1 tsp mixed black salt and sea salt, or to taste
¹/₄ tsp asafoetida
1 tsp mango powder
¹/₂ tsp cayenne pepper, or to taste
¹/₂ tsp garam masala (optional)

1 Grind the peppercorns to a powder with the cumin, ajowan, pomegranate seeds and salts.

2 Add the remaining ingredients, adjusting the quantity of cayenne pepper to taste and omitting the garam masala, if preferred, and mix well.

black peppercorns

cumin seeds

ajowan seeds

pomegranate seeds

sea salt

mango powder

asafoetida

cayenne pepper

garam masala

Green Masala

This mild masala paste, rich jewel-green in color, is tangy with fresh mint and cilantro leaves. It makes a wonderful addition to shrimp, poultry and vegetable dishes, especially those containing coconut milk, or as an addition to a simple dhal.

MAKES 17 TBSP

1 tsp fenugreek seeds
10 green cardamoms
6 cloves
2 tsp ground turmeric
2 tsp salt
4 cloves garlic, crushed
2 in piece fresh ginger root,
  peeled and finely grated
2 oz mint leaves
1 oz cilantro leaves
1 small green bell pepper, seeded
  and chopped (optional)
¼ cup cider vinegar
½ cup mixed sunflower and
  sesame oil

1 Soak the fenugreek seeds in water overnight.

2 Next day, bruise the cardamoms and dry fry them with the cloves until they give off a rich aroma. Grind these roasted spices to a powder and add the turmeric and salt.

3 Drain the fenugreek seeds, place them in a blender or food processor with the garlic, ginger, mint, cilantro leaves, green bell pepper, if using, and the vinegar. Blend the mixture to a purée, then add the salt and ground spices.

**cilantro
leaves**

**fenugreek
seeds**

**green
cardamoms**

garlic

mint leaves

cloves

**ground
turmeric**

**fresh
ginger root**

salt

**cider
vinegar**

**mixed sunflower
and sesame oil**

green bell pepper

4 Heat the oil. Add the paste and continue heating until the oil bubbles again, then remove the pan from the heat and allow to cool.

Madrasi Masala

This blend of dry and wet spices is typical of seasonings from South India. The dry spices are roasted and ground before adding garlic, finely grated ginger and vinegar to make a paste, which is then cooked in oil to develop the flavors before being stored in an airtight jar.

MAKES 1 LB

8 tbsp coriander seeds
4 tbsp cumin seeds
1 tbsp black peppercorns
1 tbsp black mustard seeds
11 tbsp ground turmeric
3-4 tsp chili powder
1 tbsp salt
8 garlic cloves, crushed
3 in piece fresh ginger root,
 peeled and finely grated
¼ cup cider vinegar
¾ cup sunflower oil

1 Heat a heavy-based frying pan and dry fry the coriander, cumin and peppercorns briefly; add the mustard seeds, tossing the mixture continuously, until the spices give off a rich aroma. Do not over-brown.

2 Grind the mixture to a fine powder, then add the turmeric, chili and salt. Add the garlic, ginger and sufficient vinegar to make a paste.

3 Heat the oil and fry the paste, stirring and turning it continuously, until the oil begins to separate from the spicy mixture.

5 Transfer the mixture to a clean jar. Make sure that there is a film of oil floating on the paste to effect an airtight seal, which will act as a preservative and make sure the paste keeps its color. Store away from strong light, or in the fridge, for 2-3 weeks.

4 Cool the paste and store it in an airtight jar away from light and preferably in a cool place. The paste will keep for about 2-3 weeks.

cider vinegar

sunflower oil

COOK'S TIP

Allow about 1-1½ tbsp for each 1 lb poultry or meat in a recipe. The paste makes a good marinade for chicken. Slash the skin and rub in 1 tbsp paste with salt and a little extra oil. Marinate the chicken for several hours before baking it on the barbecue.

coriander seeds

cumin seeds

black peppercorns

black mustard seeds

ground turmeric

chili powder

salt

garlic

fresh ginger root

Spice Pastes

Separate mounds of fresh 'wet spices' are available on market stalls throughout South-east Asia. The stall holder simply asks whether a meat, fish or vegetable curry is to be prepared and whether the preference is for a hot spicy curry or something milder. He then spoons appropriate quantities of chili, ginger, galangal, lemon grass and garlic onto a banana leaf, and folds it in a cone to take home and cook. Perhaps the banana leaf has now been superseded by the inevitable plastic bag!

Today we are able to buy ready prepared spice pastes in jars and cans that are of excellent quality, but it is fun when time allows to experiment in making up your own hot, spicy paste.

Malaysian Chicken Spice Paste

This fairly fiery paste can be toned down by reducing the number of chilies. Red onions and fresh turmeric give the paste a rich color. Blachan may appear to be an unusual ingredient, but it adds an unexpected depth of flavor, so do not be tempted to omit it. The candlenuts or macadamia nuts are included to thicken the sauce, and the lemon grass adds its own magic in this classic, basic curry paste.

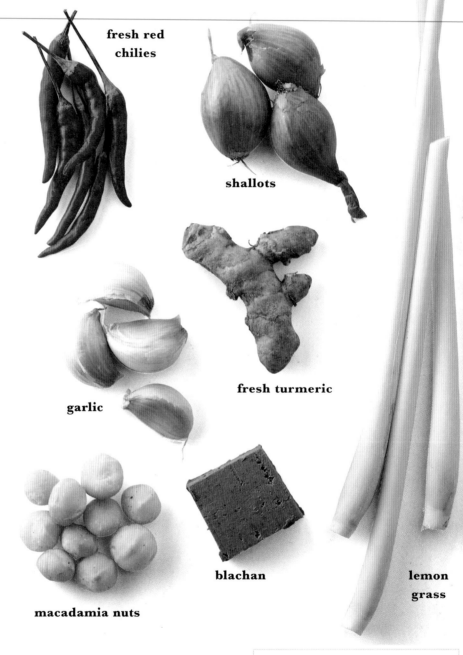

fresh red chilies

shallots

fresh turmeric

garlic

macadamia nuts

blachan

lemon grass

MAKES ABOUT 12 OZ

6 fresh red chilies, seeded and sliced
3 red onions or 12 shallots, roughly chopped
4 garlic cloves
1 in piece fresh turmeric root, peeled and sliced or 1 tsp ground turmeric
10 candlenuts or macadamia nuts
1 in cube blachan, prepared
3 lemon grass stalks

1 Place the chilies, onions or shallots, garlic, turmeric, nuts and blachan in a food processor.

2 Trim the root end from the lemon grass and slice the lower 2½ in bulbous section into small pieces.

3 Add the lemon grass to the remaining ingredients and process them to a fine paste. Use the paste at once or store in an airtight glass jar in the fridge for a few days or in a plastic container in the freezer.

COOK'S TIP

The top section of the lemon grass can be bruised and added to the curry during cooking, then removed before serving.

Thai Red Curry Paste

Krueng gaeng phed *is the Thai name for this paste, which is used for meat, poultry and vegetable dishes.*

Makes about 6 oz

- 10 fresh red chilies, seeded and sliced, or 1½ tbsp chili powder
- 4 oz dark red onions or shallots, sliced
- 4 garlic cloves
- 3 lemon grass stalks, lower part of stem sliced and bruised
- ½ in piece greater galangal, peeled, sliced and bruised
- 4 cilantro sprigs, stems only
- 1-2 tbsp peanut oil
- 1 tsp grated magrut or grapefruit peel
- ½ in cube of blachan, prepared
- 1 tbsp coriander seeds
- 2 tsp cumin seeds
- 1 tsp salt

1 Pound the chilies or chili powder, onions or shallots, garlic, bruised lemon grass, galangal and the stems from the cilantro sprigs in a mortar, to a paste, gradually adding the oil. Alternatively, purée the ingredients in a food processor or blender. Add the grated magrut or grapefruit peel and the blachan.

2 Dry-fry the coriander and cumin seeds, then turn them into a mortar and grind them to a powder. Add the ground spices to the paste with the salt and mix well.

3 Use the paste at once or place in a glass jar. Cover with plastic wrap and an airtight lid, then store in the fridge. The paste will keep for 3-4 weeks. Alternatively freeze the paste in small plastic containers, making a note of the quantity.

red chilies

peanut oil

red onion

blachan

garlic

greater galangal

lemon grass

cumin seeds

salt

green chilies

magrut

Green Curry Paste

Gaeng khiev wan *is the green paste, made using the same ingredients as for red curry paste, but with green chilies in place of the red chilies, white onion instead of a red one, and adding the leaves from the cilantro to strengthen the color.*

white onion

fresh cilantro

coriander seeds

Thai Nam Prik Sauce

This is the most famous of all Thai sauces. It can be served on its own, stirred into a helping of plain cooked rice, or it can be offered as a dip for vegetable crudités, either raw or lightly blanched. Despite the fact that the quantities and proportions vary from cook to cook, the ingredients remain constant.

MAKES 10 OZ

1 cup dried shrimp, soaked in water for 15 minutes and drained

½in cube blachan, prepared

3-4 garlic cloves, crushed

3-4 fresh red chilies, seeded and sliced

2 oz peeled cooked shrimp (optional)

a few sprigs of cilantro

8-10 tiny baby eggplants (optional)

3-4 tbsp lemon or lime juice

2 tbsp fish sauce, or to taste

1 tbsp brown sugar, or to taste

1 Pound the soaked shrimp, blachan, garlic and chilies together in a mortar. Alternatively, process the ingredients in a food processor or blender. Add the cooked shrimp, if using, and the cilantro stems and leaves. Pound the ingredients again until combined.

2 Remove the stalks from the eggplants, if using, and gradually pound them into the sauce.

3 Add the lemon or lime juice, fish sauce and sugar to taste. A little water may be added if a thinner sauce is required.

brown sugar

lemon juice

fish sauce

fresh red chilies

dried shrimp

blachan

fresh cilantro

peeled cooked shrimp

garlic

Mus-sa-man Curry Paste

<u>Makes 8 oz</u>

10 fresh red chilies, seeded and sliced, or 1½ tbsp chili powder
4 oz dark-red onions or shallots, sliced
4 garlic cloves, peeled
3 lemon grass stalks, lower part of stem sliced and bruised
½ in piece greater galangal, peeled sliced and bruised
a little peanut oil
4 sprigs cilantro, stems only
1 tsp grated grapefruit peel or magrut
½ in cube blachan, prepared
6 green cardamoms
1 tbsp coriander seeds
2 tsp cumin seeds
1 tsp salt
½ tsp ground cloves
½ tsp ground cinnamon

1 Lightly fry the fresh chilies, if using, with the onions or shallots, garlic, bruised lemon grass and galangal in the oil, stirring continuously. This initial frying will enhance the flavors.

2 Turn the mixture into a food processor or blender, add the chili powder, if using, and process to a smooth paste. Add the stems from the cilantro sprigs, the grapefruit peel or magrut and blachan. Process the mixture again until combined.

3 Bruise the cardamons and dry fry with the coriander and cumin seeds and salt. Remove the seeds from the cardamoms, discarding the pods, and pound the spices in a mortar. Add the cloves and cinnamon. Process the ground spices with the paste until thoroughly combined. Use as required or store in the fridge for 2-3 weeks.

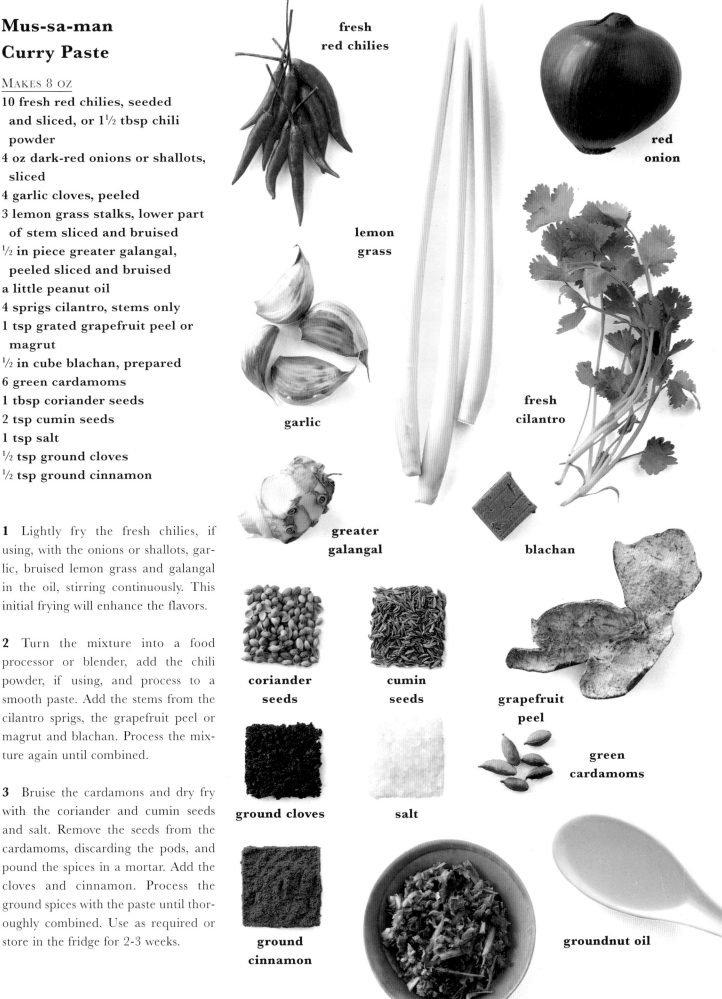

fresh red chilies

red onion

lemon grass

garlic

fresh cilantro

greater galangal

blachan

coriander seeds

cumin seeds

grapefruit peel

green cardamoms

ground cloves

salt

ground cinnamon

groundnut oil

Sambals

In this context the sambal is an accompaniment that is spooned discreetly on the side of your plate, as others would a little mustard, simply to add a kick to a main course. Additionally the chili sambal can be used when time is short or fresh chilies are not to hand both in the sambal kecap or the sambal blachan recipes. A ready-made 'chopped chili' product is now available *from most large supermarkets, which reflects our increasing interest in spicy foods.*

A sambal can also be a spicy chili sauce, which may contain a variety of foods from meat balls to cubes of fish, hard-cooked eggs or vegetables and will be found under the recipe for sambal goreng in Indonesian cookbooks.

Chili Sambal

Sambal ulek, to give this sambal its *Indonesian name, will keep for 4-6 weeks in an airtight jar in the fridge, so it is worth making up a reasonable quantity at a time if you frequently cook Indonesian-style dishes. Use a stainless steel or plastic spoon to measure out the sauce as required. This sauce is fiercely hot, and it will irritate the skin, so should you get any on your fingers, immediately wash them well in soapy water.*

MAKES 1 LB
1 lb fresh red chilies, seeded
2 tsp salt

1 Plunge the chilies into a pan of boiling water and cook them for 5-8 minutes.

2 Drain the chilies and then grind them in a food processor or blender, without making the paste too smooth.

3 Turn the paste into a glass jar, stir in the salt and cover with a piece of wax paper or wrap before screwing on the lid.

4 Store the sambal in the fridge. Spoon it into small dishes to serve as an accompaniment, or use it as suggested in recipes.

fresh red chilies

salt

Sambal Kecap

This Indonesian sauce or sambal can be served as a dip for satays instead of the usual peanut sauce, particularly with beef and chicken, and it is also good with deep fried chicken.

<u>MAKES 10 TBSP</u>
**1 fresh red chili, seeded and
  finely chopped
2 garlic cloves, crushed
4 tbsp dark soy sauce
4 tsp lemon juice or 1-1½ tbsp
  tamarind juice
2 tbsp hot water
2 tbsp deep-fried onion
  slices (optional)**

1 Mix the chili, garlic, soy sauce, lemon or tamarind juice and hot water in a bowl.

2 Stir in the onion slices, if using, and leave to stand for 30 minutes before serving.

Sambal Blachan

Serve this sambal, which is best made in small quantities, as an accompaniment to rice meals. Vary the amount of chili and blachan to taste, but it will be hot and pungent nevertheless.

<u>MAKES 2 TBSP</u>
**2-4 fresh red chilies, seeded
salt
½ in cube blachan,
  prepared
juice of ½ lemon or lime**

1 Cut the chilies in half lengthwise. Pound them to a paste in a mortar, adding a little salt.

2 Add the blachan and lemon or lime juice to taste.

dark soy sauce

lemon juice

deep-fried
onion slices

red chili

garlic

fresh
red chilies

blachan

salt

lemon
juice

347 🐌

African Spice Mixtures

Highly spiced food is eaten with relish throughout the African continent. The spices were brought by Arab traders and merchants over the centuries from biblical times. Many of the cooks are women, and recipes are passed down through the generations by families meeting and preparing food together for *feasts, festivals and weddings so that culinary knowledge and traditional recipes are kept alive. Of the four following recipes, harissa is the best known and is quite simple to make at home, though it is now available from many supermarkets in small jars, which should be stored in the fridge once opened.*

Harissa

This chili-based condiment with a definite kick is widely used in Moroccan, Tunisian and Algerian cooking. It is served neat as a side dish in which to dip pieces of broiled and barbecued meat, stirred into soups and stews or added to the sauce for couscous. Harissa is sometimes added to a purée of skinned and seeded fresh tomatoes and offered as a dip for kebabs or snacks. When added to natural yogurt, harissa is an excellent marinade for pork and chicken.

MAKES ½ CUP

12 dried red chilies
1 tbsp coriander seeds
2 tsp cumin seeds
2 garlic cloves
½ tsp salt
4-6 tbsp olive oil

1 Discard the stems and some of the seeds from the chilies, then soak the chilies in warm water for 30 minutes, until softened.

2 Meanwhile, dry fry the coriander and cumin seeds to bring out the flavor and grind them to a powder.

3 Pound the garlic with the salt, then add the drained chilies and pound the mixture until it is smooth.

4 Add the spices and gradually pound in the oil, trickling it in and mixing until the sauce is well blended and of a mayonnaise-like consistency.

5 Use the harissa at once or transfer it to an airtight jar. Flood the surface with a little more olive oil to make a seal. Cover closely and store in a cool place or in the fridge for up to 3 weeks.

VARIATION

For a less pungent sauce, use only 4-6 dried red chilies. Broil and skin 2 red bell peppers and reserve the seeds, adding at the end to give texture to the sauce. Purée the peppers until smooth and mix all the ingredients as above.

dried red chilies

olive oil

coriander seeds

garlic

cumin seeds

salt

Berbere

This is an Ethiopian blend of spices added to many local dishes, from baked fish dishes to chicken stews. The name is pronounced 'bari-baray'.

MAKES SCANT ½ CUP
10 dried red chilies
8 white cardamoms
1 tsp cumin seeds
1 tsp coriander seeds
1 tsp fenugreek seeds
8 cloves
1 tsp allspice berries
2 tsp black peppercorns
1 tsp ajowan seeds
1 tsp ground ginger
½ tsp ground nutmeg
2 tbsp salt

1 Discard the stalk end and some of the seeds from the chilies.

2 Heat a heavy-based frying pan. Bruise the cardamom pods and add them to the pan with the cumin, coriander, fenugreek, cloves, allspice, peppercorns and ajowan seeds. Toast the spices, shaking the pan over a medium heat, until they give off a rich aroma and just begin to turn color.

3 Remove the seeds from the cardamoms and then grind all the roasted spices to a fine powder. Mix in the ginger, nutmeg and salt.

4 Use at once or transfer to an airtight jar and store away from strong light; alternatively place in an airtight polythene container in the freezer.

dried red chilies

white cardamoms

allspice berries

black peppercorns

cumin seeds

coriander seeds

ajowan seeds

ground ginger

fenugreek seeds

cloves

ground nutmeg

salt

349

Ras el Hanout

Every Moroccan spice merchant has a particular recipe for ras el hanout, which means 'head of the shop'. The mix can contain upwards of twenty different spices, including cinnamon, cardamom, chili, cumin, coriander, cloves, salt, peppercorns, ginger, nutmeg, turmeric and a sprinkling of dried flowers, plus the occasional ingredient renowned for its aphrodisiac qualities. Nothing is left out or to chance! The spice mixture is always sold whole, then ground by the cook as and when required.

black peppercorns    **coriander seeds**    **cumin seeds**

cloves    **green cardamoms**   **ground turmeric**

cinnamon stick

ground ginger   **salt**

dried red chilies

nutmegs

dried flowers

La Kama

La Kama is a Moroccan mixture that is very popular in Tangier – it is altogether simpler than the complex ras el hanout and features a modest five spices. Use to flavor soups and stews – this is especially good with lamb.

MAKES 3 TBSP

1 in piece cinnamon
  stick
2 tsp black peppercorns
2 tsp ground ginger
2 tsp ground turmeric
¼ tsp ground nutmeg

1 Dry fry or roast the cinnamon and peppercorns in a heavy-based frying pan to release their flavor.

2 Grind the roasted spices to a powder and mix with the ginger, turmeric and nutmeg.

3 Use at once or store in an airtight jar, away from strong light.

black peppercorns

ground ginger

ground turmeric

cinnamon stick

ground nutmeg

Tsire Powder

This simple spice mixture is used as a coating for kebabs throughout West Africa. The raw meat is dipped first in oil or beaten egg and then in the spice mixture. A little of the mixture is scattered over the cooked meat before serving.

MAKES 4 TBSP

½ **cup salted peanuts**
1 **tsp mixed spice**
½-1 **tsp chili powder**
salt

1 Grind the peanuts to a coarse powder in a mortar, blender or food processor, then add the ground mixed spice, chili powder and a little salt.

2 Use at once or transfer to an airtight container and store in a cool place for up to 6 weeks.

chili powder

ground mixed spice

salt

salted peanuts

COOK'S TIP

Mixed spice is a ready ground, commercial spice mixture, sometimes called pudding spice, that contains allspice, cinnamon, cloves, ginger and nutmeg.

Barbecue Spice Mixtures

Barbecuing is perhaps the most primitive yet delicious method of cooking whereby pieces of meat, poultry or fish are rendered even more delicious with the addition of an aromatic blend of spices and herbs. These are either rubbed into the flesh a short time before cooking or converted into a marinade. Dry spice mixtures will keep for several months in a cool, dark place.

Barbecue Spice Mixture

<u>MAKES ABOUT 4 TBSP</u>

2 tsp celery seeds
1 tsp paprika
1 tsp ground nutmeg
1 tsp chili powder
1 tsp garlic powder
1 tsp onion salt
2 tsp dried marjoram
1 tsp salt
1-2 tsp light brown sugar
1 tsp freshly ground
  black pepper

1 Grind the celery seeds to a powder, then add to the remaining ingredients. Use the spice mixture immediately or transfer it to an airtight jar and store in a cool place.

celery seeds

paprika

ground nutmeg

chili powder

garlic powder

onion salt

dried marjoram

salt

light brown sugar

ground black pepper

<u>COOK'S TIP</u>

For a marinade, simply add this mixture to a glass of red or white wine with a few slices of onion and stir in 4 tbsp garlic-flavored oil.

Juniper Barbecue Spice

This pungent blend of spices is perfect for duck breasts, beef, venison and ostrich steaks. For a marinade, add this mixture to a small glass of gin along with 1-2 chopped shallots and a couple of rosemary sprigs.

MAKES 4 TBSP
2 tbsp juniper berries
1 tsp black peppercorns
½ tsp salt
1 tsp ground allspice
1 tbsp soft brown sugar

1 Grind the juniper berries and peppercorns finely with the salt. Mix in the allspice and sugar.

2 Rub the spice mixture on to meats before cooking them on the barbecue.

juniper berries

salt

black peppercorns

ground allspice

soft brown sugar

Old-fashioned Philadelphia Spice Powder

Use this as a seasoning for a pork joint or rub it on to steaks or chops. Do this well ahead of roasting or barbecuing the meat to allow the flavors to develop.

MAKES 2-3 TBSP
8 cloves
1 tsp chili powder
½ tsp ground nutmeg
¼ tsp ground mace
1 tsp dried basil
1 tsp dried thyme
2 dried bay leaves
salt

1 Grind the cloves to a coarse powder, then add the other ingredients and continue grinding until fine.

2 Use at once or store in an airtight container, away from strong light.

cloves

chili powder

bay leaves

ground nutmeg

ground mace

dried basil

dried thyme

salt

353

Cajun Spice Mix

The name Cajun evolved from the corruption of 'Acadian', the French settlers who left Canada after the English took over in 1755. They eventually settled in Louisiana, where the exchange of cooking techniques and dishes between the Creoles and the French began. This spice mixture can be used as a seasoning for the famous jambalaya and gumbo, as well as for fish steaks, chicken or meat. If you plan to make up the mixture in advance, prepare the dry spice ingredients and store them in an airtight container. When the mixture is required, chop the onion and garlic in a food processor and add to the spice mixture.

MAKES ABOUT 10 TBSP

1 tsp black peppercorns

1 tsp cumin seeds

1 tsp white mustard seeds

2 tsp paprika

1 tsp chili powder or cayenne pepper

1 tsp dried oregano

2 tsp dried thyme

1 tsp salt

2 garlic cloves, chopped

1 onion, sliced

1 Dry fry or roast the peppercorns, cumin and mustard seeds over a medium heat to release their flavors.

2 Grind the roasted spices to a fine powder, then add the paprika, chilli or cayenne, oregano, thyme and salt and grind again.

3 If it is to be used immediately, add the spices to the finely chopped garlic and onion in a blender or food processor and process until well combined.

garlic

dried oregano

white mustard seeds

salt

black peppercorns

chili powder

onion

cumin seeds

paprika

dried thyme

Chinese Five Spice Powder

The aroma of this spice always seems to dominate Chinese supermarkets. The mixture is made up of equal quantities of Szechuan pepper, cinnamon or cassia, cloves, fennel seeds and star anise. Use in chicken, pork and red-cooked meat dishes with soy sauce and, of course, to season Chinese spareribs. Grind all the ingredients to a fine powder and store in an airtight container.

Szechuan pepper

cassia

cloves

star anise

fennel seeds

CHINESE SPICED SALT

A magical accompaniment to crisp-skinned barbecued or roast chicken: the cooked chicken is dipped into the seasoning before it is eaten. Thoroughly mix 1 tbsp salt and ½ tsp five spice powder. Divide it among four small shallow dishes.

Chinese five spice powder

salt

VARIATION

To make salt and cinnamon mix, toast the salt in a heavy-based frying pan until it is just beginning to turn in color, then remove it from the heat and stir in 1 tsp ground cinnamon and a pinch of Chinese five spice powder. Use as above.

Chinese Roasted Salt and Pepper

This seasoning is best made up as required. It is particularly good as a dip for Szechuan duck, which is first steamed and then deep fried to obtain a really crisp skin. The pieces of duck are dipped in the roasted salt and pepper mixture and eaten with steamed flower rolls. This mixture is also delicious with deep fried chicken, shrimp and roasted meats, especially pork.

SERVES 4-6
2 tbsp salt
2 tsp freshly ground black pepper

1 Heat the salt and pepper in a heavy-based frying pan over a medium heat, shaking the pan continuously until the pepper aroma is evident. Leave to cool.

ground black pepper

salt

Sweet Spice Mixtures

Pickling Spice

This typically British mixture can be bought ready-mixed, but keen cooks enjoy experimenting with different flavors. Sometimes the spices are crushed before they are added to the mixture; for other recipes, the spices are tied into a muslin bag, which can be removed after cooking. In some recipes, the bag of spices may be boiled with the vinegar, then allowed to infuse. The spices are then discarded and the flavored vinegar is used in the pickle.

white peppercorns

allspice berries

coriander seeds

cloves

mustard seeds

dried red chilies

dried bay leaves

cinnamon stick

dried ginger root

MAKES 8 TBSP

1 tbsp coriander seeds
1 tbsp mustard seeds
1 tbsp black or white
  peppercorns
1 tbsp cloves
1 tbsp allspice berries
3-4 dried red chilies
1 in piece dried ginger root
1 in piece cinnamon stick
  (optional)
3 dried bay leaves (optional)

1 Mix all the spices. Tie them in a piece of muslin and use as directed in a recipe.

2 Alternatively, place the spices in a stainless steel or enamelled saucepan and pour in vinegar. Heat gently until boiling, allow to cool, then strain the vinegar and discard the spices.

3 To make cold spice vinegar, add the spices to a jar or bottle of vinegar and leave to infuse for 1-2 days. Strain and use as required; the spices may be discarded or used to flavor another bottle of vinegar.

Apple Pie Spice

This spice mixture is a perfect flavoring combination for the universally popular apple pie. Some cooks prefer to leave the cloves whole. Use in stewed fruit, fruit sauces and fruit pies filled with plums, pears or rhubarb as well as apples.

MAKES 4-5 TSP

1 tsp ground or whole cloves
1 tbsp ground cinnamon
½-1 tsp ground nutmeg

1 Mix the spices and use at once or store in an airtight container away from strong light.

ground cloves

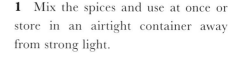

ground cinnamon

ground nutmeg

Mixed Spice or Pudding Spice

This is another typically British spice mix, which can be bought ready ground. It is used in a variety of cakes and puddings, such as fruit cake, gingerbread and Christmas pudding. Make it up or buy it in small quantities as the mixture soon loses its rich flavor. Allspice, cinnamon, cloves, nutmeg and ginger are the usual blend of spices, but some cooks like to add a few cardamom and coriander seeds.

1 tsp allspice berries
1 in cinnamon stick
1 tsp cloves
1 tsp ground nutmeg
1 tsp ground ginger

1 Grind the allspice, cinnamon and cloves to a fine powder and mix well with the nutmeg and ginger. Use at once or store in an airtight jar away from strong light.

allspice berries

cloves

ground nutmeg

ground ginger

cinnamon stick

Quatre Epices

As the name indicates, this is a blend of four spices; it is a favorite seasoning for French charcuterie and Arabian cooking. The proportions can be varied to suit the food or dish. Equivalent quantities of allspice and cinnamon can be substituted for white pepper and ginger respectively.

MAKES 5 TBSP
3 tbsp ground white pepper
1 tbsp ground nutmeg
1 tsp ground cloves
1 tbsp ground ginger

1 Mix all the spices and use at once or store in an airtight jar away from strong light.

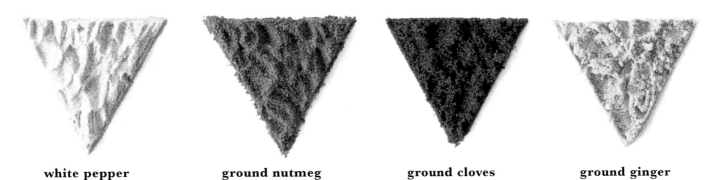

white pepper   **ground nutmeg**   **ground cloves**   **ground ginger**

Flavored Aromatic Oils

Few gifts give more pleasure than those that are hand-made to suit the recipient. Aromatic spiced oils are a perfect example: they give the impression that hours have been spent in their preparation when they are, in truth, quick and simple to make. Plan ahead and collect attractive corked wine bottles if you do not want to invest in bought bottles. If you can afford to buy bottles, you will find a wide selection available from mail order catalogs as well as high street stores. The bottles must be pristine clean and cork stoppers are preferable. Wash them well and clean them with a proprietary sterilizing solution if necessary (look for wine-making sterilizing agents or solutions for clean-ing babies' bottles), leave upside down on the draining rack to dry completely.

There are no hard and fast rules on the type of oil or the spices to use, except that they should be complementary. For instance, extra virgin olive oil is an ideal oil for Mediterranean spices and herbs; groundnut oil goes well with the Oriental flavors of lemon grass and ginger; nut oils, like walnut and hazelnut, are wonderful flavored with coriander seeds and cinnamon sticks for adding to salad dressings to serve with pasta. Remember to label the bottles so that there is no possible doubt about the flavor of the oil!

Ginger, Garlic and Shallot Oil

Often referred to as the 'trinity' of flavors used in Oriental recipes, this is ideal for fish, shellfish and chicken. For 2 cups oil, peel and lightly bruise a $2^{1}/_{2}$ in piece fresh ginger root and place in a clean bottle with the oil, 2 garlic cloves (left whole) and 3 small peeled shallots. Cover tightly and leave in a cool dark place for 2 weeks. Taste the oil and then strain it into a clean bottle if the flavors are strong enough. If the flavor is not sufficiently pronounced, leave the oil for another week before using. Label clearly and store.

garlic

fresh ginger

shallots

Garlic and Spice Aromatic Oil

Almost fill a clean bottle with best virgin olive oil. For 2¹/₂ cups oil, peel and halve a large garlic clove, then add it to the bottle with 3 whole red chilies, 1 tsp coriander seeds, 3 allspice berries, 6 black peppercorns, 4 juniper berries and 2 bay leaves. Cover tightly and leave in a cool dark place for 2 weeks. If the flavor is not sufficiently pronounced, leave the oil for another week before using. Label clearly and store or wrap decoratively as a gift.

juniper berries

fresh bay leaves

**dried
red chilies**

allspice berries

coriander seeds

black peppercorns

Lemon Grass and Lime Leaf Oil

Almost fill a clean bottle with peanut oil. Trim and discard the root end from a lemon grass stalk. Lightly bruise the bulbous end and cut the stem into lengths to fit in to the bottle. Tear 3-4 lime leaves into pieces to release more flavor. Slip the pieces of lemon grass into the bottle with the lime leaves. Cover tightly and leave in a cool dark place for 2 weeks. Label and store. If the flavor is not sufficiently pronounced, leave the oil for another week before using.

kaffir lime leaves

lemon grass

cinnamon sticks

Cinnamon- and Coriander-spiced Nut Oil

Almost fill a clean bottle with walnut or hazelnut oil. Add a cinnamon stick and 2 tsp coriander seeds. Seal and leave in a cool dark place for 2 weeks. Taste the oil and then strain it into a clean bottle if it is sufficiently well flavored. Label and store.

Alternatively, omit the coriander seeds and add a long piece of pared lemon or orange rind. Use to make dressings and mayonnaise to serve with fish and poultry dishes.

coriander seeds

Spiced Vinegars

Vinegar is an essential ingredient in every kitchen, and flavored vinegars add another dimension in the preparation of dressings, mayonnaise, marinades, sauces and preserves. Use white or red wine vinegar, sherry or cider vinegar as a medium for a huge range of spice flavors. Malt vinegar is best left as a condiment for British fish and chips or for pickling and preserving.

Flavored vinegar can be made in two ways: where strong flavors are used and/or required, for example with garlic, the vinegar is heated to extract the maximum flavor. When using milder spices, steep them in the cold vinegar for up to a fortnight before tasting to check on the flavor.

Garlic Vinegar

Crush 3-4 garlic cloves and pound them in a mortar, then place in a stainless steel or glass mixing bowl. Meanwhile, heat about 1 cup white wine vinegar or cider vinegar until just boiling and pour it over the garlic. Leave to cool. Then add a further 1 cup cold vinegar. Pour into a clean jar, cover tightly and leave for 2 weeks, or less for a milder flavor. Shake the jar occasionally. Strain the vinegar into a clean bottle, adding two or three unpeeled garlic cloves to the vinegar for identification. The liquid must completely fill the bottle. Cover tightly and label, then store in a cool dark place.

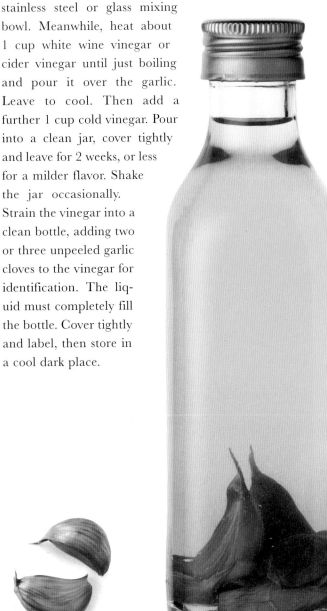

garlic

Gingered Vinegar

Follow the instructions for garlic vinegar, using rice wine vinegar and ginger instead of garlic. Use a 2 in piece of fresh ginger root for every $2^{1}/_{2}$ cups vinegar. Use in Oriental recipes, such as sweet and sour or Szechuan-style dishes.

fresh ginger

Fennel Seed Vinegar

Select a clean preserving jar not a narrow-topped bottle. Place 2 tbsp fennel seeds in the jar for every $2^{1}/_{2}$ cups white wine vinegar. Cover and leave in a cool dark place for 2-3 weeks, shaking the jar from time to time, until the flavor is as intense as you require. Strain the vinegar into clean bottles, label and store in a cool place away from direct sunlight. Use the vinegar in salad dressings and to sharpen herb sauces.

celery seeds

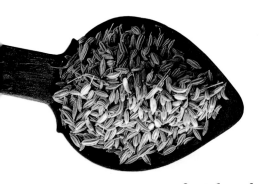

fennel seeds

VARIATION

This spiced vinegar can be made with other seeds, try celery or dill.

dill seeds

Chili Vinegar

Use a clean preserving jar. Place 1 oz (about 8) dried red chilies in the jar. Heat $2^{1}/_{2}$ cups red wine vinegar or sherry vinegar until just boiling, then pour it into the jar. Cool, cover tightly and allow to infuse for 2 weeks, shaking the jar occasionally. Taste, for flavor and strain when sufficiently strong, pouring the vinegar into a clean bottle. Make sure that the bottle is full to the top. Cover tightly, label and store. Use to pep up soups and sauces or to deglaze a pan after cooking venison or beef steaks.

dried red chilies

Chili Ho Ho

An old colonial-style vinegar to add pep and character to rather dull soups, sauces and stews. Fill a clean bottle – a pretty wine bottle will do – with lots of small red chilies. Top up with sherry vinegar. Cover tightly or seal with a cork and leave for 2 weeks, shaking occasionally. Use a few drops at a time and top up with more of the sherry vinegar to keep the ho ho going for months. Label and store in a cool dark place. The ho ho can also be made with sherry, gin or vodka instead of sherry vinegar.

small red chilies

Spiced Drinks

Cardamom, cinnamon, cloves, ginger and nutmeg flavors all have an affinity with hot or cold drinks, alcoholic or otherwise. In India tea is sometimes flavored with cardamoms, cinnamon and cloves.

Coffee may have originated from either the Yemen or Ethiopia where it is mentioned in records from the 6th century. As tastes became more sophisticated and coffee became an international drink, different ways of serving it were devised.

Cardamom Tea

In India, this tea may be served with very sweet sweetmeats or savory snacks. If you wish to drink it black, then reduce the quantity of tea by half or it will be too strong to be enjoyable.

SERVES 4

8 green cardamoms
5 cups cold water
4 tsp orange pekoe tea or
 4 tea bags
small strip of pared orange rind
sugar and freshly boiled milk,
 to serve

VARIATION

Use 1 cinnamon stick instead of the cardamoms.

green cardamoms

1 Split the cardamom pods. Boil the water and cardamoms in a large saucepan, then reduce the heat and simmer for 3-4 minutes. Remove from heat and allow to infuse for 10 minutes.

2 Just before serving, warm a teapot, add the tea and the orange rind. Bring the infused liquid to a boil and pour it into the teapot. Brew for 2-3 minutes.

3 Serve the tea with sugar and freshly boiled milk for a traditional flavor.

cloves

Grace's Easy Iced Lemon Tea

An ideal container is the plastic container in which you buy orange juice. Wash it well and fill with hot, not boiling, water and 1 tsp bicarbonate of soda to render it free of flavor. Rinse well before using.

1 Place all the ingredients in a clean container. Cover tightly and place in the fridge overnight (at least) for the flavors to infuse.

2 Strain into glasses and serve decorated with cucumber, lemon or orange slices and some more mint leaves.

SERVES 6

7½ cups cold water
8-10 cloves
1 cinnamon stick
3-4 Earl Grey or Lapsang
 Souchong tea bags
juice of 2 lemons, strained
6 tbsp sugar, or to taste
6-8 mint leaves
DECORATION
cucumber, lemon or orange slices
mint leaves

cinnamon stick

Spiced Tea

This tea, masala chah or chai, is a delicious drink to round off an Indian meal. Traditionally it would be served with milk and plenty of sugar, but many people find it more refreshing when served black.

SERVES 4

5 cups cold water
1 cinnamon stick
4 green cardamoms
3 cloves
2 tsp orange pekoe tea or
   2 tea bags
sugar to taste (optional)

cloves

green cardamoms

1 Boil the water with the cinnamon stick, cardamoms and cloves. Draw off the heat and allow to infuse for about 10 minutes.

2 Add the tea or tea bags and sugar, if used, and bring to a boil again, then simmer gently for 3-4 minutes.

3 Taste the tea and strain it into a warmed teapot or jug, then serve it at once. Float one or two cardamoms in each cup, if you like.

cinnamon stick

Masala for Tea

In Bombay, masala chai *is always offered to guests as a welcoming drink. The masala mixture is ground and stored in an airtight jar until required.*

MAKES 6 TBSP

12 green cardamoms
1 tbsp black peppercorns
6 cloves
2 tbsp ground ginger

1 Split the cardamoms and scrape out the tiny black seeds. Grind them with the peppercorns and cloves to a fine powder: a coffee grinder is ideal for this. Then mix well with the ground ginger.

2 Use at once or store in an airtight jar away from strong light. Add ½ tsp to a pot of freshly made tea.

black peppercorns

cloves

Café Brûlot

This flaming mixture of coffee, spice and brandy is a speciality of the southern states of the USA. A fondue pot is ideal for making the coffee at the table: when the spice and brandy mixture is warm, it is ignited before strong black coffee is added. It is often performed with great panache in restaurants, where the waiter pours the coffee from a ladle down a long strip of orange rind into the pan.

SERVES 4–6

**pared rind of 1 orange,
  in one long strip**
**pared rind of 1 lemon,
  in one long strip**
4 sugar lumps
6 cloves
1 cinnamon stick
¾ cup brandy
**3-4 tbsp curaçao or
  orange liqueur**
2 cups strong black coffee

1 Assemble all the ingredients. Place the orange and lemon rinds in a pan. Add the sugar, cloves, cinnamon, brandy and curaçao or orange liqueur. Heat until the sugar dissolves, stirring continuously.

2 Have the coffee ready; ignite the brandy mixture, then slowly add the coffee in a thin stream. Serve at once with a cinnamon stick and orange rind garnish, if you like.

cloves

**cinnamon
sticks**

Southern Iced Spiced Coffee

Another classic coffee from the southern states of the USA. This one is served chilled and makes a refreshing summer-time drink.

SERVES 4

**4 cups freshly made strong
  black coffee**
4 cinnamon sticks
6 cloves
3-4 tbsp sugar, or to taste
**4 tbsp Tia Maria or
  coffee liqueur**
plenty of ice cubes

1 Pour the coffee into a large bowl. Add the cinnamon sticks, cloves and sugar to taste. Stir well and leave for at least an hour to infuse.

2 Strain the coffee into a large jug, then add the liqueur and ice cubes. Serve in chilled glasses.

cinnamon sticks

cloves

Mocha on a Cloud

Vanilla is used to flavor this coffee and chocolate combination. Add a cinnamon stick to each glass to stir the cream.

SERVES 6

5 cups milk
1 vanilla bean or 2-3 drops
  natural vanilla extract
2½ cups freshly made strong
  black coffee
sugar to taste
3 tbsp vanilla sugar
4 oz unsweetened chocolate
⅔ cup whipping cream, whipped
6 cinnamon sticks and ground
  nutmeg, to serve

1 Pour 3 cups milk into a saucepan. Add the vanilla bean, if using, and place the pan over a low heat until hot, but not boiling. Set aside to infuse for 10 minutes, then remove the vanilla bean.

2 Mix the coffee with the remaining milk in a large heatproof jug. Add sugar to taste but do not make the mixture too sweet as the hot milk will also be sweetened.

3 Return the saucepan of milk to the heat and add the vanilla sugar with the vanilla extract, if using. Bring to a boil, then reduce the heat. Break the chocolate into squares and add them to the milk. Heat gently, whisking until the chocolate has melted.

4 Pour the chocolate milk into the jug and whisk until frothy.

5 Serve in tall mugs or glasses, topped with whipped cream, a cinnamon stick and a sprinkling of nutmeg.

vanilla sugar

ground cinnamon

natural vanilla extract

ground nutmeg

vanilla beans

367

Mulled Wine

Cinnamon, cloves, ginger and nutmeg add spice to this winter warmer.

cloves

SERVES 6-8

1 cinnamon stick

8 cloves

**few pinches each of ground
   ginger and nutmeg**

1 orange, sliced

1 lemon, sliced

2 tbsp dark brown sugar

3 cups red wine (1 bottle)

4 tbsp brandy

½ cup water

VARIATION

To make a lemon- and sherry-flavored Bishop, replace the orange with a lemon and use sherry instead of port. Prepare in the same way. Add the strained juice of another lemon, if required.

1 Put the cinnamon stick, cloves, ginger, nutmeg, orange and lemon in a large saucepan or casserole. Add the sugar, wine, brandy and water.

2 Place over a low heat and stir to dissolve the sugar. Do not overheat or allow to boil because this evaporates the alcohol. Heat gently until required, then ladle into cups or heatproof glasses.

The Bishop

A clove-studded orange is used to impart a warm, spicy flavor to this festive drink.

SERVES 8

1 orange

12 cloves

12 allspice berries, ground

3 cups port

3-4 tbsp sugar, or to taste

1 Preheat the oven to 325°F. Stud the orange with the cloves and wrap loosely in foil. Bake for 45 minutes.

2 Cut the baked orange into quarters and place them in a saucepan. Add the allspice, port and sugar to taste. Heat gently until warm, without allowing the port to boil. Serve in warmed glasses with a slice of clove-studded orange, to decorate.

allspice berries

Jamaican Rum Punch

Ground allspice, mace and cinnamon sticks are used to flavor this cider-based punch.

<u>SERVES 8-10</u>

10 allspice berries
1 blade mace
2 cinnamon sticks
5 cups sweet cider
3 tbsp dark Jamaican rum
3 tbsp brandy, or to taste

1 Place the allspice, mace and cinnamon in a saucepan with the cider. Heat the mixture very gently for 20-30 minutes, without boiling.

2 Add the rum and brandy. Serve hot, in warmed glasses.

allspice berries

cinnamon sticks

**ground
black pepper**

Tequila Maria

In Mexico, this spicy drink might be decorated with exotic Bougainvillaea or hibiscus flowers.

<u>SERVES 2</u>

**¹⁄₂ tsp freshly grated horseradish
  or 2 tsp horseradish**
**generous pinch of freshly ground
  black pepper**
generous pinch of celery salt
³⁄₄ cup tomato juice
¹⁄₄ cup tequila
dash of Worcestershire sauce
dash of Tabasco sauce
juice of 1 lime
pinch of dried oregano
a few ice cubes
plenty of crushed ice
2 lime slices, to decorate

1 Mix all the ingredients in a large jug. Add a few ice cubes and mix again. Taste for seasoning.

2 Half fill two glasses with crushed ice. Pour in the tequila Maria and serve, decorated with lime slices.

**fresh
horseradish**

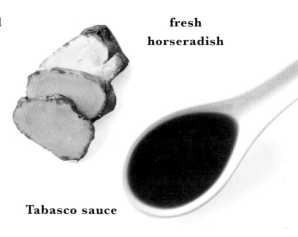

Tabasco sauce

SPICES IN THE HOME

Spices for Decoration and Fragrant Gifts

Today we associate spices mainly with cooking, but at one time spices played a much larger role in the home – their fragrance was used to scent the air, and it was thought that they had antiseptic qualities and could both prevent disease and ward off insects. Spice bags were carried around or hung from a belt, and fragrant bowls and boxes of pot pourri were used to scent the air. Included here are some traditional ideas for using spices in the home: clove-scented pomanders, festive spiced gingerbread cookies and pot pourri, and, to make as gifts for keen cooks, spice baskets, cinnamon bundles and chili ropes.

Pomanders

Pomanders are delightful Christmas gifts. Make them three or four weeks before Christmas so that they have time to mature. Attach long ribbons so that they can be hung in the wardrobe or on a door knob, where they last for ages.

MAKES 1 POMANDER
1 thin-skinned orange
300-400 cloves
1 tsp ground cinnamon
1 tsp ground orris root
ribbon or velvet cord

ground cinnamon

1 Wash and dry the chosen fruit. Use a skewer to puncture the skin of the fruit all over in an attractive pattern. This will make it easier to push in the cloves, which should completely cover the surface of the fruit.

2 Place the cinnamon and orris root in a plastic bag and toss the orange in the mixture until well coated. Place the orange in a flat basket lined with foil and leave it for 3-4 weeks to dry out and harden. Turn the fruit occasionally. If you make a number of pomanders, it is important to prevent the fruits from touching each other while they are drying out as they may turn moldy. Tie a length of ribbon or velvet cord around the fruit.

cloves

VARIATIONS

Lemons and limes can also be made into pomanders. Tie a ribbon around the fruits, leaving a length to tie them by. Puncture and stud with cloves as described left. Leave one or two segments without cloves, or cover the whole fruit if you prefer.
Kumquats or mandarin oranges, studded with cloves and prepared as for a pomander, may be added to a wreath made from fir cones, bay leaves and cranberries threaded on to wire.

Gingerbread Tree Decorations

These cookies are traditionally made at Christmas time in Scandinavia. Ginger and cinnamon are always used to spice the mixture, but ½ tsp ground cloves may also be added. Decorate the cookies with silver and gold dragées if you like. Stick them to the icing while it is still soft.

MAKES ABOUT 30-40
2 cups all-purpose flour
1 tsp baking powder
2 tsp ground ginger
1 tsp ground cinnamon
4 tbsp butter or margarine
4 tbsp soft brown sugar
2 tbsp corn syrup
DECORATION
1 cup confectioners' sugar, sifted

1 Preheat the oven to 350°F. Grease two cookie sheets. Sift the flour, baking powder, ginger and cinnamon into a bowl.

2 Melt the butter or margarine, sugar and syrup together in a saucepan over a gentle heat. Add the melted mixture to the dry ingredients and mix to a dough.

3 Gather the dough into one piece and knead it on a lightly floured surface until it is smooth. If the dough is too soft to roll, allow it to rest for a few minutes.

4 Roll out the dough and cut out Christmas shapes – stars, Christmas trees and angels using the appropriate cutters. Use a skewer to make a hole in each cookie for the ribbon to be threaded through after cooking. Place on the sheets and bake for 10-12 minutes, or until lightly brown and firm.

5 While the cookies are still warm, make sure that the holes are big enough for ribbons to be threaded through them. Transfer to a wire rack to cool.

6 Place the confectioners' sugar in a bowl and mix in a little water, adding it from a teaspoon and beating to make a thick glacé icing. Put the icing in a small paper piping bag and use to decorate the cookies.

7 When the icing has dried, thread ribbons through the cookies. Tie the cookies on to the Christmas tree or a garland decoration.

COOK'S TIP

Eat the cookies on the day they are hung. For longer keeping, each cookie may be wrapped in plastic wrap and sealed with freezer tape on the back.

Pots Pourris

Summer and Spice

Mix 4 cups dried rose petals with 1 cup mixed rosemary, lemon thyme and lavender flowers. Add the very finely grated rind of 1 lemon and 1 orange. Leave for about 24 hours, then add 2 tsp lightly crushed cloves and 1 tsp crushed allspice berries. Add 1 tbsp ground orris root to fix the perfume. Lightly toss the mixture daily for a week, then transfer to bowls or boxes.

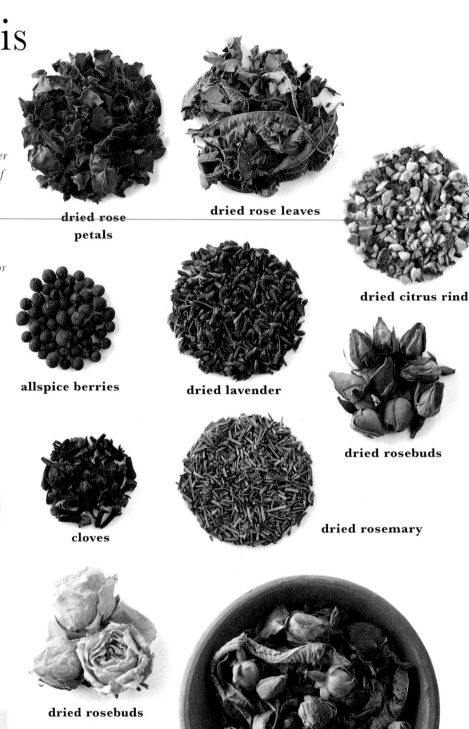

dried rose petals

dried rose leaves

dried citrus rind

allspice berries

dried lavender

dried rosebuds

cloves

dried rosemary

dried rosebuds

VARIATIONS

Combine equal quantities of dried rosemary, rose petals and lemon verbena with lightly crushed cloves. Use to fill small muslin bags, gather them up into a purse shape and tie with ribbon. Combine a handful of dried wallflowers and rosemary flowers with 1 tsp grated nutmeg and 3 tbsp ground orris root. Fill muslin bags as above. Tie the bags on the backs of chairs or leave one in the guest room, under the pillow.

Cottage Garden Mix

Combine a mixture of rose petals, orange blossom, lavender and honeysuckle. Spread the petals on a wooden tray and leave to dry in a warm, dry place, turning occasionally, for several days. Add 1 tsp ground cinnamon, 6 lightly crushed cloves and 1 tbsp ground orris root to each 5 cups petals. Add 1-2 drops rose perfume oil and 2 tsp brandy and transfer to bowls or boxes.

Spice Baskets

These make useful and interesting gifts. Choose small baskets, line them with pretty patterned fabric, tissue paper or a banana leaf. Fill with a collection of spices. If you like, pick a theme for each basket, for example pack spices for Thai cooking, seasoning mixtures for Indian cooking or spice mixtures to mull warming drinks. Or just make a selection from the following:

cinnamon sticks tied in a bundle
with ribbon or rafia
whole nutmegs
cardamoms packed in a
cellophane or muslin bag
coriander seeds and cumin seeds
in packed muslin 'purses'
vanilla beans
a few lemon grass stalks and
lime leaves
a bundle of fresh red and
green chilies
dried pomegranates

dried red chilies

KITCHEN DEVIL

To make a dried chili rope, thread red chilies on to a long piece of fine string and hang them in a cool airy place. They should retain their rich color and can be used when quite dry.

CINNAMON BUNDLES

Tie 3 cinnamon sticks and a piece of dried orange peel together with a tartan ribbon.

small
green chilies

COOKING WITH SPICES

SOUPS AND APPETIZERS

Hot and Sour Shrimp Soup

How hot this soup is depends upon the type of chili used. Try tiny Thai chilies if you really want to go for the burn.

SERVES 6

8 oz raw shrimp, in shells
2 lemon grass stalks
6¼ cups vegetable stock
4 kaffir lime leaves
2 slices peeled fresh
    ginger root
4 tbsp Thai fish sauce
4 tbsp fresh lime juice
2 garlic cloves, crushed
6 scallions, chopped
1 fresh red chili, seeded and cut
    into thin strips
generous 1½ cups oyster
    mushrooms, sliced
fresh cilantro leaves and kaffir
    lime slices, to garnish

1 Peel the shrimp and set them aside. Put the shells in a large saucepan.

COOK'S TIP

It is important that the shrimp are only heated through and not overcooked, or they will become tough.

2 Lightly crush the lemon grass and add the stalks to the pan with the stock, lime leaves and ginger. Bring to a boil, lower the heat and simmer for 20 minutes.

3 Strain the stock into a clean pan, discarding the shrimp shells and aromatics. Add the fish sauce, lime juice, garlic, scallions, chili and mushrooms. Bring to a boil, lower the heat and simmer for 5 minutes. Add the peeled shrimp and cook for 2-3 minutes. Serve, garnished with cilantro leaves and lime slices.

Provençal Fish Soup with Rouille

Although many of the tiny rock fish traditionally used in this recipe are not available away from the Mediterranean, this version is still full of Provençal flavors and is served with an authentic chili-spiked rouille.

SERVES 4-6

2 tbsp olive oil
1 leek, sliced
2 celery stalks, chopped
1 onion, chopped
2 garlic cloves, chopped
4 ripe tomatoes, chopped
1 tbsp tomato paste
$^2/_3$ cup dry white wine
1 bay leaf
1 tsp saffron strands
2¼ lb mixed fish fillets and prepared shellfish
fish trimmings, bones and heads
salt and ground black pepper
croûtons and grated Gruyère
   cheese, to serve
ROUILLE
1 slice white bread, crusts
   removed
1 red bell pepper, cored, seeded
   and quartered
1-2 fresh red chilies, seeded
   and chopped
2 garlic cloves, crushed
olive oil (optional)

1 Make the rouille. Soak the bread in 2-3 tbsp cold water for 10 minutes. Meanwhile, broil the red bell pepper quarters, skin side up, until the skin is charred and blistered. Put into a polythene bag and leave until cool enough to handle. Peel off the skin. Drain the bread and squeeze out the excess moisture.

2 Roughly chop the pepper quarters and place in a blender or food processor with the bread, chilies and garlic. Process to a fairly coarse paste, adding a little olive oil, if necessary. Scrape the rouille into a small bowl and set it aside.

3 Heat the olive oil in a large saucepan. Add the leek, celery, onion and garlic. Cook gently for 10 minutes until soft. Add the tomatoes, tomato paste, wine, bay leaf, saffron, any shellfish and the fish trimmings. Bring to a boil, lower the heat, cover and simmer for 30 minutes.

4 Strain through a colander pressing out the liquid. Cut the fish fillets into large chunks and add to the strained soup. Cover and simmer for 5-10 minutes until the fish is cooked.

5 Strain through a colander into a clean pan. Put half the cooked fish into a blender or food processor with about 1¼ cups of the soup. Process for just long enough to blend, while retaining some texture.

6 Stir all the fish back into the remaining soup. Add salt and pepper to taste. Reheat gently. Serve the soup with the rouille, croûtons and cheese.

Butternut Squash Soup with Curried Horseradish Cream

The combination of cream, curry powder and horseradish makes a wonderful topping for this beautiful golden soup.

SERVES 6

1 butternut squash
1 cooking apple
2 tbsp butter
1 onion, finely chopped
1-2 tsp curry powder
3¾ cups chicken or vegetable
  stock
1 tsp chopped fresh sage
⅔ cup apple juice
salt and ground black pepper
curry powder, to garnish
CURRIED HORSERADISH CREAM
4 tbsp heavy cream
2 tsp horseradish sauce
½ tsp curry powder

1 Peel the squash, remove the seeds and chop the flesh. Peel, core and chop the apple.

2 Heat the butter in a large saucepan. Add the onion and cook, stirring occasionally, for 5 minutes until soft. Stir in the curry powder. Cook to bring out the flavor, stirring constantly, for 2 minutes.

3 Add the stock, squash, apple and sage. Bring to a boil, lower the heat, cover and simmer for 20 minutes until the squash and apple are soft.

4 Meanwhile, make the horseradish cream. Whip the cream in a bowl until stiff, then stir in the horseradish sauce and curry powder. Cover and chill until required.

5 Purée the soup in a blender or food processor. Return to the clean pan and add the apple juice, with salt and pepper to taste. Reheat gently, without allowing the soup to boil.

6 Serve the soup in individual bowls, topping each portion with a spoonful of horseradish cream and a dusting of curry powder. Garnish with a few lime shreds, if you like.

Spiced Lentil Soup

A subtle blend of spices takes this warming soup to new heights. Serve it with crusty bread for a satisfying lunch.

SERVES 6

2 onions, finely chopped
2 garlic cloves, crushed
4 tomatoes, roughly chopped
½ tsp ground turmeric
1 tsp ground cumin
6 cardamoms
½ cinnamon stick
1 cup red lentils
14 oz can coconut milk
1 tbsp fresh lime juice
salt and ground black pepper
cumin seeds, to garnish

1 Put the onions, garlic, tomatoes, turmeric, cumin, cardamoms, cinnamon and lentils into a saucepan with 3¾ cups water. Bring to a boil, lower the heat, cover and simmer gently for 20 minutes or until the lentils are soft.

2 Remove the cardamoms and cinnamon stick, then purée the mixture in a blender or food processor. Press the soup through a strainer, then return it to the clean pan.

3 Reserve a little of the coconut milk for the garnish and add the remainder to the pan with the lime juice. Stir well. Season with salt and pepper. Reheat the soup gently without boiling. Swirl in the reserved coconut milk, garnish with cumin seeds and serve.

COOK'S TIP

If the tomatoes do not have much flavor, stir in a little tomato purée or use a small can of tomatoes.

Crab Spring Rolls and Dipping Sauce

Chili and grated ginger add a hint of heat to these sensational treats. Serve them as an appetizer or with other Chinese dishes.

SERVES 4-6

1 tbsp peanut oil
1 tsp sesame oil
1 garlic clove, crushed
1 fresh red chili, seeded and
  finely sliced
1 lb pack fresh stir-fry
  vegetables
1 in piece fresh ginger root,
  grated
1 tbsp dry sherry or rice wine
1 tbsp soy sauce
12 oz fresh dressed crab-meat
  (brown and white meat)
12 spring roll wrappers
1 small egg, beaten
oil, for deep frying
salt and ground black pepper
lime wedges and fresh cilantro,
  to garnish
1 quantity Indonesian sambal
  kecap, for dipping

1 Heat a wok briefly, then add the peanut and sesame oils. When hot, stir-fry the crushed garlic and chili for 1 minute. Add the vegetables and ginger and stir-fry for 1 minute more, then drizzle over the sherry or rice wine and soy sauce. Allow the mixture to bubble up for 1 minute.

2 Using a slotted spoon, transfer the vegetables to a dish. Set aside until cool, then stir in the crab-meat and season with salt and pepper.

> #### COOK'S TIP
>
> *Spring roll wrappers are available in many supermarkets as well as Oriental grocers. If you are unable to find them, use filo pastry instead. Keep the wrappers - and the filled rolls - covered with plastic wrap, as they will rapidly dry out if exposed to the air.*

3 Soften the spring roll wrappers, following the directions on the packet. Place some of the filling on a wrapper, fold over the front edge and the sides and roll up neatly, sealing the edges with a little beaten egg. Repeat with the remaining wrappers and filling.

4 Heat the oil in the wok and fry the spring rolls in batches, turning several times, until brown and crisp. Remove with a slotted spoon, drain on paper towels and keep hot while frying the remainder. Serve at once, garnished with lime wedges and cilantro, with the dipping sauce.

Chick-pea and Coriander Cakes with Tahini

These spicy little cakes are equally good served hot or cold. For a more substantial snack, tuck them into pockets of pitta bread with salad.

SERVES 4

15 oz cans chick-peas
2 garlic cloves, crushed
1 bunch scallions (white parts only), chopped
2 tsp ground cumin
2 tsp ground coriander
1 fresh green chili, seeded and finely chopped
2 tbsp chopped fresh cilantro
1 small egg, beaten
2 tbsp all-purpose flour
seasoned flour, for shaping
oil, for shallow frying
salt and ground black pepper
lemon wedges and fresh cilantro, to garnish

TAHINI AND LEMON DIP
2 tbsp tahini
juice of 1 lemon
2 garlic cloves, crushed

1 Drain the chick-peas thoroughly. Tip them into a blender or food processor and process until smooth. Add the garlic, scallions, cumin and ground coriander. Process again until well mixed.

2 Scrape the mixture into a bowl and stir in the chili, fresh cilantro, egg and flour. Mix well and season with salt and pepper. If the mixture is very soft add a little more flour. Chill for about 30 minutes to firm the mixture.

3 Make the dip. Mix the tahini, lemon juice and garlic in a bowl, adding a little water if the sauce is too thick. Set aside.

4 Using floured hands, shape the chick-pea mixture into 12 cakes. Heat the oil in a frying pan and fry the cakes in batches for about 1 minute on each side, until crisp and golden. Drain on paper towel and serve with the dip and lemon and cilantro garnish.

VARIATION

Another quick and easy sauce is made by mixing plain yogurt with a little chopped chili and fresh mint.

Spiced Dolmades

These dolmades contain sumac, a spice with a sharp lemon flavor. It is available from specialist food shops.

**20 vacuum-packed vine leaves
  in brine**
½ cup long grain rice
3 tbsp olive oil
1 small onion, finely chopped
⅔ cup pine nuts
3 tbsp raisins
2 tbsp chopped fresh mint
½ tsp ground cinnamon
½ tsp ground allspice
2 tsp ground sumac
2 tsp lemon juice
2 tbsp tomato purée
salt and ground black pepper
**lemon slices and fresh mint
  sprigs, to garnish**

1 Rinse the vine leaves well under cold running water, then drain. Bring a saucepan of lightly salted water to a boil. Add the rice, lower the heat, cover and simmer for 10-12 minutes, until almost cooked. Drain.

2 Heat 2 tbsp of the olive oil in a frying pan, add the onion and cook until soft. Stir in the pine nuts and cook until lightly browned, then add the raisins, mint, cinnamon, allspice and sumac, with salt and pepper to taste. Stir in the rice and mix well. Leave to cool.

VARIATION

Fresh vine leaves may be used but must be blanched in boiling water first to make them pliable.

3 Line a saucepan with any damaged vine leaves. Trim the stalks from the remaining leaves and lay them flat. Place a little filling on each. Fold the sides over and roll up each leaf neatly. Place the dolmades side by side in the leaf-lined pan, so that they fit tightly.

4 Mix 1¼ cups water with the lemon juice and tomato purée in a bowl. Add the remaining olive oil. Pour over the dolmades and place a heatproof plate on top to keep them in place.

5 Cover the pan and simmer the dolmades for 1 hour until all the liquid has been absorbed and the leaves are tender. Transfer to a platter, garnish with lemon slices and mint and serve hot or cold.

Marinated Feta Cheese with Capers

Marinating cubes of feta cheese with herbs and spices gives a marvellous flavor. Serve on toast or with salad.

2 cups feta cheese
2 garlic cloves
½ tsp mixed peppercorns
8 coriander seeds
1 bay leaf
1-2 tbsp drained capers
fresh oregano or thyme sprigs
olive oil, to cover
hot toast, to serve

1 Cut the feta cheese into cubes. Thickly slice the garlic. Mix the peppercorns and coriander seeds in a mortar and crush lightly with a pestle.

2 Pack the feta cubes into a large preserving jar with the bay leaf, interspersing layers of cheese with garlic, crushed peppercorns and coriander, capers and the fresh oregano or thyme sprigs.

3 Pour in enough olive oil to cover the cheese. Close tightly and leave to marinate for two weeks in the fridge.

4 Lift out the feta cubes and serve on hot toast, sprinkled with a little of the oil from the jar.

VARIATION

Add stoned black or green olives to the feta cheese in the marinade.

Spicy Potato Wedges with Chili Dip

For a healthy snack with superb flavor, try these dry-roasted potato wedges. The crisp spice crust makes them irresistible, especially when served with a chili dip.

<u>SERVES 2</u>

2 baking potatoes,
  about 8 oz each
2 tbsp olive oil
2 garlic cloves, crushed
1 tsp ground allspice
1 tsp ground coriander
1 tbsp paprika
salt and ground black pepper

DIP

1 tbsp olive oil
1 small onion, finely chopped
1 garlic clove, crushed
7 oz can chopped tomatoes
1 fresh red chili, seeded and
  finely chopped
1 tbsp balsamic vinegar
1 tbsp chopped fresh cilantro,
  plus extra to garnish

1 Preheat the oven to 400°F. Cut the potatoes in half, then into 8 wedges.

2 Place the wedges in a saucepan of cold water. Bring to a boil, then lower the heat and simmer gently for 10 minutes or until the potatoes have softened slightly. Drain well and pat dry on paper towels.

3 Mix the oil, garlic, allspice, coriander and paprika in a roasting tin. Add salt and pepper to taste. Add the potatoes to the pan and shake to coat them thoroughly. Roast for 20 minutes, turning the potato wedges occasionally, or until they are browned, crisp and fully cooked.

4 Meanwhile, make the chili dip. Heat the oil in a saucepan, add the onion and garlic and cook for 5-10 minutes until soft. Add the tomatoes, with their juice. Stir in the chili and vinegar. Cook gently for 10 minutes until the mixture has reduced and thickened, then check the seasoning. Stir in the fresh cilantro and serve hot, with potato wedges. Garnish with salt and fresh cilantro.

COOK'S TIP

To save time, parboil the potatoes and toss them with the spices in advance, but make sure that the potato wedges are perfectly dry and completely covered in the mixture.

Baby Onions and Mushrooms à la Grecque

There are many variations of this classic dish, but they always contain coriander seeds.

SERVES 4

2 carrots
12 oz baby onions
4 tbsp olive oil
½ cup dry white wine
1 tsp coriander seeds,
  lightly crushed
2 bay leaves
pinch of cayenne pepper
1 garlic clove, crushed
12 oz button mushrooms
3 tomatoes, peeled, seeded
  and quartered
salt and ground black pepper
3 tbsp chopped fresh parsley,
  to garnish

1 Peel the carrots and cut them into small dice. Peel the baby onions and trim the tops and roots.

2 Heat 3 tbsp of the olive oil in a deep frying pan. Add the carrots and onions and cook, stirring occasionally, for about 20 minutes until the vegetables have browned lightly and are beginning to soften.

3 Add the white wine, coriander seeds, bay leaves, cayenne, garlic, button mushrooms and tomatoes, with salt and pepper to taste. Cook, uncovered, for 20-30 minutes until the vegetables are soft and the sauce has thickened.

COOK'S TIP

Don't trim too much from either the top or root end of the onions: if you do, the centers will pop out during cooking.

4 Transfer to a serving dish and leave to cool. Cover and chill until needed. Before serving, pour over the remaining olive oil and sprinkle with the parsley. Serve with crusty bread.

VARIATION

This treatment is ideal for a single vegetable or a combination. Try leeks, fennel or artichokes, with or without baby onions.

Turkey, Juniper and Peppercorn Terrine

This is an ideal dish for entertaining, as it can be made several days in advance. If you prefer, arrange some of the pancetta and pistachios as a layer in the middle of the terrine.

SERVES 10-12

8 oz chicken livers, trimmed
1 lb ground turkey
1 lb ground pork
8 oz cubes pancetta
½ cup shelled pistachio nuts, roughly chopped
1 tsp salt
½ tsp ground mace
2 garlic cloves, crushed
1 tsp drained green peppercorns in brine
1 tsp juniper berries
½ cup dry white wine
2 tbsp gin
finely grated rind of 1 orange
8 large vacuum-packed vine leaves in brine
oil, for greasing

1   Chop the chicken livers finely. Put them in a bowl and add the turkey, pork, pancetta, pistachio nuts, salt, mace and garlic. Mix well.

2   Lightly crush the peppercorns and juniper berries and add them to the mixture. Stir in the white wine, gin and orange rind. Cover and chill overnight to allow the flavors to mingle.

3   Preheat the oven to 325°F. Rinse the vine leaves under cold running water. Drain them thoroughly. Lightly oil a 5 cup terrine or loaf pan. Line the terrine or pan with the leaves, letting the ends hang over the sides. Pack the mixture into the terrine or pan and fold the leaves over to enclose the filling. Brush lightly with oil.

4   Cover the terrine with its lid or with foil. Place it in a roasting tin and pour in boiling water to come halfway up the sides of the terrine. Bake for 1¾ hours, checking the level of the water occasionally, so that the roasting tin does not dry out.

5   Leave the terrine to cool, then pour off the surface juices. Cover with plastic wrap, then foil and place weights on top. Chill overnight. Serve at room temperature with a pickle or chutney such as spiced kumquats or red pepper and chili jelly.

Baba Ganoush with Lebanese Flatbread

Baba Ganoush is a delectable eggplant dip from the Middle East. Tahini – a sesame seed paste with cumin – is the main flavoring, giving a subtle hint of spice.

SERVES 6

2 small eggplants
1 garlic clove, crushed
4 tbsp tahini
¼ cup ground almonds
juice of ½ lemon
½ tsp ground cumin
2 tbsp fresh mint leaves
2 tbsp olive oil
salt and ground black pepper
LEBANESE FLATBREAD
4 pita breads
3 tbsp toasted sesame seeds
3 tbsp fresh thyme leaves
3 tbsp poppy seeds
⅔ cup olive oil

1 Start by making the Lebanese flatbread. Split the pita breads through the middle and carefully open them out. Mix the sesame seeds, chopped thyme and poppy seeds in a mortar. Crush them lightly with a pestle to release the flavor.

2 Stir in the olive oil. Spread the mixture lightly over the cut sides of the pita bread. Grill until golden brown and crisp. When cool, break into rough pieces and set aside.

3 Grill the eggplants, turning them frequently, until the skin is blackened and blistered. Remove the peel, chop the flesh roughly and leave to drain in a colander.

COOK'S TIP

It may be easier to split the pita breads if they are warmed slightly, either under the grill or in the oven.

4 Squeeze out as much liquid from the eggplants as possible. Place the flesh in a blender or food processor. Add the garlic, tahini, ground almonds, lemon juice and cumin, with salt and pepper to taste and process to a smooth paste. Roughly chop half the mint and stir into the dip.

5 Spoon into a bowl, scatter the remaining leaves on top and drizzle with olive oil. Serve with the Lebanese flatbread.

FISH AND SEAFOOD

Mussels and Clams with Lemon Grass and Coconut Cream

Lemon grass has an incomparable flavor and is widely used in Thai cookery, especially with seafood. If you have difficulty obtaining the clams for this recipe, use a few extra mussels instead.

SERVES 6

4-4½ lb mussels
1 lb baby clams
½ cup dry white wine
1 bunch scallions, chopped
2 lemon grass stalks, chopped
6 kaffir lime leaves, chopped
2 tsp Thai green curry paste
7 fl oz coconut cream
2 tbsp chopped fresh cilantro
salt and ground black pepper
garlic chives, to garnish

1 Clean the mussels by pulling off the beards, scrubbing the shells well and removing any barnacles. Discard any mussels that are broken or which do not close when tapped sharply. Wash the clams.

2 Put the wine in a large saucepan with the scallions, lemon grass, lime leaves and curry paste. Simmer until the wine has almost evaporated.

COOK'S TIP

Buy a few extra mussels in case there are any which have to be discarded.

3 Add the mussels and clams to the pan, cover tightly and steam the shellfish over a high heat for 5-6 minutes, until they open.

4 Using a slotted spoon, transfer the mussels and clams to a heated serving bowl and keep hot. Discard any mussels and clams that remain closed. Strain the cooking liquid into a clean pan and simmer to reduce to about 1 cup.

5 Stir in the coconut cream and cilantro, with salt and pepper to taste. Heat through. Pour the sauce over the mussels and clams and serve, garnished with garlic chives.

Sardines in Escabeche

This spicy marinade is widely used in Spain and Portugal as a traditional means of preserving fish, poultry or game. It is good with fried fish.

SERVES 2-4

16 sardines, cleaned

seasoned flour

2 tbsp olive oil

roasted red onion, green pepper and tomatoes, to garnish

MARINADE

6 tbsp olive oil

1 onion, sliced

1 garlic clove, crushed

3-4 bay leaves

2 cloves

1 dried red chili

1 tsp paprika

½ cup wine or sherry vinegar

½ cup white wine

salt and ground black pepper

1 Cut the heads off the sardines and split each of them along the belly. Turn them over so that the backbone is uppermost. Press down along the backbone to loosen it, then carefully lift out the backbone and as many remaining bones as possible.

2 Close the sardines up again and dust them with seasoned flour. Heat the olive oil in a frying pan and fry the sardines for 2-3 minutes on each side. Remove the fish from the pan and allow to cool, then place in a single layer in a large shallow dish.

VARIATION

White fish can be prepared in this way, but the method is particularly successful with oily fish such as herrings or sprats.

3 To make the marinade, add the olive oil to the oil remaining in the frying pan. Fry the onion and garlic gently for 5-10 minutes until soft. Add the bay leaves, cloves, chili and paprika, with pepper to taste. Fry, stirring, for another 1-2 minutes.

4 Stir in the wine or sherry vinegar, white wine and a little salt. Allow to bubble up then pour over the sardines. When cool, cover and chill overnight or for up to three days. Serve, garnished with onion, pepper and tomatoes.

Cajun Blackened Fish with Papaya Salsa

This is an excellent way of cooking fish, leaving it moist in the middle and crisp and spicy on the outside.

SERVES 4

1 quantity cajun spice, without the onion and garlic

4 x 8-10 oz skinned fish fillets, such as snapper or bream

¼ cup butter, melted

PAPAYA SALSA

1 papaya

½ small red onion, diced

1 fresh red chili, seeded and finely chopped

3 tbsp chopped fresh cilantro

grated rind and juice of 1 lime

salt

lime and cilantro, to garnish

1   Start by making the salsa. Cut the papaya in half and scoop out the seeds. Remove the skin, cut the flesh into small dice and place it in a bowl. Add the onion, chili, cilantro, lime rind and juice, with salt to taste. Mix well and set aside.

> ### COOK'S TIP
>
> *Cooking fish in this way can be a smoky affair, so make sure the kitchen is well ventilated or use an extractor fan.*

2   Preheat a heavy-based frying pan over a medium heat for about 10 minutes. Spread the cajun spice on a plate. Brush the fish fillets with melted butter then dip them in the spices until well coated.

3   Place the fish in the hot pan and cook for 1-2 minutes on each side until blackened. Serve at once with the papaya salsa. Garnish with lime and coriander.

Caribbean Fish Steaks

West Indian cooks love spices and use them to good effect. This quick and easy recipe is a typical example of how chilies, cayenne and allspice can add an exotic accent to a tomato sauce for fish.

SERVES 4

3 tbsp oil

6 shallots, finely chopped

1 garlic clove, crushed

1 fresh green chili, seeded and finely chopped

14 oz can chopped tomatoes

2 bay leaves

¼ tsp cayenne pepper

1 tsp crushed allspice

juice of 2 limes

4 cod steaks

1 tsp brown sugar

2 tsp angostura bitters

salt

1   Heat the oil in a frying pan. Add the shallots and cook for 5 minutes until soft. Add the garlic and chili and cook for 2 minutes, then stir in the tomatoes, bay leaves, cayenne pepper, allspice and lime juice, with a little salt to taste.

VARIATION

Almost any robust fish steaks or fillets can be cooked in this way. Try haddock or swordfish. The sauce is also good over grilled pork chops.

2   Cook gently for 15 minutes, then add the cod steaks and baste with the tomato sauce. Cover and cook for 10 minutes or until the steaks are cooked. Transfer the steaks to a warmed dish and keep hot. Stir the sugar and angostura bitters into the sauce, simmer for 2 minutes then pour over the fish. Serve with steamed okra or green beans.

Crabcakes with Ginger and Wasabi

leaf image *Wasabi – a Japanese horseradish mustard – is available as a powder or a paste. It is very hot so should be used sparingly.*

SERVES 6

1 lb fresh dressed crab meat
  (brown and white meat)
4 scallions, finely chopped
1 in piece of fresh root ginger,
  grated
2 tbsp chopped fresh cilantro
2 tbsp mayonnaise
½-1 tsp wasabi paste
1 tbsp sesame oil
1-2 cups fresh bread crumbs
salt and ground black pepper
oil, for frying

DIPPING SAUCE
1 tsp wasabi paste
6 tbsp soy sauce

1 Make the dipping sauce by mixing the wasabi and soy sauce in a small bowl. Set aside.

2 Mix the crab meat, scallions, ginger, cilantro, mayonnaise, wasabi paste and sesame oil in a bowl. Stir in a little salt and pepper and enough bread crumbs to make a mixture that is firm enough to form patties, but is not too stiff.

3 Chill for 30 minutes then form the mixture into 12 cakes. Heat a shallow layer of oil in a frying pan and fry the crabcakes for about 3-4 minutes on each side, until browned. Serve with lettuce leaves and kaffir lime slices, accompanied by the dipping sauce, garnished with chili and scallion slices.

> ### COOK'S TIP
> *Fresh crab meat will have the best flavor, but if it is not available, use frozen or canned crab meat.*

Stir-fried Five Spice Squid with Black Bean Sauce

Squid is perfect for stir-frying as it should be cooked quickly. The spicy sauce makes the ideal accompaniment.

<u>SERVES 6</u>

1 lb small cleaned squid
3 tbsp oil
1 in piece fresh ginger
  root, grated
1 garlic clove, crushed
8 scallions, cut diagonally into
  1 in lengths
1 red bell pepper, seeded and cut
  into strips
1 fresh green chili, seeded and
  thinly sliced
6 mushrooms, sliced
1 tsp five spice powder
2 tbsp black bean sauce
2 tbsp soy sauce
1 tsp sugar
1 tbsp rice wine or dry sherry

COOK'S TIP

As with all stir-fried dishes it is important to have all the ingredients ready before you start to cook.

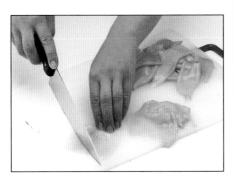

1 Rinse the squid and pull away the outer skin. Dry on paper towels. Slit the squid open and score the outside into diamonds with a sharp knife. Cut the squid into strips.

2 Heat a wok briefly and add the oil. When it is hot, stir-fry the squid quickly. Remove the squid strips from the wok with a slotted spoon and set aside. Add the ginger, garlic, scallions, red bell pepper, chili and mushrooms to the oil remaining in the wok and stir-fry for 2 minutes.

3 Return the squid to the wok. Stir in the five spice powder, black bean sauce, soy sauce, sugar and rice wine or sherry. Bring to a boil and cook, stirring, for 1 minute.

Cod and Shrimp Green Coconut Curry

If you have a jar of green masala in the store-cupboard, this curry takes just minutes to make!

SERVES 4

1½ lb cod fillets, skinned
6 tbsp green masala
¾ cup canned coconut milk or scant 1 cup coconut cream
6 oz peeled shrimp, raw or cooked
fresh cilantro, to garnish
basmati rice, to serve

1 Cut the skinned cod fillets into 1½ in pieces.

2 Put the green masala and coconut milk or cream into a frying pan. Heat to simmering and simmer gently for 5 minutes, stirring occasionally.

VARIATION

Any firm fish, such as monkfish, can be used instead of cod. Whole fish steaks can be cooked in the sauce, but allow an extra 5 minutes' cooking time and baste them with the sauce from time to time.

3 Add the cod and shrimp (if raw) and cook for 5 minutes. If using cooked shrimp, then add them and heat through. Garnish with cilantro and serve at once with rice.

Piri-piri Shrimp with Aïoli

Piri-piri is a Portuguese hot pepper sauce. The name literally means small chilli.

SERVES 4

1 fresh red chili, seeded and finely chopped
½ tsp paprika
½ tsp ground coriander
1 garlic clove, crushed
juice of ½ lime
2 tbsp olive oil
20 large raw shrimp in shells, heads removed and deveined
salt and ground black pepper
AïOLI
⅔ cup mayonnaise
2 garlic cloves, crushed
1 tsp Dijon mustard

1 Make the aïoli. Mix the mayonnaise, garlic and mustard in a small bowl and set aside.

VARIATION

The piri-piri marinade can be used for all types of fish. It is also very good with chicken, although this will need to be marinated for longer.

2 Mix the chili, paprika, coriander, garlic, lime juice and olive oil in a bowl. Add salt and pepper to taste. Place the shrimp in a dish. Add the spice mixture and mix well. Cover and leave in a cool place for 30 minutes.

3 Thread the shrimp onto skewers and broil or barbecue, basting and turning frequently, for 6-8 minutes until pink. Serve with the aïoli, garnished with two or three extra chilies, if you like.

Marrakesh Monkfish with Chermoula

Chermoula is a Moroccan spice mixture, which is used as a marinade for meat, poultry and fish.

SERVES 4

1 small red onion, finely chopped
2 garlic cloves, crushed
1 fresh red chili, seeded and finely chopped
2 tbsp chopped fresh cilantro
1 tbsp chopped fresh mint
1 tsp ground cumin
1 tsp paprika
generous pinch of saffron strands
4 tbsp olive oil
juice of 1 lemon
salt
1½ lb monkfish fillets, skinned
salad and pita bread, to serve

1 To make the chermoula, mix the onion, garlic, chili, cilantro, mint, cumin, paprika, saffron, olive oil, lemon juice and salt in a bowl.

2 Cut the monkfish into cubes. Add them to the spice mixture in the bowl. Mix well to coat, cover and leave in a cool place for 1 hour.

COOK'S TIP

If you use bamboo or wooden skewers, soak them in cold water for about 30 minutes before draining and threading them. This helps to prevent the skewers from scorching.

3 Thread the monkfish on to skewers and place on a rack over a broiler. Spoon over a little of the marinade.

4 Broil the monkfish skewers, close to the heat, for about 3 minutes on each side, until cooked through and lightly browned. Serve with salad and warm pita bread.

Salmon Marinated with Thai Spices

This recipe takes a suggestion from the Scandinavian cooks and transforms it with Thai spices.

SERVES 4-6

tail piece of 1 salmon, about 1½ lb, cleaned and prepared (see Cook's tip)

4 tsp coarse sea salt

4 tsp granulated sugar

1 in piece fresh ginger root, grated

2 lemon grass stalks, coarse outer leaves removed, thinly sliced

4 kaffir lime leaves, finely chopped or shredded

grated rind of 1 lime

1 fresh red chili, seeded and finely chopped

1 tsp black peppercorns, coarsely crushed

2 tbsp chopped fresh cilantro

cilantro and kaffir limes, to garnish

CILANTRO AND LIME DRESSING

⅔ cup mayonnaise

juice of ½ lime

2 tsp chopped fresh cilantro

1 Remove all the bones from the salmon (a pair of tweezers is the best tool). In a bowl, mix together the salt, sugar, ginger, lemon grass, lime leaves, lime rind, chili, peppercorns and cilantro.

2 Place one quarter of the spice mixture in a shallow dish. Place one salmon fillet, skin down, on top of the spices. Spread two-thirds of the remaining mixture over the flesh then place the remaining fillet on top, flesh side down. Sprinkle the rest of the spice mixture over the fish.

COOK'S TIP

Ask your fishmonger to scale the fish, split it lengthwise and remove it from the backbone in two matching fillets.

3 Cover the fish with foil, then place a board on top. Add some weights, such as clean cans of fruit. Chill for 2-5 days, turning the fish daily in the spicy brine.

4 Make the dressing by mixing the mayonnaise, lime juice and chopped cilantro in a bowl.

5 Scrape the spices off the fish. Slice it as thinly as possible. Serve with the lime dressing, garnished with cilantro and wedges of kaffir limes.

POULTRY AND GAME

Moroccan Harissa-spiced Roast Chicken

The spices and fruit in this stuffing give the chicken an unusual flavor and help to keep it moist.

SERVES 4-5

3-3½ lb chicken
2-4 tbsp garlic and spice
  aromatic oil
a few bay leaves
2 tsp clear honey
2 tsp tomato paste
4 tbsp lemon juice
⅔ cup chicken stock
½-1 tsp harissa

STUFFING
2 tbsp butter
1 onion, chopped
1 garlic clove, crushed
1½ tsp ground cinnamon
½ tsp ground cumin
1⅓ cups dried fruit, soaked for
  several hours or overnight in
  water to cover
¼ cup blanched almonds,
  finely chopped
salt and ground black pepper

COOK'S TIP

If you do not particularly like mixed dried fruit, use a single variety such as apricots instead.

1 Make the stuffing. Melt the butter in a saucepan. Add the onion and garlic and cook gently for 5 minutes until soft. Add the ground cinnamon and cumin and cook, stirring, for 2 minutes.

2 Drain the dried fruit, chop it roughly and add to the stuffing with the almonds. Season with salt and pepper and cook for 2 minutes more. Tip into a bowl and leave to cool.

3 Preheat the oven to 400°F. Stuff the neck of the chicken with the fruit mixture, reserving any excess. Brush the garlic and spice oil over the chicken. Place the chicken in a roasting tin, tuck in the bay leaves and roast for 1-1¼ hours, basting occasionally with the juices, until cooked.

4 Transfer the chicken to a carving board. Pour off any excess fat from the roasting tin. Stir the honey, tomato paste, lemon juice, stock and harissa into the juices in the roasting tin. Add salt to taste. Bring to a boil, lower the heat and simmer for 2 minutes, stirring frequently. Meanwhile, reheat any excess stuffing. Carve the chicken, pour the sauce into a small bowl and serve with the stuffing and chicken.

Fragrant Chicken Curry with Thai Spices

This is perfect for a party as the chicken and sauce can be prepared in advance and combined at the last minute.

SERVES 4

3 tbsp oil
1 onion, roughly chopped
2 garlic cloves, crushed
1 tbsp Thai red curry paste
4 oz creamed coconut dissolved
  in 3¾ cups boiling water
2 lemon grass stalks,
  roughly chopped
6 kaffir lime leaves, chopped
⅔ cup plain strained yogurt
2 tbsp apricot jam
1 cooked chicken, about
  3-3½ lb
2 tbsp chopped fresh cilantro
salt and ground black pepper
kaffir limes leaves, shredded
  coconut and fresh cilantro,
  to garnish
boiled rice, to serve

1 Heat the oil in a saucepan. Add the onion and garlic and fry over a low heat for 5-10 minutes until soft. Stir in the curry paste. Cook, stirring, for 2-3 minutes. Stir in the diluted creamed coconut then add the lemon grass, lime leaves, yogurt and apricot jam. Stir well. Cover and simmer for 30 minutes.

2 Process the sauce in a blender or food processor, then strain it back into a clean pan, pressing as much of the puréed mixture as possible through the strainer.

3 Remove the skin from the chicken, slice the meat off the bones and cut it into bite-size pieces. Add to the sauce.

4 Bring the sauce back to simmering point. Stir in the fresh cilantro and season with salt and pepper. Serve with rice, garnished with extra lime leaves, shredded coconut and cilantro.

COOK'S TIP

If you prefer the sauce a little thicker, stir in a little more creamed coconut after adding the chicken.

Turkey Sosaties with a Curried Apricot Sauce

This is a South African way of cooking meat or poultry in a delicious sweet and sour sauce spiced with curry powder.

SERVES 4

1 tbsp oil
1 onion, finely chopped
1 garlic clove, crushed
2 bay leaves
juice of 1 lemon
2 tbsp curry powder
4 tbsp apricot jam
4 tbsp apple juice
salt
1½ lb turkey fillet
4 tbsp low fat cream or yogurt

1 Heat the oil in a saucepan. Add the onion, garlic and bay leaves and cook over a low heat for 10 minutes until the onion is soft. Add the lemon juice, curry powder, apricot jam and apple juice, with salt to taste. Cook gently for 5 minutes. Leave to cool.

VARIATION

This marinade is traditionally used with lamb, but is equally good with cubes of steak or pork fillet or chicken.

2 Cut the turkey into ¾ in cubes and add to the marinade. Mix well, cover and leave in a cool place and marinate for at least 2 hours or overnight in the fridge. Thread the turkey on to skewers, allowing the marinade to run back into the bowl. Broil or barbecue the sosaties for 6-8 minutes, turning several times, until cooked.

3 Meanwhile, transfer the marinade to a pan and simmer for 2 minutes. Stir in the cream or yogurt and serve with the sosaties.

Spicy Indonesian Chicken Satay

This spicy marinade quickly gives an exotic flavor to tender chicken breasts. The satays can be cooked on a barbecue or under a broiler.

SERVES 4

4 skinless, boneless chicken breasts, about 6 oz each
1 quantity sambal kecap, with the deep-fried onions separate

1 Cut the chicken breasts into 1 in cubes and place in a bowl with the sambal kecap. Mix thoroughly. Cover and leave in a cool place to marinate for at least 1 hour. Soak 8 bamboo skewers in cold water for 30 minutes.

2 Tip the chicken and marinade into a strainer placed over a saucepan and leave to drain for a few minutes. Set the strainer aside.

3 Add 2 tbsp hot water to the marinade and bring to a boil. Lower the heat and simmer for 2 minutes, then pour into a bowl and leave to cool. When cool, add the deep fried onions.

4 Drain the skewers, thread them with the chicken and broil or barbecue for about 10 minutes, turning regularly until the chicken is golden brown and cooked through. Serve with the sambal kecap as a dip.

Roast Rabbit with Three Mustards

In France rabbit and mustard are a popular combination. In this recipe each of the three different mustards adds a distinctive flavor to the dish.

SERVES 4

1 tbsp **Dijon mustard**
1 tbsp **tarragon mustard**
1 tbsp **whole-grain mustard**
3-3½ lb **rabbit portions**
1 large **carrot, sliced**
1 **onion, sliced**
2 tbsp **fresh chopped tarragon**
½ cup **dry white wine**
⅔ cup **heavy cream**
salt and ground black pepper
fresh tarragon, to garnish

VARIATION

If the three different mustards are not available, use one or two varieties, increasing the quantities accordingly. The flavor will not be quite as interesting, but the dish will still taste good!

1 Preheat the oven to 400°F. Mix the mustards in a bowl and spread over the rabbit. Put the carrot and onion slices in a roasting pan and scatter the tarragon over. Pour in ½ cup of water, then arrange the meat on top.

2 Roast for 25-30 minutes, basting frequently with the juices, until the rabbit is tender. Remove the rabbit to a heated serving dish and keep hot. Using a slotted spoon, remove the carrot and onion slices from the roasting pan and discard.

3 Place the roasting pan on the hob and add the white wine. Boil to reduce by about two-thirds. Stir in the cream and allow to bubble up for a few minutes. Season with salt and pepper then pour over the rabbit and serve, garnished with fresh tarragon.

Venison in Guinness with Horseradish and Mustard Dumplings

Mustard, juniper berries and bay leaves combine with lean dark venison to create a casserole with a rich flavor and wonderful aroma.

SERVES 6

1 tbsp olive oil
1½ lb stewing venison, cut
  into cubes
3 onions, sliced
2 garlic cloves, crushed
1 tbsp flour
1 tsp mustard powder
6 juniper berries, lightly crushed
2 bay leaves
1⅔ cups Guinness
2 tsp light brown sugar
2 tbsp balsamic vinegar
salt and ground black pepper

DUMPLINGS

1½ cups self-rising flour
1 tsp mustard powder
generous ½ cup shredded
  beef suet
2 tsp horseradish sauce

1 Preheat the oven to 350°F. Heat the oil in a flameproof casserole. Fry the meat, a few pieces at a time, until browned. As each batch browns, remove it to a plate. Add the onions, with a little more oil, if necessary. Cook, stirring, for 5 minutes until soft. Add the garlic, then return the venison to the pan.

2 Mix the flour and mustard in a small bowl, sprinkle over the venison and stir well until the flour has been absorbed. Add the juniper berries and bay leaves and gradually stir in the Guinness, sugar and vinegar. Pour over enough water to cover the meat. Season with salt and pepper and bring to simmering point.

3 Cover and transfer the casserole to cook in the oven for 2-2½ hours, until the venison is tender. Stir the casserole occasionally and add a little more water, if necessary.

4 About 20 minutes before the end of the cooking time, make the dumplings. Sift the flour and mustard into a bowl. Season with salt and pepper and mix in the suet. Stir in the horseradish sauce and enough water to make a soft dough. With floured hands, form into six dumplings. Place these gently on top of the venison. Return the casserole to the oven and cook for 15 minutes more, until the dumplings are well risen and cooked. Serve at once.

Spiced Grilled Poussins

The cumin and coriander coating on the poussins keeps them moist during broiling as well as giving them a delicious and unusual flavor.

SERVES 4

2 garlic cloves, roughly chopped
1 tsp ground cumin
1 tsp ground coriander
pinch of cayenne pepper
½ small onion, chopped
4 tbsp olive oil
½ tsp salt
2 poussins
lemon wedges, to garnish

1 Combine the garlic, cumin, coriander, cayenne pepper, onion, olive oil and salt in a blender or food processor. Process to make a paste that will spread smoothly.

VARIATION

Chicken portions and quail can also be cooked in this way.

2 Cut the poussins in half lengthwise. Place them skin side up in a shallow dish and spread with the spice paste. Cover and leave to marinate in a cool place for 2 hours.

3 Broil or barbecue the poussins for 15-20 minutes, turning frequently, until cooked and lightly charred on the outside. Serve immediately, garnished with lemon wedges.

Chicken with 40 Cloves of Garlic

This recipe is not as alarming as it sounds. Long slow cooking makes the garlic soft and fragrant and the delicious flavor permeates the chicken.

SERVES 4-6

½ lemon
fresh rosemary sprigs
3-4½ lb chicken
4 or 5 heads of garlic
4 tbsp olive oil
salt and ground black pepper
steamed fava beans and scallions, to serve

1 Preheat the oven to 375°F. Place the lemon half and the rosemary sprigs in the chicken. Separate 3 or 4 of the garlic heads into cloves and remove the papery husks, but do not peel. Slice the top off the other garlic head.

COOK'S TIP

Make sure that each guest receives an equal portion of garlic. The idea is to mash the garlic into the pan juices to make an aromatic sauce.

2 Heat the oil in a large flameproof casserole. Add the chicken, turning it in the hot oil to coat the skin completely. Season with salt and pepper and add all the garlic.

3 Cover the casserole with a sheet of foil, then the lid, to seal in the steam and the flavor. Cook for 1-1¼ hours until the chicken is cooked. Serve the chicken with the garlic, accompanied by steamed fava beans and scallions.

Mediterranean Duck with Harissa and Saffron

Harissa is a fiery chili sauce from North Africa. Mixed with cinnamon, saffron and preserved lemon, it gives this colorful casserole an unforgettable flavor.

Serves 4

1 tbsp olive oil
4-4½ lb duck, quartered
1 large onion, thinly sliced
1 garlic clove, crushed
½ tsp ground cumin
1⅔ cups duck or chicken stock
juice of ½ lemon
1-2 tsp harissa
1 cinnamon stick
1 tsp saffron strands
⅓ cup black olives
⅓ cup green olives
peel of 1 preserved lemon,
   rinsed, drained and cut into
   fine strips
2-3 lemon slices
2 tbsp chopped fresh cilantro
salt and ground black pepper
cilantro sprigs, to garnish

1 Heat the oil in a flameproof casserole. Add the duck quarters and cook until browned all over. Remove with a slotted spoon and set aside. Add the onion and garlic to the oil remaining in the casserole and cook for 5 minutes until soft. Add the cumin and cook, stirring, for 2 minutes.

2 Pour in the stock and lemon juice, then add the harissa, cinnamon and saffron. Bring to the boil. Return the duck to the casserole and add the olives, preserved lemon peel and lemon slices. Season with salt and pepper.

3 Lower the heat, partially cover the casserole and simmer gently for 45 minutes until the duck is cooked through. Discard the cinnamon stick. Stir in the chopped cilantro and garnish with the cilantro sprigs.

Tea-smoked Duck Breasts

Smoking spiced duck breasts over fragrant tea leaves gives them a slightly smoky flavor, which is not too overpowering.

SERVES 2-4

2 duck breasts

4 tbsp seven seas curry powder or Singapore-style curry powder

1 tbsp soy sauce

½ cup long grain rice

½ cup sugar

2 tbsp Earl Grey tea leaves

stir-fried bok choy, to serve

VARIATION

Whole chicken and duck, chicken portions, quail, other game or fish steaks can be smoked in the same way. Fish does not need to be steamed first. A whole bird will take about 1 hour.

1 Pat the duck breasts dry with paper towels. Rub the curry powder all over the meat. Pour water into a wok to the depth of 2-3 in.

2 Place the duck on a steaming rack over the water. Cover the wok and steam the duck breasts for 20-30 minutes, depending on the thickness of the meat. Remove the duck and sprinkle with soy sauce. Set aside.

3 Wash and dry the wok and line with two sheets of foil. Mix together the raw rice, sugar and tea. Spread the mixture in the bottom of the lined wok. Place the duck breasts on the steaming rack above the tea mixture. Put the lid on and seal the rim with damp paper towels.

4 Place the wok over a medium heat. As soon as you can smell that it has started smoking leave it, undisturbed, for 10-15 minutes. Remove from the heat and leave, covered, for 15 minutes more. Discard the rice. Cut the duck breasts into thin slices and serve warm or cold with bok choy.

BEEF, LAMB AND PORK

Beef Teryaki

Mirin, which is used in this ginger and garlic marinade, is a sweetened sake, widely used in Japanese cooking. However, it is difficult to find outside Japanese grocers, so a medium-sweet sherry can be used instead.

SERVES 4

1 tbsp oil

4 tbsp soy sauce

2 tbsp mirin or medium sherry

1 tsp soft light brown sugar

1 tbsp ginger juice (see
 Cook's tip)

1 garlic clove, crushed

1½-2 lb rump steak, about 1 in
 thick, in one piece if possible

sansho pepper

1 daikon radish (mooli), peeled,
 2 tbsp wasabi paste and fresh
 cilantro sprigs, to garnish

1 Mix the oil, soy sauce, mirin or sherry, sugar, ginger juice and garlic in a large shallow dish. Add the steak and turn to coat both sides. Leave in a cool place to marinate for at least 4 hours, turning from time to time.

2 Preheat a broiler, ridged cast iron broiling pan or barbecue and broil the steak for 3-5 minutes on each side. Season with sansho pepper.

3 To prepare the Japanese-style garnish, grate the daikon radish and squeeze out as much liquid as possible. Place a little pile of grated daikon, a dessertspoonful of wasabi paste and a cilantro sprig on each of four plates.

4 With a sharp knife, slice the steak into thin diagonal slices and arrange on the plates with the garnish.

COOK'S TIP

To make ginger juice, peel and grate a piece of ginger root and squeeze out the liquid.

Black Bean Chili con Carne

Two chilies add plenty of fire to this Tex-Mex classic.

SERVES 6

1¼ cups dried black beans
1¼ lb braising steak
2 tbsp oil
2 onions, chopped
1 garlic clove, crushed
1 fresh green chili, seeded and finely chopped
1 tbsp paprika
2 tsp ground cumin
2 tsp ground coriander
14 oz can chopped tomatoes
1¼ cups beef stock
1 dried red chili, crumbled
1 tsp hot pepper sauce
1 fresh red bell pepper, seeded and chopped
2 tbsp fresh cilantro leaves
salt
plain boiled rice, to serve

1   Put the beans in a saucepan. Add water to cover, bring to a boil and boil vigorously for 10-15 minutes. Drain, tip into a clean bowl, cover with cold water and leave to soak for about 8 hours or overnight.

2   Preheat the oven to 300°F. Cut the beef into very small dice. Heat the oil in a large flameproof casserole. Add the onion, garlic and green chili and cook them gently for 5 minutes until soft. Using a slotted spoon transfer the mixture to a plate.

3   Increase the heat and brown the meat, then stir in the paprika, cumin and ground coriander.

4   Add the tomatoes, stock, dried chili and hot pepper sauce. Drain the beans and add them to the casserole, with enough water to cover. Bring to simmering point, cover and cook in the oven for 2 hours. Stir the casserole occasionally and add extra water, if necessary, to prevent it from drying out.

5   Season with salt and add the red bell pepper. Return to the oven and cook for 30 minutes more, until the meat and beans are tender. Scatter over the cilantro and serve with rice.

Wild Boar Chops with Romesco Sauce

Romesco is a fiery Spanish sauce that takes its name from the small dried red peppers used for making it in Catalonia. It is often served cold as a dip for vegetables, but it is equally delicious served hot with broiled meat and fish.

<u>Serves 4</u>

4 wild boar loin chops, about
  6 oz each
olive oil, for shallow frying
braised Savoy cabbage, to serve
Romesco sauce
3 dried red chilies
⅔ cup olive oil
1 slice white bread, crusts
  removed
3 garlic cloves, chopped
3 tomatoes, peeled, seeded and
  roughly chopped
¼ cup ground almonds
4 tbsp balsamic vinegar
4 tbsp red wine vinegar
salt and ground black pepper

VARIATION

Wild boar is increasingly available in good butchers and large supermarkets. However, if you can't find it, thick pork loin chops can be used instead and are equally delicious with this spicy sauce.

1 To make the romesco sauce, slit the chilies and remove the seeds, then leave the chilies to soak in warm water for about 30 minutes until soft. Drain the chilies, dry them on paper towels, then chop finely.

2 Heat 3 tbsp of the olive oil in a frying pan and fry the bread until golden on both sides. Lift out with a slotted spoon and drain on paper towels, then crumble into a blender or food processor.

3 Add the garlic to the oil remaining in the frying pan and cook gently for 2-3 minutes until softened, then leave to cool for a few minutes.

4 Add the chilies, tomatoes and ground almonds to the fried bread in the food processor. Tip in the garlic, with the oil in which it was cooked. Blend to a paste.

5 With the motor running, gradually add the remaining olive oil and then the balsamic and red wine vinegars. When the sauce is smooth, scrape it into a bowl and stir in salt and pepper to taste. Cover and chill for 2 hours.

6 Season the boar chops with pepper. Heat the olive oil in a heavy-based frying pan and fry the chops for about 15 minutes on each side, until golden brown and cooked through.

7 When the chops are almost cooked, place the romesco sauce in a saucepan and heat it gently. If it is too thick, stir in a little boiling water. Serve with the wild boar chops, accompanied by braised Savoy cabbage.

COOK'S TIP

Remember to wash your hands and the knife and chopping board thoroughly after preparing the chilies.

Roast Lamb with Apricot, Cinnamon and Cumin Stuffing

Cinnamon and cumin make perfect partners for apricots in the bulgur stuffing in this easy-to-carve joint.

SERVES 6-8

½ cup bulgur
2 tbsp olive oil
1 small onion, finely chopped
1 garlic clove, crushed
1 tsp ground cinnamon
1 tsp ground cumin
¾ cup ready-to-eat dried
   apricots, chopped
⅔ cup pine nuts
1 boned shoulder lamb, about 4-
   4½ lb
½ cup red wine
½ cup lamb stock
salt and ground black pepper
mint sprigs, to garnish

1 Place the bulgur in a bowl and add warm water to cover. Leave to soak for 1 hour, then drain thoroughly.

2 Heat the oil in a saucepan. Add the onion and crushed garlic and cook for 5 minutes until soft. Stir in the cinnamon, cumin, apricots and pine nuts, with salt and pepper to taste. Leave to cool. Preheat the oven to 350°F.

3 Open out the shoulder of lamb and spread the stuffing over. Roll up firmly and tie tightly with string. Place in a roasting pan. Roast for 1 hour, then pour the red wine and stock into the roasting pan. Roast for 30 minutes more. Transfer the joint to a heated plate, cover with tented foil and allow the meat to rest for 15-20 minutes before carving.

4 Meanwhile, skim the surface fat from the wine-flavored stock in the roasting pan. Place the pan over a high heat and allow the gravy to bubble for a few minutes, stirring occasionally to incorporate any sediment. Carve the lamb neatly, arrange the slices on a serving platter and pour over the gravy. Serve at once, garnished with mint.

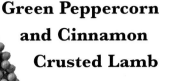

Green Peppercorn and Cinnamon Crusted Lamb

Racks of lamb are perfect for serving at dinner parties. This version has a spiced crumb coating.

SERVES 6

2 oz ciabatta bread
1 tbsp drained green peppercorns in brine, lightly crushed
1 tbsp ground cinnamon
1 garlic clove, crushed
½ tsp salt
2 tbsp butter, melted
2 tsp Dijon mustard
2 racks of lamb, trimmed
4 tbsp red wine
1⅔ cups lamb stock
1 tbsp balsamic vinegar
fresh vegetables, to serve

VARIATION

The spicy crumbs also make a tasty coating for chicken pieces, fish or chops.

1 Preheat the oven to 425°F. Break the ciabatta into pieces, spread out on a cookie sheet and bake for 10 minutes or until pale golden. Process in a blender or food processor to make crumbs.

2 Tip the crumbs into a bowl and add the green peppercorns, cinnamon, garlic and salt. Stir in the melted butter. Spread the mustard over the lamb. Press the crumb mixture on to the mustard to make a thin even crust. Put the racks in a roasting pan and roast for 30 minutes, covering the ends with foil if they start to over-brown.

3 Remove the lamb to a carving dish and keep hot under tented foil. Skim the fat off the juices in the roasting pan. Stir in the wine, stock and vinegar. Bring to a boil, stirring in any sediment, then lower the heat and simmer for about 10 minutes until reduced to a rich gravy. Carve the lamb and serve with the gravy and vegetables.

Lamb Tagine

Combining meat, dried fruit and spices is typical of Middle Eastern cooking. This type of casserole takes its name from the earthenware pot (tagine) in which it is traditionally cooked.

SERVES 4-6

½ **cup dried apricots**

2 **tbsp olive oil**

1 **large onion, chopped**

2¼ **lb boneless shoulder**
  lamb, cubed

1 **tsp ground cumin**

1 **tsp ground coriander**

1 **tsp ground cinnamon**

grated rind and juice of ½ **orange**

1 **tsp saffron strands**

1 **tbsp ground almonds**

about 1¼ **cups lamb or**
  chicken stock

1 **tbsp sesame seeds**

salt and ground black pepper

fresh parsley, to garnish

couscous, to serve

COOK'S TIP

If you do not have time to soak the apricots use the ready-to-eat variety and add extra stock to replace the soaking liquid.

1   Cut the apricots in half and put in a bowl with ⅔ cup water. Leave to soak overnight.

2   Preheat the oven to 350°F. Heat the olive oil in a flameproof casserole. Add the onion and cook gently for 10 minutes until soft and golden.

3   Stir in the lamb. Add the cumin, coriander and cinnamon, with salt and pepper to taste. Stir to coat the lamb cubes in the spices. Cook, stirring, for 5 minutes.

4   Add the apricots and their soaking liquid. Stir in the orange rind and juice, saffron, ground almonds and enough stock to cover. Cover the casserole and cook in the oven for 1-1½ hours until the meat is tender, stirring occasionally and adding extra stock, if necessary.

5   Heat a heavy-based frying pan, add the sesame seeds and dry fry, shaking the pan, until golden. Sprinkle the seame seeds over the meat, garnish with parsley and serve with couscous.

Turkish Kebabs with Tomato and Olive Salsa

The mix of aromatic spices, garlic and lemon gives these kebabs a wonderful flavor – a fiery salsa makes the perfect accompaniment.

<u>SERVES 4</u>

2 garlic cloves, crushed
4 tbsp lemon juice
2 tbsp olive oil
1 dried red chili, crushed
1 tsp ground cumin
1 tsp ground coriander
1¼ lb lean lamb, cut into
　1½ in cubes
8 bay leaves
salt and ground black pepper
TOMATO AND OLIVE SALSA
1½ cups mixed pitted green and
　black olives,
　roughly chopped
1 small red onion, finely chopped
4 plum tomatoes, peeled and
　finely chopped
1 fresh red chili, seeded and
　finely chopped
2 tbsp olive oil

1 Mix the garlic, lemon juice, olive oil, chili, cumin and coriander in a large shallow dish. Add the lamb cubes, with salt and pepper to taste. Mix well. Cover and marinate in a cool place for 2 hours.

2 Make the salsa. Put the olives, onion, tomatoes, chili and olive oil in a bowl. Stir in salt and pepper to taste. Mix well, cover and set aside.

3 Remove the lamb from the marinade and divide the cubes among four skewers, adding the bay leaves at intervals. Broil over a barbecue, on a ridged iron broiling pan or under a hot broiler, turning occasionally, for 10 minutes, until the lamb is browned and crisp on the outside and pink and juicy inside. Serve with the salsa.

Veal Escalopes with Ruby Grapefruit and Ginger

The ginger and pink peppercorns give the grapefruit sauce a subtle spiciness without being overpowering.

SERVES 4

4 veal escalopes

2 tbsp butter

1 tbsp olive oil

juice of 1 large ruby grapefruit

²/₃ cup chicken stock

2 tsp grated fresh ginger root

1 tsp pink peppercorns, drained and lightly crushed

1 tbsp cold butter

salt

GARNISH

1 ruby grapefruit

oil, for shallow frying

1 Start by making the garnish. Wash and dry the grapefruit, then pare off thin strips of rind, using a citrus zester. Scrape off any pith that remains attached to the strips. Cut the grapefruit in half. Squeeze the juice from half the grapefruit into a small bowl, add the strips of pared rind and leave to macerate for 1 hour. Cut the other half grapefruit into wedges and reserve.

2 Drain the strips of rind and pat them dry with paper towels. Heat oil to a depth of ¹/₂ in in a small saucepan and add the strips. As soon as they are brown strain the strips through a strainer into a bowl. Discard the oil in the bowl.

3 Place the veal escalopes between two sheets of wax paper and beat them with a rolling pin until they are about ¹/₈ in thick. If the escalopes are very large, cut them into neat pieces.

4 Melt the butter and the oil in a heavy-based frying pan. Fry the veal, in batches if necessary, for 1 minute on each side. Remove the escalopes to a heated dish and keep hot.

5 Add the grapefruit juice, stock and grated ginger to the pan. Allow to boil until reduced by half. Strain the sauce into a saucepan, add the peppercorns and heat through. Whisk in the butter and season with salt. Pour the sauce over the veal, then garnish with fried grapefruit rind and reserved wedges.

427

Tsire Koftas with Avocado and Melon Salsa

Tsire powder makes a lovely crunchy coating for the meat on these kebabs.

SERVES 4-6

1½ lb lean ground lamb
2 tbsp Greek-style yogurt
1 small onion, finely chopped
1 garlic clove, crushed
¼ tsp chili powder
1 egg, beaten
double quantity tsire powder
salt and ground black pepper
mint leaves, to garnish

VARIATION

Use minced beef in place of lamb.

SALSA

1 ripe avocado
juice of 1 lime
8 oz melon, peeled, seeded and
    cut into small dice
4 scallions, very finely chopped
1 fresh red chili, seeded and
    finely chopped

1   Make the salsa. Cut the avocado in half, remove the stone and peel off the skin. Dice the flesh finely and toss it with the lime juice in a bowl. Add the melon, scallions and chili, with salt and pepper to taste. Cover closely and leave to stand for 30 minutes.

2   Put the minced lamb in a food processor with the yogurt, onion, garlic and chili powder. Add a little salt and pepper and process until smooth.

3   Divide the lamb mixture into 12 portions and shape each one into a sausage shape. Push a pre-soaked bamboo skewer into each kofta and press the meat on to the stick.

4   Dip each kofta in egg, then roll it in the tsire powder. Cook over a barbecue or under a hot broiler for 10 minutes, turning occasionally until cooked. Serve with the avocado and melon salsa, garnished with mint leaves.

Paprika Pork with Fennel and Caraway

Fennel always tastes very good with pork, and combined with caraway seeds adds an aromatic flavor to this Middle European dish.

SERVES 4

1 tbsp olive oil
4 boneless pork steaks
1 large onion, thinly sliced
14 oz can chopped tomatoes
1 tsp fennel seeds, lightly
  crushed
½ tsp caraway seeds, lightly
  crushed
1 tbsp paprika
2 tbsp sour cream
salt and ground black pepper
paprika, to garnish
buttered noodles and poppy
  seeds, to serve

COOK'S TIP

Always buy good quality paprika and replace it regularly as it loses its distinctive flavor very quickly.

1 Heat the oil in a large frying pan. Add the pork steaks and brown on both sides. Lift out the steaks and put them on a plate.

2 Add the onion to the oil remaining in the pan. Cook for 10 minutes, until soft and golden. Stir in the tomatoes, fennel, caraway seeds and paprika.

3 Return the pork to the pan and simmer gently for 20-30 minutes until tender. Season with salt and pepper. Lightly swirl in the sour cream and sprinkle with a little paprika. Serve with noodles, tossed in butter and sprinkled with poppy seeds.

Baked Maple Ribs

The only way to eat these spicy ribs is with your fingers. So provide plenty of paper napkins!

SERVES 6

2 tbsp oil

1 onion, cut into thin wedges

1 garlic clove, crushed

scant ½ cup maple syrup

1 tbsp soy sauce

1 tbsp tomato ketchup

1 tbsp Worcestershire sauce

1 tsp ground ginger

1 tsp paprika

1 tsp mustard powder

1 tbsp red wine vinegar

1 tsp Tabasco sauce

2¼ lb pork spare ribs

1 Preheat the oven to 400°F. Heat the oil in a saucepan, add the onion and garlic and cook for about 5 minutes until soft.

2 Add the maple syrup, soy sauce, tomato ketchup, Worcestershire sauce, ginger, paprika, mustard powder, wine vinegar and Tabasco sauce. Bring to a boil, lower the heat and simmer for 2 minutes.

3 Place the ribs in a roasting pan, pour over the sauce and turn the ribs to coat them completely. Cover the pan with foil and bake the ribs for 45 minutes. Remove the foil and bake for 15 minutes more, basting occasionally. The ribs should be sticky and tender.

COOK'S TIP

Make sure you use real maple syrup and not maple-flavored syrup for this recipe.

Jerk Pork

This is a Jamaican way of spicing meat or poultry before roasting in the oven or over a fire.

SERVES 4

1 tbsp oil

2 onions, finely chopped

2 fresh red chilies, seeded and finely chopped

1 garlic clove, crushed

1 in piece fresh ginger root, grated

1 tsp dried thyme

1 tsp ground allspice

1 tsp hot pepper sauce

2 tbsp rum

grated rind and juice of 1 lime

salt and ground black pepper

4 pork chops

fresh thyme, small red chilies and lime wedges, to garnish

1 Heat the oil in a frying pan. Add the onions and cook for 10 minutes until soft. Add the chilies, garlic, ginger, thyme and allspice and fry for 2 more minutes. Stir in the hot pepper sauce, rum, lime rind and juice.

VARIATION

Chicken joints or a whole chicken can also be coated with this delicious spicy paste before roasting.

2 Simmer until the mixture forms a dark paste. Season with salt and pepper and leave to cool. Rub the paste over the chops. Put them in a shallow dish, cover and chill overnight.

3 Preheat the oven to 375°F. Place the chops on a rack in a roasting pan and roast for 30 minutes until fully cooked. Serve at once, garnished with fresh thyme, chilies and lime wedges.

VEGETABLES AND SALADS

Vegetable Korma

The blending of spices is an ancient art in India. Here the aim is to produce a subtle, aromatic curry rather than an assault on the senses.

SERVES 4

¼ cup butter
2 onions, sliced
2 garlic cloves, crushed
1 in piece fresh ginger
  root, grated
1 tsp ground cumin
1 tbsp ground coriander
6 cardamoms
2 in cinnamon stick
1 tsp ground turmeric
1 fresh red chili, seeded and
  finely chopped
1 potato, peeled and cut into
  1 in cubes
1 small eggplant
1½ cups mushrooms, thickly
  sliced
1 cup French beans, cut into
  1 in lengths
4 tbsp plain yogurt
⅔ cup heavy cream
1 tsp garam masala
salt and ground black pepper
fresh cilantro sprigs, to garnish
poppadums, to serve

1 Melt the butter in a heavy-based saucepan. Add the onions and cook for 5 minutes until soft. Add the garlic and ginger and cook for 2 minutes, then stir in the cumin, coriander, cardamoms, cinnamon stick, turmeric and chili. Cook, stirring for 30 seconds.

2 Add the potato, eggplant and mushrooms and about ¾ cup water. Cover the pan, bring to a boil, then lower the heat and simmer for 15 minutes. Add the beans and cook, uncovered, for 5 minutes.

VARIATION

Any combination of vegetables can be used for this korma, including carrots, cauliflower, broccoli, peas and chick-peas.

3 With a slotted spoon, remove the vegetables to a warmed serving dish and keep hot. Allow the cooking liquid to bubble up until it reduces a little. Season with salt and pepper, then stir in the yogurt, cream and garam masala. Pour the sauce over the vegetables and garnish with cilantro. Serve with poppadums.

Dhal with Tadka

Boost your pulse rate with this delectable dish of red lentils with a spicy topping.

SERVES 4

¼ cup butter

2 tsp black mustard seeds

1 onion, finely chopped

2 garlic cloves, finely chopped

1 tsp ground turmeric

1 tsp ground cumin

2 fresh green chilies, seeded and finely chopped

1 cup red lentils

1¼ cups canned coconut milk

1 quantity tadka or coriander baghar

fresh cilantro, to garnish

1 Melt the butter in a large heavy-based saucepan. Add the mustard seeds. When they start to pop, add the onion and garlic and cook for 5-10 minutes until soft.

2 Stir in the turmeric, cumin and chilies and cook for 2 minutes. Stir in the lentils, 4 cups water and coconut milk. Bring to a boil, then cover and simmer for 40 minutes, adding water if needed. The lentils should be soft and should have absorbed most of the liquid.

3 Prepare the tadka or baghar and pour immediately over the lentil (dhal) mixture. Garnish with cilantro leaves and serve at once, with naan bread to mop up the sauce.

VARIATION

This dish is excellent made with mung dhal, the yellow split mung bean that is widely used in Indian cookery.

435

Glazed Sweet Potatoes with Ginger and Allspice

Fried sweet potatoes acquire a candied coating when cooked with ginger, syrup and allspice. Cayenne cuts through the sweetness.

SERVES 4

2 lb sweet potatoes
¼ cup butter
3 tbsp oil
2 garlic cloves, crushed
2 pieces stem ginger, finely chopped
2 tsp ground allspice
1 tbsp syrup from ginger jar
salt and cayenne pepper
2 tsp chopped fresh thyme, plus a few sprigs to garnish

1 Peel the sweet potatoes and cut into ½ in cubes. Melt the butter with the oil in a large frying pan. Add the sweet potato cubes and fry, stirring frequently, for about 10 minutes until they are just soft.

2 Stir in the garlic, ginger and allspice. Cook, stirring, for 5 minutes more. Stir in the ginger syrup, salt, a generous pinch of cayenne pepper and the fresh thyme. Stir for 1-2 minutes more, then serve scattered with thyme sprigs.

COOK'S TIP

Some sweet potatoes have white flesh and some have yellow. Although they taste similar, the yellow-fleshed variety look particularly colorful and attractive.

Roasted Root Vegetables with Whole Spice Seeds

Roast these vegetables alongside a joint or whole chicken and they virtually look after themselves.

SERVES 4

3 parsnips, peeled
3 potatoes, peeled
3 carrots, peeled
3 sweet potatoes, peeled
4 tbsp olive oil
8 shallots, peeled
2 garlic cloves, sliced
2 tsp white mustard seeds
2 tsp coriander seeds, lightly crushed
1 tsp cumin seeds
2 bay leaves
salt and ground black pepper

1 Preheat the oven to 375°F. Bring a saucepan of lightly salted water to a boil. Cut the parsnips, potatoes, carrots and sweet potatoes into chunks. Add them to the pan and bring the water back to a boil. Boil for 2 minutes, then drain the vegetables thoroughly.

2 Pour the olive oil into a large heavy roasting pan and place over a moderate heat. Add the vegetables, shallots and garlic. Fry, tossing the vegetables over the heat until they are pale golden at the edges.

3 Add the mustard seeds, coriander seeds, cumin seeds and bay leaves. Cook for 1 minute, then season with salt and pepper. Transfer the roasting pan to the oven and roast for 45 minutes, turning occasionally, until the vegetables are crisp and golden and cooked through.

VARIATION

Vary the selection of vegetables according to what is available. Try using swede or pumpkin instead of, or as well as, the vegetables suggested.

Mexican Tortilla Parcels

Seeded green chilies add just a flicker of fire to the spicy filling in these parcels – perfect as an appetizer or snack.

SERVES 4

1½ lb tomatoes
4 tbsp sunflower oil
1 large onion, finely sliced
1 garlic clove, crushed
2 tsp cumin seeds
2 fresh green chilies, seeded
  and chopped
2 tbsp tomato paste
1 vegetable bouillon cube
7 oz can corn kernels, drained
1 tbsp chopped fresh cilantro
1 cup grated Cheddar cheese
8 wheatflour tortillas
cilantro leaves, shredded lettuce
  and sour cream, to serve

1 Peel the tomatoes: place them in a heatproof bowl, add boiling water to cover and leave for 1 minute. Lift out with a slotted spoon and plunge into a bowl of cold water. Leave for 1 minute, then drain. Slip the skins off the tomatoes and chop the flesh.

2 Heat half the oil in a frying pan and fry the onion with the garlic and cumin seeds for 5 minutes, until the onion softens. Add the chilies and tomatoes, then stir in the tomato paste. Crumble the bouillon cube over, stir well and cook gently for 5 minutes, until the chili is soft but the tomato has not completely broken down. Stir in the corn and fresh cilantro and heat gently to warm through. Keep warm.

3 Sprinkle grated cheese in the middle of each tortilla. Spoon some tomato mixture over the cheese. Fold over one edge of the tortilla then the sides and finally the remaining edge, to enclose the filling completely.

4 Heat the remaining oil in a separate frying pan and fry the filled tortillas for 1-2 minutes on each side until golden and crisp. Serve with cilantro, shredded lettuce and sour cream.

COOK'S TIP

Mexican wheatflour tortillas are available in most supermarkets. They are very useful to keep in the cupboard as a wrapping for a variety of meat, chicken and vegetable mixtures.

Vegetable Couscous with Saffron and Harissa

A North African favorite, this spicy dish makes an excellent meal for vegetarians.

SERVES 4

3 tbsp olive oil
1 onion, chopped
2 garlic cloves, crushed
1 tsp ground cumin
1 tsp paprika
14 oz can chopped tomatoes
1¼ cups vegetable stock
1 cinnamon stick
generous pinch of
  saffron strands
4 baby eggplants, quartered
8 baby zucchini, trimmed
8 baby carrots
1⅓ cups couscous
15 oz can chick-peas, drained
¾ cup prunes
3 tbsp chopped fresh parsley
3 tbsp chopped fresh cilantro
2-3 tsp harissa
salt

1 Heat the olive oil in a large saucepan. Add the onion and garlic and cook gently for 5 minutes until soft. Add the cumin and paprika and cook, stirring, for 1 minute.

2 Add the tomatoes, stock, cinnamon stick, saffron, eggplants, zucchini and carrots. Season with salt. Bring to a boil, cover, lower the heat and cook for 20 minutes until the vegetables are just tender.

3 Line a steamer, metal strainer or colander with a double thickness of muslin. Soak the couscous according to the instructions on the packet. Add the chick-peas and prunes to the vegetables and cook for 5 minutes. Fork the couscous to break up any lumps and spread it in the prepared steamer. Place on top of the vegetables, cover, and cook for 5 minutes until the couscous is hot.

4 Stir the parsley and cilantro into the vegetables. Heap the couscous on to a warmed serving plate. Using a slotted spoon, arrange the vegetables on top. Spoon over a little sauce and toss gently to combine. Stir the harissa into the remaining sauce and serve separately.

Orange and Red Onion Salad with Cumin

Cumin and mint give this refreshing salad a Middle Eastern flavor. Choose small seedless oranges if you can.

SERVES 6

6 oranges
2 red onions
1 tbsp cumin seeds
**1 tsp coarsely ground
  black pepper**
1 tbsp chopped fresh mint
6 tbsp olive oil
salt
**fresh mint sprigs and black
  olives, to serve**

1 Slice the oranges thinly, working over a bowl to catch any juice. Then, holding each orange slice in turn over the bowl, cut around with scissors to remove the peel and pith. Slice the onions thinly and separate the rings.

COOK'S TIP

It is important to let the salad stand for 2 hours, so that the flavors develop and the onion softens slightly. However, do not leave the salad for much longer than this before serving.

2 Arrange the orange and onion slices in layers in a shallow dish, sprinkling each layer with cumin seeds, black pepper, mint, olive oil and salt to taste. Pour over the orange juice left over from slicing the oranges.

3 Leave the salad to marinate in a cool place for about 2 hours. Just before serving, scatter the salad with the mint sprigs and black olives.

Spanish Salad with Capers and Olives

Make this refreshing salad in the summer when tomatoes are sweet and full of flavor.

SERVES 4

4 tomatoes
½ cucumber
1 bunch scallions
**1 bunch purslane or
  watercress, washed**
8 pimiento-stuffed olives
2 tbsp drained capers
DRESSING
2 tbsp red wine vinegar
1 tsp paprika
½ tsp ground cumin
1 garlic clove, crushed
5 tbsp olive oil
salt and ground black pepper

1 Peel the tomatoes: place them in a heatproof bowl, add boiling water to cover and leave for 1 minute. Lift out with a slotted spoon and plunge into a bowl of cold water. Leave for 1 minute, then drain. Slip the skins off the tomatoes and dice the flesh finely. Put in a salad bowl.

2 Peel the cucumber, dice it finely and add it to the tomatoes. Trim and chop half the scallions, add them to the salad bowl and mix lightly.

3 Break the purslane or watercress into small sprigs. Add to the tomato mixture, with the olives and capers. Make the dressing. Mix the wine vinegar, paprika, cumin and garlic in a bowl. Whisk in the oil and add salt and pepper to taste. Pour over the salad and toss lightly. Serve with the remaining scallions.

COOK'S TIP

Serve this salad as soon as possible after adding the dressing.

Gado Gado

The peanut sauce on this traditional Indonesian salad owes its flavor to galangal, an aromatic rhizome that resembles ginger.

SERVES 4

9 oz white cabbage, shredded

4 carrots, cut into matchsticks

4 celery stalks, cut
 into matchsticks

4 cups beansprouts

½ cucumber, cut
 into matchsticks

fried onion, salted peanuts and
 sliced chili, to garnish

PEANUT SAUCE

1 tbsp oil

1 small onion, finely chopped

1 garlic clove, crushed

1 small piece galangal, peeled
 and grated

1 tsp ground cumin

¼ tsp chili powder

1 tsp tamarind paste
 or lime juice

4 tbsp crunchy
 peanut butter

1 tsp soft brown sugar

1 Steam the cabbage, carrots and celery for 3-4 minutes until just tender. Leave to cool. Spread out the beansprouts on a large serving dish. Arrange the cabbage, carrots, celery and cucumber on top.

2 Make the sauce. Heat the oil in a saucepan, add the onion and garlic and cook gently for 5 minutes until soft. Stir in the galangal, cumin and chili powder and cook for 1 minute more. Add the tamarind paste or lime juice, peanut butter and sugar. Mix well.

COOK'S TIPS

As long as the sauce remains the same, the vegetables can be altered at the whim of the cook and to reflect the contents of the vegetable rack or chiller. Pour the sauce over the salad and toss lightly or serve it in a separate bowl.

3 Heat gently, stirring occasionally and adding a little hot water, if necessary, to make a coating sauce. Spoon a little of the sauce over the vegetables and garnish with fried onions, peanuts and sliced chili. Serve the rest of the sauce separately.

Sesame Duck and Noodle Salad

This salad is complete in itself and makes a lovely summer lunch. The marinade is a marvellous blend of spices.

<u>SERVES 4</u>
2 duck breasts
1 tbsp oil
5 oz sugarsnap peas
2 carrots, cut into
  3 in sticks
8 oz medium egg noodles
6 scallions, sliced
salt
2 tbsp cilantro leaves,
  to garnish
MARINADE
1 tbsp sesame oil
1 tsp ground coriander
1 tsp five spice powder
DRESSING
1 tbsp garlic vinegar
1 tsp light brown sugar
1 tsp soy sauce
1 tbsp toasted sesame seeds
  (see Cook's tip)
3 tbsp sunflower oil
2 tbsp sesame oil
ground black pepper

1 Slice the duck breasts thinly across and place them in a shallow dish. Mix all the ingredients for the marinade, pour over the duck and mix well to coat thoroughly. Cover and leave in a cool place for 30 minutes.

2 Heat the oil in a frying pan, add the slices of duck breast and stir-fry for 3-4 minutes until cooked. Set aside.

3 Bring a saucepan of lightly salted water to a boil. Place the sugarsnap peas and carrots in a steamer that will fit on top of the pan. When the water boils, add the noodles. Place the steamer on top and steam the vegetables, while cooking the noodles for the time suggested on the packet. Set the steamed vegetables aside. Drain the noodles, refresh them under cold running water and drain again. Place them in a large serving bowl.

4 Make the dressing. Mix the vinegar, sugar, soy sauce and sesame seeds in a bowl. Add a generous grinding of black pepper, then whisk in the oils.

5 Pour the dressing over the noodles and mix well. Add the sugarsnap peas, carrots, scallions and duck slices and toss to mix. Scatter the cilantro leaves over and serve.

COOK'S TIP

To toast the sesame seeds, place them in a dry heavy-based frying pan and heat gently, stirring frequently, until they are lightly browned.

PIZZA, PASTA AND GRAINS

Chili, Tomato and Olive Pasta

The sauce for this pasta packs a punch, thanks to the robust flavors of red chilies, anchovies and capers.

SERVES 4

3 tbsp olive oil
2 garlic cloves, crushed
2 fresh red chilies, seeded
    and chopped
6 drained canned anchovy fillets
1½ lb ripe tomatoes, peeled,
    seeded and chopped
2 tbsp sun-dried tomato paste
2 tbsp drained capers
1 cup pitted black olives,
    roughly chopped
3 cups penne
salt and ground black pepper
chopped fresh basil, to garnish

1 Heat the oil in a saucepan and gently fry the garlic and chili for 2-3 minutes. Add the anchovies, mashing them with a fork, then stir in the tomatoes, sun-dried tomato paste, capers and olives. Add salt and pepper to taste. Simmer gently, uncovered, for 20 minutes, stirring occasionally.

2 Meanwhile, bring a large pan of lightly salted water to a boil and cook the penne according to the instructions on the packet, or until *al dente*. Drain and immediately stir into the sauce. Mix thoroughly, tip into a heated serving dish, garnish with basil and serve at once.

COOK'S TIP

If ripe well-flavored tomatoes are not available, use two 14 oz cans chopped tomatoes.

Spaghettini with Garlic and Olive Oil

It is essential to use a good quality virgin olive oil and a brightly colored fresh red chili for this simply delicious pasta sauce.

SERVES 4

350 g/12 oz spaghettini
5 tbsp virgin olive oil
3 garlic cloves, finely chopped
1 fresh red chili, seeded
    and chopped
1½ cups drained sun-dried
    tomatoes in oil, chopped
2 tbsp chopped fresh parsley
salt and ground black pepper
freshly grated Parmesan cheese,
    to serve

1 Bring a large saucepan of lightly salted water to a boil. Add the pasta and cook according to the instructions on the packet, or until *al dente*. Towards the end of the cooking time, heat the oil in a second large pan. Add the garlic and chili and cook gently for 2-3 minutes. Stir in the sun-dried tomatoes and remove from the heat.

COOK'S TIP

Save the oil from the jar of sun-dried tomatoes for adding to salad dressings.

2 Drain the pasta thoroughly and add to the hot oil. Return to the heat and cook for 2-3 minutes, tossing the pasta to coat the strands in the sauce. Season with salt and pepper, stir in the parsley and transfer to a warmed serving bowl. Scatter with grated Parmesan cheese and serve.

Pastitsio

*Macaroni in a cheese sauce is
layered with cinnamon and
cumin-spiced minced beef to
make a Greek version of lasagne.*

SERVES 4-6

2 cups macaroni
2 tbsp olive oil
1 large onion, finely chopped
2 garlic cloves, crushed
1 lb ground steak
1¼ cups beef stock
2 tsp tomato paste
1 tsp ground cinnamon
1 tsp ground cumin
1 tbsp chopped fresh mint
¼ cup butter
⅓ cup all-purpose flour
½ cup milk
½ cup plain yogurt
1½ cups grated Kefalotiri
  cheese
salt and ground black pepper

1 Bring a saucepan of lightly salted water to the boil. Add the macaroni and cook for 8 minutes, or according to the instructions on the packet, until *al dente*. Drain, rinse under cold water and drain again. Set aside. Preheat the oven to 375°F.

2 Heat the oil in a frying pan, add the onion and garlic and cook for 8-10 minutes until soft. Add the ground steak and stir until browned. Stir in the stock, tomato paste, cinnamon, cumin and mint, with salt and pepper to taste. Cook gently for 10-15 minutes until the sauce is thick and flavorsome.

3 Melt the butter in a saucepan. Stir in the flour and cook for 1 minute. Remove the pan from the heat and gradually stir in the milk and yogurt. Return the pan to the heat and cook gently for 5 minutes. Stir in half the cheese and season with salt and pepper. Stir the macaroni into the cheese sauce.

COOK'S TIP

*If Kefalotiri cheese is unavailable, use
a well flavored Cheddar cheese
or similar.*

4 Spread half the macaroni mixture over the base of a large gratin dish. Cover with the meat sauce and top with the remaining macaroni. Sprinkle the remaining cheese over the top and bake for 45 minutes or until golden brown on top.

Hot Pepperoni Pizza

There is nothing more mouth-watering than a freshly baked pizza, especially when the topping includes pepperoni and red chilies.

SERVES 4

2 cups strong bread flour

2 tsp fast acting dried yeast

1 tsp sugar

$\frac{1}{2}$ tsp salt

1 tbsp olive oil

$\frac{3}{4}$ cup mixed hand-hot milk and water

TOPPING

14 oz can chopped tomatoes, well drained

2 garlic cloves, crushed

1 tsp dried oregano

8 oz mozzarella cheese, coarsely grated

2 dried red chilies, crumbled

8 oz pepperoni, sliced

2 tbsp drained capers

fresh oregano, to garnish

1 Sift the flour into a bowl. Stir in the yeast, sugar and salt. Make a well in the center. Stir the olive oil into the milk and water, then stir the mixture into the flour. Mix to a soft dough.

2 Knead the dough on a lightly floured surface for 5-10 minutes until it is smooth and elastic. Return it to the clean, lightly oiled, bowl and cover with plastic wrap. Leave in a warm place for about 30 minutes or until the dough has doubled in bulk.

3 Preheat the oven to 425°F. Turn the dough out on to a lightly floured surface and knead lightly for 1 minute. Divide it in half and roll each piece out to a 10 in circle. Place on lightly oiled pizza trays or cookie sheets. To make the topping, mix the drained tomatoes, garlic and oregano in a bowl.

COOK'S TIP

If time is short, use ready-made pizza bases or scone bases.

4 Spread half the mixture over each round, leaving a margin around the edge. Set half the mozzarella aside. Divide the rest between the pizzas. Bake for 7-10 minutes until the dough rim on each pizza is pale golden.

5 Sprinkle the crumbled chilies over the pizzas, then arrange the pepperoni slices and capers on top. Sprinkle with the remaining mozzarella. Return the pizzas to the oven and bake for 7-10 minutes more. Scatter over the oregano and serve at once.

Singapore Noodles

Dried mushrooms add an intense flavor to this lightly curried dish. Use Oriental mushrooms if possible.

SERVES 4

1/3 **cup dried Chinese mushrooms**

8 oz fine egg noodles

2 tsp sesame oil

3 tbsp peanut oil

2 garlic cloves, crushed

1 small onion, chopped

1 fresh green chili, seeded and thinly sliced

2 tsp curry powder

4 oz green beans, topped, tailed and halved

1 cup Chinese leaves, thinly shredded

4 scallions, sliced

2 tbsp soy sauce

1 cup cooked shrimp, peeled and deveined

salt

1 Place the mushrooms in a bowl. Cover with warm water and soak for 30 minutes. Drain, reserving 2 tbsp of the soaking water, then slice.

2 Bring a saucepan of lightly salted water to a boil and cook the noodles according to the directions on the packet. Drain, tip into a bowl and toss with the sesame oil.

VARIATION

Ring the changes with the vegetables used in this dish. Try snowpeas, broccoli, bell peppers or baby sweetcorn. The shrimp can be omitted or substituted with ham or chicken.

3 Heat a wok and add the peanut oil. When it is hot, stir-fry the garlic, onion and chili for 3 minutes. Stir in the curry powder and cook for 1 minute. Add the mushrooms, green beans, Chinese leaves and scallions. Stir-fry for 3-4 minutes until the vegetables are crisp-tender.

4 Add the noodles, soy sauce, reserved mushroom soaking water and shrimp. Toss over the heat for 2-3 minutes until the noodles and shrimp are heated through.

Jambalaya

This popular Cajun dish has something in common with paella, but is distinguished by the addition of fiery spices.

SERVES 4

2 tbsp oil

8 oz boneless skinless
  chicken, cubed

8 oz chorizo sausage, cut
  into chunks

3 celery stalks, chopped

1 red bell pepper, seeded
  and chopped

1 green bell pepper, seeded
  and chopped

1 quantity Cajun spice mix,
  including onion and garlic

generous 1 cup long grain rice

7 oz can chopped tomatoes

2½ cups chicken stock

celery leaves, to garnish

1 Heat the oil in a large heavy-based frying pan. Fry the chicken and chorizo sausage until lightly browned. Remove from the pan with a slotted spoon and set aside. Add the celery and red and green bell peppers and fry for 2-3 minutes. Return the chicken and sausage to the pan.

VARIATION

Raw jumbo shrimp can be added with the rice. Alternatively, duck and ham may be used instead of chicken and sausage.

2 Stir in the Cajun spice mix and cook, stirring, for 2-3 minutes more. Stir in the rice and add the tomatoes and stock. Bring to a boil and stir.

3 Turn the heat to low, cover the pan and simmer gently for 15-20 minutes until the rice is tender and the liquid has been absorbed. Garnish and serve.

COOK'S TIP

This dish is very hot. If a milder result is preferred, use less chili powder in the Cajun spice mix.

Thai Fried Rice

This recipe uses jasmine rice which is sometimes known as Thai fragrant rice.

SERVES 4

½ cup coconut milk powder
1⅓ cups jasmine rice
2 tbsp peanut oil
2 garlic cloves, chopped
1 small onion, finely chopped
1 in piece fresh ginger
  root, grated
8 oz boneless, skinless chicken
  breasts, cut into ½ in dice
1 red bell pepper, seeded
  and diced
4 oz drained canned
  corn kernels
1 tsp chili oil
1 tbsp hot curry powder
salt
2 eggs, beaten
scallions shreds, to garnish

1 In a saucepan, whisk the coconut milk powder into 2 cups water. Add the rice, bring to a boil and stir once. Lower the heat to a gentle simmer, cover and cook for 10 minutes or until the rice is tender and the liquid has been absorbed. Spread the rice on a cookie sheet and leave until completely cold.

2 Heat the oil in a wok, add the garlic, onion and ginger and stir-fry for 2 minutes. Push the vegetables to the sides of the wok, add the chicken to the center and stir-fry for 2 minutes. Add the rice and stir-fry over a high heat for 3 minutes more.

3 Stir in the pepper, corn, chili oil, curry powder and season with salt. Toss over the heat for 1 minute. Stir in the beaten egg and cook for 1 minute more. Garnish with shredded scallions and serve.

COOK'S TIPS

It is important that the rice is completely cold before it is fried and the oil should be very hot, or the rice will absorb too much oil.
Add some sliced baby corn cobs along with the rice, if you like.

Pilau Rice with Whole Spices

This fragrant rice dish makes a perfect accompaniment to any Indian meal.

SERVES 4-6

generous pinch of
  saffron strands
2½ cups hot chicken stock
¼ cup butter
1 onion, chopped
1 garlic clove, crushed
½ cinnamon stick
6 cardamoms
1 bay leaf
generous 1 cup basmati rice,
  rinsed and drained
⅓ cup white raisins
1 tbsp oil
½ cup cashew nuts

1 Add the saffron strands to the hot stock and set aside. Heat the butter in a large saucepan and fry the onion and garlic for 5 minutes. Stir in the cinnamon stick, cardamoms and bay leaf and cook for 2 minutes.

COOK'S TIP

To rinse the rice, stir it around in several changes of water until the water is clear. Drain thoroughly before cooking.

2 Add the rice and cook, stirring, for 2 minutes more. Pour in the stock and add the white raisins. Bring to a boil, stir, then lower the heat, cover and cook gently for 15 minutes or until the rice is tender and the liquid has all been absorbed.

3 Meanwhile, heat the oil in a frying pan and fry the cashew nuts until browned. Drain on paper towels. Scatter over the rice and serve.

Couscous Salad

This is a spicy variation on a classic tabbouleh, which is traditionally made with bulgur wheat, not couscous.

<u>SERVES 4</u>

3 tbsp olive oil
5 scallions, chopped
1 garlic clove, crushed
1 tsp ground cumin
1½ cups vegetable stock
1 cup couscous
2 tomatoes, peeled and chopped
4 tbsp chopped fresh parsley
4 tbsp chopped fresh mint
1 fresh green chili, seeded and
  finely chopped
2 tbsp lemon juice
salt and ground black pepper
toasted pine nuts and grated
  lemon rind, to garnish
crisp lettuce leaves, to serve

1 Heat the oil in a saucepan. Add the scallions and garlic. Stir in the cumin and cook for 1 minute. Add the stock and bring to a boil.

2 Remove the pan from the heat, stir in the couscous, cover the pan and leave it to stand for 10 minutes, until the couscous has swelled and all the liquid has been absorbed. If using instant couscous, follow the instructions on the packet.

3 Tip the couscous into a bowl. Stir in the tomatoes, parsley, mint, chili and lemon juice, with salt and pepper to taste. If possible, leave to stand for up to an hour to allow the flavors to develop fully.

4 To serve, line a bowl with lettuce leaves and spoon the couscous salad into the center. Scatter the toasted pine nuts and grated lemon rind over, to garnish.

Bulgur and Lentil Pilaf

Bulgur is a very useful pantry ingredient. It has a nutty taste and texture and only needs soaking before serving in a salad or warming through for a hot dish.

SERVES 4

½ cup green lentils
⅔ cup bulgur wheat
1 tsp ground coriander
1 tsp ground cinnamon
1 tbsp olive oil
8 oz sliced bacon, chopped
1 red onion, chopped
1 garlic clove, crushed
1 tsp cumin seeds
2 tbsp roughly chopped
  fresh parsley
salt and ground black pepper

COOK'S TIP

Look out for Puy lentils, which have a superior flavor, aroma and texture.

1 Soak the lentils and bulgur separately in cold water for 1 hour, then drain. Tip the lentils into a pan. Stir in the coriander, cinnamon and 2 cups water. Bring to a boil, then simmer until the lentils are tender and the liquid has been absorbed.

2 Meanwhile, heat the olive oil and fry the bacon until crisp. Remove and drain on paper towels. Add the red onion and garlic to the oil remaining in the pan and fry for 10 minutes until soft and golden brown. Stir in the cumin seeds and cook for 1 minute more. Return the bacon to the pan.

3 Stir the drained bulgur into the cooked lentils, then add the mixture to the frying pan. Season with salt and pepper and heat through. Stir in the parsley and serve.

BREADS, BUNS AND QUICK BREADS

Focaccia with Green Peppercorns and Rock Salt

The combination of green peppercorns and a fruity olive oil gives these open-textured Italian flatbreads a delectable flavor.

MAKES 1 LOAF

3 cups bread flour
½ tsp salt
2 tsp fast-rising yeast
2 tsp drained green peppercorns
  in brine, lightly crushed
1½ tbsp fruity extra virgin
  olive oil
about 1 cup hand-hot water
4 tsp roughly crushed rock salt,
  for the topping
basil leaves, to garnish

1 Sift the flour and salt into a mixing bowl. Stir in the yeast and crushed peppercorns. Make a well in the center and stir in 1 tbsp of the olive oil, with enough of the hand-hot water to make a soft dough.

2 Turn the dough out on to a lightly floured surface and knead for about 10 minutes until smooth and elastic. Return to the clean, lightly oiled bowl, cover with plastic wrap and leave in a warm place until doubled in bulk.

3 Turn the dough out on to a floured surface and knead lightly for 2-3 minutes. Place on an oiled cookie sheet and pat out to a rough oval. Cover with a clean cloth and leave for 30 minutes until the dough puffs up.

4 Preheat the oven to 375°F. With your fingers, make a few dimples in the surface of the dough. Drizzle the remaining olive oil over, then sprinkle with the crushed rock salt. Bake the focaccia for 25-30 minutes until pale gold. Scatter with basil leaves and serve warm.

COOK'S TIP

Instead of one large loaf, you could make two medium or four individual loaves.

Spiced Naan Bread

Indian naan bread is traditionally baked in a fiercely hot tandoori oven. However, good results can be achieved at home by using a combination of a hot oven and a broiler.

MAKES 6

4 cups all-purpose flour
1 tsp baking powder
½ tsp salt
1 sachet fast-rising yeast
1 tsp superfine sugar
1 tsp fennel seeds
2 tsp black onion seeds
1 tsp cumin seeds
⅔ cup hand-hot milk
2 tbsp oil, plus extra
** for brushing**
⅔ cup natural yogurt
1 egg, beaten

VARIATION

Vary the spices used by adding chopped chili to the mixture, or sprinkling with poppy seeds before baking.

1 Sift the flour, baking powder and salt into a mixing bowl. Stir in the yeast, sugar, fennel seeds, black onion seeds and cumin seeds. Make a well in the center. Stir the hand-hot milk into the flour mixture, then add the oil, yogurt and beaten egg. Mix to form a ball of dough.

2 Turn the dough out on to a lightly floured surface and knead it for 10 minutes until smooth. Return to the clean, lightly oiled bowl and roll the dough to coat it with oil. Cover the bowl with plastic wrap and set aside until the dough has doubled in bulk.

3 Put a heavy cookie sheet in the oven and preheat the oven to 475°F. Also preheat the broiler. Knead the dough again lightly and divide it into six pieces. Keep five pieces covered while working with the sixth. Quickly roll the piece of dough out to a tear-drop shape (see right), brush lightly with oil and slap the naan on to the hot cookie sheet. Repeat with the remaining dough.

4 Bake the naan in the oven for 3 minutes until puffed up, then place the cookie sheet under the broiler for about 30 seconds or until the naan are lightly browned. Serve hot or warm as an accompaniment to an Indian curry.

Chili Cheese Muffins

These muffins are flavored with chili paste, which is available in tubes or jars.

MAKES 12

1 cup self-rising flour
1 tbsp baking powder
1 tsp salt
2 cups fine cornmeal
1¼ cups grated mature
  Cheddar cheese
4 tbsp butter, melted
2 large eggs, beaten
1 tsp chili paste
1 garlic clove, crushed
1¼ cups milk

Chili Cornbread

This golden yellow cornbread spiked with chili makes an excellent accompaniment to soups and salads.

MAKES 9 SLICES

2 eggs
1⅞ cups buttermilk
¼ cup butter, melted
½ cup all-purpose flour
½ tsp ground mace
1 tsp baking soda
2 tsp salt
2¼ cups fine cornmeal
2 fresh red chilies, seeded and
  finely chopped
shredded red chilies and
  sea salt, to serve

1 Preheat the oven to 400°F. Thoroughly grease 12 deep muffin pans or line the pans with paper cake cases. Sift the flour, baking powder and salt into a bowl, then stir in the cornmeal and 1 cup of the grated cheese.

2 Pour the melted butter into a bowl and stir in the eggs, chili paste, crushed garlic and milk.

3 Pour on to the dry ingredients and mix quickly until just combined.

4 Spoon the batter into the prepared muffin pans, scatter the remaining cheese on top and bake for 20 minutes until risen and golden brown. Leave to cool for a few minutes before turning the muffins out on to a wire rack to cool completely.

COOK'S TIP

Take care not to over-mix the muffin mixture or they will be heavy. Stir the mixture just enough to combine the ingredients roughly.

1 Preheat the oven to 400°F. Line and grease a 9 x 3 in loaf pan. In a large bowl, whisk the eggs until frothy, then whisk in the buttermilk and melted butter.

2 Sift the flour, mace, baking soda and salt together and gradually stir into the egg mixture. Fold in the cornmeal a little at a time, then stir in the fresh chilies.

3 Pour the mixture into the prepared pan and bake for 25-30 minutes until the top is firm to the touch.

4 Leave the loaf to cool in the pan for a few minutes before turning out. Scatter over the red chilies and sea salt, then cut into slices and serve warm.

COOK'S TIP

For a loaf with a more rustic appearance, use medium or coarse cornmeal.

Chelsea Buns

These traditional sticky buns, packed with spice and fruit, are always popular.

MAKES 9

2 cups bread flour

2 tsp fast-rising dried yeast

1 tsp superfine sugar

¹/₂ tsp salt

2 tbsp unsalted butter, softened

¹/₂ cup hand-hot milk

1 egg, beaten

³/₄ cup confectioners' sugar, for the glaze

COOK'S TIP

Do not be tempted to try to hurry the rising process by putting the dough in an oven or similar hot place to rise. Excessive heat will kill the yeast.

FILLING

¹/₄ cup unsalted butter, softened

¹/₄ cup soft brown sugar

²/₃ cup mixed dried fruit

1 tsp ground cinnamon

¹/₂ tsp ground nutmeg

¹/₄ tsp ground cloves

1 Grease a 7 in square cake pan. Sift the flour into a mixing bowl. Stir in the yeast, superfine sugar and salt. Rub in the butter until the mixture resembles bread crumbs, then make a well in the center and pour in the milk and beaten egg. Beat together vigorously to make a soft dough.

2 Knead the dough on a floured surface for 5-10 minutes until smooth. Return it to the clean, lightly oiled bowl, cover with plastic wrap and leave in a warm place until doubled in bulk. Turn out on to a floured surface. Knead lightly and roll out the dough to give a rectangle. This should measure about 12 x 9 in.

3 Spread the dough with the softened butter and sprinkle with the brown sugar, dried fruit, cinnamon, nutmeg and ground cloves. Roll up from a long side and cut into 9 pieces. Place in the prepared pan, cut sides up. Cover with lightly oiled plastic wrap and leave in a warm place for 45 minutes or until the buns are well risen.

4 Preheat the oven to 375°F. Bake the buns for 30 minutes until golden. Leave to cool in the pan for 10 minutes, then transfer, in one piece, to a wire rack to cool. Mix the confectioners' sugar with enough water to make a thin glaze and brush over the buns. Pull the buns apart to serve.

Cornish Saffron Buns

Saffron gives these buns a brilliant golden color and a distinctive flavor.

MAKES 12

³/₄ cup milk

¹/₂ tsp saffron strands

¹/₄ cup superfine sugar

400 g/14 oz/3¹/₂ cups bread flour

1 sachet fast-rising dried yeast

¹/₂ tsp salt

3 tbsp butter, melted

2 eggs, beaten

1 Put the milk and saffron strands in a saucepan and slowly bring to a boil. Remove from the heat, stir in the sugar and leave for about 5 minutes until the mixture is hand hot.

2 Sift the flour into a bowl and stir in the yeast and salt. Make a well in the center. Add the melted butter and half the egg to the milk, then mix with the dry ingredients to make a dough. Turn the dough out on to a lightly floured surface and knead for 10 minutes.

COOK'S TIP

Buy fresh saffron for the best flavor and do not keep it for too long.

3 Divide the dough into 12 pieces and roll into balls. Place on greased cookie sheets and cover with a cloth. Leave to rise until the buns have doubled in size.

4 Preheat the oven to 375°F. Glaze the tops of the buns with the remaining beaten egg and bake for 15-20 minutes until they are golden and sound hollow when rapped with your knuckle underneath. Cool on a wire rack.

Barm Brack

This customary Irish spiced bread is made and eaten at Halloween. It used to be customary to bake a wedding ring in the mixture in the belief that whoever retrieved it would be married within the year.

MAKES 1 x 9 IN ROUND LOAF

6 cups all-purpose flour
¹⁄₂ tsp mixed spice
1 tsp salt
1 sachet fast-rising dried yeast
¹⁄₄ cup superfine sugar
1¹⁄₄ cups hand-hot milk
²⁄₃ cup hand-hot water
¹⁄₄ cup butter, softened
1¹⁄₃ cups sultanas
¹⁄₃ cup currants
¹⁄₃ cup chopped mixed peel
milk, for glazing

1 Sift the flour, mixed spice and salt into a bowl. Stir in the yeast and 1 tbsp of the superfine sugar. Make a well in the center and pour in the milk and water.

2 Mix well, gradually incorporating the dry ingredients to make a sticky dough. Place on a lightly floured board and knead the dough until smooth and no longer sticky. Put into a clean bowl. Cover with plastic wrap and leave in a warm place for 1 hour until well risen and doubled in bulk.

3 Preheat the oven to 400°F. Knead the dough lightly on a floured surface. Add the remaining ingredients, apart from the milk, to the dough and work them in. Return the dough to the bowl, replace the plastic wrap and leave to rise for 30 minutes.

4 Grease a 9 in round loaf pan. Pat the dough to a neat round and fit it into the pan. Cover and leave in a warm place for about 45 minutes until it has risen to the top of the pan. Brush lightly with milk and bake for 15 minutes. Cover the loaf with foil, reduce the oven temperature to 350°F and bake for 45 minutes more, or until the bread is golden and sounds hollow when rapped underneath. Cool on a wire rack.

Swedish Spice Bread

Cardamom and caraway seeds are widely used in Scandinavian cooking. At Christmas, dried fruit and candied peel are added to this recipe to make a traditional julekake.

MAKES 1 X 9 IN ROUND LOAF

2 tbsp butter
3 tbsp well-flavored
 clear honey
2 cups bread flour
2 cups rye flour
$\frac{1}{2}$ tsp salt
1 sachet fast-rising dried yeast
1 tsp ground cardamom
1 tsp ground caraway seeds
$\frac{1}{2}$ tsp ground star anise
2 tbsp superfine sugar
grated rind and juice of
 1 small orange
$\frac{3}{4}$ cup lager
4 tbsp boiling water
1 egg, beaten
GLAZE
1 tbsp clear honey

COOK'S TIP

For a more decorative loaf, scatter chopped candied citrus peel or browned flaked almonds over the top, after brushing with honey.
As the dough tends to be rather sticky, knead it in a mixer or food processor if you have one, using a dough hook or blade.

---

1 Melt the butter with the honey in a small saucepan, then leave to cool. Sift the flours and salt into a bowl. Tip any rye remaining in the sieve into the bowl. Stir in the yeast, cardamom, caraway, star anise, superfine sugar and orange rind.

2 Mix the lager with the boiling water in a jug. Stir the orange juice and beaten egg into the melted butter and honey, then stir the mixture into the flour. Add enough of the warm lager to make a soft and slightly sticky, but manageable dough.

3 Place the dough on a lightly floured surface and knead for 5 minutes until smooth and elastic. Place in an oiled bowl, cover and leave to rise until doubled in bulk. Knead briefly, then divide the dough in two. Roll out each piece into a long snake.

4 Grease a 9 in round loaf pan. Starting at the edge of the prepared pan, coil the dough around and around to the center, joining the second piece to the first with a little water. Cover with oiled plastic wrap and leave until doubled in size. Preheat the oven to 375°F. Bake the bread for 10 minutes, then turn the oven down to 325°F and bake for 40-50 minutes more, until the bread is lightly browned and sounds hollow when rapped underneath.

5 Make the glaze by mixing the honey with 1 tbsp hot water, then brush the mixture over the hot bread. Leave the loaf on a wire rack to cool. Cut into slices and serve with butter.

Stollen

Stollen is an Austrian spiced fruit bread with a marzipan filling. Although it is traditionally served at Christmas, it is delicious at any time, served warm or cold or toasted and buttered.

SERVES 10

¼ cup currants
½ cup raisins
¼ cup chopped mixed peel
¼ cup candied cherries, rinsed, dried and quartered
2 tbsp rum
¼ cup butter
¾ cup milk
2 tbsp superfine sugar
3 cups bread flour
¼ tsp salt
½ tsp ground nutmeg
½ tsp ground cinnamon
seeds from 3 cardamoms
1 sachet fast-rising dried yeast
grated rind of 1 lemon
1 egg, beaten
⅓ cup flaked almonds
6 oz marzipan
melted butter, for brushing
sifted confectioners' sugar, for dusting

1 Place the currants, raisins, mixed peel and cherries in a bowl. Stir in the rum and set aside. Combine the butter, milk and superfine sugar in a saucepan and heat gently until the sugar has dissolved and the butter has just melted. Cool until hand-hot.

2 Sift the flour, salt, nutmeg and cinnamon into a bowl. Crush the cardamom seeds and add them to the flour mixture. Stir in the dried yeast. Make a well in the center and stir in the milk mixture, lemon rind and beaten egg. Beat to form a soft dough.

3 Turn on to a floured surface. With floured hands, knead the dough for about 5 minutes. It will be quite sticky, so add more flour if necessary. Knead the soaked fruit and flaked almonds into the dough until just combined.

4 Return the dough to the clean, lightly oiled bowl, cover with plastic wrap and leave in a warm place for up to 3 hours until doubled in bulk.

5 Turn the dough on to a floured surface. Knead for 1-2 minutes, then roll out to a 10 in square. Roll the marzipan to a sausage shape slightly shorter than the length of the dough and place in the center. Fold one side over to cover the marzipan and repeat with the other side, overlapping in the center. Seal the ends.

6 Place the roll, seam side down, on a greased cookie sheet. Cover with oiled plastic wrap and leave in a warm place until doubled in bulk. Preheat the oven to 375°F.

7 Bake the Stollen for 40 minutes, or until it is golden and sounds hollow when rapped underneath. Brush the hot Stollen generously with melted butter and dredge heavily with sifted confectioners' sugar.

Orange and Coriander Brioches

The warm spicy flavor of coriander combines particularly well with orange.

2 cups bread flour
2 tsp fast-rising dried yeast
½ tsp salt
1 tbsp superfine sugar
2 tsp coriander seeds,
  coarsely ground
grated rind of 1 orange
2 eggs, beaten
¼ cup unsalted butter, melted
1 small egg, beaten, to glaze

1 Grease 12 individual brioche pans. Sift the flour into a mixing bowl and stir in the yeast, salt, sugar, coriander seeds and orange rind. Make a well in the center, pour in 2 tbsp hand-hot water, the eggs and melted butter and beat to make a soft dough. Turn the dough on to a lightly floured surface and knead for 5 minutes until smooth and elastic. Return to the clean, lightly oiled bowl, cover with plastic wrap and leave in a warm place for 1 hour until doubled in bulk.

2 Turn on to a floured surface, knead again briefly and roll into a sausage. Cut into 12 pieces. Break off a quarter of each piece and set aside. Shape the larger pieces of dough into balls and place in the prepared pans.

3 With the end of a floured wooden spoon, press a hole in each dough ball. Shape each small piece of dough into a little plug and press into the holes.

COOK'S TIP
These individual brioches look particularly attractive if they are made in special brioche pans. However, they can also be made in muffin pans.

4 Place the brioche pans on a cookie sheet. Cover with lightly oiled plastic wrap and leave in a warm place until the dough rises almost to the top of the pans. Preheat the oven to 425°F. Brush the brioches with beaten egg and bake for 15 minutes until golden brown. Scatter over extra orange rind to decorate, if you like, and serve the brioches warm with butter.

CAKES AND COOKIES

Spiced Caribbean Christmas Cake

There is a taste of the tropics in this spicy fruit cake spiked with brandy, rum and port.

MAKES 1 X 9 IN CAKE

1½ lb luxury dried mixed fruit

⅔ cup prunes, chopped

⅔ cup dried mango or papaya pieces, chopped

½ cup candied cherries, quartered

3 tbsp brandy

3 tbsp rum

3 tbsp port

4 tbsp cherry brandy

1 tbsp apple pie spice

½ tsp salt

2 tsp vanilla extract

1 tbsp treacle

2¼ cups self-rising flour

1½ cups raw sugar

generous 1 cup butter, softened

6 eggs, beaten

1 Combine the mixed fruit, prunes, mango or papaya pieces and candied cherries in a saucepan. Add the brandy, rum, port, cherry brandy, apple pie spice, salt, vanilla extract, treacle and 4 tbsp water. Bring to a boil, then simmer gently for 15 minutes.

2 Set the fruit mixture aside to cool. Leave overnight or, if time allows, place in a large screwtop jar and chill for up to 1 week.

3 Preheat the oven to 275°F. Grease and line a 9 in round cake pan. Sift the flour into a large mixing bowl. Add the raw sugar, softened butter and eggs. Beat the mixture thoroughly until well combined. Gradually fold in the macerated fruit mixture.

> #### COOK'S TIP
>
> *This is a very rich moist cake and does not need marzipan or icing, but, if you do want to decorate it, a glazed nut and glacé fruit topping looks good and tastes delicious.*

4 Pour the mixture into the prepared pan, do not level the surface and bake for 3½-4 hours until cooked through. Place a sheet of wax paper over the cake after about 3 hours if it appears to be browning too quickly.

5 Leave the cake to cool in the pan for 45 minutes, then transfer it to a wire rack to cool completely. Wrap in wax paper and store in an airtight pan. If possible, keep the cake for 1 month before cutting.

Honey Spice Cake

Use a strongly flavored honey such as chestnut honey, which will not be over-whelmed by the spices.

MAKES 8-10 SLICES

²/₃ **cup butter**
1½ **cup brown sugar**
³/₄ **cup clear honey**
1³/₄ **cups self-rising flour**
½ **tsp ground ginger**
½ **tsp ground cinnamon**
¼ **tsp caraway seeds**
¼ **tsp ground cloves**
2 **eggs, beaten**
3 **cups confectioners' sugar**
crushed sugar, to decorate

COOK'S TIP

This cake benefits from being kept for a day before eating.

1 Preheat the oven to 350°F. Grease a 3³/₄ cup fluted mold. Put the butter, sugar, honey and 1 tbsp water into a saucepan. Heat gently until the butter has melted and the sugar has dissolved. Remove from the heat and cool for 10 minutes.

2 Sift the flour into a bowl and mix in the ginger, cinnamon, caraway seeds and ground cloves. Make a well in the center. Pour in the honey mixture and the eggs and beat well until smooth. Pour the batter into the prepared mold.

3 Bake for 40-50 minutes until the cake is well risen and a skewer inserted into the center comes out clean. Leave to cool in the pan for 2-3 minutes, then remove to a wire rack to cool.

4 Make the icing. Sift the confectioners' sugar into a bowl. Stir in enough warm water to make a smooth, flowing icing. Spoon carefully over the cake so that it is evenly coated. Decorate with crushed sugar.

Lemon Poppy Seed Cake

Pouring lemon syrup over this makes it marvelously moist, while the poppy seeds add texture and extra flavor.

MAKES 12 SQUARES OR DIAMONDS

1/3 **cup poppy seeds**
1/2 **cup butter, softened**
3/4 **cup superfine sugar**
2 **eggs, beaten**
finely grated rind of 1 lemon
1 1/2 **cups self-rising flour, sifted**
4 **tbsp milk**
TOPPING
juice of 1 lemon
1/2 **cup sugar**
lemon rind, to decorate

1 Preheat the oven to 350°F. Grease a 9 x 7 in cake pan, about 1 in deep. Line it with parchment paper. Grind the poppy seeds in a clean coffee grinder or place between 2 sheets of plastic wrap and crush with a rolling pin.

2 Beat the butter and sugar in a bowl until light and fluffy. Gradually beat in the eggs. Stir in the lemon rind. Fold in the flour, alternately with the milk, then fold in the poppy seeds.

3 Spoon the mixture into the prepared pan and level the surface. Bake for about 45 minutes until the cake is well risen and pale golden.

COOK'S TIP

If you warm the lemon in a microwave for a few seconds on High, it will yield more juice.

4 While the cake is baking mix the lemon juice and sugar in a bowl. Remove the cake from the oven and, without taking it out of the pan, immediately pour the mixture evenly over the surface.

5 Leave the cake in the pan until completely cold, then cut into squares or diamonds. Decorate with fine strips of lemon rind.

Ginger Cake

Three forms of ginger make this the ultimate cake for all lovers of the versatile spice.

MAKES 12 SQUARES

2 cups self-rising flour
1 tbsp ground ginger
1 tsp ground cinnamon
½ tsp baking soda
½ cup butter
½ cup brown sugar
2 eggs
1½ tbsp corn syrup
1½ tbsp milk
TOPPING
6 pieces stem ginger, plus
  4 tsp syrup, from the jar
1 cup confectioners' sugar
lemon juice

1 Preheat the oven to 325°F. Grease a shallow 7 in square cake pan and line with parchment paper.

2 Sift the flour, ginger, cinnamon and baking soda into a bowl. Rub in the butter, then stir in the sugar.

3 Make a well in the center. In a bowl, whisk together the eggs, syrup and milk. Pour into the dry ingredients and beat until smooth and glossy.

4 Spoon into the prepared pan and bake for 45-50 minutes until well risen and firm to the touch. Leave in the pan for 30 minutes, then remove to a wire rack to cool completely.

COOK'S TIP

This cake benefits from being kept in an airtight pan for a day before eating.

5 Cut each piece of stem ginger into quarters and arrange the pieces on top of the cake.

6 Sift the confectioners' sugar into a bowl and stir in the ginger syrup and enough lemon juice to make a smooth icing. Put the icing into a wax paper icing bag and drizzle over the top of the cake. Leave to set, then cut the cake into squares.

Ginger-topped Shortbread Fingers

Topping a ginger short-bread base with a sticky ginger topping may be gilding the lily, but it tastes delicious!

MAKES ABOUT 40

2 cups all-purpose flour

1 tsp ground ginger

6 tbsp superfine sugar

3 pieces stem ginger, finely chopped

¾ cup butter

TOPPING

1 tbsp corn syrup

¼ cup butter

4 tbsp confectioners' sugar, sifted

1 tsp ground ginger

1 Preheat the oven to 350°F. Grease a shallow rectangular 11 x 7 in jelly roll pan. Sift the flour and ground ginger into a bowl and stir in the sugar and stem ginger.

2 Rub in the butter until the mixture begins to stick together. Press the mixture into the prepared pan and smooth over the top with a metal spatual. Bake for 40 minutes until the ginger short-bread base is very lightly browned.

3 Make the topping. Put the syrup and butter in a small saucepan. Heat gently until both have melted. Stir in the confectioners' sugar and ginger. Remove the pan from the oven and pour the topping over the base while both are still hot. Allow to cool slightly, then cut into fingers. Remove to wire racks to cool completely.

COOK'S TIP

Use the syrup from the jar of stem ginger instead of corn syrup in the topping, if you prefer.

Apple and Cinnamon Muffins

These spicy muffins are quick and easy to make and are perfect for serving for breakfast or tea.

MAKES 6 LARGE MUFFINS

1 egg, beaten

3 tbsp superfine sugar

½ cup milk

¼ cup butter, melted

1¼ cups all-purpose flour

1½ tsp baking powder

¼ tsp salt

½ tsp ground cinnamon

2 small eating apples, peeled cored and finely chopped

TOPPING

12 brown sugar lumps, roughly crushed

1 tsp ground cinnamon

1 Preheat the oven to 400°F. Line six large muffin pans with paper cases. Mix the egg, sugar, milk and melted butter in a large bowl. Sift in the flour, baking powder, salt and cinnamon. Add the chopped apple and mix roughly.

2 Spoon the mixture into the prepared muffin cases. Make the topping by mixing the crushed sugar lumps with the cinnamon. Sprinkle over the uncooked muffins. Bake for 30-35 minutes until well risen and golden. Cool on a wire rack.

COOK'S TIP

Do not overmix the muffin mixture – it should be lumpy.

Vanilla Streusel Bars

The crumbly topping on this cake makes a crunchy contrast to the moist vanilla-flavored sponge underneath.

MAKES ABOUT 25

1½ cups self-rising flour
1 tsp baking powder
¾ cup butter, softened
¾ cup vanilla sugar
3 eggs, beaten
1½ tsp pure vanilla extract
1-2 tbsp milk
STREUSEL TOPPING
1 cup self-rising flour
6 tbsp butter
6 tbsp vanilla sugar
confectioners' sugar, to finish

1 Preheat the oven to 350°F. Lightly grease and line a shallow 9 x 7 in baking pan.

2 Make the topping. Sift the flour into a bowl and rub in the butter until the mixture resembles coarse bread crumbs. Stir in the vanilla sugar and set aside.

3 Sift the flour and baking powder into a bowl. Add the butter, vanilla sugar and eggs. Beat well until the mixture is smooth, adding the vanilla extract and just enough milk to give a soft dropping consistency.

4 Spoon the mixture into the prepared pan. Sprinkle the Streusel topping over the surface and press down to cover. Bake for 45-60 minutes until browned and firm. Cool in the pan for 5 minutes, then turn out on to a wire rack to cool completely. Cut into bars when cool.

COOK'S TIP

Cover the cake loosely with foil if the topping browns too quickly.

Chocolate Lebkuchen

Cut this nutty spice cake into small squares to serve with after-dinner coffee instead of chocolates.

Makes 24

3 eggs

1 cup superfine sugar

1 cup all-purpose flour

1 tsp ground cinnamon

¼ tsp ground cloves

¼ tsp ground nutmeg

¼ tsp ground cardamom

2 cups unblanched almonds, coarsely ground

¼ cup candied lemon peel, finely chopped

¼ cup candied orange peel, finely chopped

⅓ cup unsweetened chocolate, grated

½ tsp grated lemon rind

½ tsp grated orange rind

2 tsp rosewater

ICING

1 egg white

2 tsp cocoa powder, mixed with 1 tbsp boiling water and cooled

generous 1 cup confectioners' sugar

2 tbsp sugar crystals

1 Preheat the oven to 325°F. Base-line a 12 x 9 in jelly roll pan with rice paper.

2 Whisk the eggs and superfine sugar in a large bowl until thick and pale. Sift the flour, cinnamon, ground cloves, nutmeg and cardamom. Stir in all the remaining dry ingredients.

3 Spread in the prepared pan and brush with the rosewater. Bake for 30-35 minutes until firm.

4 Make the icing. Stir the egg white into the cocoa mixture, sift in the confectioners' sugar and mix. Spread over the cake while still warm. Sprinkle with sugar crystals. Return to the oven for 5 minutes. Cut into squares when cold.

COOK'S TIP

Do not worry when the top of the cake cracks when you cut it; it is meant to be like that!

Spiced Cocktail Crackers

These savory crackers are ideal for serving with pre-dinner drinks. Each of the spice seeds contributes to the flavor.

<u>MAKES 20-30</u>

1¼ cups all-purpose flour
2 tsp curry powder
½ cup butter
¾ cup grated Cheddar cheese
2 tsp poppy seeds
1 tsp black onion seeds
1 egg yolk
cumin seeds, to decorate

1   Grease two cookie sheets. Sift the flour and curry powder into a bowl.

2   Rub in the butter until the mixture resembles bread crumbs, then stir in the cheese, poppy seeds and black onion seeds. Stir in the egg yolk and mix to a firm dough. Wrap the dough in plastic wrap and chill for 30 minutes.

3   Roll out the dough on a floured surface to a thickness of about ⅛ in. Cut into shapes with a cookie cutter. Arrange on the prepared cookie sheets and sprinkle with the cumin seeds. Chill for 15 minutes.

4   Preheat the oven to 375°F. Bake the crackers for about 20 minutes until crisp and golden. Serve warm or cold.

> COOK'S TIP
>
> *These biscuits are at their best when freshly baked. Make the dough in advance and chill until required.*

Cinnamon-spiced Pastelitos

These melt-in-the-mouth cinnamon and vanilla crackers are traditionally served at Mexican weddings. They are perfect for serving with coffee.

<u>MAKES ABOUT 40</u>

1 cup butter, softened
¼ cup superfine sugar
2 cups all-purpose flour
1 cup cornstarch
1 tsp pure vanilla extract
½ cup confectioners' sugar
1 tsp ground cinnamon

1   Preheat the oven to 325°F. Grease two or three cookie sheets. In a bowl, cream the butter with the superfine sugar until light and fluffy. Sift the flour and cornstarch together and gradually work into the creamed butter and sugar mixture with the vanilla extract.

2   Roll heaped teaspoons of the mixture into balls and place on the cookie sheets. Bake for 30 minutes or until pale golden.

3   Sift the confectioners' sugar and ground cinnamon into a bowl. While the cookies are still warm, toss them in the confectioners' sugar mixture. Leave on a wire rack to cool, then store in an airtight pan for up to 2 weeks.

> COOK'S TIP
>
> *The cookie mixture can be prepared in a food processor.*

DESSERTS

Pear Tart Tatin with Cardamom

Cardamom is a spice that is equally at home in sweet and savory dishes. It is delicious with pears.

SERVES 2-4

¼ **cup butter, softened**
¼ **cup superfine sugar**
seeds from 10 cardamoms
8 oz puff pastry, thawed if frozen
3 ripe pears

1 Preheat the oven to 425°F. Spread the butter over the base of a 7 in heavy-based cake pan or an ovenproof omelet pan. Spread the sugar evenly over the bottom of the pan. Scatter the cardamom seeds over the sugar. On a floured surface, roll out the pastry to a circle slightly larger than the pan. Prick the pastry lightly, support it on a cookie sheet and chill.

2 Peel the pears, cut out the cores and slice them lengthwise into halves. Arrange the pears, rounded side down, on the butter and sugar. Set the cake pan or omelet pan over a medium heat until the sugar melts and begins to bubble with the butter and juice from the pears. If any areas are browning more than others, move the pan, but do not stir.

3 As soon as the sugar has caramelized remove the pan carefully from the heat. Place the pastry on top, tucking the edges down the sides of the pan. Transfer to the oven and bake for 25 minutes until the pastry is well risen and golden.

4 Leave the tart in the tin or pan for 2-3 minutes until the juices have stopped bubbling. Invert the pan over a plate and shake to release the tart. It may be necessary to slide a spatula underneath the pears to loosen them. Serve the tart warm with cream.

COOK'S TIP

Choose fairly large round pears for this tart rather than the more elongated varieties.

American Pumpkin Pie

This spicy sweet pie is traditionally served at Thanksgiving, or at Hallowe'en to use the pulp from the hollowed-out pumpkin lanterns.

SERVES 8

1¾ cups all-purpose flour

½ tsp salt

scant ½ cup unsalted butter

1 egg yolk

FILLING

2 lb piece of pumpkin

2 large eggs

6 tbsp brown sugar

4 tbsp corn syrup

1 cup heavy cream

1 tbsp pumpkin pie spice

½ tsp salt

confectioners' sugar, for dusting

1 Sift the flour and salt into a mixing bowl. Rub in the butter until the mixture resembles bread crumbs, then mix in the egg yolk and enough iced water (about 1 tbsp) to make a dough. Roll the dough into a ball, wrap it up in plastic wrap and chill it for at least 30 minutes.

2 Make the filling. Peel the pumpkin and remove the seeds. Cut the flesh into cubes. Place in a heavy-based saucepan, add water to cover and boil until tender. Mash until completely smooth, then leave in a srainer set over a bowl to drain thoroughly.

3 Roll out the pastry on a lightly floured surface and line a 9-10 in loose-bottomed flan pan. Prick the base and line with wax paper and baking beans. Chill for 15 minutes. Preheat the oven to 400°F. Bake the flan case for 10 minutes, remove the paper and beans, return the flan case to the oven and bake for 5 minutes more.

4 Lower the oven temperature to 375°F. Tip the pumpkin pulp into a bowl and beat in the eggs, sugar, syrup, cream, spice and salt. Pour the mixture into the pastry case. Bake for 40 minutes or until the filling has set. Dust with confectioners' sugar and serve at room temperature.

Clementines with Star Anise and Cinnamon

This fresh dessert, delicately flavored with mulling spices, makes the perfect ending for a festive meal.

SERVES 6

1½ cups sweet dessert wine
6 tbsp superfine sugar
6 star anise
1 cinnamon stick
1 vanilla bean
1 strip thinly pared lime rind
2 tbsp Cointreau
12 clementines

1 Put the wine, sugar, star anise and cinnamon in a saucepan. Split the vanilla bean and add it to the pan with the lime rind. Bring to a boil, lower the heat and simmer for 10 minutes. Allow to cool, then stir in the Cointreau.

2 Peel the clementines, removing all the pith and white membranes. Cut some clementines in half and arrange them all in a glass dish. Pour over the spiced wine and chill overnight.

VARIATION

Tangerines or oranges can be used instead of clementines.

Pistachio Halva Ice Cream

Halva is made from sesame seeds and is available in several flavors. This ice cream, studded with chunks of pistachio-flavored halva, is as unusual as it is irresistible.

SERVES 6

3 egg yolks
½ cup superfine sugar
1¼ cups light cream
1¼ cups heavy cream
4 oz pistachio halva
chopped pistachio nuts,
  to decorate

1 Turn the freezer to its lowest setting. Whisk the egg yolks with the superfine sugar in a bowl until thick and pale. Pour the light cream into a small saucepan and bring to a boil. Stir the hot cream into the egg yolk mixture.

2 Transfer the mixture to a double boiler or a heatproof bowl placed over a pan of boiling water. Cook, stirring continuously, until the custard is thick enough to coat the back of a spoon. Strain into a bowl and leave to cool.

COOK'S TIP

Use an ice cream machine, if you have one, to make the ice cream.

3 Whisk the heavy cream lightly, then whisk in the cooled custard. Crumble the halva into the mixture and stir in gently.

4 Pour the mixture into a freezer-proof container. Cover and freeze for 3 hours or until half set. Stir well, breaking up any ice crystals, then return to the freezer until frozen solid.

5 Remove the ice cream from the freezer about 15 minutes before serving so that it softens enough for scooping, and to allow the full flavor to develop. Decorate with chopped pistachio nuts.

Ginger and Lemon Desserts with Vanilla Custard

The flavors of lemon and ginger complement each other perfectly in these light little desserts.

SERVES 8

3 lemons

3 oz drained stem ginger, plus 2 tbsp syrup from the jar

4 tbsp corn syrup

1½ cups self-rising flour

2 tsp ground ginger

½ cup butter, softened

½ cup superfine sugar

2 eggs, beaten

3-4 tbsp milk

VANILLA CUSTARD

⅔ cup milk

⅔ cup heavy cream

1 vanilla bean, split

3 egg yolks

1 tsp cornstarch

2 tbsp superfine sugar

1 Preheat the oven to 325°F. Grease eight individual ovenproof bowls. Set one lemon aside for the sauce. Grate the rind from the remaining lemons and reserve in a bowl. Remove all the pith from one of the grated lemons and slice the flesh into eight thin rounds. Squeeze the juice from the second grated lemon. Chop the stem ginger.

2 In a small bowl, mix 1 tbsp of the ginger syrup with 2 tbsp of the corn syrup and 1 tsp of the lemon juice. Divide among the greased ovenproof bowls. Place a slice of lemon in the bottom of each bowl.

3 Sift the flour and ground ginger into a bowl. In a separate bowl, beat the butter and sugar together until pale and fluffy. Gradually beat in the eggs, then fold in the flour mixture and add enough milk to give a soft dropping consistency. Stir in the reserved grated lemon rind. Spoon into the ovenproof bowls.

4 Cover each bowl with foil and stand in a roasting pan. Add boiling water to come halfway up the bowls. Overwrap with foil, sealing well. Bake for 30-45 minutes, until cooked through.

5 Meanwhile make a lemon and ginger sauce. Grate the rind and squeeze the juice from the remaining lemon. Place in a saucepan with the remaining ginger syrup and corn syrup. Bring to a boil, lower the heat and simmer for 2 minutes. Keep warm.

6 Make the custard. Mix the milk and cream in a pan. Add the vanilla bean. Heat to just below boiling. Remove from the heat and leave for 10 minutes. Whisk together the egg yolks, cornstarch and sugar until light, then strain in the hot milk and cream. Whisk until blended, then return to the clean pan and heat, stirring, until thick. Turn out the desserts, spoon over the sauce and serve with the custard.

Churros with Cinnamon Syrup

Deep fried choux puffs tossed in sugar flavored with star anise are a popular Mexican dessert. They are traditionally served with a cinnamon syrup.

SERVES 4-6

¼ cup unsalted butter
⅔ cup all-purpose flour, sifted
2 eggs, beaten
oil, for deep frying
shreds of pared orange rind,
  to decorate
STAR ANISE SUGAR
5 star anise
6 tbsp superfine sugar
CINNAMON SYRUP
½ cup superfine sugar
2 star anise
1 cinnamon stick
2 tbsp orange juice

1 Make the star anise sugar. Put the star anise and sugar into a mortar and grind with a pestle until very fine. Sift into a bowl.

2 To make the cinnamon syrup, mix the sugar and ⅔ cup water in a saucepan. Add the star anise and cinnamon stick. Heat, stirring occasionally until the sugar has dissolved, then boil without stirring for 2 minutes. Stir in the orange juice and set aside.

3 Melt the butter in a saucepan. Add ⅔ cup water and bring to a boil. Add the flour, all at once, and beat thoroughly until the mixture leaves the sides of the pan. Cool slightly, then vigorously beat in the eggs, a little at a time. Spoon the churro mixture into a large piping bag fitted with a large star nozzle.

4 Heat the oil to 350°F or until a cube of bread browns in 1 minute. Fry a few churros at a time: pipe the paste into the oil, cutting off 1 in lengths with a knife. Each batch will take 3-4 minutes. The churros are ready when they float to the surface of the oil and are golden. Drain the churros on paper towels and keep hot while you are cooking successive batches.

5 Toss the churros in the star anise sugar. Decorate with the shreds of orange rind. Pour the cinnamon syrup into a small bowl and serve with the hot churros.

487

Kulfi with Cardamom

Kulfi is a delicately spiced Indian ice cream, which is traditionally made in individual containers. Yogurt pots or dariole moulds are ideal, but it can be made like other ice cream in a large container if you prefer.

SERVES 6

**2 litres/3½ pints/8 cups
  creamy milk**
12 cardamoms
175 g/6 oz/¾ cup caster sugar
**25 g/1 oz/¼ cup blanched
  almonds, chopped**
**toasted flaked almonds and
  cardamoms, to decorate**

1 Place the milk and cardamoms in a large heavy-based pan. Bring to the boil then simmer vigorously until reduced by one-third. Strain the milk into a bowl, discarding the cardamoms, then stir in the sugar and almonds until the sugar is dissolved. Cool.

COOK'S TIP

Use a large pan for reducing the milk as there needs to be plenty of room for it to bubble up.

2 Pour the mixture into a freezer-proof container, cover and freeze until almost firm, stirring every 30 minutes. When almost solid, pack the ice cream into six clean yogurt pots. Return to the freezer until required, removing the pots about 10 minutes before serving and turning the individual ices out. Decorate with toasted almonds and cardamoms before serving.

Pears in Mulled Wine

The red wine gives the pears a deep ruby colour, and the spices contribute a lovely warm flavour.

SERVES 4

1 bottle full-bodied red wine
1 cinnamon stick
4 cloves
½ tsp grated nutmeg
½ tsp ground ginger
8 peppercorns
175 g/6 oz/¾ cup caster sugar
thinly pared rind of ½ orange
thinly pared rind of ½ lemon
8 firm ripe pears

1 Pour the wine into a heavy-based saucepan into which the pears will fit snugly when standing upright. Stir the cinnamon stick, cloves, nutmeg, ginger, peppercorns, caster sugar and citrus rinds into the wine.

COOK'S TIP

Serve the pears with a mascarpone cream, made by combining equal quantities of mascarpone cheese and double cream, and adding a little vanilla essence for flavour.

2 Peel the pears, leaving the stalks intact, and stand them in the pan. The wine should only just cover the pears. Bring the liquid to the boil, lower the heat, cover and simmer very gently for 30 minutes or until the pears are tender. Using a slotted spoon, transfer the pears to a bowl.

3 Boil the poaching liquid until it has reduced by half and is syrupy. Strain the syrup over and around the pears and serve hot or cold.

Fruit Platter with Chat Masala

The spicy sour flavor of chat masala may seem a little strange at first, but it can become quite addictive!

SERVES 6

1 pineapple
2 papayas
1 small melon
juice of 2 limes
2 pomegranates
chat masala, to taste
sprigs of mint, to decorate

COOK'S TIP

If you do not have time, or the spices to hand, to make chat masala, simply season the fruit with ground black pepper.

1 Peel the pineapple. Remove the core and any remaining 'eyes', then cut the flesh lengthwise into thin wedges. Peel the papayas, cut them in half and then into thin wedges. Halve the melon and remove the seeds from the middle. Cut it into thin wedges and remove the skin.

VARIATION

The selection of fruit can be varied according to what is available. Apples and bananas make a simple salad, or guava and mango a more exotic combination.

2 Arrange the fruit on six individual plates and sprinkle with the lime juice. Cut the pomegranates in half and scoop out the seeds, discarding any pith. Scatter the seeds over the fruit. Serve, sprinkled with a little chat masala to taste. Scatter over a few sprigs of mint if you have some.

Caribbean Bananas with Ground Allspice and Ginger

Tender baked bananas in a rich and spicy sauce – a dessert for those with a sweet tooth!

SERVES 4

2 tbsp butter
8 firm ripe bananas
juice of 1 lime
scant ½ cup dark brown sugar
1 tsp ground allspice
½ tsp ground ginger
seeds from 6 cardamoms, crushed
2 tbsp rum
pared lime rind, to decorate
whipping cream, to serve

1 Preheat the oven to 400°F. Use a little of the butter to grease a shallow baking dish large enough to hold the bananas snugly in a single layer. Peel the bananas and cut them in half lengthwise. Arrange the bananas in the dish and pour over the lime juice.

VARIATION

For a version which will appeal more to children, use orange juice instead of lime and omit the rum.

2 Mix the sugar, allspice, ginger and cardamom in a bowl. Scatter the mixture over the bananas. Dot with the remaining butter. Bake, basting once, for 15 minutes, or until the bananas are soft.

3 Remove the dish from the oven. Warm the rum in a small pan or metal soup ladle, pour it over the bananas and set it alight. As soon as the flames die down, decorate the dessert with the pared lime rind and serve each portion with a dollop of cream.

PRESERVES AND CHUTNEYS

Moroccan Spiced Preserved Lemons

Salt is all that you need to preserve lemons, but adding spices gives them an aromatic flavor.

MAKES ABOUT 2 LB

6 unwaxed lemons, washed
6 tbsp sea salt
2 tbsp black peppercorns
4 bay leaves
6 cardamoms
1 cinnamon stick
sunflower oil

1 Cut the lemons lengthwise into quarters. Layer the lemon quarters and salt in a strainer placed over a bowl and leave to drain for 2 days.

> COOK'S TIP
>
> *The chopped preserved peel from preserved lemons is used in couscous, tagines and other Middle Eastern chicken and fish dishes.*

2 Pack the lemon quarters tightly into one or two clean preserving jars with the peppercorns, bay leaves, cardamoms and cinnamon stick.

3 Pour in sunflower oil to cover the lemons, seal the jar and leave for 3-4 weeks before using.

Roasted Red Bell Pepper and Chili Jelly

The hint of chili in this glowing red jelly makes it ideal for spicing up hot or cold roast meat. The jelly is also good stirred into sauces.

MAKES ABOUT 2 LB

8 red bell peppers, quartered
  and seeded
4 fresh red chilies, halved
  and seeded
1 onion, roughly chopped
2 garlic cloves, roughly chopped
1 cup water
1 cup white wine vinegar
1½ tsp salt
2 cups preserving sugar
½ oz sachet powdered pectin
  (about 5 tsp)

1 Place the bell peppers, skin side up, on a rack in a broiling pan. Broil until the skins blister and blacken. Place in a polythene bag until cool enough to handle, then remove the skins.

2 Purée the red bell peppers with the chilies, onion, garlic and water in a blender or food processor. Press the purée through a nylon strainer set over a bowl, pressing hard with a wooden spoon, to extract as much juice as possible. There should be about 3 cups.

3 Scrape the purée into a large stainless steel pan. Add the vinegar and salt. In a bowl, mix the sugar and pectin, then stir into the liquid. Heat gently until both the sugar and pectin have dissolved, then bring to a full rolling boil. Boil, stirring frequently, for exactly 4 minutes.

4 Remove the jelly from the heat and pour into warm sterilized jars. Leave to cool and set, then cover.

> COOK'S TIP
>
> *It is not essential to use preserving sugar, but it produces less scum.*

Clementine and Coriander Marmalade

Coriander has a warm spicy flavor, which goes particularly well with clementines and lemons.

MAKES ABOUT 6 LB

3-3½ lb clementines
6 unwaxed lemons
2 tbsp coriander seeds, roasted and roughly crushed
12 cups water
6 cups preserving sugar

1 Wash the clementines and lemons, then cut them in half. Squeeze all the fruit and pour the juice into a large saucepan.

2 Scrape all the pith from the citrus shells and tie it, with the pips and half the crushed coriander seeds, in a piece of muslin. Add the bag to the juice.

3 Slice the clementine and lemon peels into fine shreds and add them to the pan with the water.

4 Bring the water to a boil, lower the heat and simmer for 1½ hours, or until the clementine and lemon peel is very soft. Remove the muslin bag. Holding it over the pan, squeeze it between two saucers.

5 Add the sugar and the remaining coriander seeds to the pan and stir over a low heat until dissolved. Boil rapidly until setting point is reached. Skim the surface of the marmalade, then leave it to stand for 30 minutes, stirring occasionally to distribute the peel evenly. Pour into warm sterilized jars and cover with waxed paper discs. Seal the jars when cool and store them in a cool dry place.

COOK'S TIP

To test for a set, spoon a little marmalade on to a cold saucer. If a wrinkled skin forms within a few minutes it is ready for skimming.

Spiced Kumquats

Cloves and other spices are combined with kumquats to make a perfect accompaniment for baked ham.

MAKES ABOUT 2 LB

1¼ lb kumquats
1½ cups white wine vinegar
2½ cups sugar
1 cinnamon stick
15 cloves
6 allspice berries

1 Cut the kumquats into quarters and remove the pips. Place the kumquats in a large heavy-based saucepan and pour in just enough water to cover. Bring to a boil, then lower the heat and simmer gently until the fruit is tender.

COOK'S TIP

If you prefer, tie the spices in a muslin bag and remove them before bottling.

2 With a slotted spoon, remove the kumquats and set them aside. Add the vinegar, sugar, cinnamon stick, cloves and allspice berries to the cooking liquid. Bring to a boil, stirring occasionally. Return the kumquats to the pan, lower the heat and simmer for 30 minutes.

3 With a slotted spoon, remove the kumquats from the syrup and place in warm sterilized jars. Boil the syrup until thick and syrupy. Pour over the kumquats, cover and leave for at least 2 weeks before using.

Fresh Tomato, Onion and Cilantro Chutney

Indian chutneys of this type are not meant to be kept, but are used in much the same way as salsas, and eaten when freshly made. Fresh chili is used with cayenne pepper to make the relish quite hot.

SERVES 4-6

2 tomatoes
1 red onion
1 fresh green chili, seeded and finely chopped
4 tbsp chopped fresh cilantro
juice of 1 lime
½ tsp salt
½ tsp ground paprika
½ tsp cayenne pepper
½ tsp cumin seeds, roasted and ground

1 Dice the tomatoes and onion finely. Place them in a bowl.

2 Add the chili, cilantro, lime juice, salt, paprika, cayenne and ground cumin seeds. Mix well and serve as soon as possible.

Bread and Butter Pickles

This is a traditional American pickle with a distinctive blend of whole spices. The celery seeds combine particularly well with the cucumber, and the mustard seeds add a little fire and also look attractive in the jar.

MAKES ABOUT 4-4½ LB

2 lb cucumbers, cut into ¼ in slices
2 onions, thinly sliced
¼ cup salt
1½ cups cider vinegar
1½ cups sugar
2 tbsp white mustard seeds
2 tsp celery seeds
½ tsp ground turmeric
½ tsp black peppercorns

1 Put the cucumbers and onions in a large bowl. Add the salt and mix well. Fit a plate inside the bowl, pressing down on the cucumber mixture. Add a weight to compress the vegetables even more, and leave for 3 hours. Drain the cucumber and onions, rinse under cold running water and drain again.

2 Put the vinegar, sugar, mustard seeds, celery seeds, ground turmeric and peppercorns in a large saucepan. Bring to a boil, stirring to dissolve the sugar. Add the drained cucumber and onions. As soon as the mixture comes to a boil again, remove the pan from the heat.

3 Spoon the pickle into warm sterilized preserving jars, making sure the vegetables are covered with the liquid. Cover with airtight, vinegar-proof lids and store for at least 1 month before using.

Christmas Chutney

This savory mixture of spices and dried fruit takes its inspiration from mincemeat, and makes a delicious addition to a festive buffet.

MAKES 2-3½ LB

1 lb cooking apples, peeled, cored and chopped

3 cups luxury mixed dried fruit

grated rind of 1 orange

2 tbsp mixed spice

⅔ cup cider vinegar

2 cups soft brown sugar

1 Place the apples, dried fruit and orange rind in a large saucepan. Stir in the mixed spice, vinegar and sugar. Heat gently, stirring until all the sugar has dissolved.

COOK'S TIP

Watch the chutney carefully towards the end of the cooking time, as it has a tendency to catch on the bottom of the pan. Stir frequently at this stage.

2 Bring to a boil, then lower the heat and simmer, for 40-45 minutes, stirring occasionally, until the mixture is thick. Ladle into warm sterilized jars, cover and seal. Keep for 1 month before using.

Green Tomato Chutney

This is a classic chutney to make at the end of summer when the last tomatoes on the plants refuse to ripen. Preparing your own pickling spice makes it easy to add exactly the right amount of spiciness to balance the sweet and sour flavors.

MAKES ABOUT 5½ LB

4-4½ lb green tomatoes, roughly chopped

1 lb cooking apples, peeled, cored and chopped

1 lb onions, chopped

2 large garlic cloves, crushed

1 tbsp salt

3 tbsp pickling spice

2½ cups cider vinegar

2 cups sugar

1 Place the tomatoes, apples, onions and garlic in a large saucepan. Add the salt. Tie the pickling spice in a piece of muslin and add to the pan.

2 Pour in half the vinegar and bring to a boil. Lower the heat and simmer for 1 hour, or until the chutney is thick, stirring frequently.

3 Dissolve the sugar in the remaining vinegar and add to the chutney. Simmer for 1½ hours until the chutney is thick, stirring. Remove the muslin bag from the chutney. Spoon the hot chutney into warm sterilized jars. Cover with airtight, vinegar-proof lids and store for at least 1 month before using.

COOK'S TIP

Use a jam funnel to transfer the chutney into the jars. Wipe the jars and label them when cold.

Index

Acknowledgements

Photographs:
(Herbs) All photographs for this section of the book are by John Freeman and Michelle Garrett, apart from those on p40 (left), 41, 58, 40 (right), 79 (hollyhocks), 81 (sea thrift), 85 (knapweed), 86 (chamomile), 91 (rocket), 94 (herb robert), 97 (woad), 99 (lavender), 102 (mallow), 111 (greater plantain), 117 (savory) and 121 (variegated Russian comfrey), which were kindly lent by Jenny Balfour-Paul, Jacqui Hurst and the Garden Picture Library respectively. The pictures on p11 (bottom), 12 (top and bottom left) and 13 (right) were lent by Visual Arts Library.

Photographs:
(Spices) With the exceptions noted below, all photographs in this section of the book are by William Adams-Lingwood: Tony Stone Worldwide, p256, 258, 259 (top left and bottom right), 260 and 261; Image Bank, p257, 262, 263 (bottom right); Zefa Picture Library, p259 (centre); and Anthony Blake Photo Library, p263 (top).